The Case for Work

The Case for Work

Jean-Philippe Deranty

OXFORD
UNIVERSITY PRESS

OXFORD
UNIVERSITY PRESS

Great Clarendon Street, Oxford, OX2 6DP,
United Kingdom

Oxford University Press is a department of the University of Oxford.
It furthers the University's objective of excellence in research, scholarship,
and education by publishing worldwide. Oxford is a registered trade mark of
Oxford University Press in the UK and in certain other countries

Published in the United States of America by Oxford University Press
198 Madison Avenue, New York, NY 10016, United States of America

British Library Cataloguing in Publication Data

Data available

Library of Congress Control Number: 2024940119

ISBN 9780192887146

DOI: 10.1093/oso/9780192887146.001.0001

Printed and bound by
CPI Group (UK) Ltd, Croydon, CR0 4YY

Acknowledgements

This book builds on years of collaborative research on work with colleagues and friends from Europe, the UK, and Australia. It attempts to defend and to develop from a new perspective the many ideas about work I have gained from reading them and from talking with them, as well as ideas we produced together in joint publications and collective research projects. I hope that the book's arguments do justice to our previous efforts and to everything I've learnt from them. The book is deeply inspired by their writing and their scholarship. My thoughts about work have also been shaped by the collaboration with postgraduate students on their projects. Many insights in this book were gained from reading and discussing their research. I would like to acknowledge this debt. Several friends and colleagues have provided not only intellectual inspiration but also direct hands-on support to help me complete the manuscript, through the reading of drafts, correcting my hesitant English and providing important conceptual and structural comments. I would like to thank most especially Mike Olson, Emmanuel Renault, and Keith Breen, as well as Thomas Corbin, Simon Lumsden, Alison Ross, and Richard Menary for all their input and advice. The book is dedicated to the three companions of my life and a little furry mate.

Contents

Introduction

i.1 The Book's Purpose and Method

This book is about the centrality of work. It offers an account of why work is a significant aspect of human life, as a form of individual experience and as an institution of human societies, and why many arguments denouncing and rejecting this significance are mistaken or ill-directed.

For many people outside of academia, it is obvious that work is an important part of human lives. The work people do for a wage continues to determine the financial situation of the majority. For many, work directly impacts their physical and mental health. There can be many detrimental or even dangerous aspects of work for human health, but if work is well organized, it can also have many benefits. For many, work is an opportunity to learn, to develop skills and acquire expertise. For most people still, the social standing attached to occupations matters a lot. Many people see their professional activity as a key aspect of their identity. For many, even if there is much to complain about their experiences at work, it is through work that they enjoy social connections. Often it is at work that friendships are formed, and many people find their life partners through work. Work occupies the mind and the time of many people, and many feel empty when they don't work. For many, not being able to work, or not working as much as they would like, or not working in their preferred area is a source of deep dissatisfaction, which shows how important work is in a negative way. Work also remains a cultural value in many societies. It often takes the form of an explicit moral command, the expectation that everyone who is able should make genuine efforts to contribute to the community to the best of their ability. As one of the main sources of individual and collective wealth, work continues to be a key concern of public policy and one of the most important items raised in political debates. As a result of this ongoing, multifold importance of work, many academic disciplines take aspects of work as their thematic focus: economics, organization and management studies, industrial

The Case for Work. Jean-Philippe Deranty, Oxford University Press. © Jean-Philippe Deranty (2024).
DOI: 10.1093/oso/9780192887146.003.0001

relations, organizational psychology, the sociology of work, business ethics and business history, labour law, and many other specialized enquiries still.

In the theoretical humanities and social sciences, however, a growing trend questions the importance of work and advocates a 'post-work' ethos (Frayne 2016, 2024; Breen and Deranty 2021a, 2021b, Breen and Deranty 2024; Deranty 2022 for reviews of the recent literature; Granter 2021 on the long history behind this recent trend). This trend has become popular among intellectuals, journalists, artists, and progressives. It has made its way into areas of public policy, notably through the latest advocacy for universal basic income and as one of the rationales for the four-day week (Lewis et al. 2023). Although social theorists and philosophers have criticized aspects of modern work since the beginning of the Industrial Revolution, the most influential reference for post-work theory is the body of writings by André Gorz (1980, 1982, 1985, 1989, 1994, 1999, 2018; see Granter and Aroles 2023), in which all of the themes that are mentioned in the next paragraphs are already articulated and woven together.

For post-work theorists, work is a value of the past. Many argue that this is the case for simple empirical reasons because the expansion of automation (Srnicek and Williams 2015; Susskind and Susskind 2015; Danaher 2019a, 2021; Susskind 2020) and other imminent technological breakthroughs (Mason 2015; Bastani 2018) make the need for work redundant. Many post-work theorists, however, do not tether their critiques of work to the projection of a real 'end of work' (Hester and Stronge 2020). What they question rather is the 'work society' (Donaldson and Kymlicka 2019), that is, the mode of social organization characteristic of modern society, in which waged work became the institution through which people were financially supported, socially integrated, enjoyed full citizenship, and through which they defined their social identity. A seminal book arguing in this way, which became the bridge between Gorz's work and current post-work theorizing, is Kathi Weeks' *The Problem with Work* (2011).

The first set of reasons brought up against the 'work society' is that the organization of work today makes it difficult for a growing number of people to enjoy these old promises attached to work, as it becomes increasingly precarious, in relation to pay and conditions. Work for many has become a source of deep insecurity, material, social and even existential (Bauman 1998; Sennett 1998; Standing 2016). Even workers in higher occupations face precariousness (Horgan 2021). For post-work theorists, these old promises were intrinsically problematic anyway. Integration through work is deeply exclusionary, first for those who cannot or do not want to work (Van Parijs 1995; Frayne 2015), but also because discrimination based on race, culture, sexuality, or gender is often expressed and entrenched through work (Chamberlain 2018). In the work society, the work to which the 'goods' mentioned above are attached in fact excludes many forms of social contribution, notably domestic work and care work. Some strands of feminist scholarship, notably 'materialist' feminism of the 1970s, are a major source of inspiration for a number of post-work theorists (Weeks 2011; Hester and Srnicek 2023).

Another issue of modern work is that it undermines freedom: not only are the majority forced to work to survive but work organizations place citizens in situations of obedience and arbitrary control by external authorities. Also, work is so entrenched as a subjective preference and as the centre of social organization, it remains an imperative for individuals and an obsession for government policy, even though there is less and less of it to go around (Livingstone 2017), and even when it produces no real value, or is in fact utterly meaningless (Graeber 2018) or even destructive. Even work that produces some value can be destructive if all externalities are considered, notably the impact on human health and on the environment (Cholbi 2018b; Hoffmann and Frayne 2023). But even work that is necessary should be contained and minimized as much as possible, since genuinely human endeavours begin with autonomy and the capacity to engage with self, others and the world freely (Weeks 2011; Danaher 2017, 2019b). Given the intrinsic badness of work and the increasing gap between the promises of work and what work really means for most today, the continuing grip it continues to hold on people's mentalities and governments' imagination can only be explained by the force of ideology or as being a typical case of 'adaptive preference' (Cholbi 2018a).

The purpose of this book is to 'make the case' for work amidst this concert of voices projecting and advocating its demise. A properly positive case for work is presented in the second part of the book, in Chapters 10–14. We will see in a moment (i.4) how this positive case for work is constructed. Chapter 9, which explores the ambivalent status of work in feminist scholarship provides the hinge between this positive case for work and the negative first part. This shift from critique towards constructive approval turns on a conceptual extension of a key concept of feminist theorizing, the concept of social reproduction.

The first part of the book, Chapters 1–8, reconstructs the case against work. This part does not restrict itself to the current discussions, as the arguments and counter-arguments are already clearly set out in existing publications (see Frayne 2016; Danaher 2019a; Deranty 2022; Breen and Deranty 2024; Celentano et al. 2024). Instead, the book's first part reframes post-work and anti-work positions by exploring the main theoretical traditions (from the

Western canon) that have inspired critiques of work across the many dimensions noted above. This archaeological work is important to conduct because these classical bodies of scholarship represent a formidable background informing current dismissals of work. Even if all the arguments made by contemporary post-work theorists were successfully rebutted, there would still remain a number of momentous philosophical and social-theoretical points denying the importance of work from a variety of perspectives. Some other formulations or empirical variations on key arguments drawn from this background would continue to cast doubt on work's significance. Indeed, major strands of work-related disciplinary enquiries, in sociology, labour relations, management, and organization studies, which are often overlooked by post-work theorists, provide these empirical and conceptual variations on themes and ideas from the major authors, sometimes over a long history within these disciplines. Furthermore, contemporary anti-work and post-work theorists often draw on the argumentative weight of these seminal references to establish their positions. For example, the mere mention of the term 'work ethic' conjures up all the critical dimensions noted by Max Weber in his landmark study (Chapter 2). The term does a lot of argumentative work by itself, because of the force and influence of Weber's demonstration it appeals to. Or the contrast between work activities and what are supposed to be freer, more authentic forms of human action leans on the distinction between *praxis* and *poiesis* inherited from Greek philosophy and rejuvenated in striking fashion by Hannah Arendt in *The Human Condition* as well other leading neo-Aristotelian thinkers (Chapter 5). This philosophical background plays an important role in today's debate, by lending its leverage to arguments that emphasize the heteronomy built into work activities. To make the case for work, therefore, the lineages between those classical references and current anti- and post-work arguments need to be made fully visible. Each chapter in this first part is thus dedicated to one major tradition from which critical arguments against work have emerged. In the course of this historical-conceptual exploration, the main post-work accounts, as well as Gorz's seminal texts, find their place and are referenced as reformulations, applications, and extensions of these older strands of critique.

The underlying aim of this first part is to begin to make the case for work in a dialectical way. In most chapters, significant conceptual and methodological contradictions, flaws and hesitations, and sometimes empirical mistakes, can be highlighted in the critiques of work. The contemporary versions are caught up in these immanent criticisms. In Chapters 1 (historicist objections) and 8 (objections from social and political theory), however, the rebuttal of these criticisms requires the extended arguments presented in the second part. These two chapters therefore remain aporetic, that is, present versions of the case against work to which only chapters in the second part (Chapters 13 and 14 respectively) are able to respond.

The order of chapters in this first part is broadly dictated by two organizing principles, but the progression there is not as linear as in the second part, which means that the chapters in this first part can be read in relative independence from each other. The first organizing principle centres on the historical background from which critical arguments 'against work' are made. Chapters 1–5 (exploring post-work arguments in the footsteps of Weber, Marx, Foucault, and post-Aristotelian philosophy) study theories whose critiques of modern work rely on an extensive contrast with earlier modes of social organization. Chapter 6 (Nietzsche and post-Nietzschean philosophy, including Heidegger) looks at critiques of modern work that are less interested in historical comparison and focus on work as a pathology of the present, which they view as one of the main symptoms of modern nihilism. Chapters 7 and 8 (objections from technology and from social and political theory) look towards the immediate and long-term futures of work.

The second organizing principle is archaeological in a broad thematic sense. Chapter 1 sets the scene by articulating the historicist concerns that are mentioned in most contemporary anti-work and post-work arguments. Following it, the order of chapters loosely reflects the scope of each author's appeal for contemporary critiques of work. Most or perhaps all current post-work theorists use the term 'work ethic' or similar expressions in their denunciation of the centrality of modern work. Max Weber's shadow spreads across most of the post-work landscape, we might say. While several influential post-work theorists today do not reference Marx, many others do (Gorz, Weeks, and Frayne in particular), and in any case, the link between modern work and the constraints placed on it by the rules of capitalist economy is thematized by all of them. But the Marxian shadow doesn't cover as much theoretical territory as the Weberian one, to pursue the metaphor. And while post-Nietzschean references feature in important post-work writings (Weeks, Chamberlain), they are foreign to many others.

In order to present the argument that is made in the second part, we need first to briefly explain what is meant by 'work' in this book.

i.2 What Is Meant by 'Work'?

Besides the usual issues that arise as soon as one attempts to define an everyday concept, two extra reasons linked to this book's project make such an attempt even more problematic. The first is the great diversity of cultural, social, political, and economic realities and the many dimensions of experience that are implied in discussions of work across the many authors mentioned in the previous section. For Aristotle and his heirs, work is problematic when it overtakes other kinds of activity in importance. For many post-work theorists, the 'problem with work' is the place formal employment has taken in modern people's lives. For many critical philosophers in the French and German traditions, the pathologies associated with the modern work ethic point to deep cultural ills, at a metaphysical level, we might say. Work means different things in each one of those cases, even if there are overlaps between these meanings. A second issue, which stems from the book's approach, relates to the core assumptions that run implicitly in the first part and are made explicit in the second. The claim that work is central draws on the analysis of the ways in which particular dimensions of work activities mobilize subjective resources and imply specific social relations. The underlying assumption is that there are material and social dimensions to working activities that implicate human persons and their interactions to such a degree that they are bound to have a strong impact on them as individuals and on their collective life. 'Central' then means that, because of these impacts, work shapes individual identities, for the better, when work goes well, or for worse when it does not go well in some way. And similarly for the collectives. But such an analysis seems to reach for aspects of work beyond the particular meanings that a particular society attaches to it at a particular time. It seems to make essentializing, transhistorical claims about work activities. These kinds of claims are completely outmoded in contemporary philosophy and social theory (Jaeggi 2018 formulates sophisticated arguments to explain why). In relation to work specifically, Baudrillard's demolition of Marx in his influential 1968 *The Mirror of Production* seems to mount a definitive rejection of essentialist, humanist approaches. Indeed, post-work theorists think that the belief in work's central importance, more than being a theoretical mistake is in fact a cultural illusion (Frayne 2015), or as we saw, an 'adaptive preference' (Cholbi 2018a).

Despite these portentous objections, the argument in the second part unabashedly takes it as its grounding assumption that there are characteristic features of work, as a particular kind of human activity, which are intrinsic to it, and which have a demonstrable impact on the bodies and minds of human beings as well as on the organization of their collectives, in all kinds of cultural and historical contexts. The book's wager, for which much evidence is evinced in the second part, is that, once these features of work are identified, it becomes clear that work is a type of activity that is bound to have a profound impact on individual and social life, whatever the cultural and historical contexts. Chapter 11 surveys a large amount of historical and anthropological scholarship to defend this idea factually. The chapter also takes up the worries just noted about essentialist and transhistorical claims. However, given the large question mark that these worries will undoubtedly represent for many readers before we get to that chapter, it is worth while making a few simple points already in this introduction, to try and assuage them until then.

The anthropological perspective that the questionable assumption suggests is in actual fact not difficult to accept. It seems utterly trivial to say that all human societies work, if work is taken in a basic sense, namely, as an intentional activity that humans engage in to fulfil many of their needs. Hegel is a good reference here, as he made it the basic starting point of his analysis of work in the *Philosophy of Right* (Hegel 1991, 231). Work, he wrote, is a 'mediation' between needs and means to satisfy them: particular 'means' are 'acquired and prepared for similarly particularised needs'. In other words, work is about fulfilling specific needs by mobilizing the means appropriate for that. As the paragraphs preceding this definition made clear, this is the specific way in which humans keep themselves alive, by fulfilling subsistence needs, and how they ensure their well-being, by fulfilling needs beyond subsistence. Marx after him constantly emphasized the same basic fact. He did so not just in his writings of 1844, which many might dismiss for their essentialist-sounding talk of 'species-being'. He made that point at the start of every description of human social orders, as a foundational given on which to build his analyses of particular modes of production, for example in the *German Ideology* (2000, 177), in the general introduction of the *Grundrisse* (2000, 381), in volume one of Capital (1991 [1867], 127) and in many other texts. A passage from the *Contribution to the Critique of Political Economy* of 1861 shows that he made Hegel's basic definition of work his own: 'Real labour is purposeful activity aimed at the creation of a use value, at the appropriation of natural material in a manner which corresponds to particular needs' (1988 [1861–1863], 55). In a famous letter (of July 1868 to Louis Kugelmann), he emphasized the trivial nature of this fact, which means however, precisely, that it is valid across societies and across history:

> Every child knows a nation which ceased to work, I will not say for a year, but even for a few weeks, would perish. Every child knows, too, that the masses of products corresponding to the different needs required different and quantitatively determined masses of the total labor of society. That this necessity of the distribution of social labor in definite proportions cannot possibly be done away with by a

> particular form of social production but can only change the mode of its appearance, is self-evident. No natural laws can be done away with. What can change in historically different circumstances is only the form in which these laws assert themselves.
>
> **(Marx and Engels 2010, 47)**

Axel Honneth (2023, 117–121) has highlighted the odd discrepancy between the formality of the definitions of work to be found in Hegel and Marx, which cover all 'needs' and 'means', and the way they restrict work to the use of natural resources for the fulfilling of subsistence needs when they give concrete content to these terms. We take up this difficulty in Section 12.1. This problematic restriction, however, does not affect the generic definition we can draw from these two major philosophers of work. Accordingly, work at its most basic is simply the activity enabling humans to fulfil many of their needs. Of course, there are many needs that do not require work for their satisfaction. The definitions of Hegel and Marx already provide the conceptual elements helping to demarcate work in this context: work is any activity fulfilling 'needs' when purposeful action mobilizing some instrumentality ('means') is required for it. Or, to emphasize a related aspect: work is an activity that is engaged in with the aim of producing an output that is of value for someone. The output to which value is attached, in the most general sense of being valuable to someone, can be a material object but it can also be a change in someone's circumstances which from their perspective is useful, whether it be repairing a burst pipe in their basement, tending their broken leg, or providing professional support if their mental health is ailing.

Saying that all human societies are work societies in this trivial sense is not saying that every human society acknowledges work as an important aspect of its social life, and that work is always a central cultural value. It just means that one of the things (many) individuals do in a human society is work. It does not mean that only humans work either. The claim is simply that humans, qua humans, engage in a particular kind of activities that we call work. Work is one of the characteristic features of the human species, alongside religion, war, art, living in a particular kinship form, having one's actions constrained by moral rules that can be enforced through symbolic and material punishment, and so on. This anthropological view of work is precisely the one adopted by anthropologists who study work (Applebaum 1992; Spittler 2016). Noting that Marx consistently thought of humans as a working species, in other words, that there was an anthropological layer in his conception of work is important because Marx is for many theorists a major reference point for defending a historicist approach against what they view as essentialist, ethnocentric or anachronistic claims. As a matter of fact, Marx had no compunction grounding his historicist method on an anthropological basis. Making the point that all human societies have to work in no way excludes the acknowledgement of the cultural specificity of work experiences and work institutions at a given time and in a particular society. Anthropologists of work, or Marx, have no issue holding the two perspectives concurrently, and it is no problem for them to do so as the two sets of considerations are situated at different levels. One is a general, analytical, external way of describing human societies, the other focuses hermeneutically on the substantial content of particular, historical forms of social life.

Equally, saying that all human societies work, in the generic sense just defined, is not refuted by pointing out that some activities are viewed as work in some societies but not in others, or as Hannah Arendt famously outlined it, that there are different categories of working activities, to which different values are attached. The general necessity to work does not specify how a particular society carves out its own form of life, how it describes its own reproductive activities, what values are attached to different spheres of activity and indeed of non-activity, or what kind of social recognition is attached to which activities. Since the levels of description are different, it is entirely possible that in a given society some purposeful activities are essential to fulfil needs, activities that therefore count as work in the general, analytical sense, but are not described as work in that society's value system. This is typically what happens with care work in long periods of modern societies. The feminist perspective we study in Chapter 9 highlights the danger inherent in rejecting the general, analytical perspective on the basis of a substantive, particular one. This amounts to refusing to call care a form of work, on the grounds that in many societies, in modern capitalism in particular, many activities performed by women have not been recognized as work, their role in the overall economic organization was overlooked, and what women did was interpreted as being simply an expression of their femininity. This example shows how important it is to hold on to the difference separating levels of analysis, between the formal, general one, and the particular, substantial one.

Once the trivial point about human societies is accepted, that all human societies have to work because needs have to be fulfilled, a simple conception of work comes into view, which is already sufficient to give some flesh to the idea of the centrality of work. In a moment, four features of working activities will be highlighted that analytically derive from the basic conception of human work just mentioned. They provide an initial specification of the conception of work that operates in the background of the book's first part and is made fully explicit in the second part. Before we look at these features of work though, the earlier methodological issue needs to be tackled, that work as it is discussed in the first part covers many different aspects and the classical authors mentioned do not all mean work in the sense discussed here.

In answer to that, it can be pointed out that the aspects of work discussed by these authors must have some relationship to the generic definition of work we are starting with since the latter is entailed in any basic, realistic view of what a human society requires to function at all. An example will make this clearer. If critiques of the work ethic are raised in the legacy of Max Weber's most famous book, this is an argument against a particular way of linking work in formal employment to an individual's overall life plan, their hope of redemption and the meaning of their life. It does not seem to be an argument against work understood as an activity that is necessary to fulfil socially defined needs. But there can be a modern work ethic only because modern individuals, like all human individuals, have to work, or at least many of them. The general sense of work is a necessary condition for there to be a modern work ethic.

Highlighting this twofold link, both a discrepancy and a necessary connection, between the basic, anthropological, and more specific meanings of work, is important for several reasons. First, it helps to better identify arguments against work that only target particular aspects of it in particular historical circumstances, but which do not amount to a rejection of the importance of work when the latter is considered from the general point of view of a needs-fulfilling activity. Indeed, sometimes criticisms that target historical organizations of work include a reference to the goods of work that are sacrificed in that set-up, such as social connections or the potential for developing expertise. Sometimes, a counter-model of work is even proposed (typically by Gorz in his later writings, 1994, 80–84; 1999, 72–78; 2018, 126–131; see Bowring 2002 for an argument along similar lines and Chamberlain 2018, 110–112 for a recent post-work criticism of this). In all such situations, the rejection of work is only relative. It is not work itself that is challenged, but a particular organization of work. Often the criticisms of factual aspects of work organizations are undoubtedly on point, for instance, those that Michael Cholbi lists in his influential 2018 article debunking the notion of a 'duty to work'. But that does not make it an argument against work as such. When the critique of work targets empirical aspects of its organization, not only does the general meaning of work remain valid, it also continues to raise specific challenges, which are captured in simple yet unavoidable questions, such as: given that human societies have to organize work among their members and given how impactful work is for subjectivities, how should such an organization be set up so that it is fair to all, both from the point of view of the distribution of work outputs, and the distribution of the goods and bads of these activities?

i.3 Four Features of Work

Four basic but significant dimensions of work can be drawn from the anthropological outlook, as belonging analytically to work activities. It is useful to mention them here already because it is the effect of those features on human minds and bodies and the need to organize these effects collectively that explains why work is 'central' to human life. Part II of the book will explain these mechanisms at length, but it is important to introduce them here already so that the fundamental perspective of the book is clear from the beginning. These four features of work are identified in a compelling fashion by Hegel in his conceptual analysis of work in the *Philosophy of Right* (1991, 228–239; see Schmidt-am-Busch 2001 for a thorough analysis of Hegel's concept of work). This section draws heavily on this passage.

The first dimension is that work is an *instrumental* kind of human action. That is, its primary aim is to produce an output, not to engage in the action as an end in itself. Even if in some happy circumstances work is engaged in for its own sake and is in that situation akin to a form of *praxis*, this motivation only comes as an addition to what distinguishes work from other kinds of action. Hegel captured this dimension via the concept of 'means', *Mittel*. All work is 'mediation', *Ver-mittl-ung*, that is, an employment of means to secure the means for the realization of an end. The essential 'mediatedness' of work comes out clearly if we consider that many needs are not 'primary' needs, that is needs that are the ultimate, final cause of work actions (the point where the work process ends), but rather are needs for yet other means in a chain including different parts and processes: some other artefacts or pieces of artefacts or parts of infrastructure or forms of support for the workers doing the work, all of which are required for the realization of the final end (the final, needed output). Furthermore, that final output is usually not itself the ultimate end of the work action. Humans don't usually work to produce outputs for the sake of it, except in pathological situations. The 'for the sake of' of the work action is an output, but the output itself has its own 'for the sake of', namely the need to fulfil. Indeed, the working agent might have her own motivation for producing this needs-fulfilling output, whether drawing an income from it, or demonstrating her skills, or avoiding punishment.

Work, the mediation of means and needs, is mediation, or instrumentality, through and through: some means are needed to produce other means which are needed to fulfil needs which are themselves the means for other ultimate needs.

It might well be that the need fulfilled is 'a false need', for example, a need manufactured by marketing to increase consumption. Or indeed, because we are so used to working, it might be true that many jobs today have no other purpose than to keep us working without fulfilling any 'genuine' needs or even any need at all, as the 'bullshit jobs' thesis holds (Graeber 2018). But even if many of the needs fulfilled by work are in fact not genuine, this does not prevent the fact that work definitionally is about fulfilling needs by producing outputs. Work that does not produce real outputs is just sham work, but the fact that there is sham work does not affect the definition of work. Indeed, without that definition, we wouldn't know those types of work are a sham.

A second key dimension of work as an instrumental kind of action is that it harbours an intrinsic *technical* dimension. There are simply better and worse ways to fulfil needs by providing the output required. The technical dimension relates first of all to the needs themselves: the need can be fulfilled better or not so well. There is an intrinsic instrumental normativity to needs-fulfilment. But different types of work-action can fulfil the same need and yet be ranked among each other, on a range of different standards. This is the case notably in relation to efficiency, if one kind of action uses fewer resources than another, in terms of working time, or of the material resources or tools used. Cultural factors also come into play. Particular societies and indeed particular professions develop their own understanding of what it is to do the job well, or what adequate needs-satisfaction is. In one community, resource economy might be a strong consideration compared to the quality of service; in another society, it might be the aesthetics of the output; in others, the satisfaction of the person to whom the work output is addressed might be paramount. Professional experts have their own evaluation of the output and of the work that produced it, compared with non-experts. The general point is that no work escapes technical adjudication. All work is under the constraint of technical normativity, and because of that it demands of the working agent an acquisition and mastery of the techniques involved.

Thirdly, all work is a *socially embedded gesture* in several ways. We noted already the cultural dimension of technical evaluations. All work mobilizes knowledge that is not purely technical but also steeped in cultural values. Working activities as a result are subjected to social judgements on the basis of the cultural-technical normativities they mobilize. In many cases the addressee of work is not the working self, but another person, a real, identified person, or an anonymous other, or society as a whole or a part of society (for instance repairing a road in a local community). Work therefore usually brings with it the necessity to exchange, to communicate, to haggle over price and the terms of exchange, to discuss product quality, and so on. The sociality of work is also an inherent aspect of its instrumentality: work is addressed *to* someone. It is a feature of the work activity that its outputs are intended *for* someone, often someone other than the working self.

Another obvious aspect of work's intrinsic sociality is that an individual human being cannot have all of their individual needs fulfilled by their own work alone. Rather, the exchange of their work outputs against the work outputs of others is made necessary for the satisfaction of all of their needs. This other-dependence obtains simply as a result of the finitude of an individual person's intellectual and physical capacities. Additionally, as soon as technological complexity has passed a certain threshold, key aspects of need-fulfilment depend on the availability of infrastructures and material processes that cannot be produced by a single individual but require coordination of many individual efforts to be built, operated and maintained, such as roads, bridges, airports, pyramids, cathedrals, castles, common houses, parliaments, public grounds, an electricity or an internet network, and so on. Thirdly, many important needs require the use of single yet complex tools, weapons, machines, instruments, which are beyond the productive capacities of a single individual, notably because they require specialized knowledge and it is by definition impossible for one individual to master every kind of it. This means that even work whose output is addressed to the self retains an intrinsic social component. Working on one's piano skills by practising a piece requires the use of a piano, an instrument no individual is able to produce by themselves, simply considering the raw material that is necessary for it, let alone the complex assemblage of the instrument. In short, the division of labour makes human individuals inherently dependent upon other individuals for the fulfilment of all of their needs in many different ways. Through her work, even work addressed to herself, and even more clearly in the case of work addressed to others, the self relates in many different ways to the others to whom she is related for the satisfaction of her needs. Indeed, through the division of labour, all work is in a sense both other- *and* self-directed. In working, the human individual knows more or less clearly, she fulfils her own needs by fulfilling those of others.

Finally, a fourth dimension of work derives from the three features highlighted, namely that it is a form of action under *many, severe constraints*. In work, humans truly enter the 'realm of necessity', as Marx famously wrote, and as Hegel already stated (1991, 221). A work action is first of all under *the double sway* of the external ends for which it is pursued, namely a particular output and the need to which the output corresponds. It is *also under the sway* of social judgements, evaluating its efficacy in fulfilling the needs for which it is performed, and all the normativity involved in the instrumental, technical, and cultural dimensions of all work. As a result of all these dimensions, all work implies forms of *exertion* for the self: an expenditure of subjective forces, intellectual, physical, and emotional, to achieve the tasks, to learn what has to be learnt, to maintain the efforts, to sustain the gaze of the others, the challenge of having to communicate with them, and so on. All work, therefore, is *toil* in many ways.

These four analytical features of work are foundational building blocks in the original 'case for work' that is presented in the second part of the book.

i.4 Making the Case for Work

The case for work begins at Chapter 9, with a study of feminist theorizing of work. The gendered dimensions of the organization of modern work are an important aspect of the latter's critique. Many of the injustices and harms suffered by women are linked to the organization of work and the cultural understandings that frame it, and feminist concerns therefore play an important role in post-work theory (Weeks 2011; Hester and Srnicek 2023). However, many feminist theorists have been clear on the distinction that needs to be held between the extant organization of work, which can entrench social exclusions and discriminations, and the positive impact that work can have in the lives of women, notably in their struggles for emancipation, but also for the collective more broadly if it is organized correctly. Indeed, it is in feminist theorizing, notably in analyses based on the key notion of social reproduction, that the view of work as the set of activities necessary for subsistence and well-being both at the individual and collective level is most clearly and substantially developed. A maximal extension of this notion borrowed from feminist theory, covering all aspects of individual and social life, is the foundation upon which the case for work is built in the second part of the book.

Chapter 10 explores what this extension of social reproduction entails for the conception of work and defends the latter against objections. A key aim of this chapter is to emphasize the sheer amount of work, across all sectors of society, that is required for the production and reproduction of human life.

Chapter 11 begins the case for work's centrality by studying a variety of sources in history and anthropology, which all indicate that working activities have played a major role in individual and collective lives in many societies before and outside Western modernity. Historical and ethnographic studies belie the widespread view, often cited in post-work writings, that work is an invention of modernity. Based on the distinction noted above and already formulated by Marx, between a general concept of work used in the analysis of social systems, and particular understandings used in cultural analysis, the chapter responds to the accusations of ethnocentrism and anachronism.

Chapter 12 has a twofold aim. The first is to respond to one of the major objections left unanswered in the dialectical exploration of the 'case against work' in the first part, namely that it is wrong to refer to a form of experience and a set of institutions as being 'central' given the complexity of human societies, particularly modern societies, and the plurality of dimensions making up the identity of human subjects, particularly modern subjects. The rejoinder this chapter formulates is that this objection relies on an inaccurate view of work as being a sphere of social life. The view from social reproduction shows clearly that there is work going on in all social spheres. The centrality of work then hangs not on it being a more important sphere than others, since it is not a sphere at all, but rather on the actions included as having prime importance in some way. The chapter shows why and how this is the case. The chapter pursues a second aim, which is to highlight the many different ways in which work is central in a social sense. A key lesson from this chapter is that the notion of the centrality of work has different meanings, depending on context.

Chapter 13 puts in place the perspective from which the centrality of work is advocated in the remainder of the book. This is the perspective 'from necessity'. The different strands of necessity built into work are outlined. From this, the centrality of work in individual life is demonstrated: it is precisely in forcing individual subjects to face multi-dimensional necessity that work not only allows them to grow, to 'self-develop', but can even become the vector for their freedom. The chapter explores this notion of self-development and the conception of freedom attached to it. Freedom arises from the facing of necessity, not from attempting to escape it and work, precisely because it is the direct attempt to meet necessity, is an eminent conduit for freedom.

Chapter 14 argues in a similar fashion in relation to politics and the collective organization of necessity. The different dimensions of this organization of necessity are described and three core meanings of political centrality are distinguished on the basis of it. The first extends the analyses from the first chapter: only a collective organization of work can ensure the latter provides the conditions for freedom and self-development of all. The second meaning is critical and negative. The organization of work creates a number of 'pressure points' for individuals and groups in society, that is, aspects of their social existence in which the fairness or equality of collective organization might appear problematic. Work is politically central, because the pressures felt at these points render it a key vector to question the overall justice of the organization of social cooperation, and on the basis of that questioning, to potentially transform it. The third sense is positive. Work is politically central as a constitutive condition of democratic politics, first because a democratic organization is the condition for solving the issues of justice and equality just raised, and second because work is the space where individuals can develop the dispositions that are necessary for sustaining democratic collective life.

The Conclusion takes up one final objection, which seems to arise out of the view from necessity adopted in the second part: that this perspective might demonstrate the significance of responding to necessity, but a truly human life begins only after this has been done, as Marx seemed to argue with his famous metaphor of the two realms. The conclusion shows why this dualism of two realms and of separate times of human existence can be questioned, which then suggests that work is central even in activities and experiences outside of work.

This book is an attempt to add an original, personal contribution to years of collaborative research on the centrality of work with colleagues from Europe, Australia, and the UK. It marks the culmination of a four-year research project funded by the Australian Research Council (DP190103116). As part of this project, a comprehensive online repository has been built (onwork.edu.au), to collate the rich literatures across the humanities and social sciences that nourish the 'case' for and against work. An online newsletter (https://onwork.substack.com/) documents progress in this online library and offers dedicated studies of authors and themes. Interested readers can consult these resources for further references.

It is time now to begin the long, dialectical journey through the negative arguments against the centrality of work, before the positive case for work can be made in the second half of the book.

PART I

THE CASE AGAINST WORK

1
A Modern Value

This chapter takes up what forms the background of most post-work and anti-work arguments, namely the reference to premodern and non-Western social organizations.

The critique of the 'work society', the denunciation of the centrality and 'hegemony' of work, conjures up alternative visions of human lifeforms that *would not* be organized around work as their most fundamental value. In many post-work and anti-work writings, these counter-images are developed in an explicit fashion, in the form of programmatic statements of a more or less utopian nature, appeals for substantial cultural shifts and more or less radical institutional transformations, like the shorter working week, universal basic income, all the way to luxury communism. A second type of counter-image also plays an important role in critiques of the work society, referring this time to pre-modern and non-Western societies. In this case, examples of alternative social organizations highlight modes of living in which work simply *was not* the central organizing value for collective and subjective life. References to societies that were historically or culturally distant from modern, capitalist society are used by work critics to demystify the modern work ethic by showing that strong subjective investment in work and the central role of work in social organization are historically specific, do not rely on some hard-wired nature of being human, or a structural law of all human societies. Observing other cultures in which, for instance, the most important value in social life is performing one's obligations to kin, rather than being a zealous productive agent or striving to optimize one's human and financial capital, shows that the importance we grant work is not 'natural' or universal but rather the product of a particular imaginary that is specific to Western modernity, and, more precisely, specific to capitalism.

Historical genealogies of the rise of the work ethic attempt to retrace where this particular social formation came from, when it was born, and from which confluence of cultural and material circumstances it emerged. Having been shown to be the outcome of particular contexts, the work ethic is up for grabs, as it were, as the circumstances that saw its rise were not always present and are now changing significantly, notably under the pressure of technological

The Case for Work. Jean-Philippe Deranty, Oxford University Press. © Jean-Philippe Deranty (2024).
DOI: 10.1093/oso/9780192887146.003.0002

developments and economic shifts. The possibility of an overhaul of the work ethic in the near future thus finds a factual ground for many work critics in the historical and ethnographic record.

This first objection to the centrality of work based on the contrast between Western modernity and other examples of human lifeforms can be called the *historical contingency objection*. It is associated with another, normative objection. As the next chapters will illustrate, genealogical accounts of the rise of the modern work ethic usually combine with diagnostic accounts of the new pathological social traits that appear with it. In genealogies of work's centrality, work pathologies usually feature as major symptoms of modernity's destructive tendencies; indeed, work centrality is identified as the direct cause of many modern social pathologies. We might call this the *social pathology objection* to the modern work ethic.

This attempt to undermine the ideological force of the work ethic through gestures of cultural distantiation is shared by many of the authors who are part of the 'post-work' constellation. It finds influential antecedents in the seminal references that are studied in the next chapters. The writings of Weber, Marx, Foucault, Nietzsche, Heidegger, all contribute in their own way to this historical attempt at debunking the modern work ethic. Each one of these classical references provides its own version of a critical genealogy of the work ethic. The writings published by André Gorz in the 1980s, which remain a substantive resource for post-work thinking, are a key mediating resource between these references and contemporary post-work thinking for this historical dimension, as on so many other aspects. In each one of his books (Gorz 1982, 1985, 1989, 1994) Gorz emphasized, usually at the start of his analyses, the historical contingency of the modern work ethic. The start of the *Critique of Economic Reason*, the most comprehensive account of his post-work position, is typical in this regard:

> 'Work' as we know it, is a modern invention. Work in the form in which we recognize and perform it, and to which we give a central place in the life of the individual and of society, was invented, then subsequently generalized only with the coming of industrialism.
>
> **(Gorz 1989, 14)**

However, it is the book by another leading French theorist of work though, Dominique Méda's 1995 *Work: A Value on the Way to Extinction*, that we use here as our lead, as it provides a condensed, representative precis of how historical and ethnographic evidence is deployed to contrast the modern sense of work with that of other, non-Western cultures. In the second and third chapters of her book (see a later rendition in Méda and Vendramin 2017, 7–47), Méda wants to demonstrate that it is only in modern, capitalistic societies that economic activity and the organization of material production became the central institutions through which individuals develop a sense of self and achieve status, the integration of individuals in the collective is imagined, and the community conceives of its most efficient and important mode of collective action. Correspondingly, Méda insists, it is only following the cultural rupture of modernity that a singular notion of 'work' comes to the fore and can meaningfully refer to all these different aspects of social life at the same time. In other cultures, Méda argues, no such term that would encapsulate all these social logics at once exists:

> Anthropological research shows that we can't find a similar sense of work in the societies anthropologists have studied. Some don't even have a distinct word to distinguish productive activities from other modes of human behaviour and have no term or notion that would sum up the idea of work in general.
>
> **(Méda 1995, 32)**

Méda's reliance on anthropological research to emphasize the specificity of modern work draws on a programme of research in France in the 1980s and 1990s, led among others by Maurice Godelier, to study comparatively different cultural representations of work (Godelier 1980; Chamoux 1994; Freyssenet 1999). One thing this research brought to light is that in some pre-modern and some non-Western societies, a generic term for productive activities might exist, but usually extends to activities Western societies would not call 'work', for instance, magical action by a shaman. Or there might be words to designate engaging in activities that cause suffering and pain, as in the etymological roots of 'labour', but that are not specifically attached to ideas of productive activity. Méda cites Philippe Descola's ethnographic studies of the Achuar people of the Amazon as a vivid illustration of the uniqueness of the modern work concept (later published in Descola's first book, 1994, as well as Descola 1996). In Achuar language, not only is there no generic term for 'work', but there isn't even a single term to designate general productive processes, like 'fishing' or 'gardening', the two activities at the heart of Achuar economic life. Descola's later magnum opus, *Beyond Nature and Culture* (2013), further amplified the uniqueness of the Western notion of work, showing how it reflected a 'productivist' ontology that was only one possibility among other ways to carve out the natural world and understand the place of humans in it (see 2013, 325 in particular).

As Méda argues, what explains that diverse social functions and types of activity can all be assembled under the single category of 'work' is the emergence of a properly capitalist form of market economy and the cultural beliefs that accompany capitalism's fixation on the ceaseless creation of abstract value. Work is viewed by moderns as the decisive factor behind the creation of wealth and the most fundamental value of the new society, because it makes it possible both to measure and multiply that wealth. It can subsume other meanings associated with it, precisely because the new social model of which it has become the central principle itself makes other social values (the satisfaction of needs, status, social integration, cooperation) dependent upon the mechanisms of wealth-production. On this narrative, the year 1776—the publication year of Adam Smith's *Wealth of Nations*, in which the labour theory of value is reprised and the modern view of society as the outcome of a giant exchange of work outputs is explicitly promulgated—marks the definitive birthdate for the modern concept of work, the moment when work in the singular becomes the central value in social organizations. The new outlook that Smith develops in his text anticipates the economic perspective that becomes hegemonic in the next century, from the classical political economists to Marx and beyond. On this outlook, the social bond finds its root in the division of labour and the exchange of commodities; the wealth of nations is equated to the output of material goods created by human work; and individuals are considered mainly from the point of view of their labour-power or entrepreneurial capacity. This concrete power that ensures the creation of use-values becomes an abstract entity when it is exchanged in the market in the form of the commodity it has helped to produce, and in the labour market where it is exchanged for a wage. Such singling out of Smith's classic by Méda as radical 'rupture' in social imaginaries is representative of a most commonly shared assumption among critics of the centrality of work.

Other social theorists, Gorz for instance (1985, 1989), add to the narrative of a conceptual and ontological distinguishing of work as a separate sphere of social life in modernity a focus on the concrete social features through which this is expressed. Accordingly, whereas premodern work was not conducted separately from the spaces, times, and relations that made up the general web of life, modern work is performed outside the home (the *oikos* for the Greeks), leads to the creation of specific social relations, and is performed in times clearly demarcated from the rest of social time.

The detour through long history and cultural comparison thus emphasizes the great variability in the way human societies envisage and name the different parts of their social organization and how they see them interacting.

Whilst modern societies see themselves as national communities with the division of labour as their backbone, other societies operate on a reversed logic as it were. Instead of making economic activity the crucible in which other social functions come together, in other societies material production is embedded in social and religious practices that have primacy over work. Activities to ensure subsistence are performed in all human societies, but in most of them, the aims, means, and distribution of products are governed by logics other than technical, instrumental, or financial ones. In the societies of the Western Pacific studied by Malinowski in a classic of anthropology (Malinowski 2001 [1922]), which Méda cites abundantly, a great surplus is produced for no strictly 'economic' reason but rather to display power and status. The largest part of productive activities is conducted for others to whom one owes particular obligations (the affines, relatives by marriage), and the largest part of the outputs is not kept by the person who produces them. Individuals can display high levels of skill and intensity, notably in building canoes, the central artefact of that society, but these physical and technical exertions are governed by magical beliefs and rites which lend specific meaning to the actions. While the activities of the Trobrianders appear to share many of the features of any agricultural and craft work in modern Western societies, in terms of skills mobilized, technique, and the complexity of labour processes, they are in fact entirely different in respect of the deep cultural logics that define the very meaning and the ultimate purpose of the aims and means of working.

These differences in cultural self-conceptions raise sceptical doubts about the epistemological standing of arguments for the centrality of work. The fact that different societies represent social reality differently to themselves, and that, as a result, the psychological, cultural, and social dimensions that are attached to what modern individuals call 'work' are captured in a different imaginary and are reflected in different vocabularies means that speaking of 'the' centrality of work is to commit a basic ethnocentric or anachronistic mistake, imposing one social ontology onto others that are irreducibly different. This is a third objection arising from the historical and ethnographic record, the *ethnocentric objection.*

This objection has a major methodological implication, which might be called the *nominalist challenge.* The great historical and social variability in the self-representations of what people make and do means that there is, in fact, no settled concept of work. Indeed, there is no reason to limit the scope of this challenge to just a comparison between modern and premodern or non-Western societies. It might well be that different modern societies themselves in fact think of work slightly differently, as a result for instance of their specific cultural and economic histories. In this case, once again, 'the' centrality of work has no stable referent.

This nominalist challenge has *methodological* but also deeper, even more portentous *ontological* implications. Methodologically, the lack of stable referent means social scientists must approach work and work issues by adopting the perspective that the culture they study itself takes on its many activities to know what is explicitly defined as work within it. In different societies, different activities will be brought together under a term that might connect with some meanings of modern work but not to others, and those "work" activities will be linked to specific, culturally infused connotations, like pleasure and toil, or freedom and heteronomy, in ways that are specific each time. Already this methodological challenge weakens greatly the talk of 'the' centrality of work, since such centrality, if it exists, is different in different cultures. More deeply though, as Marie-Noelle Chamoux asks in concluding her 1994 article: 'does work exist at all if it is not thought and lived as such?' If a society does not describe some of its productive or technical activities with a term that is equivalent to modern 'work', does work even exist as a social reality for that society? In doing what they do, individuals in that society believe they perform social obligations for instance. Why should the external observer insist that they in fact work? In the cultural realm, representations might well be intrinsic components of reality. The ontology of society might well be directly dependent on the way the collective imagines it.

Aside from references to non-Western cultures, pre-modern understandings are also mobilized to isolate the modern work ethic. Here, the reference point for work critics is often ancient Greek and Roman societies (Gorz 1989, 164–165; Livingstone 2017, 40; Frayne 2015, 24, to cite just three examples). Classical expert studies confirm the uniqueness of the modern conception of work, even within the Western cultural sphere (Finley 1999 [1973]; Vernant 2006). Dominique Méda explains why this is a choice example (Méda 1995, 37). First, Greek and Roman institutions, literature and philosophy have left deep roots in modern Western culture. And yet their basic attitude to work is markedly different from the modern work ethic. Second, ancient writers have left sustained, sophisticated accounts showing, firstly, how there was no homogeneous conception of work corresponding to the modern one, and second explaining why work and workers were held in such low esteem amongst the different types of human activities and social relations. As such, these writings can be taken to encompass 'a kind of ideal-type of societies in which work is not glorified, in the name of other activities'. Ancient writings are thus a privileged source to once again study an example of a society in which work was not central, and in fact, the notion itself did not exist as such. To cite a highly influential Roman source, a famous passage in Cicero's *On Duties* sums up the ancient vision:

> all those workers who are paid for their labour and not for their skill have servile and demeaning employment; for in their case the very wage is a contract of servitude. Those who buy from merchants and sell again immediately should also be thought of as demeaning themselves. For they would make no profit unless they told sufficient lies, and nothing more dishonourable than falsehood. All handcraftsmen are engaged in a demeaning trade; for there can be nothing well-bred about the workshop.
>
> **(Cicero 1991, 57)**

Work for many of the ancient writers was generally the realm of heteronomy. There are important exceptions, for instance Hesiod's description of free farming work in *Work and Days*, though he takes that to correspond to an archaic stage in Athenian history (Vernant 2006). For the most part, however, activities of work are viewed as being either hard labour, *ponos*, which are so obviously punishing they are clear negations of any kind of freedom and virtue, misshaping the body, mind and character of the individual, or as craft activities, engaged in by *technites*, which are performed in the service of others and therefore, again, as putting the person in a situation of servility. Craft activities are also heteronomous because they are engaged in for the purpose of producing a particular outcome, not because the individual would demonstrate their worth through them or would perfect their person by engaging in them. They are 'interested' activities, in every way, activities that slaves typically engage in. These activities are necessary to produce the means to sustain oneself, those which at the time when independent Greek cities were at their peak, were performed in the *oikos*, the home. Freedom flourishes outside that realm, in spaces and temporalities in which the human being engages in activities that correspond most eminently to what is highest in human nature. For the ancients, this occurs in civic activity and in philosophy.

The lesson drawn from classical cultures is not just that they offer a series of eminent and influential denunciations of work. Beyond the negative case, a positive lesson is also drawn from them by modern thinkers, namely, the way in which they defined the social bond, citizenship, individual and collective freedom and their interdependencies, independently of the economic sphere, and in particular of the sphere of production (Méda 1995, 44). As Arendt develops the argument in emphatic fashion in her political philosophy, beyond all the inegalitarian aspects of their social organization that offend our modern sensitivities, the Greek writers showed eminently how individual and collective freedom can flourish in reciprocal dependence but on the basis of a strict separation from the spheres of reproduction and production. The reference to the historical roots of Western culture, which demonstrate a stark contrast when it comes to work, thus provide a historical basis for a major conceptual distinction which continues to be held in modern political thought, the one Marx himself alluded to in the famous passage on the realm of freedom and the realm of necessity. We might call this the *realm of necessity objection.*

To recap then, critical analyses of the centrality of work often draw upon historical genealogies and comparative studies that show how appealing to work as a preeminent notion for understanding the organization of society is a modern invention. Such a historical perspective leads to several objections: the historical contingency objection; the pathology objection; the ethnocentric objection; the nominalist challenge, with its methodological and ontological implications; and the realm of necessity objection.

To maintain the flow of this first part of the book, these objections will be responded to only in the second part, notably in Chapter 11. For now, we must turn to the most influential articulation of these objections, to be found in Max Weber's analysis on the modern work ethic.

2
The Work Ethic

Max Weber's famous reconstruction of the emergence and content of the 'Protestant work ethic' provides the starting point for many critics of work and features in many accounts of 'post-work society' (e.g., Gorz 1989, 15; Méda 1995, 141–145; Weeks 2011, 37–78; Frayne 2015, 24–29; Chamberlain 2018, 4). Many social theorists have expanded upon Weber's initial thesis to characterize later developments of capitalism, from Gramsci's analyses of the Fordist model of production in the 1930s (Gramsci 1992), to more recent analyses of neoliberal capitalism (Fleming 2015). This chapter reviews the main features of Weber's famous historical thesis and considers how they are put to use by work critics. It then outlines the problems that arise from these extensions. The range of social phenomena that the denunciation of the modern 'work ethic' targets has become so vast since the publication of Weber's classic, that the category risks losing any firm reference in social reality. The historical tenour of the thesis has been subjected to serious scholarly criticism and might not provide the factual basis work critics might hope for. And Weber's practice as a sociologist was much more attuned to aspects of the modern work experience that speak to its importance for individuals and working communities.

2.1 The Rational Organization of Formally Free Labour

Weber made the point that capitalism predated developments in Calvinism. Many earlier economic forms could already be called 'capitalistic', as particular individuals and groups in different cultural areas, going back to fairly ancient history, already engaged in the ruthless pursuit of profit (Weber 1992, xxxiii). On the other hand, older, more direct, and brutal forms of capitalization continue to be witnessed in modern capitalism, typically those that contemporary materialist feminists refer to as 'expropriation', as we will see later in Chapter 10. What makes modern capitalism different, Weber argues, is a new attitude to work, 'the rational organization of (formally) free labour' (1992, xxxiv).

The Case for Work. Jean-Philippe Deranty, Oxford University Press. © Jean-Philippe Deranty (2024).
DOI: 10.1093/oso/9780192887146.003.0003

The rationality at play here consists in the systematization of calculation, conducted with exacting precision and the incessant search for increases in efficiency to maximize the profits to be made on the basis of returns on investment. Weber's account of the work ethic in his 1904–1905 study famously focuses on the 'spiritual' and ethical innovations explaining the rise of a modern form of capitalism in the West. These innovations, however, acted alongside other institutional aspects, all of which he also thought of as outcomes of rationalization processes. These, as listed by an expert commentator who draws on the full gamut of texts Weber dedicated to the rise of modern capitalism, include:

> capital accounting, private ownership of the means of production, shared rights in enterprise and property, unrestricted competitive markets, rational technology and organization (including work discipline and division of labour in the firm), modern science, calculable formally rational law and administration (with trained and specialized bureaucrats), a free labour market, and the separation of business from the household.
>
> **(Etzrodt 2008, 53)**

These organizational, institutional, technological, and scientific dimensions of modern capitalism can also take their place in a critique of the modern centrality of work. We find them mentioned in the accounts that will be explored in the next chapters, whether the latter draw inspiration from, or conversely, in the case of Nietzsche and even Marx, have directly inspired the Weberian account. The connections between other major critical theories of modern society and Weber's analysis of rationalization processes have been well studied: whether in relation to Lukacs' analysis of reification, Adorno and Horkheimer's dialectic of modernity, Foucault's genealogy of disciplinary regimes, or Habermas' colonization thesis. And the disciplines of management studies and organization theory owe a lot to his study of modern bureaucracy. This is just to say that references to aspects of Weber's immensely rich body of writings can be found in many critical accounts of work and organizations of work. However, it is his focus on the psychological and ethical motivations behind modern capitalism, underpinned by religious views about individual redemption, that has most particularly fed the scepticism about the centrality of work in modern society.

As was just recalled, the rationalization thesis holds that a calculating, profit-maximizing attitude is applied to all the factors involved in production.

However, the rationalization of all the factors involved in economic activity is fundamentally underpinned by the rationalization of labour:

> all these peculiarities of Western capitalism have derived their significance in the last analysis only from their association with the capitalistic organization of labour. Even what is generally called commercialization, the development of negotiable securities and the rationalization of speculation, the exchanges, etc., is connected with it. For without the rational capitalistic organization of labour, all this, so far as it was possible at all, would have nothing like the same significance, above all for the social structure and all the specific problems of the modern Occident connected with it. *Exact calculation—the basis of everything else—is only possible on a basis of free labour* (emphasis JPD).
>
> **(Weber 1992, xxxvi)**

The 'rational organization of formally free labour' denotes not just the systematic development and application of institutional and scientific knowledge, of new techniques and norms, but also and most fundamentally the adaptation of minds, souls, and bodies to the new rationality. The extension of the logic of calculable profitability across all social and institutional factors, in the end, depends on the individuals who are to carry out the actions making profits possible. Every single individual who participates in this system needs to adopt dispositions that make this logic of calculation operative. If individuals, or groups of individuals, behave in ways that escape the logic of calculation, this hampers the fluid unfolding of the system:

> Capitalism cannot make use of the labour of those who practice the doctrine of undisciplined *liberum arbitrium*, any more than it can make use of the businessman who seems absolutely unscrupulous in his dealings with others.
>
> **(Weber 1992, 21)**

The free labourer is a person whose integration in the social system is such that they have internalized what the system demands for its reproduction. The old ways of ensuring individual compliance resorted to direct social obligation, notably in settings where economic activity relied upon bonds of kinship, and on direct force and oppression, via techniques of compulsion framed by the political and legal systems, notably through the institutions of serfdom and slavery. Yet, while dependent and forced labour might provide opportunities to extract profit in fairly controlled ways, economic efficiency increases dramatically if individuals themselves adopt appropriate dispositions and modes of behaviour. What the logic of constant wealth accumulation requires is that

> Labour (...) be performed as if it were an absolute end in itself, a calling. But such an attitude is by no means a product of nature. It cannot be evoked by low wages or high ones alone, but can only be the product of a long and arduous process of education.
>
> **(Weber 1992, 27)**

Such a process of education applies to each individual and across generations. For modern capitalism to emerge, a violent break with the past was necessary, one that had to be strong enough to uproot old attitudes and beliefs, which made people inclined to work only so much as they would need to reproduce the existing way of life. Weber characterizes this latter attitude with the generic term 'traditionalism'. The revolutionary impact of Protestantism, according to him, is that it offered new narratives of salvation, with corresponding prescriptions and prohibitions, that completely overturned such a traditionalist approach to life journeys. The new creed provided the deep motivations, new promises of redemption and threats of damnation that motivated individuals to regard their occupation as a duty imposed by the highest authority, one through which they could prove their inclusion among the blessed. This is the initial Lutheran meaning of 'calling' or *Beruf*, according to Weber: to accept one's occupation in social life as a way of serving God through earthly activity (1992, 39–47). To this, Calvin and especially his followers added the angst-inducing idea of predestination. The answer to this existentially threatening vision was that one could only ascertain one's election through constant dedication to work, where financial success would demonstrate on earth one's election in the next life:

> Asceticism looked upon the pursuit of wealth as an end in itself as highly reprehensible; but the attainment of it as a fruit of labour in a calling was a sign of God's blessing. And even more important: the religious valuation of restless, continuous, systematic work in a worldly calling, as the highest means to asceticism, and at the same time the surest and most evident proof of rebirth and genuine faith, must have been the most powerful conceivable lever for the expansion of that attitude toward life which we have here called the spirit of capitalism.
>
> **(Weber 1992, 116)**

Weber made it clear that the motivating power behind these beliefs quickly waned in its significance. As soon as the new economic organization took on its momentum, religiously based motivations were no longer needed to ensure individual compliance (1992, 19). As the original religious inspiration disappeared, however, it left behind basic ethical traits which remained in place throughout modernity, as functional requisites of the new capitalistic life form.

2.2 Creative Extensions

This sense that the religious origins of the modern work ethic continue to operate in changed yet uninterrupted ways throughout all the later transformations of capitalist culture probably plays a significant part in making Weber's historical thesis so powerfully suggestive for contemporary critical social theorists and post-work theorists. The thesis does not just provide a precise, seemingly well-informed historical background that appears to ground the work ethic in established facts. Just as importantly it suggests an adequate descriptive language, the language of religiosity and of supreme existential stakes, that seems particularly well suited to account for the psychological depth at which the modern work ideology enlists individuals, enjoining them to define themselves through their economic activity and their occupation.

Because of the simple yet compelling nature of the religious perspective, new features seem to be fittingly added to the list of psychological and behavioural traits belonging to the 'work ethic', as natural additions or extensions of it. Such features include the rejection of idleness and the praise of sustained, utility-driven activity; the identification of the person with her occupation; the alleged character-building power of work; the belief that 'God only helps those who help themselves', that 'people get what they deserve and deserve what they get', in other words, that each should take full individual responsibility for their social fate; the social premium accorded to wealth; the obsession with money; the myth of the daring entrepreneur, the slogan common in US politics according to which 'makers are better than loafers' (Brudney 2022), or 'makers' better than 'takers'.

Other traits can be noted. As Weber already stated, the centralization of life around work is rational from the point of view of profit maximization but deeply irrational in respect to other ends (1992, 32, 33, 38). Following Weber's own description, Kathi Weeks emphasizes that the life-orientations built into the modern work ethic are anything but rational from the point of view of a holistic, eudaimonic consideration of individuals' existences. Weber had made the point in relation to the original neo-Calvinist asceticism (1992, 18). This suggests an important extension for later critics of work: even after the initial condemnation of hedonism and consumption was lifted, the irrational drive to work as an end in itself continues on right until today. Work continues to be treated as an absolute good, something intrinsically valuable. This deep irrationality of the work ethic is captured in the absurd catchphrase, 'living to work', which Weber had already formulated as that 'a man exists for the sake of his business instead of the reverse' (1992, 32). This irrationality is all the more striking in today's context, post-work theorists argue, given that automation will arguably destroy increasing numbers of jobs, making the duty to work further and further out of touch with economic reality (Srnicek and Williams 2015; Danaher 2019a). Beside the paradox of an ethic of constant activity premised on the contempt for consumption, another, more basic paradox is that a lot of work in fact produces bad outcomes for society, or indeed incurs many costs for the individuals working (Cholbi 2018a, 2018b). The obsession with work built into the modern work ethic makes us overlook these negative aspects of work.

The work ethic is also synonymous with loss of freedom in several senses. First, in the objective sense that the new rationality is materialized in coercive organizations and controlling social expectations. This has been illustrated in great detail by Elizabeth Anderson (2023) as a 'hijacking' performed by the wealthier classes to repress egalitarian elements present in initial formulations. In a subjective sense, the modern work ethic alienates individuals from richer forms of life and forms of positive freedom. The new ethical worldview, as Weber's famous metaphor goes, entraps individuals as it turns into a 'shell as hard as steel'. That is, it develops into a system of institutions and social expectations such that there is no escaping the imperative of constant valorization and utilitarian calculation. Those who refuse to engage in that logic cannot survive (1992, 20). In such a 'cosmos', individuals famously turn into 'specialists without insight and hedonists without heart' (1992, 124).

The values that come to be inculcated into each new generation are not just those of hard toil as moral duty, accumulation without enjoyment of the riches it can buy or the happiness it might enable, but also a whole series of values that are external to the activity of work itself but radiate from it, as it were: obedience and deference to authority, fear of the master, punctuality, self-control, a regressive attitude to bodily functions and pleasures, an exclusionary stance towards those who can't contribute. As the initial bourgeois phase of work ethic in the nineteenth century became a hurdle to capitalist expansion, the imperative for workers to work hard and for the bourgeois to acquire wealth was transformed into the imperative to consume, again as an end in itself, and not as a means to a higher end (Weeks 2011, 49).

In the fable of the ant and the cicada, the ant is representative of the work ethic. It is deaf to the pleas from the cicada who risks dying as winter comes. The cicada had not made sufficient provisions during summer, as it was too busy singing and dancing. As the fable shows, meanness of heart, selfishness, and harshness, towards oneself and towards others, can also be related to the work ethic. A massive psychological literature was spawned after the Second World War to try and break down into personality traits, analyse through psychometric scales, and measure statistically the psychological profiles of different populations in their attitudes towards work. In his review of the many attempts by psychologists to put Weber's thesis into measurable metrics, Adrian Furnham (1990) highlights all the disparate social and individual psychological characteristics that have been attributed to the Protestant work ethic. These include, to note just a few: the justification of capitalism; sexual repression and the condemnation of hedonism; the exploitation of nature and ecological destruction; a spirit of violence and militarism; the rise of modern science.

Finally, as Kathi Weeks notes, the work ethic has served as a 'deep discursive reservoir on which to draw to obscure and legitimate processes and logics of racial, gender, and nationalist formations past and present' (Weeks 2011, 62). Commitment to the work ethic through the positive identification with waged work allowed portions of the American working class to distinguish themselves from other groups, notably women who performed unwaged work, and non-white groups, especially African-Americans, who could be associated with slave work or against whom the suspicion of bad working habits could be raised. Pride in being a waged worker could complement the pride in being male and being white. It was used as a moral principle to justify the social marginalization of women in the times of the male-breadwinner model, and today still of the descendants of nineteenth-century slavery, as well as of all non-white groups, including immigrants.

2.3 A Protean Catchphrase

Since its initial formulation, the work ethic thesis has thus become a protean formula that encompasses all kinds of psychological, ethical, sociological, and political realities. The term has immediate intuitive appeal for critics of neoliberal capitalism, for the reasons we have just highlighted. Indeed, critical mention of the modern 'work ethic' as a rupture from traditional worldviews often represents the initial starting point for critiques of the centrality of work. The content of the category, however, has become highly variable.

In Gramsci's *Prison Notebooks*, two decades after the publication of Weber's classic, a link was already made between the new social-economic-cultural organization appearing in the United States in the aftermath of the First World War and some defining features of the old Protestant work ethic. Gramsci noted that the new formation, which he already termed 'Fordism', and its attendant cultural forms, gave new shape to old puritanical practices, and produced 'a renaissance of the pioneer morality' (1992, 304). Gramsci drew attention to a whole gamut of new social, cultural, and psychological dimensions that were transformed in the new industrial phase of capitalism in the early twentieth century: new relations between the sexes; the generalization of Taylorist techniques, as a way to discipline bodies and souls; renewed attempts to inculcate useful physical and psychological attributes, such as the capacity for hard toil, punctuality, exactitude, self-control; and new forms of control over hedonistic tendencies, notably alcohol consumption and sexual pleasure. Most importantly, Gramsci highlighted the function that mass consumption through higher wages played in pacifying the working classes and ensuring compliant participation in the system.

A few decades after Gramsci's analyses, on the other side of the Second World War, the term 'Fordism' designated a different social-cultural context and a different interpretation of key societal norms. Many of the phenomena highlighted by Gramsci continue to feature in critical analyses of post-war Fordism, notably the emphasis on the gendered division of labour, the patriarchal model of the family wage (Wilson 1977; Pateman 1988), and the role of consumption both as a structural condition of the capitalist economy and as an inherent factor of destabilization that requires constant surveillance (Aglietta 2001). All these features, however, had to cover new social and psychological realities given the entirely new context.

The 'work ethic' has thus been put to use in the most diverse historical contexts, to designate a large number of psychological, cultural and ethical phenomena and many features of social and bureaucratic practices, all with varying content. Is such high variability in the descriptive content of the work ethic thesis a benefit or a problem for arguments against work centrality? Kathi Weeks thinks that the malleability of the work ethic diagnosis is an asset precisely because it allows the basic insights gained from Weber's classic to be adapted to changing circumstances. But if the term's reference is so elastic, one might well wonder if it designates anything specific in the end. From the point of view of Weber's own practice, which aimed for rigorous accuracy in the use of sociological categories and paid great attention to differences between historical cultures, the fluctuations in what the concept comes to designate in social reality and the great many uses it was put to after his death is problematic. Given the great variability of the term's meaning, one might wonder if it has not become a placeholder, a vague reference that draws on the aura of a great sociologist and his most famous concept to highlight whatever a social critic wants to denounce in a particular culture of work. Indeed, in many post-work texts, critique of 'the' modern work ethic is often rather a critique of a particular work ethic, namely the one that dominates at the time and place in which the social or political theorist is writing. Elizabeth Anderson's recent genealogy (2023) can be viewed from this perspective as a substantive, critical reconstruction of the contested history of the work ethic in the English-speaking sphere. The local specificity of a criticized work ethic becomes particularly visible when theorists list egregious traits that are not to be found in other, contemporaneous lifeworlds. This occurs typically when an American or British theorist targets issues of work, or cultural dimensions of work ideology, that are specific to their country or do not exist with that level of severity in other countries (on the variability of expectations towards work across different nations, see Méda and Vendramin 2017, 49–91). American and British theorists are mentioned here because they are the most represented in contemporary anti-, and post-work literature, and some of the pathologies of modern work they highlight are most acute in their own countries, at least among the richest nations. For instance, the encroachments on personal freedom Elizabeth Anderson notes in the case of US corporations do not compare with what European labour law gives employers and managers licence to do (Anderson 2017). The general point is that as the reference of the term 'modern work ethic' in social reality has become so varied, it risks appearing almost void, an easy catchphrase without determinate content, thereby undermining the arguments that sought to gain historical and sociological weight through its reference.

2.4 A Problematic Reference

This problematic aspect of the work ethic argument is compounded by the fact that, for historians who studied the links between capitalism and Protestantism, the historical basis of the thesis is largely discredited (Eisenstadt 1968; Little 1970; Giddens 1992; Hamilton 2000; Chalcraft and Harrington 2001; Zafirovski 2019 for a recent account of the literature). In the words of one of the experts on the relationship between monotheisms and the rise of capitalism, 'there is in fact not much in the various parts of Weber's thesis which stands up to examination' (Hamilton 2000, 171).

The causal role of puritanism has been rejected, as many of the first 'modern' capitalists who appeared in Weber's sense were in fact Catholics who had migrated from absolutist Spain, France, and Italy and did not convert to the reformed faiths (Hamilton 2000, 162–163). The role of Sephardic Jews expelled from Portugal and Spain has also been highlighted (Sombart 2015 [1911]). Rather than Calvin, historians have argued that the intellectual sources of the modern capitalistic spirit were to be found in late Renaissance thinking, notably Erasmus and Machiavelli and, in England, in Locke and the British Enlightenment. On a methodological level, many have questioned the causal link between religion and economic action, arguing that neo-Calvinists might well have adapted their teachings to new social-economic realities, rather than religion influencing economic behaviour.

The theological roots of the new spirit of capitalism have also been construed differently. Weber's reading of Franklin, of Calvin, and of the neo-Calvinists (Bunyan and Baxter in particular) on which his thesis mostly relied has been roundly rejected. If anything, the Reformers objected to older theological justifications of financial gain (see Brentano's early criticism, 1923). Crucially, the convoluted explanation Weber put forward to resolve the paradoxical asceticism of neo-Calvinists has been judged a non sequitur as it relies upon a mistaken theological interpretation of neo-Calvinist thought in the seventeenth century, which no longer held to the idea of predestination. Even the notion of calling had shifted and no longer applied to earthly activities (Mackinnon 1988; Hamilton 2000, 168). Most significantly, the notion of 'calling' and the idea that doing one's work was pleasing to God, were shown to be old tropes of Christian theology, going back to the New Testament. Brentano already made the point (1923, 389–405) that Luther's *Beruf* was in fact a translation in German by the Augustinian monk of the old concept of '*vocatio*' and, did not mean, even for the reformers, the type of earthly activity Weber had viewed in it.

These criticisms rob the arguments against work of the footing in history and historical sociology they might have hoped to gain from the reference to Weber's thesis. What passes for a recent shift in cultural norms and psychological attitudes might well in fact have had a much longer history. In turn, the core claim that the centrality of work is a historical phenomenon tightly connected to the rise of modern capitalism can no longer ground itself in a linear narrative about the psychological and cultural transformations of modernity. In the second part of the book, we will examine alternative accounts of the significance of work, which show that the importance placed on professional identity is not necessarily reducible to the capitalistic work ethic.

Finally, focusing exclusively on this reference is to make highly selective use of the work of Max Weber. *The Protestant Work Ethic* is his most cited book in contemporary debates on work, but it is only a snippet of the immensely rich and detailed body of writings he dedicated to work, whether in his enquiry into the different attitudes to economic activity in the great monotheistic religions (Weber 1978, 399–611), or in his extensive analyses of the rise of modern capitalism (Weber 1961; see Zafirovski 2019 for the complex links between the Protestant Work Ethic and other parts of Weber's writings). In particular, throughout his career, Weber engaged in fine-grained sociological enquiries about aspects of modern work. In an old but still unsurpassed study, Paul Lazarsfeld and Anthony Oberschall reviewed the moments in Weber's life when he stepped out of the archival records to engage in concrete enquiries of contemporary industrial sociology: investigations on rural labour in 1890 and 1893; a study of the occupational choices and experiences of industrial workers in 1907; a study of the 'Psycho-Physical Aspects of Industrial Work' in a textile mill; a critical review of a large survey of heavy industry workers conducted between 1907 and 1911; and his initiation of an empirical inquiry into the press when he became secretary-treasurer of the German Sociological Society (Lazarsfeld and Oberschall 1965). Lazarsfeld and Oberschall are particularly interested in the many innovations Weber introduced in techniques of sociological analysis as he took part or indeed himself conducted these studies, from the crafting of survey questionnaires, the application of modern statistics, including the coding of qualitative data, to refining the link between quantitative and qualitative dimensions. The article also draws attention to the types of concerns Weber showed regarding work. These concerns encompassed the fundamental attitudes of workers to their activity and the place of work in their lives, in a way that overlapped with the perspective developed in the *Protestant Work Ethic*. Indeed, the 1907 study of the textile mill directly quoted the book. However, the studies included many other aspects of work experience, which no longer matched the framework of the famous 1905 book. In particular, Weber focused a number of these investigations on the impact of working conditions and work activities upon the individuals involved, their occupational choices and life aspirations. These enquiries examined concrete aspects of working activities, the precise organization of tasks, the relationships to management, and the interplay between life outside work and life in work, which are precisely the types of concerns that are brought forward in claiming that work is 'central'. Indeed, even if Weber's political aims did not resemble our own, his concern for how workers engaged in their work was driven precisely by the conviction that work is a central institution for the modern state. Reading only *The Protestant Work Ethic* misrepresents Weber's position.

Let us see now how it is with the second major reference in this context, how the writings of Karl Marx are variously appealed to by different critics and defenders of work.

3
Abstract Labour

A second important trope in arguments against the centrality of work, one that intersects with Weber-inspired denunciations of the work ethic, draws on Marx's critical analyses of capitalism. Marx remains a live reference for many contemporary post-work theorists, like Kathi Weeks or David Frayne. Gorz's seminal writings of the 1980s began as a critique of Marxist discourse in his time, but they remained deeply inspired by some aspects of Marx's thought and by post-Marxist critical social theory. Beyond texts that thematize post-work society explicitly, sophisticated readings of Marx in the last decades focused on *Capital* and the concepts of *abstract labour* and *value* as a social form have presented Marx as a critical theorist who made it theoretically impossible to talk positively about the centrality of work. These readings have had a deep impact on contemporary social and political theory. Their authoritative reconstructions of Marx add substantial weight to rejections of the centrality of work since they present the thinker who is supposed to be the philosopher of work par excellence as providing arguments against work. This chapter reviews these influential readings and attempts to show that they face serious challenges, stemming from within Marx's own writings. Before it does that, the chapter considers other readings of Marx that provide arguments in favour of work.

Marx scholarship is incredibly complex and dense. The profusion of texts and debates to consider challenges the cognitive capacities of any single reader. On any doctrinal point, divergent statements can be found across Marx's immense corpus, for instance between his very early texts of the 1840s and the mature texts leading to and including *Capital*, all the way to the later writings. Indeed, that corpus is still in the process of being thoroughly edited. In his mature works of political economy, Marx constantly revised his formulations, notably between different editions of *Capital*. Some interpreters mobilize these variations to mount key arguments in support of their readings. Many interpreters correct the letter of his texts in the spirit of what they take to be his research programme, or for their own agendas, so that independent considerations, of a logical, historical, economic-theoretical, or political nature, beyond the already thorny issues of interpretation, are brought into

The Case for Work. Jean-Philippe Deranty, Oxford University Press. © Jean-Philippe Deranty (2024).
DOI: 10.1093/oso/9780192887146.003.0004

the debate. Some major historical interpretations become focal points for contemporary debates and disagreements, for example in recent years, Isaak Rubin's *Essays on Marx's Theory of Value* (1972 [1923]). Historical schools of Marx interpretation develop along national lines, sometimes ignoring, sometimes interacting with each other. And Marx interpretations vary according to epistemological traditions. Analytical Marxists don't cite Marxists trained in Critical Theory, structuralism, post-colonial studies, or feminist theory, and vice-versa. Critical Theory itself is split between post-Habermassians and adherents of the first generation. The former, who are institutionally dominant, rarely acknowledge the latter who in turn tend to cite the former only in a polemical fashion.

Acknowledging such startling complexity is important before Marxian arguments against work are considered. There simply is no one-best way of reading Marx. Readings of Marx arguing that for him true emancipation is emancipation *from* work have to contend with interpretations that contrarily argue that for him emancipation is emancipation *in* and *through* work, or indeed via a new kind of work. *Five main pathways* through this interpretive maze can be singled out for their relevance in debates on the centrality of work. The third, fourth, and fifth of the approaches studied below emphatically reject the centrality of work. Before we look at them, it is important to introduce readings that more classically highlight the different ways in which work is central for Marx. Many of these readings are reference points in the second part of the book when the case for work is made.

3.1 Normative and 'Traditional' Accounts of Work in Marx

The first of these positive approaches vindicates the view of Marx as the philosopher of work par excellence. These are philosophical readings that draw on Marx to present conceptual accounts of what work allows human beings to achieve, as individuals, regarding the development of their capacities, their self-realization, and their overall flourishing, and between themselves as social and political beings (for instance Elster 1985, especially at 521–527, 1986; Brudney 1998; Wood 2004; Sayers 2011; Fischbach 2023; Kandiyali 2014; Foster 2017).

The 1844 'Economic-Philosophical Manuscripts', and the notes on James Mill are often a particular focus in these analyses since they propound detailed formulations of the developmental and socializing power of work. The 1844 manuscripts famously argue that work is an essential feature of being human, that 'productive life is species-life, (...) life producing life'. And, since 'the whole character of a species, its generic character, is contained in its manner of vital activity', 'free conscious activity is the species characteristic of man' (Marx 2000 [1844a], 90). This expresses a normative concept of work, whereby unalienated work is work which allows humans to actualize their full humanity, which concretely means fully developing their cognitive and practical powers and their creativity. In that text, science and art are the ultimate manifestations of what work allows humans to express and how it is the pathway for them to realize their essence, within themselves and in the objective world. In his notes on James Mill, the young Marx insisted particularly on the fact that work is not just a way for my 'personality', 'individuality', or 'peculiarity' to be actively affirmed, that is, both developed and expressed. Work is also a concrete, practical way to establish sociality. Through unalienated work, I can have 'the direct enjoyment of realizing that I have satisfied a human need', 'by my work' I have 'fashioned for another human being the object that met his need'. Through (free) work, therefore, the young Marx argued, each can 'doubly affirm themselves and their fellow human beings' (Marx 2000 [1844a], 132).

These philosophical interpretations often attribute a consistent view of work to Marx, from these early texts, all the way to the texts of the 1850s and 1860s. A passage in Booknote VI of the *Grundrisse*, in which Marx takes Adam Smith's early definition of work as disutility to task, is often cited as key evidence of such continuity:

> It seems quite far from Smith's mind that the individual, 'in his normal state of health, strength, activity, skill, facility ', also needs a normal portion of work, and of the suspension of tranquility. Certainly, labour obtains its measure from the outside, through the aim to be attained and the obstacles to be overcome in attaining it. But Smith has no inkling whatever that this overcoming of obstacles is in itself a liberating activity—and that, further, the external aims become stripped of the semblance of merely external natural urgencies and become posited as aims which the individual himself posits—hence as self-realization, objectification of the subject, hence real freedom, whose action is, precisely, labour.
>
> **(Marx 1973 [1857], 611–612)**

The arguments mounted in these readings are thus arguments of philosophical anthropology. Even when they include analyses of Marx's critique of work under capitalism, they endorse general, normative claims about the impact of work activities on different features of being human and on social and political relations, independently of the specific historical formation in which those activities are deployed. The injustices and pathological effects of exploitation, alienation, reification, and domination as structural features of the capitalist mode of production, are interpreted as inversions and perversions of the normative ideal of work.

A *second* approach can be delineated, which might be called the 'traditional' one, following Moishe Postone in his seminal book *Time, Labor, Social Domination* (Postone 1993). This type of approach overlaps in many ways with the previous family of readings as it also uses an anthropological and transhistorical lens to discuss work. The emphasis, in this case, is not so much on the normative model of work, but rather on the institutions of capitalist society, notably private property and the market, as instruments of exploitation and immiseration of the working class. The focus is mainly critical and political. The collective organization of social labour and the shared experiences of work are the classical leverage points from which that unjust system can be opposed and overthrown to lead to an emancipated society. An important strand of Marx reading of this kind is the first wave of the Frankfurt School, as represented notably in the texts published by Max Horkheimer and Herbert Marcuse in the 1930s (Marcuse 1970 [1941], 272–273; Horkheimer 2002). An extract from Horkheimer's long study on authority can be cited for the purposes of illustration. The final page of the 'Authority' section is a neat summary of a 'traditional' take on work:

> If the goods men need in order to live no longer originate in an economy of seemingly free producers, of whom some because of poverty must hire themselves out to others, while the latter manufacture goods not according to human needs but according to what their own solvency requires, and if, instead, such goods originate in the rationally guided efforts of mankind, then the freedom of the abstract individual, who proves really to be in chains, will become the collaborative work of concrete men whose genuine freedom will be limited only by nature and its necessities. In disciplined work men will take their place under an authority, but the authority will only be carrying out the plans that men have made and have decided to implement. The plans themselves will no longer be the result of divergent class interests, for the latter will have lost their foundation and been converted into communal effort. The command of another will express his personal interests only because it also expresses the interests of the generality.
>
> **(Horkheimer 2002, 97)**

One exegetical emphasis identified by Postone that demarcates traditional readings is the tension between forces of production and relations of production, which Marx famously articulated in the 1859 Preface, as the main factor in social evolution. Linked to this is the positive valuation of industrial progress. This provides another sense of the centrality of work, namely the capacity of industrial labour to stimulate tremendous progress in science and technology and thereby achieve hitherto unknown levels of social wealth. By creating material abundance, work becomes the precondition for the emancipation of humanity. This is a paradoxical form of work centrality, since this power of labour to create the material conditions of emancipation relies on the historical necessity of class society. The emphasis is on the future benefits for humanity that lay in modern industrial work (see Cohen 2000 [1978], 193–215). In fact, the positivity of modern, industrial labour can be twofold in some of these readings. It is not only as a historical precondition of socialism, through the release of productive forces across society, that modern industrial labour has value. For readers of Marx who stress the productivity and technological advancement unleashed by capitalism, it can even be the scientific organization of work as an activity that can serve as an inspiration for a future socialist society. Lenin is a good example as his early denunciation of Taylorism was later replaced by an enthusiastic embrace, as he came to see it as a condition for the success of the new Soviet society (Scoville 2001).

3.2 Struggle against Work and Refusal of Work

In the first group of Marx readings that result in negative appraisals of work, it is the centrality of *capitalistic* work that is rejected, but work remains a central experience for individuals and a central institution for the collective in the vision of an emancipated society. The tremendous development in productive forces unleashed by capitalism remains the historical precondition for a new form of liberated work. The difference between normative and traditional readings and the next readings to be discussed is that in the latter, the denunciation of work is more virulent, and many passages make it sound as though it is work as such that is rejected. The autonomist, 'operaist' tradition stemming from Italy is the paradigm example of such an approach. This line of Marx reading, centred on the 'struggle against work' and the 'refusal of work' is a source of inspiration for many post-work accounts, most especially Kathi Weeks in *The Problem with Work*.

'Struggle against work' and the 'refusal of work', as Italian autonomism first articulated them (Tronti 2019 [1965], 259–263), are both theoretical conclusions and political rallying calls. As theoretical mottoes, they are premised on a reading of Marx that emphasizes the structural antagonism at the heart of the capitalist organization of production. Rather than locating this antagonism in property institutions and market mechanisms, autonomism emphasizes the tension at the structural level of the process of surplus-value creation. That process, as is well-known, relies on the transformation of the capacity of workers to produce specific outputs with concrete use-value into abstract labour, which thereby becomes the 'substance of value'. Work, which is initially the capacity to produce use-values that fulfil real needs, matters only as a producer of value, through the commodification of its outputs, and as being itself a bearer of exchange-value, through the wage. An individual capacity that can be mobilized for collective goods is thus objectified and commodified. Following this transformation, a series of antagonistic forms of work confront each other in capitalistic society: objective labour mobilizes subjective labour, dead labour commands living labour, surplus labour takes precedence over necessary labour.

The specificity of the autonomist approach is that, for it, these transformations do not occur simply through the processes of circulation, commodification, and valorization, since they rely also primordially on antagonistic social relations. For these readings, the agents involved continue to be opposed in terms of class but become increasingly autonomous even as they remain intertwined in capitalistic relations. This unity is maintained through direct and indirect forms of domination, via social and cultural mechanisms on top of economic and directly political ones. The major thrust behind these interpretations is to read Marx's critique of political economy 'politically', not only as an alternative economic theory, or even as a 'critical theory' as the next school does. The point of the critique of political economy is to be a political denunciation in and of itself, a direct taking of sides in the struggle between fundamental classes whose interests, worldviews and needs diverge radically (Cleaver 2000 for a continuation of this project), and who hold radically diverging projects for the future of humanity.

A useful text to focus on for these kinds of Marx readings is the lecture course on the *Grundrisse* held by Antonio Negri in Paris in 1978, which was published in English as *Marx Beyond Marx* (1991 [1867]). In reconstructing the core of Marx's mature thinking, the theory of surplus-value, Negri described the development of the two antagonistic social poles just mentioned: 'on the one hand, exchange value is autonomised in money and in capital, and on the other, use value is autonomised as the working class'

(1991 [1867], 72). He emphasized the oppressive force holding together those two social groups, even as they become increasingly autonomous from each other:

> only exploitation as a political process of domination and constriction, as a generalized command over society, determines at once value and surplus value. The level of the initial antagonism is so strong that only exploitation, constraint, force can succeed in resolving it.
>
> **(Negri 1991 [1867], 74)**

Negri read the famous shift from formal to real subsumption as the moment when the two fundamental collective subjects, capital, and the working class, become fully autonomous. As real subsumption provides the social and material conditions forcing the working class to come together as one, at the same time that class unifies and asserts itself as an antagonistic class. In doing so, the working class demonstrates that it can continue to exist as such beyond the wage relation that ties it to the capitalistic class:

> The constitution of social capital is paralleled by the emergence of the social class of workers, who are at first unified by capital at the level of its social development, and secondly by themselves—in material composition and identity—by the destruction of the exchange relation as a basis of the associated existence of the workers. We have thus seen the explosion of the form antithetic to the collective force of capital, to its expansion: a new subject is now on the terrain.
>
> **(Negri 1991, 125)**

From this perspective, work under capitalism is more than just the source of value. As the antagonism between the fundamental classes becomes increasingly acute, work becomes the principal means by which capitalists maintain their domination, their power of 'constraint and force', over the workers. A key passage for this reading is the 'Fragment on Machines' in Notebook VII of the *Grundrisse*, where Marx identified a terminal structural flaw in the logic of surplus-extraction: the push to reduce the part of labour in wealth production through technological innovation and eventually through full automation would spell the end of the logic of value and thereby of capitalism itself. In his 1978 lectures, Negri interpreted this text as the culmination of the logic of separation and antagonism. On the one hand, by making full use of the productive powers of machines, 'capital presses to reduce labour time to a minimum'. This directly helps it in its attempt to control and exploit living labour. At the same time, however, capital continues to depend on labour time as the measure of value. In reducing labour time to a minimum, capital is driven by its own logic to extinguish the process of valorization (Marx 1973 [1857], 705). At that point, the law of value becomes purely formal. That is, it continues to rule not just production but social life as a whole, yet increasingly fails to fulfil its core capitalist function. It has become a pure instrument of domination: 'the *form of value is pure and simple command, the pure and simple form of politics*' (Negri 1991, 148).

Negri's 1978 lectures presented a precis of autonomist thinking through a creative reading of the *Grundrisse*, but that movement had begun to crystallize more than a decade earlier, around the radical militancy that spread through the industrial cities of Northern Italy from the early 1960s onwards (Cleaver 2017, 56–65) and then in the early 1970s in the adoption of some of its key analyses among socialist circles in the USA (Federici 1995 [1974]. The 'refusal of work' motto can be traced back to texts by radical sociologists in the *Quaderni Rossi* at that time. In Mario Tronti's 'Factory and Society', for instance, there is one of the first references to the concept of the 'social factory', a major motivation behind the refusal of work. The antagonism of labour towards capital forces the latter to respond. Capital does this, first, through a rearrangement of its own internal (industrial, financial, organizational) composition, but also through the attempt to colonize 'the whole of society' so that society comes to exist 'as a function of the factory and the factory extends its exclusive domination over the whole of society' (Cleaver 2017, 60; Tronti 2019 [1965], 52). Negri reprised and extended this idea in his lectures, describing the process by which the logic of surplus value extraction was generalized from factories to all social institutions, in a process of 'socialization of surplus-value' (Negri 1991, 88). On this reading, real subsumption spreads to all social spheres, translating in particular into the duty to work as an injunction pursued via all kinds of policies and institutional programmes. The family and the school in particular are two spheres where capital seeks to extend its control over the working class in order to prepare it for surplus work. We see here why social reproduction theory, to which we'll turn in the second part of the book, finds in autonomist readings of Marx a major source of theoretical inspiration. The refusal of work initially comprised all the actions at the points of production, that aimed to interrupt capitalist production, such as wildcat strikes, sabotage, absenteeism. More broadly, though, it includes the rejection of the institutional policies and discourses that aim at the 'setting-to-work' of the entire population.

From the perspective of such readings of Marx, the centrality of work thus names the heart of capitalist domination to the extent that class exploitation is not just an economic phenomenon but also determines cultural, social, and political practices, and is relayed in normative discourses designed to make people work. In contrast to analyses of the modern work ethic, the autonomist approach seeks to debunk not just an ideological construct and its underlying social logic, but also to actively oppose this logic at the places where it is deployed, first in workplaces, but then also in the other spheres of life where work for capitalism seeks to impose its demands on bodies, psyches, and relationships.

Yet, what demarcates an autonomist approach from other Marxian schools is also its insistence on the growing power of dominated society as it increasingly escapes the grasp of capitalist domination, for reasons that are internal to capitalism (the self-undermining of the law of value, the paradoxical effects of automation on profits in the long run) and as a result of the assertion of that force's own 'constituent power'. In autonomist readings, this power of society is explicitly identified with 'social labour', the work of all individuals combined to reproduce society, or, in reference to a category mostly used in the *Grundrisse* rather than in *Capital*, 'living labour', the capacity of life to create and reproduce itself, as opposed to the dead nature of invested capital. Reappropriations of autonomist thinking in the post-work literature retrieve only the critical part of it. They leave behind that other dimension, the emphasis on social and living labour, which entails a case for a different type of work, one the autonomists think can already be witnessed in its outline at the heart of capitalist oppression (see a succinct and clear formulation in Negri 2009).

This positive case for work that is to be found in autonomist readings of Marx derives logically from the idea that capitalism is premised on the unity in separation of antagonistic classes that become increasingly autonomous from each other. The antagonistic stance that the working class opposes to capitalist exploitation is not a reactive attitude, not just a rejection of domination that remains defined by what it opposes. This opposition is grounded in a positive, 'constituting power' whose heart is precisely the capacity to work outside of capitalistic logic. Negri leans on the end of the 'Fragment on Machines' to describe that stage when the socialization of surplus-value reaches its limits and turns into its opposite, thereby liberating the creative and socially productive power of work. As the law of value becomes obsolete, capitalism reaches its ultimate limit. The process of valorization creates its own antithesis, namely 'worker self-valorization'. This is a process of valorization that is the exact inverted image of capital self-valorization: it creates real social wealth as opposed to surplus-value; use value and not exchange value; it fulfils needs of social reproduction rather than the need to accumulate based on domination; it is universal rather than hegemonic:

> Capital seeks a continual reduction in necessary labor in order to expand the proportion of surplus value extorted, but the more it succeeds individually with

> workers taken one by one, the more necessary labour benefits the collectivity and is reappropriated by absorbing the great collective forces that capital would like to determine purely for its own account. The compression of necessary individual labour is the expansion of necessary collective labour and it constructs a 'social individual,' capable not only of producing but also of enjoying the wealth produced.
>
> **(Negri 1991, 145)**

On this other side of capitalism, the central factor of the new society comes to light, namely work with emancipated features: living labour controlling dead labour; necessary labour taking precedence over surplus-labour; labour-time transformed by the expansion of 'free time', where free time itself has been transformed and rather than being an escape from labour-time in fact benefits it, which means that the boundary between labour and free time itself has been dissolved. As Marx writes at the conclusion of the 'Fragment on Machines':

> Free time, which is both idle time and time for higher activity—has naturally transformed its possessor into a different subject, who then enters into the direct production process as this different subject.
>
> **(Marx 1973 [1857], 712)**

This vision of work as a living resource that capitalism attempts to bind and exploit, but which can burst open the system's straitjacket once its collective power has been organized (which capitalism unwittingly helps to do), has remained a constant source of inspiration in Negri's later work. This can be traced notably in the writings with Michael Hardt, where proletarian self-valorization is reconceptualized as constituent biopower, the capacity to reproduce and create life, individual and collective, as in this representative passage:

> As it contests the dead labour accumulated against it, living labour always seeks to break the fixed territorializing structures, the national organizations, and the political figures that keep it prisoner. With the force of living labour, its restless activity, and its deterritorializing desire, this process of rupture throws open all the windows of history. When one adopts the perspective of the activity of the multitude, its production of subjectivity and desire, one can recognize how globalization, insofar as it operates a real deterritorialization of the previous structures of exploitation and control, is really a condition of the liberation of the multitude.
>
> **(Hardt and Negri 2001, 52)**

In this reading of Marx, then, it is only the centrality of capitalistic work that is 'refused'. Work itself, as the liberated activity of individuals who produce their own lives and their collective freely, is in fact the central factor of life beyond capitalism.

3.3 Technological Rejections of the Work Ethic

A *fourth* approach also emphasizes the liberating power entailed in the technological and scientific development triggered by capitalistic competition. Thinkers who take up this approach (Srnicek and Williams 2015; Bastani 2018; Dyer-Whitherford, Kjosen, and Steinhoff 2019) see a critical survey in Noonan 2020) argue that the new wave of automation powered by artificial intelligence will make the necessity to work obsolete. Like non-Marxist authors such as John Danaher and Michael Cholbi, they believe that work is inherently freedom-undermining. In contrast with autonomists, and in direct opposition to humanist and traditional readings, these thinkers believe the emancipatory potential in technology, therefore, lies in the emancipation from work itself, not simply emancipation from exploited and alienated work. This line of Marxist reading can find echoes and in turn adds its own voice to technologically based utopian reflections, for instance xenofeminism (Hester 2018). An early reference for this approach is Paul Lafargue's *Right to be Lazy* (2012 [1883]). The obsolescence of the centrality of work in this case stems not just from it being the ideological expression of the capitalistic extraction of surplus-value. It is also based on a definitive, empirical obsolescence, made possible by the power of the 'automatic system of machinery', as Marx already anticipated it.

There are no explicit or even implicit acknowledgements of the importance of work within or beyond its capitalistic forms in this line of Marx reading, unlike in the other approaches outlined in this chapter. To mount a case for work against these kinds of arguments, the empirical thesis on which it is based (that work, as a matter of fact, is fated to disappear) first needs to be evaluated. We do this in Chapter 7 regarding the debate on technological unemployment, and by reference to work as activity of social reproduction in Chapters 10, 12, and 13. In these last chapters, which make up 'the case for work', the normative claim that work is an important part of living a human life-form, individually and collectively, is made against the accelerationist contempt for work. As said before, this normative case for work is made in direct reference to Marx.

3.4 Value-Form Theory

A *fifth* approach in Marxist scholarship that is directly relevant to this book's concerns is one in which the centrality of work appears to be rejected most thoroughly, apparently without giving an alternative account. This includes the many readings of Marx that identify the categories of *value* and *abstract labour* as the decisive concepts in his critique of modern capitalism. For this other large family of readings, it is wrong to endorse the centrality of work because Marx's critique of capitalism is founded on the idea that it is precisely that centrality that is the lynchpin of capitalism as a new mode of social organization. Endorsing the centrality of work would be to endorse what lies at the heart of the system he wants to thoroughly criticize and help to overcome. Formulated in very general terms, the core idea sounds similar to the one that autonomists also hold: that the centrality of work cannot be defended since it is a central ideological tenet in the unjust and pathological order to be denounced. Beyond this superficial overlap, however, the precise arguments underlying the positions we are now looking at are different, and often position themselves critically towards the most famous autonomist views (see for instance Heinrich 2004 for sarcastic remarks on Negri; see other prominent criticisms in Bonefeld 2014, 62, 197; Holloway 2009, 2010).

Debates around the correct interpretation of Marx's theory of value and how to use it in contemporary critical theory are so complex, even a book-length study would not be able to cover all the main authors and schools. These debates span decades, with many tracing their origins in Rubin's 1923 *Essays on Marx's Theory of Value*. Particular schools of value-form theory have developed in different national contexts and often don't talk to each other. The 'new Marx reading' that began in the late 1960s in Germany has only been partially translated into English, and many of the proponents of these debates, notably the foundational writings of Reichelt and Backhaus (see Eleb 2018, 367–385), remain unknown outside that country. There is a prominent English version of value-form reading (for instance Arthur 2004) and an Italian one (Bellofiore 2018). In France, the work of Jean-Marie Vincent (1987) already put forward many of the themes and arguments propounded by these other readings, but he is never cited by them (he is cited by Kathi Weeks, see 2011, 101–103). There is an influential, early school of value-form reading in Japan (Kuruma 1957; Uno 1980).

Of course, the many authors who insist on value as a social form and on abstract labour as the 'substance of value' have diverging views on many methodological and hermeneutic points. However, they also share some key assumptions in their approaches to Marx, which differentiate them from other strands of Marx scholarship. Many value-form theorists highlight the importance of Hegel's *Logic* for reading *Capital*, even though they operationalize this reference in different ways. *Capital* is the centre of these interpretations, as opposed to other texts by Marx. Even though there are key differences with Althusserian structuralism, the defiance towards anthropological arguments is shared and critical theories based on the 'form of value' make arguments of a 'structuralist' kind. Most especially the *Grundrisse* and the 'Fragment on Machines' are dismissed as not being truly relevant to a properly Marxist approach, contrary to autonomist readings (see Bellofiore, Starosta, and Thomas 2013, notably the chapter by Heinrich (Heinrich 2013, 197–213). As with Althusser and his school, discussions centre on the interpretation of the first chapter of volume one of *Capital*, in which Marx presents a dialectical analysis of the value category. Many authors in this strand think that Marx's method in *Capital* offers much more than just a critique of political economy; they find in it the programme for a genuinely critical theory of modern society. Many locate their readings of Marx explicitly in the ambit of Frankfurt School critical theory, in the footsteps of Adorno and the first generation, in opposition to Habermas and post-Habermassians.

In what sense is work 'central' for these readers of Marx, in such a way that this centrality is precisely one of the fundamental reasons why capitalism is a social formation that is deficient and needs to be overcome? As the first volume of *Capital* explains right from the start, what characterizes modern society in comparison with other historical formations is that in it the needs of individuals are fulfilled not simply through the exchange of useful goods, but rather through the exchange of commodities: 'the wealth of societies in which the capitalist mode of production prevails appears as an "immense collection of commodities"; the commodity appears as its elementary form' (Marx 1991 [1867], 27). Commodities are goods that have a double character: they can fulfil a real need and thus have use-value, but they also have value from their exchange. In capitalism, while use-values matter, they matter as 'bearers' or as the 'bodies' of exchange-value. This means that they are produced not so much with the view to helping to fulfil a need directly, but rather to be exchanged. In capitalist society, it is the exchange of the products of labour, not labour directly, that allows individuals to acquire the goods with which they can fulfil their needs. This means that individuals relate to each other not as co-providers or co-contributors, by exchanging the outputs of their concrete efforts, but as sellers and purchasers of commodities. What makes commodities commensurable to each other regardless of their immense variety is labour, but 'abstract' labour as a producer of exchange-value, not 'concrete' labour that produces specific use-values. Commodities, the products of labour whose main quality is their capacity to be exchanged rather than their use-values, are 'merely congealed quantities of homogeneous human labour, i.e. of human labour-power expended without regard to the form of its expenditure' (Marx 1991 [1867], 182). Abstract labour is 'the substance' of value.

Since human interactions in capitalist society are mediated by commodity exchange, with their value as their determining feature (not their use-value), and since value is congealed labour abstracted from any specific feature, congealed abstract labour, it is therefore accurate to say, value-form theorists argue, that in capitalist society it is abstract labour that is the main form of relation between individuals. Value-form theorists of all stripes share the emphasis on the abstraction of labour as the underlying mediating mechanism of capitalist society, and they base their critique of that society on some formulation of the idea that the value-form spreads to all spheres of society as a result, including in the categories with which individuals represent to themselves their own social life, notably through the categories of economic science. By making value-creation the sole purpose of economic organization, capitalism thereby makes the abstraction of value, and with it the abstraction characteristic of its substance, abstract labour, the form of society in all of its main characteristics. Value form determines the form of society and with this process, the abstraction that characterizes value under capitalism becomes 'real'.

To outline more specifically how Marxist critics who emphasise abstract labour and the value-form reject the centrality of work, it is useful to focus on Moishe Postone's 1993 *Time, Labour, and Social Domination*. This book is particularly emblematic firstly from the point of view of the history of this line of Marx readings. It is the lynchpin between the critical theories of Adorno and Horkheimer and many contemporary critical theorists who also identify 'real abstraction' as the key critical category. Independently of its historical place in Marx scholarship, Postone's classical study presents in a particularly lucid fashion some of the key themes and arguments that value-form theorists highlight about work, even if other critical theorists disagree with him on some aspects (for instance Bonefeld 2014 on the exact political consequences to draw from the critical analysis of modern society).

Postone has a succinct way of formulating why readings of Marx like his reject the centrality of work, when work is defined along similar lines as at the start of this book, namely as a concrete activity producing use-values, whose features are such that it becomes the vector of crucial personal, social and political 'goods'. As Postone constantly reminds his readers, the true focus of critical theory should not be 'a critique of capitalism *from the standpoint of* labor', but rather, 'a critique *of* labor in capitalism'.

The introduction formulates in clear terms why the emphasis on value and the form of value lead to the rejection of the centrality of work:

> My reading of Marx's critical theory focuses on his conception of the centrality of labour to social life, which is generally considered to lie at the core of his theory. I argue that the meaning of the category of labour in his mature works is different from what traditionally has been assumed: it is historically specific rather than transhistorical. In Marx's mature critique, the notion that labour constitutes the social world and is the source of all wealth does not refer to society in general, but to capitalist, or modern, society alone. Moreover, and this is crucial, Marx's analysis does not refer to labour as it is generally and transhistorically conceived—a goal-directed social activity that mediates between humans and nature, creating specific products in order to satisfy determinate human needs—but to a peculiar role that labour plays in capitalist society alone.
>
> **(Postone 1993, 6)**

From the point of view of this reading, while it is correct to claim that work is central in modern, capitalistic society, the concept of work that is relevant in this case is highly specific and not what is meant by 'centrality of work' as discussed in the introduction and as will be discussed in the second part of the book. The work that is central under capitalism for Marx does not equate with a generic concept of work activity, which, as a type of activity, would apply in any human society at any historical time. It is not work as 'a goal-directed social activity that mediates between humans and nature, creating specific products in order to satisfy determinate human needs'. This sense of work is a trivial aspect of any historical formation. In fact, in this concrete sense, work is not really 'central'. In pre-capitalist societies, other social relations have greater importance, whether they more directly embody a religious world-view of fundamental importance for the group, or they express other, more direct forms of interpersonal dependence, such as obligations based on tradition or kinship (Postone 1993, 149). Under capitalism, by contrast, work is indeed central, but not as concrete labour, not as creator of use-values, but rather as abstract labour, as substance of value whose essential goal is the universal exchangeability of its outputs.

To say that abstract labour is central in capitalist society is a way to characterize the 'form of social interdependence' that is specific to that society. Postone exposes with great clarity the core idea underpinning value-form readings: namely, that in a society that is organized around commodity production, where abstract labour is, therefore, the central social mediation, abstraction has become 'real'. This claim that abstraction has become real is the underlying motto for a large strand of critical theory inspired by Marx.

First there is a direct link between the abstraction of labour as a social mediator in capitalism, and the ideas of alienation and domination. The link is well explained in a passage like this one:

> because the social relations that essentially characterize this society are constituted by labor, they exist only in objectified form. They have a peculiar objective and formal character, are not overtly social, and are characterized by the totalizing antinomic duality of the concrete and the abstract, the particular and the homogeneously general. The social relations constituted by commodity determined labor do not bind people to one another in an overtly social fashion; rather, labor constitutes a sphere of objectified social relations which has an apparently nonsocial and objective character and ... is separate from, and opposed to, the social aggregate of individuals and their immediate relations.
>
> **(Postone 1993, 154)**

By relating to each other through the prism of value, that is, from an instrumental point of view, social agents unwittingly produce a social world whose mechanism is itself governed by laws deriving from the law of valorization and over which they appear to have no control. The social world therefore appears alien to them. As individuals feel alien to their own collective life, the laws governing this objectivity come to dominate them. This domination is no longer the direct domination of some individuals over others on the basis of tradition or ideological justifications, but abstract domination of individual and collective life by the detached objectivity of self-reproducing capital:

> alienation refers to a process of the historical constitution of human powers which is effected by labor objectifying itself as a socially mediating activity. Through this process, an abstract, objective social sphere emerges, which acquires a life of its own and exists as a structure of abstract domination over and against the individuals.
>
> **(162)**

As individual lives and their life together are dominated by a system of abstract value production that they themselves reproduce but from which they are estranged, the abstraction at the heart of that system radiates through all the dimensions of social and subjective life, in what Postone calls 'a continuum of abstraction'. Or, in *Capital* Postone writes, Marx aims to describe 'the constitution of historically specific social forms that are forms of social objectivity and subjectivity simultaneously' (218).

The process of abstraction touches the process of work itself. That is, the labour process is itself organized in formal ways, through purely quantitative, analytical methods that recognize as their sole valid aim the attempt to maximize the value to be realized from the exchange of the output. The worker is treated as mere labour-power, not as a human person. Her working activity is detached from the final product. The end of the activity is pure value, not use-value. No other consideration matters in the production of the output than value, and so any consequences detrimental to the individuals, in terms of physical, psychological harms, or to the collective, in terms social ills or environmental degradation, are disregarded.

Individuals relate to each other through abstract labour, that is, the capacity to create value becomes the determining factor, whatever particular output that value might be attached to. This kind of relationship where the other counts only as an element in the chain of value creation, is itself entirely abstract in the sense that it overlooks all features of the other person that are not relevant from the point of view of value, including those that would be intrinsically significant, which would define this person as who they are. The other person is treated as a mere means, a possessor of labour-power or other instrumentally valuable attributes, whose vitality can only contribute to the creation of more value. This disincarnation of individual qualities is applied not just to others, but by each person to themselves as well. When everyone counts essentially as 'mere worker', this is true of everyone's own self-relation. And abstraction becomes real in people's attitude to external, non-human reality as well, as the world is reduced to 'a secular world of "thingly" objects bound together by, and revolving around, the glittering abstractum of money' (175).

Finally, value is the goal of the mobilization of social labour under capitalism, yet labour remains a mere means since it is just what makes exchange possible. This ontological ambiguity explains why the law of self-valorization underpinning capitalism knows no bounds. As it is both a goal and a means, valorization can never reach a state that would complete it. There is always more value to be extracted somewhere, by finding or indeed by creating new sources of valorization, for instance in the exploitation of life, or of digital data. As always, these extensions of the valorization process into new areas of organic, human, and symbolic life occur whatever the costs to society, to individuals or to environments, and the many species they harbour (Postone 1993, 382–383).

Readings of Marx such as the one proposed by Postone, in which the centrality of work designates the functionally central role played by abstract labour in capitalist society, have immense argumentative power in contemporary debates on work because they present with authoritative force one compelling version of Marx's mature project. Under their lens, the thinker who was thought to be the philosopher of work par excellence turns out to be the most virulent critic of the centrality of work.

The reconstructions of the method, aims, and results of *Capital* these readers of Marx offer connect with earlier, highly influential twentieth-century social criticisms that also highlighted processes of abstraction spreading through modern society as a result of the commodification that capitalism imposes on all aspects of life. There are multiple methodological, exegetical, and descriptive differences and points of contentions around the interpretation of these earlier critical theorists and how they should be included in contemporary appropriations of Marx. This field is far too complex to review here. What matters for this book's argument is just to take note of these thematic intersections between earlier readings and contemporary ones centred on the notion of abstraction, because of the importance of this critical strand in debates on work.

A seminal early account was Lukacs' translation of the commodity fetishism metaphor at the start of *Capital* volume one (Marx 1991 [1867], 47), into the category of reification in *History and Class Consciousness* (1972 [1923]). The critical language proposed by Lukács in that seminal text had a tremendous impact on Frankfurt School critical theory (Zuidevart 2007; Hall 2011). In turn, Adorno's and Horkheimer's later writings propounded major critical descriptions of modernity as a historical time in which the abstraction spreading from the organization of the work had become so invasive it shaped the structures of individual lives, of social relations and of politics. Several contemporary Marxists who make the abstraction of value their central critical category claim these texts as their lead inspiration today, notably in 'Open Marxism' (Holloway 2009, 2010; Bonefeld 2014; Bonefeld and O'Kane 2018; Oliva and Novara 2020). However, despite the espousal of Adorno by Open Marxism, on one key aspect, Adorno's and Horkheimer's analyses appear to separate them from other contemporary value-form theorists, as they maintained a transhistorical conception of work as the central organizing factor in human societies, a view summed up in their concept of 'social labour' (see a critique in Honneth 1995a; also, Postone 1993, 118). In the *Dialectic of Enlightenment*, they famously theorized this centrality of social labour in anthropological terms, as the concrete manifestation of the species' distinctive relation to nature in the form of instrumental rationality (Adorno and Horkheimer 2002, in particular at 25–27). A noteworthy aspect of their analyses was their focus on the psychological dimensions of reification and commodification (see, e.g., Horkheimer 1947, 66 or Adorno 1967/1968). These analyses had an impact well beyond the circle of Marx and critical theory specialists and can be traced in contemporary denunciations of the obsession with work (for instance Cohen 2018). One spectacular text that can be cited to illustrate this is section 147 of Adorno's *Minima Moralia*. In it, Adorno presents an account explaining how the functional requirements placed on individual psyches in modern capitalism, which makes of individuals 'mere agents of the law of value', leads to an institutionalized form of schizophrenia. 'Under a priori saleability', that is, under the prescribed assumption that everything can and should be commodified, each self manipulates its own psychological features (character traits, affects, and emotions) so they best fit the requirements of the situation, according to valorization concerns. Authenticity is sacrificed for maximum responsiveness to the demands from the system. As a result, 'all that is left are the light, rigid, empty husks of emotions, matter transportable at will, devoid of anything personal. They are no longer the subject; rather, the subject responds to them as to his internal object. In their unbounded docility towards the ego they are at the same time estranged from it: being wholly passive they nourish it no longer' (Adorno 2005, 230). This text, and others along similar lines by Adorno, rings like a striking anticipation of the psychological impact of the neoliberal prescription for everyone to consider their own self as a 'self-entrepreneur'. The critical relevance of passages like this one is obvious. In such an account, work has indeed become psychologically central, as a reflection of it becoming central in the overall organization of society, but this only expresses the totalizing nature of reification under contemporary capitalism.

Another key figure to mention was Alfred Sohn-Rethel (1971, 1978) who proposed his own version of 'abstraction'-analysis, as we might call it, making the link between the spread of the commodity logic and the epistemological infrastructure of modern forms of knowledge. Gorz, the leading reference for contemporary post-work theory, was deeply inspired by Marx, Sohn-Rethel, and the first and second generations of Critical Theory. Accordingly, the critique of abstraction was an important inspiration for him in his writings of the 1980s (see for instance 1989, chapter 1).

From the perspectives of value-form theory, the centrality of work is problematic in two fundamental ways.

First it is problematic if work is taken in the sense of abstract, commodified labour, which is the key to understanding how capitalist society functions specifically. The centrality of work is problematic in this sense simply because it designates the central functional element of a problematic social formation, one characterized not only by exploitation and domination of those whose labour-power is commodified, but also by much wider negative cultural, social, and psychological harms that can be shown to derive from the abstraction of labour.

The centrality of work is also problematic if work is taken this time no longer in the sense of abstract labour but rather in the normative, anthropological and transhistorical sense favoured by 'traditional' readings, that is, as an activity that is both characteristic of the human species in its self-reproduction and would be the bearer of decisive developmental and social goods if emancipated. From the point of view of Marx, these readings argue, this centrality of work is problematic for reasons that are simultaneously exegetical, methodological, and political. It mistakenly assumes that Marx's reference point in his critique of capitalism would be a normative, essentialist concept of work, one that would remain the same across all periods in human history. This mistaken belief in the anthropological and transhistorical centrality of work leads to the mistaken view of Marx's political goal as being the mere liberation of such a conception of work from the chains of exploitation and domination under capitalism.

3.5 Work beyond Abstract Labour

One is fully entitled to argue that the relevant concept of work from a 'true' Marxian perspective, that is, from a perspective that wants to be faithful to Marx's true project, is of work as abstract labour. This perspective, if we follow the analyses that flow on from it, provides a critical description of the structure and functioning of capitalist economies. In fact, however, such a critical account by itself does not fully explain the reproduction of capitalist societies. For these societies to be reproduced, it is not sufficient to produce exchange value, to make money. Society itself, and the multitude of individual lives within it, need to be materially reproduced, in response to the myriad needs they have. For that, concrete use values need to be produced. Those use values and those needs might well be caught up in the logic of commodification and abstraction, but they still need to do their job as use-values, as it were, that is, fulfil needs. This is true not only because value cannot attach to a good that has no use to anyone. Value in exchange relies on demand for use value. Capitalism can certainly create false needs; the valorization process can make some goods appear valuable when in fact the motivation for making them appear so is just to create more value. As Gorz showed, in late capitalism, it is often production that drives consumption, rather than the other way around (Gorz 1985, 19–25). But even in those cases, for that process to be sustained, commodities still have to appear to have some use, otherwise, they will not be exchanged for money. And it cannot be the case that all use-values are produced just for the purpose of valorization. Concrete use values need to be produced for basic concrete reasons: because a multitude of needs, of individuals and of the collective as a collective, require these use values for their continuation, however reified or alienated individuals and the social world might be. And for this to occur, a lot of work is needed, many use values need to be produced. From a simple materialistic point of view, it cannot be sufficient to reduce the concept of work to abstract labour, even if the project is to reconstruct a true Marxian critique of capitalist society. The later chapters on social reproduction (Chapter 10) and on the social centrality of work (Chapter 12) will develop these arguments at length.

These basic points were made explicitly by Marx himself, in countless passages in his mature writings. In the Introduction we recalled the letter to Kugelmann, in which the idea of work as concrete activities reproducing individual and collective lives was clearly stated. This idea in turn, as we just made the point, leads to a concept of work that is very basic indeed, yet remains indispensable. Marx did not fail to identify this basic, analytical sense of work. This is the first sense of work at the start of *Capital*, in the very first chapter of volume one, the focus of so much debate among value-form theorists and their critics:

> Labour, as the creator of use-values, as useful labour, is a condition of human existence which is independent of all forms of society; it is an eternal natural necessity which mediates the metabolism between man and nature, and therefore human life itself.
>
> **(Marx 1991 [1867], 133)**

The first meaning of labour for Marx, then, is explicitly as a necessary, transhistorical, anthropological feature of the human species, even in the later writings. In volume three, to pick a later passage in the constellation of *Capital*, the same transhistorical meaning of work as necessary characteristic of the human species is clearly asserted:

> the productive activity of human beings in general, by which they mediate their material metabolism with nature, divested . . . of every social form and determinate character.
>
> **(Marx 1981, 954)**

Again, Marx has no compunction here about using an explicitly transhistorical, anthropological concept of work.

In chapter 7 of volume one, we find perhaps the most famous definition of work by Marx, as:

> a process between human beings and nature, a process by which human beings, through their own actions, mediate, regulate and control the metabolism between themselves and nature.... The human being sets in motion the natural forces which belong to her own body, her arms, legs, head and hands, in order to appropriate the materials of nature in a form adapted to her own needs.
>
> **(Marx 1991 [1867], 283)**

This new analytical definition adds the reference to the biological underpinnings of work for the human species: work is the activity by which particular organisms, human organisms, stay alive in the larger web of life by interacting with all kinds of beings and environments, in highly specific ways, notably by using their own organisms in their own species-defining ways. The reference to the embodied (physical, cognitive, and we might add, emotional) dimensions of work is highly relevant for the argument in this book, because it anticipates developmental arguments that will be made in Chapter 13 about the significance of work for individuals. These references also matter in regard to exegetical debates—the concern of this chapter—because they point to a semantic layer in Marx's concrete use of the work concept that directly contradicts the methodological prohibitions stemming from value-focused readings.

In this all-important first chapter on commodities, Marx also writes:

> all labour is an expenditure of human labour-power in the physiological sense, and it is in this quality of being equal, or abstract, human labour that it forms the value of commodities.
>
> **(Marx 1991 [1867], 137)**

Marx is not just saying here that to be real 'power', labour-power has to mobilize what allows working individuals to concretely produce outputs, namely their entire physiology, that is, physical, cognitive. and emotional powers. He is also saying that, to the extent that this physiological dimension of work involves the 'expenditure' of human energies, it is in fact the material basis upon which the calculation of socially necessary labour-time, itself the substance of value, becomes possible. Labour can become abstract according to this passage, to the extent that it relies on quantifiable expenditure of human physiological resources. Because they base their interpretations exclusively on the processes that allow value to be realized in circulation, through exchange, when it takes its form as exchange-value through its expression in money, value-form theorists cannot accept such formulations. As a result, they tend to reject passages like this one, in which Marx identifies a 'physiological' core in abstract labour. They can rely on Rubin's interpretation, in which the Russian scholar already argued that the category of abstract labour could not logically designate at the same time both an abstraction of concrete work activities pointing to their physiological basis and the specific form taken by labour in a historical mode of production (Rubin 1972, 2). Postone's interpretation is once again typical in this respect (see also Bonefeld 2010):

> If the category of abstract human labor is a social determination, it cannot be a physiological category (…) It is central to Marx's analysis that value be understood as a historically specific form of social wealth. That being the case, its "social substance" could not be a transhistorical, natural residue, common to human labor in all social formations. (…) The problem, then, is to move beyond the physiological definition of abstract human labor provided by Marx and analyze its underlying social and historical meaning. An adequate analysis, moreover, must not only show *that* abstract human labor has a social character; it must also investigate the historically specific social relations that underlie value in order to explain why those relations appear and, therefore, are presented by Marx, as being physiological—as transhistorical, natural, and thus historically empty.
>
> (146)

As the end of the quote implies, not only is Marx accused of being logically inconsistent, but worse still he is accused of falling prey to the obfuscation he is supposed to denounce through the method deployed in *Capital*, that is, of naturalizing and making 'transhistorical' a category that is historically specific.

Yet there is no inconsistency in holding that labour demands the expenditure of human energies, and that this physiological basis takes on historically specific forms in different modes of production (see Carchedi 2007, 2009 and in direct criticism of value-form theory, Kiciloff and Starosta 2007, 2011). Even though it is through abstract labour that value is created as value, it is still an 'expenditure of human brain, nerves, muscles and sense organs' (1991, 164) that provides the actual, material content of the labour-power that capital rents out and exploits to create surplus-value. For the purposes of this book, this is a crucial conclusion. If, as the introduction suggested and as the second part of the book will argue, work can be distinguished from other forms of human action in key analytical features, then we can acknowledge vast differences in the cultural and symbolic significance of work actions across history and between different cultures, and we can in particular hold on to the very specific character of work under capitalism, while also arguing that those analytical features of work actions do mobilize human energies in specific ways. Even if different historical periods frame work organizations and the content of work activities in specific ways, there still remain some analytically characteristic features of all work activities that need to be taken into account in studying the significance of work for subjects and the community. Indeed, Chapter 12, on the long history of work, will highlight substantial ethnographic and historical evidence to justify the claim that work has enduring individual and social impacts across diverse human societies.

In fact, in other parts of his book, Postone takes a more careful attitude, accepting that there are features of work that apply analytically to all human societies (for instance at 30, 138, and especially 382). In these passages, Postone implicitly acknowledges the point just made: an analytical concept of work is not de facto ruled out in a project that aims at specifically describing the shape of work under capitalism. If that is true, then the methodological mistake of undue 'projection' is in fact made by those who think a critique of capitalist labour by necessity rules out considering work independently of its shape under capitalism. Indeed, in one passage, Postone's unofficial acknowledgement of the very general, anthropological necessity to work opens up precisely the kind of subject-focused analysis that highlights the ambivalent impacts it can have on subjectivities:

> Marx's notion of nonalienated labor is that it is free of relations of direct and of abstract social domination; it can thereby become an activity for self-realization, hence more playlike. Yet this freedom from domination does not imply freedom from all constraints, since any human society requires labor in some form in order to survive. That labor can never be a sphere of absolute freedom, however, does not mean that nonalienated labor is unfree in the same way and to the same extent as labor constrained by forms of social domination. In other words, Marx, in denying that absolute freedom could exist in the realm of labor, was not reverting to Adam Smith's undifferentiated opposition of labor to freedom and happiness.
>
> **(1993, 33)**

In this footnote at the start of the book as well as later towards the end, Postone suggests a view of work as a type of activity involving very specific forms of constraint, in which freedom and self-realization can be achieved precisely as a result of subjects having to face those constraints. In doing this, Postone simply follows some of Marx's own analyses, which also highlight different forms of necessity and how work is the way humans take them on. The book's last chapters explore in detail what is entailed in taking this necessity to work and the necessity involved in working seriously.

As it turns out, then, the two major schools of Marx interpretation that appear to speak most decisively against the centrality of work do not provide definitive arguments against it. Value-form theory unrealistically represses the concrete reality of work with its exclusive focus on circulation as the locus where value is created. In one of its most influential references, the goods that can arise from work are even explicitly acknowledged. The refusal of work stemming from the Italian autonomist tradition is a refusal of alienated work, but an affirmation of living labour. Besides these two approaches popular in the contemporary critical humanities, many more readers of Marx take seriously all the passages in his writings in which the critique of the pathological forms work takes under capitalism is premised on normative analyses of work as a special kind of human activity. The remaining reading that needs to be addressed is the accelerationist one, which requires first that the empirical claim about the obsolescence of human labour is investigated (Section 7.3). As for its rejection of the normative claim that work is an important part of living a human life-form, individually and collectively, this is what the entire second part of the book endeavours to demonstrate. Before we come to that, another important inspiration for contemporary post-work theorists needs to be studied, namely, the writings of Michel Foucault.

4
Work as Discipline

A third major reference point for objections to the centrality of work is the body of writings of Michel Foucault. They are an important reference for several contemporary post-work theorists (for instance James Chamberlain and Kathi Weeks). However, his writings matter for debates on the centrality of work beyond their direct influence on recent post-work literature, for two main reasons. First, his detailed historical genealogies reconstructing the establishment of a 'disciplinary society' and his later analysis of new forms of power focused on the life of populations and the society- and subjectivity-shaping impact of forms of government deliver powerful *critical descriptions* of the experiences and institutions of modern work. These critical descriptions add much descriptive weight to Marx- and Weber-inspired criticisms. From the point of view of these descriptions, the centrality of work is an untenable value to hold since work is shown to be one of the main institutional spaces through which disciplinary mechanisms shape and dominate modern subjects. Foucault's writings are also significant for methodological reasons: the genealogical method is premised on a thorough rejection of ahistorical analyses of social phenomena, and of work in particular. With that, Foucault's writings appear to void anthropological arguments of their validity. His body of work can safely be regarded as one of the main influences on the thorough *historicism* and *normative relativism* that are prevalent in the contemporary humanities. These methodological tenets affect the study of work directly and directly contradict the approach to work taken in this book. Outside the humanities, Foucault's writings have had an immense influence on disciplines that take work as their specific object of study, such as critical organizational theory, critical management studies, industrial relations studies, business ethics, and the sociology of work. The impact of Foucault's critical descriptions of modern work, the authority attached to his rejection of dehistoricized analysis mean that for many today the thesis of the centrality of work is an untenable proposition one can defend only by holding on to obsolete methods with questionable normative consequences. In this chapter, we review these two sets of objections, before considering the strength of this Foucauldian case against work.

The Case for Work. Jean-Philippe Deranty, Oxford University Press. © Jean-Philippe Deranty (2024).
DOI: 10.1093/oso/9780192887146.003.0005

4.1 Discipline after Marx and Weber

The first line of objections arising from Foucault's oeuvre is thus *descriptive*. From the point of view of the genealogy of disciplinary society, to extol the centrality of work is hopelessly naive since it overlooks the many forms of domination and control targeting both the physical and psychic lives of individuals that characterize work as one of the main social fields to which disciplines apply. This view of work as one of the main objects of modern disciplinary regimes overlaps significantly with Weberian and Marxian critical diagnoses of modernity. The overlap with Weber is pursued explicitly in Foucault's early work. The *History of Madness* begins with an account of the rise of the modern 'work ethic' and the denunciation of idleness, in an alternative interpretation of the same historical moment using similar religious texts as those analysed by the great German sociologist (1961, 69). The overlap with Marx is much more extended. Throughout the 1970s, up until the first book on the *History of Sexuality* in 1976, Foucault explicitly endorsed a Marxian frame of reference (see Feldman 2019 on the Marx–Foucault relation). Indeed, many aspects of Marx's work directly anticipated Foucault's analysis of disciplinary power. Marx already used the category of discipline to analyse the methods by which capitalism attempts to make individuals pliable to the demands of its system of production. This is one of the main aspects, for example, of 'primitive accumulation', to transform peasants into proletarians by subjecting them to 'the discipline necessary for the wage system' (Marx 1991 [1867], 523). Once the industrial system is in place, the 'discipline and command of capital' (1991 [1867], 248) applies at different levels: from eliciting a general social necessity forcing the poor to work for a wage, to expressing a multitude of prescriptions and modes of controls at the point of production allowing the capitalist labour process to 'seize labour-power by its very roots' (Marx 1991 [1867], 249). As Foucault notes (1976, 175; Sakolsky 1992), Marx is the first to highlight the emerging functions of surveillance within the new factories and in life outside the factory. And Marx explicitly formulated the idea that disciplines are modes of control that work by having subjects internalize their own subjection (1973 [1857], 325.

Disciplines, as is well-known, designate institutional practices applying and perfecting new scientific and normative discourses, which are characteristic of the form taken by power in modern society. Disciplines seek to establish control over individuals, as its name suggests, but the coercion built into it is effectuated mostly at a distance and indirectly.

Bodies are controlled by being made to abide by formal rules that regulate all aspects of their being and of their conduct down to the finest of details. Minds and souls are made to conform through material and discursive strategies that seek to have individuals internalize these rules. Key to these processes are mechanisms of surveillance, observation, examination and self-examination, refined categorization, and hierarchical rankings and orderings. All these practices and their accompanying discourses intend to maximize the visibility of individual bodies so as to increase knowledge of their capacities, their modes of action and reaction, and to adjust control as closely as possible to their most minute and intimate features. Visibility ensures control, most especially through the panopticon effect, by which an individual who knows they are being observed spontaneously takes up the attitude they assume the observer wants them to take.

In the third part of *Discipline and Punish*, Foucault applies disciplinary analysis to many different spheres in the medical, penal, educational, military, and economic realms. The panoptic schema, which is at the heart of disciplines according to that book, 'is polyvalent in its applications; it serves to reform prisoners, but also to treat patients, to instruct schoolchildren, to confine the insane, to supervise workers, to put beggars and idlers to work. It [...] can be implemented in hospitals, workshops, schools, prisons. Whenever one is dealing with a multiplicity of individuals on whom a task or a particular form of behaviour must be imposed, the panoptic schema may be used' (1977 [1975], 205; see anticipatory passages in the 1973–1974 lectures, 2006, 51, and 70). The logic driving these institutional interventions is a novel mode of social organization, the 'carceral' one, a new impetus spreading throughout all kinds of institutional orders, which seeks to 'confine' individuals in new ways, following a logic of inclusion and exclusion different from those witnessed in the medieval and 'classical' age. The aim is no longer to assert power centrally by maintaining the excluded outside or at the margins of society. Instead, the new logic of internment applies to everyone as power now seeks to extend its control over the entire population in each one of its bodies, in a variety of modalities. However, even though 'surveilling and punishing' (the book's original title) are the two fundamental logics Foucault retraces underneath the myriad evolutions that mark the emergence of modern society, in many passages it is in fact clear that the norm-guided coercion of behaviours is not merely for the sake of control, but more fundamentally for the sake of extracting as much from bodies as possible. Underlying the new carceral logic remains the aim of productivity maximization. As was said at the outset, the genealogical reconstruction of new institutional and discursive logics is explicitly made compatible with a Marxian approach. In that respect, work is more than just one among other institutional spheres in which disciplines are deployed:

> the two processes—the accumulation of men and the accumulation of capital—cannot be separated; it would not have been possible to solve the problem of the accumulation of men without the growth of an apparatus of production capable of both sustaining them and using them; conversely, the techniques that made the cumulative multiplicity of men useful accelerated the accumulation of capital. At a less general level, the technological mutations of the apparatus of production, the division of labour and the elaboration of the disciplinary techniques sustained an ensemble of very close relations (cf. Marx, *Capital*, vol. 1, chapter XIII). Each makes the other possible and necessary; each provides a model for the other [...] The growth of a capitalist economy gave rise to the specific modality of disciplinary power, whose general formulas, techniques of submitting forces and bodies, in short, 'political anatomy', could be operated in the most diverse political regimes, apparatuses and institutions.
>
> **(1977 [1975], 220–221)**

In the 1972–1973 lectures on 'punitive society', the capitalist imperative underpinning the new logic of internment is emphasized even more emphatically. In those lectures, Foucault appears to closely follow the Althusserian reading (Read 2003; Legrand 2007). He establishes a formal equivalence between what he calls the prison-form and the wage-form, as two modalities by which new institutional realities shape individual experience, notably as they make new demands on individuals' time. In the last third of these lectures, Foucault shows in minute detail how the rise of new forms of confinement is linked directly to the bourgeoisie's attempt at ensuring that workers find no way of escaping the constant pressure to work. If labour-time is the key to capitalist exploitation, then all of the worker's time has to be transformed into time for labour, including in the periods of their life where the worker is not yet, or no longer, working:

> the supervision-punishment couple is imposed as an indispensable power relationship for fixing individuals to the production apparatus, for the formation of productive forces, and characterizes the society that may be called disciplinary. We have here a means of ethical and political coercion that is necessary for the body, time, life, and men to be integrated, in the form of labor, in the interplay of productive forces.
>
> **(2015, 196)**

Reading these lectures of the years 1972–1974 leading to *Discipline and Punish* further strengthens the descriptive force of all the passages in that seminal book where the experience of work is shown to be entirely dominated and shaped by the coercive, invasive, calculating control of disciplines. As the book outlines in numerous passages, new scientific discourses and bodies of regulations, new technical implements, new architectural designs combined with new organizations of time are devised and refined, all aiming to better observe, evaluate, compare, train, admonish, and directly punish workers. The impression that arises from all these descriptions is that disciplinary power and all its different modes of exertion make the oppression of modern work intense, deeply intimate, and utterly comprehensive. Beyond this empirical denunciation of modern work, the disciplinary thesis makes the thesis of the centrality of work problematic in a second, more specific sense: to the extent, namely, that work is more than just one site of disciplining but the main causal factor behind the rise of disciplines, since disciplines were developed to facilitate and intensify the exploitation of labour.

The all-encompassing dominance of disciplinary power on work was confirmed and extended in the next phase of Foucault's writing. In the first volume of the *History of Sexuality*, published the year following *Discipline and Punish*, and in the next lecture courses at the Collège de France ('Society must be defended', 1976–1977 and 'Security, Territory, Population', 1977–1978), Foucault introduced biopower as another perspective to describe the nexus of knowledge and power establishing the dominance of capitalistic imperative over subjective forces and the organization of society (see Just 2016 for a good comparison of Foucault's and Negri's uses of the bio-power category). The biopolitical nexus of power–knowledge targets the life processes as they are singularly embodied in individual citizens. Its aim is to promote the life of the population as a whole, and to achieve that purpose new knowledges combining medical, statistical, and bureaucratic perspectives are developed. The outcome is a raft of normative regulations and injunctions to individuals. In 1976, Foucault maintained the capitalistic imperative as the underlying impetus behind the deployment of biopower, using formulations that directly quoted *Discipline and Punish*:

> bio-power was without question an indispensable element in the development of capitalism; the latter would not have been possible without the controlled insertion of bodies into the machinery of production and the adjustment of the phenomena of population to economic processes [...] The adjustment of the accumulation of men to that of capital, the joining of the growth of human groups to the expansion of productive forces and the differential allocation of profit, were

> made possible in part by the exercise of bio-power in its many forms and modes of application. The investment of the body, its valorization, and the distributive management of its forces were at the time indispensable.
>
> (1978 [1976], 141)

The rhetorical force and conceptual sophistication deployed in these critical genealogies of the disciplinary power and later on in his delineations of biopower, backed by the gargantuan mass of archival detail he mobilized, made the books and lectures of the 1970s an overwhelming reference for generations of scholars in the humanities and the social sciences. This has meant in particular that these writings changed the research focus and the methods used by many in all the academic disciplines that take work as their object of study. In each one of those disciplines, a substantial critical literature has pursued Foucault's analyses from particular methodological perspectives, each with a focus on specific dimensions of work (for instance, employment conditions, unemployment policies, training and education, activities, motivations and culture in workplaces, employee–employer relations), all adding critical material to the empirical case denouncing how modern, capitalistic work is organized and experienced. It is worth mentioning a few of those disciplinary specializations. In the new field of surveillance studies, which was transformed by the 1975 book (Monahan and Muakami 2018), surveillance in the workplace is one of the major topics (Ball 2018). In labour-process theory, a mode of inquiry inspired by Harry Braverman's 1974 *Labour and Monopoly Capitalism*, which focuses on the ergonomic, organizational, and managerial procedures that are concretely deployed at the point of production to secure the creation of surplus-value, the disciplinary thesis was integrated by many scholars, even though this turn was not uncontested (Jaros 2000; O'Doherty and Willmott 2001). These empirical inquiries into modes of workplace discipline overlap with studies in the sociology of work that describe the introduction of new methods in labour processes (Sewell and Wilkinson 1992 on just-in-time) or innovations in management discourse promoting new capitalistic methods (Knights and Willmott 1989 on the worker as self-entrepreneur). All these studies provide concrete evidence of the forms of control and oppression occurring in work as a form of daily experience. Foucault's book was also immensely influential in management and organization studies (MacKinlay and Starkey 1998; *Organization* special issue volume 9 issue 4, 2002; MacKinlay 2013), where critically minded scholars found a fresh avenue to develop Weber's seminal analysis of modern bureaucracy. *Discipline and Punish*, especially the panopticon theme, inspired numerous critical studies of new management practices and management discourse at all levels, from particular firms to entire economic sectors, to shifts in macro-economic orientations and government policies, all the way to management as a practice and a scholarly field (Barratt 2004). Foucault's reference was initially often combined with other key references in French poststructuralism like Derrida, Levinas, Lyotard, and Deleuze to challenge the rationalistic, progressive bent of traditional organizational approaches. As more of the later work was translated into English, new waves of Foucault interpretation brought other parts of his work to bear on the critical study of organizations and methods of management (Raffnsøe, Mennicken, and Miller 2019). The biopolitical motto could connect with the writings of Agamben (Boland and Griffin 2023). The texts on governmentality spawned a new wave of engagement, with a renewed focus on state actions and the analysis of how government discourses and policies at different levels became enmeshed in neoliberal imperatives (Dean 2009). Peter Fleming's *The Mythology of Work* (2015) connects this rich field of Foucault-inspired critical organizational studies with the 'post-work' literature.

4.2 The Historical Relativity of Work

The first significance of Foucault's writings in debates on work is thus descriptive and turns around two key claims: modern work is one of the main spaces where disciplines are applied to individuals, and thus one of the main reasons for their coercion; moreover, the disciplinary society emerged largely from the attempts to tie individuals to the many-sided imperatives of capitalist production. Work is doubly central in this sense, and each one of those senses is negative: work is one of the main centres of modern subjection; and the organization of work is a central causal factor behind the rise of disciplinary power more generally.

Another set of objections to a positive sense of work's centrality is entailed in Foucault's genealogy of modern disciplines and biopower. These are the conceptual and methodological objections that arise once a particular social phenomenon, in our case the centrality of work, can be shown to be the product of a particular history, which occurred at a particular place and a particular time. The localization of that phenomenon entails that it is illegitimate to generalize the meanings, values, and norms constituting it to other times and other places. Such generalization is a methodological mistake from a theoretical point of view, and a moral one from a practical one, since it imposes a set of norms and values to a context in which these do not apply. It can cause direct social, political, and individual harms when such a belief in the universal validity of one's representations comes armed with superior military and economic power, as was the case in the heydays of European colonialism. Conceptually, the rejection of transhistorical claims combines with a rejection of arguments of an anthropological kind, which include dehistoricized normative claims, in other words generic claims about human beings and human societies.

We encountered versions of these objections, mobilizing different conceptual and historical resources, in each of the first three chapters of the book. In Foucault's case, the strength of methodological and conceptual objections inspired by his writings stems notably from the fact that he gives precise information about the relativity of work at both ends, so to speak, reconstructing both its emergence and the early signs of its obsolescence as a master representation. We mentioned his first book already, the *History of Madness* (1961), where, at the beginning, Foucault accounted for the historical shift that saw the rise of the modern work ethic and with it of an entirely new understanding of work. In *The Order of Things*, five years later, Foucault contrasted the defining features of the classical, the modern, and the postmodern 'epistemes'. In chapter 8 of that book, Foucault focused his analysis on texts by the Physiocrats and the Mercantilists as representatives of an economic theory consistent with the general epistemological worldview of the classical age. The main object of economic theory in this worldview is not the search for a constant increase in productivity but rather the problem of how to maintain the flow of circulation in systems of equivalence. As a result of a fundamental rupture in core epistemic attitudes with the emergence of industrial society, there is in fact only a superficial continuity between earlier economists and Smith's, and most especially Ricardo's, first delineations of modern political economy (1989, 276). In Ricardo most particularly, value as general equivalent is replaced by work as the core operative concept: 'value ceases to be a sign and becomes a product' (266). This motto sums up the new emphasis on production, that is, on the processes that enable the creation of commodities, displacing the earlier interest in the relations of equivalence among commensurable entities. In theorizing this shift, Ricardo announces the era when work functions as a central concept. Within the framework of this new episteme, economic activity is envisaged from the point of view of a creature's desperate attempt to maintain its life in conditions of increasing scarcity and hardship (277–283). The conceptual pair of scarcity and of production as the response to scarcity motivates the urge to ceaselessly increase productivity and efficiency and to reduce costs. However, as work takes on such a central place at this particular historical conjunction, its centrality is only a temporary one, fated to disappear when the episteme of which it is one of the most eminent expressions gradually recedes to be replaced by a new one. This is precisely what the end of the book famously gestured towards, with the anticipation of an 'erasure' of the human being, that is, of the anthropological assumption underpinning the modern human sciences and, more broadly, the modern worldview.

The *Birth of Biopolitics* lecture series (1978–1979) of a decade later and its analysis of German and American neoliberal doctrines can be interpreted as being precisely an attempt by Foucault to flesh out the content of this new episteme just as neoliberal discourse was also beginning to become the new mantra of governments in the West. The modern episteme replaced the earlier paradigm of equivalent values with the new paradigm of productive work. For Foucault in 1978, this paradigmatic centrality of efficient production is now itself being superseded as the conception of rational economic action advocated by neoliberal thinkers takes over. This is economic action as the optimal allocation of scarce resources to competing ends, a conception so formal it can be broadened to define the rationality of any social action. Linked to this conception is a new vision of the institutional mechanisms required to enable the efficient integration of social actors, namely, a transparent market in which agents adjust their behaviour in full knowledge of other people's preferences. Competition takes over from discipline as the privileged mode of social integration. With this, the overarching power exercised by the state in disciplinary society becomes obsolete. If the rationality of action is ensured when signals about actors' intentions and preferences can be transparently and securely communicated and individual actions can as a result be consistently coordinated, then the state's decisive function is just to create and protect this space of competition in which market mechanisms can operate unimpeded. On this reading, the industrial, disciplinary regime coinciding with the emergence of modern society, a regime that required the constant and minute regulation of individuals and of the population, gives way to a fluid society consisting of a multiplicity of networks linking discrete singularities, each seeking to maximize its own self-chosen utilities (234). In this fluid, decentralized social reality, work is no longer an injunction that has to be imposed on each and every one. Without the state having to intervene, the market situation determines the objective conditions in which each can decide for themselves, according to their own set of preferences, whether they would like to work or not, and how much. For the economic system as a whole, the bundle of incentives and negative utilities is enough to adjust the supply of labour-power needed (207).

Between the *Order of Things* and the *Birth of Biopolitics*, then, Foucault seems to present a precise historical delineation of the one moment in history, namely modern, Western, disciplinary society, when work as productive activity was as a matter of fact a centrally organizing category. That category was not central beforehand and is no longer central in the new context.

The methodological conclusions to be drawn from the historical relativizing of the centrality of work were explicitly formulated in the lectures on 'punitive society' in 1972 and 1973. In these lectures, Foucault retraced the emergence of new forms of penal practices from the middle of the eighteenth century onwards. The thrust of these inquiries was to see how new forms of criminal inquiry and internment opened the door for more general forms of social control and subjugation. This work directly prepared the material to be published as *Discipline and Punish*. As we saw, Foucault's perspective at the time was faithful to a general Marxist approach. He tied the rise of practices and institutions of disciplinary control directly to capitalistic imperatives. The overarching theme was to show how the new modalities of judicial and broader social control aimed to tie the population to the production apparatus, to make workers available for exploitation. Despite his continuous reference to Marxist themes, however, Foucault also drew methodological conclusions from the genealogical reconstruction that spoke directly against classical Marxian conceptions of work as the essence of the human being:

> It is false to say, with certain famous post-Hegelians, that labor is man's concrete existence. The time and life of man are not labor by nature; they are pleasure, discontinuity, festivity, rest, need, moments, chance, violence, and so on. Now, it is all this explosive energy that needs to be transformed into a continuous labor-power continually offered on the market. Life must be synthesized into labor-power, which involves the coercion of this system of sequestration. For exercising this coercion that transforms the time of life into labor-power, the clever ploy of industrial society was to take up the old technique of the confinement of the poor, which, in the classical age, was a way of fixing and, at the same time, suppressing those who through idleness, vagabondage, or revolt had escaped all the geographical fixations in which the exercise of sovereignty was carried out. This institution will have to be generalized and utilized, in contrast, to connect up individuals to the social apparatuses; it will be specified in accordance with a whole series of apparatuses from the factory-prison to the prison, passing through poorhouses, schools, and reformatories. Reutilized to this end, all this old system of confinement will make possible sequestration, which is actually constitutive of modes of production.
>
> **(2015 [1972–1973], 232)**

This key methodological statement was reiterated later in the year in the lectures Foucault gave in Rio de Janeiro in May 1973. In the fourth and fifth lectures, Foucault focused once again on concrete measures adopted in the early nineteenth century to ensure the entirety of workers' existence would revolve around work, how 'people's time became labour time'. A short passage is worth citing, for the clarity with which the idea that the centrality of work was actively enforced upon the population, and how it continues to be enforced in the present, is expressed:

> the creation, in the 1820s and especially the 1840s and 1850s, of savings banks and relief funds, made it possible to channel workers' savings and control how they were used. In this way, the worker's time—not just the time of his working day but his whole lifespan—could actually be used in the best way by the production apparatus. Thus, in the form of institutions apparently created for protection and security, a mechanism was established by means of which the entire time of human existence was put at the disposal of the labour market and the demands of labour. This extraction of the whole quantity of time was the first function of these institutions of subjugation. It would also be possible to show how this general control of time was exercised in the developed countries by the mechanism of consumption and advertising.
>
> **(2001 [1974], 80–81)**

What is of particular interest is the conclusion Foucault drew from these analyses, namely, an explicitly formulated methodological rejection of dehistoricized and anthropological justifications for the centrality of work:

> Someone said that man's concrete essence is labor. Actually, this idea was put forward by several people. We find it in Hegel, in the post-Hegelians, and also in Marx, the Marx of a certain period, as Althusser would say. [...] In point of fact, labor is absolutely not man's concrete essence or man's existence in its concrete form. In order for men to be brought into labor, tied to labor, an operation is necessary, or a complex series of operations, by which men are effectively—not analytically but synthetically—bound to the production apparatus for which they labor. It takes this operation, or this synthesis effected by a political power, for man's essence to appear as being labor. So I don't think we can simply accept the traditional Marxist analysis, which assumes that, labor being man's concrete essence, the capitalist system is what transforms that labor into profit, into hyperprofit [*sur-profit*] or surplus value. The fact is, capitalism penetrates much more deeply into our existence. That system, as it was established in the nineteenth century, was obliged to elaborate a set of political techniques, techniques of power, by which man was tied to

> something like labor—a set of techniques by which people's bodies and their time would become labor power and labor time so as to be effectively used and thereby transformed into hyperprofit. But in order for there to be hyperprofit, there had to be an infrapower [*sous-pouvoir*]. A web of microscopic, capillary political power had to be established at the level of man's very existence, attaching men to the production apparatus, while making them into agents of production, into workers.
> **(2001 [1974], 86–87)**

The descriptive historical analysis thus leads to a major methodological objection, one that directly anticipates objections put forward more recently by post-work scholars: namely that work is indeed central in modern society, but not based on any natural feature of the human species, or for any 'analytical' reasons that an argument in social ontology could highlight. Work is indeed central in modern society, this objection goes, but only because it *has been made* so, because it has been enforced as a central value in people's lives through a focused, determined, combined effort of all the institutions surrounding individual life. More precisely, as Foucault's texts of the early 1970s make clear, work has been made central to people's lives *by those and to further the interests of those for whom the workers work*. This directly anticipates Elizabeth Anderson's recent historical reconstruction of how the ruling classes 'hijacked' the egalitarian impulses of the initial work ethic (2023). For Foucault, a long process of refining and imposing coercive disciplines and biopolitical techniques, combining the creation and development of new knowledges and institutional technologies, spanning all social fields, from the family to school to the justice system and of course the labour market, had to unfold for this centrality to come to be. From this point of view, endorsing the centrality of work means naively taking as the consequence of the human species' natural history what is in fact the outcome of the brutal, freedom-denying history of modernity. Arguments based on anthropological or analytical grounds alone are ignorant of history and, because of this ignorance, produce only superficial explanations of the centrality of work in our lives, explanations that overlook the immense power asymmetries involved in it.

Interestingly, as the text above intimates, Foucault even suggested a counter-anthropological account, emphasizing features we will meet again soon, where the 'time and life of man', to use his words, are rather to be defined as a capacity of that unique animal to seek pleasure beyond sexual reproduction or engage in expenditure for the sake of it. These are features Foucault borrowed from Nietzsche and Bataille, two authors who exerted the strongest theoretical influence on him, as they did more generally on other French thinkers at the time. We will study that counter-anthropological account directed against the centrality of work in the next chapters.

4.3 A Foucauldian Case for Work?

Foucauldian objections to the centrality of work thus seem overwhelming. How could a 'case for work' be possibly mounted in spite of them, especially if, as the Introduction suggested, such a case relies on the claim that there are features of work activities that matter in all historical contexts, even if the precise meanings attached to the organization of work and to work activities vary across cultures?

In response to the first part of the descriptive challenge, that is, the fact that modern work is one of the main realms in modern society where individuals are subjected to the coercing effects of disciplines and biopower, a first answer can point to the wide diversity of positions defended by Foucault throughout his oeuvre. Which of Foucault's writings are appropriate to the study of work? After the work of the 'archaeological' period at the end of which the anthropological assumptions of human sciences were denounced, after the disciplinary period where work seemed to be a central locus of subjection for modern subjects, the later lectures on neoliberalism suggest that a new 'spirit of capitalism' replacing the modern episteme might have the effect of liberating work from the disciplines. These lectures can be used as reference points to undermine the empirical side of the descriptive challenge.

This alternative approach to work is made possible by the fact that in his late writings Foucault sought to correct the one-sidedness of his genealogical analyses and reaffirmed the subject as a source of agency, notably for establishing procedures of truth. He concurrently insisted on the fact that power relies, as a structural condition of its exercise, on what resists it, that 'where there is power, there is resistance' (1978 [1976], 95), that 'resistance comes first, and remains superior to the forces of the process; power relations are obliged to change with the resistance' (1982, 167). Both these aspects have inspired a large strand of critical management and organization studies focused on practices of resistance at work (MacKinlay and Starkey 1998; Barrat 2008; Mumby et al. 2017). These passages in the later writings significantly correct the picture of modern work as a site of disciplinary subjection gained from the earlier writings. With this new emphasis on subjective agency, a passage in his late work seems to open the door to an analysis of work that acknowledges its positive value for the individual. This passage is situated in the 1978–1979 lectures on neoliberalism. In the last decade, a heated debate has arrayed those who have read these lectures as an endorsement of neoliberal thinking by Foucault against those who defend the critical thrust of the lectures (Dean 2015). Whichever side one takes in this debate, it seems difficult to read the following passage in any other way but as an implicit endorsement. In turn, this signals a Foucauldian way to analyse work positively in the context of the new episteme:

> What does bringing labor back into economic analysis mean? It does not mean knowing where labor is situated between, let's say, capital and production. The problem of bringing labor back into the field of economic analysis is not one of asking about the price of labor, or what it produces technically, or what is the value added by labor. The fundamental, essential problem, anyway the first problem which arises when one wants to analyze labor in economic terms, is how the person who works uses the means available to him. That is to say, to bring labor into the field of economic analysis, we must put ourselves in the position of the person who works; we will have to study work as economic conduct practiced, implemented, rationalized, and calculated by the person who works. What does working mean for the person who works? What system of choice and rationality does the activity of work conform to? As a result, on the basis of this grid which projects a principle of strategic rationality on the activity of work, we will be able to see in what respects and how the qualitative differences of work may have an economic type of effect. So we adopt the point of view of the worker and, for the first time, ensure that the worker is not present in the economic analysis as an object—the object of supply and demand in the form of labor power—but as an active economic subject.
>
> **(2008 [1978–1979], 223)**

Taken outside of its economic context, this passage seems to speak precisely to the approach to work taken in the second part of the book: what does working mean for the person who works? What does work mean as it is 'practiced, implemented, rationalized, and calculated by the person who works'?

A second response is similar to the one expressed in the previous chapter. Even if the Foucauldian analyses of the 1970s and all the empirical, critical scholarship in work sciences they inspired are valid, they do not speak against work itself, but rather about work as it has been organized under industrial capitalism. Even if work is utterly disciplined and subjected to normalizing logics, it remains the case that individual lives and collective structures need to be reproduced, which demands a lot of work. The case for work does not argue for the positive value of current work organizations but highlights the significance of the work that needs to be done for subjectivities and for communities, because of key features of work activities. Such a case is not contradicted by the factual state of work, since it mounts its argument at a different level, in terms of features of activities and in social-ontological terms. Indeed, establishing the significance of work helps to explain the impact of unjust and pathological work organizations on subjective and collective life, and potentially the causal role played by work in forms of injustice and social pathologies. This latter consideration helps to reply to the second part of the descriptive challenge, the fact that modern work is not just thoroughly disciplined but is in fact functionally central in the deployment of disciplines, given that they aim to entrench the exploitation of workers. Work matters centrally since it is a key vector of injustice and freedom-undermining institutional practices. But the correct conclusion to draw from this critical point is not that work therefore should not matter, but rather that work matters all the more if justice and a flourishing collective life are to be established. The last chapter in the book develops all these points at length.

Finally, in response to the methodological challenges that derive from the historical relativity of work's centrality, Chapter 11 will deal with them extensively. The key there will be to demonstrate that it is legitimate to speak of work in analytical terms, independently of the specific cultural representations that frame work activities, work statuses, and work organizations differently across different cultures.

Before we consider these replies to Foucauldian worries, several other momentous critical thoughts need to be examined. One of them, to which the next chapter now turns, concerns the fundamental distinction, famously articulated by Aristotle, between actions that are intrinsically valued and actions that are merely instrumental and therefore subordinate in light of higher ends, for which work is the paradigm example.

5
Aristotelian Objections

This chapter considers objections to the centrality of work that take as their conceptual foundation the classical dichotomy distinguishing between two types of action: doing and making, *praxis* and *poiesis*, in other words, actions that are intrinsically worthwhile, in which human agents demonstrate their excellence simply by doing what that excellence consists of, like being good friends, or good citizens, as opposed to actions whose worth lies in the product they bring about, which are therefore worthwhile only instrumentally, such as actions that produce a technically useful outcome, like repairing one's roof, or producing an economically profitable commodity. Even though this dichotomy between intrinsically valuable and instrumentally valuable action is already found in Plato (2013, 119) and must have been a common intuition among the free citizens of Greek city-states, it is traditionally associated with Aristotle. As the examples above intimate, the intuition that some actions are less valuable than others because they are mere means to achieve higher, external ends applies most particularly to work, the paradigm of instrumental action. The most influential objections to the centrality of work that draw on the dichotomy of *poiesis* and *praxis* deploy critical historical narratives that resemble those we studied in the previous chapters but do so on the basis of the conceptual downgrading of work implied in the dichotomy. For these thinkers, modern work is deleterious not just because of the particular features it takes on as a specifically *modern* activity. Rather, for these thinkers there is something inherent in work, as a *distinct form of activity*, different from other forms of human activity, that is already problematic. More precisely, for all these authors, what makes *the very activity* of work, work itself, destructive of individual freedom and the cause of a breakdown in communal ethos is when this kind of activity becomes socially and culturally dominant over against other types of human activity.

5.1 The Dichotomy of *Praxis* and *Poiesis*

In Aristotle's famous formulation (see Angier 2016 for a clear summary), *praxis* is action in the proper sense, action through the performance of which

The Case for Work. Jean-Philippe Deranty, Oxford University Press. © Jean-Philippe Deranty (2024).
DOI: 10.1093/oso/9780192887146.003.0006

higher human ends are realized, like demonstrating one's freedom, or manifesting other virtues, such as being a just person, a good friend, a valuable fellow citizen, and so on. It is opposed to *poiesis*, 'productive' action that is guided by technical considerations and that aims to efficiently realize externally set ends. The distinction relies especially on the ends of action. In *praxis*, the end is the action itself: acting justly or morally is valuable in itself, is its own end. In *poiesis*, the goal of action is its outcome, its 'product' (*ergon*), the action matters only as the means to realize that end. Three passages from the *Nichomachean Ethics* and the *Metaphysics* suffice to illustrate Aristotle's view. In book 6, chapter 5 of the *Nichomachean Ethics*, he writes:

> *Poiesis* has its end in something other than itself, but *praxis* does not since its end is acting well itself.
>
> **(Aristotle 1999, 89, 1140b6)**

To emphasize the lesser character of making that results from its instrumental nature, he writes:

> where there are ends apart from the actions [*praxeis*], it is the nature of the products [*erga*] to be better than the activities [*energeiōn*].
>
> **(Aristotle 1999, 1094a5–6)**

And in the *Metaphysics*:

> Only the kind of movement in which the end is immanent is action properly speaking.
>
> **(Aristotle 1961, 1048b23)**

How is this basic distinction between types of action mobilized in critical accounts of modernity, and how does it feed a major strand of objections to the centrality of work?

The wealth of authors to consider, together with the secondary literature dedicated to them, makes the task even more daunting than in the previous three chapters, which focused on just one canonical figure. The authors who use a version of the dichotomy in important parts of their works includes, among others: Schiller and many other Romantic authors after him; Marx himself, notably in the passage in Volume III of *Capital* where he opposes the realm of freedom and the realm of necessity; Kant (as we will see); Hans-Georg Gadamer; Hannah Arendt; Michael Oakeshott; Jürgen Habermas; and Alasdair MacIntyre, to name but the most illustrious ones. The distinction plays a central role in Gorz's thinking, for whom Arendt is a major source of inspiration. The distinction is also mobilized in many post-work writings. Needless to say, it is impossible to do justice to the details of each one of the accounts just mentioned. However, for the purposes of this chapter, we can rely on the wonderfully concise yet substantive study György Márkus dedicated to the conceptual pair and its role in contemporary social criticism (Márkus 2011). This text guides the chapter's analyses, with additional insights that arise as a result of our specific focus on the issue of work's centrality.

Márkus' short study efficiently conveys the way in which the basic conceptual opposition between *praxis* and *poiesis* can become the foundation for comprehensive critical narratives of modernity. On the basis of the core conceptual distinction, two different rationalities are opposed to each other. In turn, this distinction between modes of rationality is used to underpin a whole series of other oppositions, concerning individual life, the human community, and corresponding values and norms. The underlying logic of 'making' is the attempt at the successful completion of ends posited independently of the action itself. Upon completion, the action leads to *achievements*, whose rationality is measured not just by the end achieved, but also by external criteria such as efficacy, economy of means (for instance of time spent completing the action, or of resources) and, in an economic context, profitability. The rationality that drives activity of this kind is *technical* in nature, defining the best means to be used for external ends, with the appropriate means defined by the agent's conception of utility in each case. By contrast, genuine acting consists in *accomplishments*, which are measured in terms of excellence, where the agent demonstrates particular virtues and realizes inherently good values. The rationality embodied in that kind of action is practical intelligence, *phronesis*, as opposed to *techne*. Actions that are productive, efficient, and useful are measured by standards of utility. The ultimate basis from which utilities derive their value is some conception of the good for the agent, where in this case the good is rooted in a conception of well-being. The fundamental value underpinning this sphere of action is therefore self-preservation, the reproduction and promotion of life in its merely biological sense. Genuine action, by contrast, reproduces true human life, that is life to which some meaning is given, which transcends mere survival. For many authors, this dimension is intimately linked to autonomy. The core argument is that the meaning attached to action is authentic if it has been autonomously endorsed by the agent, or indeed has been defined by her in relation to her chosen ends. This contrasts with the reasons involved in making, which remain external to the agent and are imposed by some form of necessity: the technical necessity of what are the best means for given ends, the necessity of the ends themselves (natural necessity for the reproduction of life and social necessity when that reproduction of life occurs via the economic process). Only in genuine action, therefore, do human agents affirm themselves in their capacity to act autonomously, pursuing ends they can agree with, or they have set for themselves. Because of the autonomous characteristic of genuine action, it is also the kind of action that ensures authenticity. Only in 'doing' can humans find avenues for self-affirmation, that is, for the expression of who they are as a unique person, and opportunities to realize their true self. The kind of life that authentic action makes possible is not mere organic life, but a truly human life, the 'good life', living well as opposed to simply enjoying well-being. *Poiesis* or instrumental action responds to challenges that make human life vulnerable to forms of necessity. Genuine action by contrast promotes the realization of freedom. A community in which utilitarian, technical, calculating rationality takes the upper hand is under the sway of forms of necessity. Typically, such a community is run by experts and technocrats, people who are very good at calculating the best means for chosen ends, but don't reflect on the ends themselves. Whatever the experts' benevolence, genuine political freedom is inherently limited in such a community, since technical, instrumental calculation dictates what needs to be done. The true meaning of political action is when collective decision-making itself follows the logic of genuine action, that is, the free setting of ends. In this case, participation in collective decision-making is seen by each and all as a good in itself, not merely as a means to deliver utilities for individuals and the collective.

In Aristotle, the two rationalities were embodied in social types, slaves, and craftsmen working under the orders of free citizens (Aristotle Politics VII, 8, 1944, 571–579). The freedom of free citizens thus had a negative dimension, namely, the state of not being subjected to the forms of necessity that other classes lived under: the necessities stemming from the technical aspects of production, the necessities arising from the relation of dependence to another's will in the slave or the wage relationship, and the necessity to which the very action of production as a fulfilment of needs responds (Arendt 1961, 19, 117–118; 1958, 83–83). It is on such a negative basis, that is, the absence of domination, that the positive dimension of freedom—of realizing the virtues enabling them to live well—was open for free citizens. Modern thinkers shed Aristotle's separation of humanity into the naturally unfree and the naturally free, but there remains the idea of kernels of necessity attached to work that is antithetical to freedom.

Probably the most famous and influential modern retrieval of the Greek concepts is Hannah Arendt's tripartite distinction of forms of action in the *Human Condition*. In Greek thought, Arendt reminds us, *praxis* is opposed to two different classes of 'making', which follow two different epistemic and practical rationalities and are embodied in two different social statuses (see Angier 2016): *praxis* as genuine *action* is contrasted with craftwork mobilizing technical know-how (*Werk*) and with basic, everyday work to provide for the necessities of life, the work done by slaves in ancient society (*Arbeit*). *Arbeit*, as the activities necessary for the reproduction of human life, is itself an expression of the human form of life in its 'metabolic' interaction with nature and natural necessity. *Werk*, the activity that is productive of durable objects, provides the material framework supporting the only activities that truly merit the name of 'action'. The latter are those human endeavours that break the flows of natural and human-induced causality, introduce novelty into the world, and reveal a human person for who she authentically is. Only in this latter sense can human action have true political meaning, as it is only in this latter sense that a collective genuinely decides upon its collective fate in a way that respects both individual and collective freedom.

Arendt describes modern society as promoting an exact inversion of the hierarchy that made labour ideologically inferior to work and genuine action the conduit for individual self-expression and collectively built freedom. In modernity, she argues, the rise of economic and bureaucratic imperatives means a dissolution of the political into the management of the social. This in turn means that of the three kinds of action, *Arbeit*-work becomes the most important one, the one whose logic and inherent values come to best represent the driving ethos of its society. Modern society becomes predominantly a society of 'job holders' and consumers (Arendt 1958, 319–321). Even *Werk*-work comes under the sway of labour, as the mere amelioration of life aiming towards the now absolutized ends of 'happiness' and well-being trump the other values associated with *Werk*-work, such as individual excellence and creativity. The diagnosis is repeated from a different angle in *On Revolution*, where the sharp criticism of the French revolution rests precisely on the idea that it was the first modern revolution to make happiness and not freedom the ultimate goal of emancipation. With this, Arendt argues, the seeds were planted for the totalitarian politics of the next century, in which the promise of finally overcoming human finitude led to the most radical programmes for the annihilation of personal freedom. In such a critical diagnosis, we see how self, society, culture, and politics, the four areas of concern for critical theories of modernity, are all impacted by the rising centrality of labour and its utilitarian, biologically centred values.

5.2 Play, Leisure, and Festivals

One defining feature of these accounts is the place taken by the reference to traditional forms of life in them. The critique of modernity based on the distinction between two root forms of action is, as we saw, a critique of how utility- and efficiency-driven forms of action 'took over' from the more genuine kind of human action. These critiques of modernity bemoan a gradual 'atrophy of praxis', a 'colonization' of lifeworld that should be ruled by free communication by the logic of utilitarian efficiency. As the paradigmatic example of instrumental action, work becoming central is the symptom and even, as the central factor of modern industrialism, the cause of this pathological inversion. In premodern societies, by contrast, the sphere of work was appropriately bounded and overdetermined by the higher cultural and religious values of the community.

Focusing on this aspect of post-Aristotelian critiques of work is useful because it helps to single out dimensions of the debate on work that appear most strikingly in this particular theoretical context. These are appeals to alternative modes of acting and indeed of being that are taken up again in current post-work writings.

One reference to cite here, because it makes these dimensions eminently visible and because of the tremendous influence it had on modern European culture, is Schiller's *Letters on the Aesthetic Education of Humanity*. The conceptual framework Schiller mobilizes is of course indebted to Kant, not Aristotle. Markus, however, convincingly shows that, despite the major displacement Kant effects within ethical theory as he shifts the focus of morality from the features of action to the rationality of the agent's motivation, his distinction between hypothetical and categorical imperatives, or between technical and practical rules of judgement, in the end retrieves the Aristotelian vision of genuine as opposed to merely instrumental action (Márkus 2011, 46). In its paramount expression, moral action for Kant has the same key feature Aristotle attaches to *praxis*, namely, that it is an action be pursued for its own sake. The fact that deontological and virtue-based approaches can communicate on this vision of the highest form of action demonstrates how deeply the intuition about the hierarchy of action types is rooted in Western thought.

What is interesting for our concerns is the method Schiller uses to detect the pathological overtaking of instrumental over practical action. For Schiller and generations of German writers after him, the ideal forms of ancient culture tragically manifest the ideals of harmonious individual and community life that have been lost as work and its associated values have come to the fore. Whereas in the ideal Greek past, each individual embodied a harmony between their different faculties, free citizens could all participate equally in the life of the collective, and art and science could both know and celebrate nature equally,

> in our day it is necessity, neediness, that prevails, and bends a degraded humanity under its iron yoke. Utility is the great idol of the time, to which all powers do homage and all subjects are subservient. In this great balance on utility, the spiritual service of art has no weight, and, deprived of all encouragement, it vanishes from the noisy Vanity Fair of our time. The very spirit of philosophical inquiry itself robs the imagination of one promise after another, and the frontiers of art are narrowed in proportion as the limits of science are enlarged.
>
> **(Schiller 2005, 89)**

Progress in scientific knowledge, the unprecedented development of technical powers, the increasingly detailed division of labour, and the encroachment of state controls into the individual sphere sunder human faculties, separate individuals from each other along class and professional lines, and detach individuals from communal life. All these cultural developments are spurred on by responses to 'necessity'. Only those human capacities that increase the ability to address 'neediness' are henceforth developed. As a result of this,

> Man himself, eternally chained down to a little fragment of the whole, only forms a kind of fragment; having nothing in his ears but the monotonous sound of the perpetually revolving wheel, he never develops the harmony of his being, and instead of imprinting the seal of humanity on his being, he ends by being nothing more than the living impress of the craft to which he devotes himself, of the science that he cultivates. This very partial and paltry relation, linking the isolated members to the whole, does not depend on forms that are given spontaneously; for how could a complicated machine, which shuns the light, confide itself to the free will of man?
>
> **(Schiller 2005, 100)**

What this critique of modernity as the age of utility first signals is an aesthetic dimension to the rejection of work's centrality. This is a trope that continues to reverberate today in post-work writings. This aspect of the objection goes something like this. A world in which the central value is work is ugly: morally ugly, because it is a world where the core values are narrow-mindedly pragmatic or even downright mean-spirited, ungenerous, even selfish; socially ugly, as civic bonds are instrumentalized or even destroyed, manners and politeness are shunned; and it is formally ugly, as the functional mindset is unable to create beautiful forms to replicate the beauty of the past. Such an aesthetic-moral condemnation of the modern world runs through MacIntyre's *After Virtue*, for instance. The final paragraph of that book epitomizes such a nostalgic trepidation in which contemporary times are described as being akin to the 'dark ages', whose difference in comparison with the times of the fall of Rome is only that now 'the barbarians are not waiting beyond the frontiers; they have already been governing us for quite some time' (MacIntyre 2007, 263). In Gorz's writings, the 'critique of economic reason' includes this aesthetic dimension:

> To a work culture which cuts itself off from the sensory substance of the lifeworld, corresponds the production of a world without sensory values and a hardened sensibility, which hardens thought in its turn.
>
> **(Gorz 1989, 87)**

In contrast, premodern cultures, which embedded all actions in an all-encompassing symbolic framework, could provide deep meaning even to instrumental activities, including work itself. This was shown for instance in the fact that in many traditional societies, work instruments were decorated as there was no strict separation between working and higher forms of social action (Gorz 1985, 49).

To correct the pathologies of modern times, Schiller's *Letters* appeal to a new 'aesthetic education' that would fortify and expand the powers of taste and imagination so that technical, moral, and legal modes of rational thinking would be put back in their proper place, as specialized forms of thought and of acting that ought to remain in their specific spheres. A new unity of individual powers could thereby be restored leading to a sensibility for beautiful external forms, notably those manifested by others, which would make possible a truly democratic community based on open social interactions rather than the 'zealous' enforcement of rights and duties, as the French Revolution attempted to do (Schiller 2005, 178). In true Kantian fashion, Schiller attempts to prove that this aesthetic education is a priori possible, by pointing to a faculty uniting the powers of perception and understanding, the 'play-drive', which just needs to be released from the shackles of material and formal-rational imperatives to lead humanity on the way to full emancipation. As synthesis of passivity and activity, actions driven by the play-drive inspires activities that produce their outputs by letting themselves be guided by the order and forms the agent perceives in the world (126). This kind of action stands in direct contrast with action performed by a will that seeks to realize its own ends by bending the external world to its own goals, which is paradigmatic of work. Artistic creation is the archetypal realm of human activity in which the play-drive is active. In turn, the education that beauty-producing art can provide acts on individuals and the community through taste, the development of sensibility that attunes individuals to forms in their environments, particularly the forms embodied in fellow human beings. Aesthetic sensibility has the power to heal the divisions that have emerged from industrial modernity, notably because of the division of labour and its premium on constantly refined specialization, which leads to multiple divisions: the divisions between individuals, between occupations, between faculties, between the hand and the head, between intelligence and sensibility. The ideal community created in a fully operative 'aesthetic state' is one in which each individual can recognize their genuine self in their own actions and authentically communicates with others on the basis of this authentic self-relation (176).

This famous aesthetic-political programme, which became a model for so many subsequent artistic projects in the following century, is echoed in the utopian visions of social organizations many post-work writings propose in which the rationality underpinning work would cease to be central and individual lives would be allowed once again to be directed by other values. At the most general level, this leads to demands to liberate people's time from the strictures of work and allow them to act in non-work ways, in other words, a defence of leisure against work. These demands for more leisure can denote varying content. At bottom, it is the demand famously expressed by Lafargue to be allowed to be idle, lazy, to do nothing if one so wishes (Hodgkinson 2004; O'Connor 2018). In another formulation, this demand ushers a liberal vision of justice defended by Van Parijs (1995) and Julie Rose (2016) of providing everyone with the means to 'do whatever we might wish to do' and 'what we will', without prescription of what this might entail. In Graeber's critical reflections on modern work societies, this is the reference to ways of doing and of interacting in non-Western, precapitalist societies, which show the whole range of activities humans can actually engage in when they are not obsessed with work (2018). In Kathi Weeks' *The Problem with Work*, the utopian demand that people be given the time to engage in non-work activities is a central formulation of the post-work manifesto: 'to consider and experiment with different kinds of lives, with wanting, doing, and being otherwise' (2011, 145).

More specifically, Schiller's 'play-drive' can be taken as a most famous advocacy in favour of productive activities that escape the heteronomous dimensions attached to economically determined work. These are activities that produce real outcomes, and in which the agent exercises and manifests their skills, expresses their identity, engages in social relations, but which do not stand under the yoke of necessity, whether economic or social. As we know, the archetype of this was art, but this conception of intrinsically valuable and free activity also applies to a broader category such as 'play', as in John Danaher's post-work vision centred on the 'utopia of games', practices in which human agents can continue to develop their skills and interact but no longer have to worry about real-world efficacy since machines can do all the necessary work (Danaher 2019a, 231–241, 2019b).

Finally, Schiller's aesthetic critique of the society of work points to a third major strand in nineteenth-century and later thinking, all the way to contemporary post-work literature. This is the idea that the overcoming of work as the central value will liberate human senses and human attention from being used in merely instrumental ways and will therefore make possible a freer attitude to the external world, one that no longer seeks to master and utilize it but has the capacity to take it in, to wonder at its beauties and simply let it be without trying to exploit or shape it to human interests (for instance Gorz 1985, 107).

One famous text making this kind of argument is Joseph Pieper's denunciation of modern society as society of 'total labour', in his 1948 *Leisure, the Basis of Culture* (1998, 48). This text is worth dwelling on briefly, as it helps to emphasize the religious inspiration that can underpin this last strand. Pieper's critical rendition of modernity reprises the classical tropes already encountered. That is, the modern world according to him is governed by the dictates of instrumental rationality, the demand for efficiency, needs-fulfilment, utilitarian thinking, and organization. Fundamentally, the logic of *poiesis*, of outcome- and efficiency-oriented action has become the standard by which all other forms of human actions are measured. It provides the normative framework in which different kinds of values are ranked. As it imposes its logic on genuine forms of action, knowledge, and belief and thereby undermines authentic freedom and culture, work realizes its 'totalitarian claims' (25). Like many other authors in the Aristotelian tradition, Pieper means totalitarianism in a literal sense, and sees the centrality of industrial values as the direct cause of twentieth century's various political disasters. By contrast with other neo-Aristotelian writers, however, the category Pieper stresses in opposition to *poiesis* is not *praxis* but contemplation, which entails the aesthetic aspects we just noted, but unveils a religious layer as their ultimate ground. The ugliest side of modernity according to Pieper is not just that it has made genuine action impossible, but a more radical problem, namely the increasing difficulty to engage in true *skhole*, or leisure, understood now as a state in which humans can be detached from earthly concerns and as a result can become truly open for a genuine contemplation of the world, and the transcendent cause of it. The demise of leisure, of non-utilitarian forms of sensing and thinking, is also the demise of a truly human way of being, and in particular of true culture, because only in this kind of disposition can humans transcend the status they share with animals and all other organic life and elevate themselves to the true beauty and order of the world. Leisure is 'the basis of culture' to the extent that it is what truly separates humans from other creatures. In contrast with Arendt, such a conception of *skhole* is thus not content with the dichotomy of genuine versus instrumental action but anchors the true dichotomy in the distinction between active and contemplative life. For this approach, the most authentic 'leisure' activities are to be found in religious cult; indeed the original, German title of the book is in fact 'Leisure and Cult':

> leisure can only be made possible and justifiable on the same basis as the celebration of a festival. That basis is divine worship.
>
> **(Pieper 1998 [1948], 59)**

The central problem of modernity, then, is the repression of the Christian heritage, which is manifested in individual experiences and social practices coming increasingly under the sway of utilitarian frenzy that destroys the real basis of culture. Rather than aesthetic education, this version of the critique of work from leisure ushers in the hope that humanity's ability to revel in 'festivals' can be reawakened, where true worship (not the worship of consumption and technical prowess) can arise again.

5.3 Shaky Foundations

For the authors mentioned in this chapter, the centrality of work is a major pathology because it manifests the 'atrophy' of genuine action, both at the individual and the collective level. In 'The Dichotomy of Praxis and Poiesis', György Márkus made a series of portentous objections against the attempt at criticizing modernity based on an ontological separation of types of actions. We can follow his lead and apply his concerns more specifically to issues surrounding the centrality of work.

First, Márkus' analysis alerts to how unstable the conceptual distinction is. To begin with, Aristotle himself defines action in general, including praxis, as activity that 'is for the sake of things other than themselves' (Aristotle 1999 III,

3, 1112b33; Márkus 2011, 39). In his landmark study James Murphy shows in detail how messy the apparently clear distinction between intrinsic and external ends actually is (Murphy 1993, 87–112). This was a point repeated by Kant, that 'every action has its end' (Kant 2017, 43). From an analytical perspective, Candace Vogler (2002) demonstrates that a 'calculative' view of practical reason is inevitable but does not by itself lead to all-out instrumentalism. The calculation of the proper means for a chosen end is in fact the formal structure of any practical reasoning, if only because reasoning simpliciter aims for the end of 'figuring out what to do'. The teleological nature of action therefore cannot be the conceptual marker to distinguish *praxis* from *poiesis*. All action is teleological, aims to 'produce' some output, even if it is not a material object.

Besides the form of practical reasoning, we can add a material dimension to the idea that all actions, including praxis-actions, aim to achieve some end. Being a good friend is expressed through particular actions (remembering a birthday, actively listening, providing material support, and so on), each of which has a specific end in view, which can be 'produced' more or less well. Merely being a good friend, without actually 'producing' the outcomes that give content to the idea of it, is not being a good friend at all. Or to take another example, political activity, often the specific concern of authors who want to retrieve genuine forms of *praxis*, aims to produce outcomes from the deliberations. The point of deliberation is precisely what the collective will *do*.

Furthermore, the categories of achievement and of accomplishment can designate highly heterogeneous actions, to which social valuations typically fall on both sides of the conceptual divide: harvesting and then arranging apples in a bowl and making a painting of apples in a bowl are both examples of *poietic* 'achievement'; satisfying one's hunger and helping someone in distress are both examples of 'accomplishments' resulting from *praxis*-actions.

Also, the same action can appear as *praxis* or as *poiesis*, depending on the circumstances and the point of view adopted. This is typically the case for craftwork. People who enjoy craftwork can be said to engage in *praxis*, since they produce objects for the sake of it. Yet their actions are obviously paradigm examples of *poietic* actions: the series of actions they perform are guided by technical considerations and the actions' end in view is external (making a dress, a table). Indeed, these workers might well find in other people using and enjoying, and perhaps even admiring and cherishing, the product of their work, one of the leading motivations for their actions. In recent discussions of Marx's famous passage on the two realms, this aspect of 'working for others' has been especially emphasized (Kandiyali and Gomberg

2024, who take the example of the US furniture maker George Nakashima). In such cases, poietic activities are therefore pursued both for intrinsic and extrinsic reasons. In fact, if the enjoyment of others is an intrinsic part of the making of an output, then it becomes difficult to decide what are intrinsic and extrinsic ends to the making of that output.

Finally, as we saw, for the tradition in which Schiller is a key reference point, it is typically a productive activity, delivering an external object, the work of art, that is tasked with reuniting the different modalities of being in the world and being with others that allegedly became sundered in modern conditions. As Christopher Shaw shows (1991), this led to the vision of a higher form of work for which artistic practice is the model. This aesthetic utopia of redeemed work remained an inspiration for successive generations of artists and intellectuals in nineteenth-century England, from Coleridge, Carlysle, Ruskin, to William Morris. We should include Oscar Wilde in this list, with 'The Soul of Man under Socialism' (Wilde 2001 [1891]) as a prime example of this tradition. Such a utopia of work was a major strand in nineteenth-century socialism, as the vision of creative, freely chosen activity that would allow each individual to express and realize their individual 'soul', was pitted against the pathological traits of real Victorian labour and was made the central mode of individual expression and the vector for the realization of a free collective. In Germany, through the influence of Kant and Schiller, a similar Romantic trait was also prominent. Its legacy can be found in Marx's critique of work as disutility at the end of the *Grundrisse*, where the paradigm example of composing music is chosen as an example of work that is intrinsically valuable and allows the agent to achieve self-realization (Marx 1973 [1857], 611). This Kantian-Marxian strand continues all the way into twentieth-century critical theory. It is prevalent for instance in Marcuse's focus on the aesthetic dimensions of emancipation, pointing not only to the significance of artistic practice and artistic enjoyment as spheres in which the deepest human drives are visible, but more generally to the need for liberation of sensation and perception (Marcuse 1966 [1955], 172–197; 2007).

If all intentional actions have a calculative form and entail a material aspect; if typical examples of *praxis* and of *poiesis* designate highly heterogeneous examples with social valuations typically striding the line between them; and if archetypal examples of *poiesis* also have *praxis*-dimensions, then the line separating 'genuinely practical' and 'productive' actions is not at all as clear as first appeared. And if that is the case, it is difficult to see how such a shaky conceptual foundation could ground a strict hierarchy of freedom-enabling versus freedom-undermining practices, on which a complex, weighty scaffolding of social criticism could then be erected. Depending on the circumstances and the agents' attitudes to their activity, there might be occurrences of work in which the poietic side is not repressive of the *praxis* side at all, where in fact engaging in *poiesis* is also engaging in *praxis*. There might be forms of work individuals undertake at least partly for their own sake, because they help individuals acquire particular 'goods' through the act of working, goods that are intrinsically valuable to them, even as these activities also achieve the production of some use-value, including perhaps a monetary value, in the form of a wage for instance.

Because of the influence Arendt's distinction between labour, work and action has played in twentieth-century social and political thought, it is useful to apply these points to her approach. If we take the example of the work involved in social reproduction as it is discussed by feminist scholars, and as we will study in detail in Chapters 9 and 10, it is typically described, not as 'labour', but as a form of work in the sense of *Werk*. This work creates its own material 'outputs', namely the new generation of individuals who will rejuvenate the collective, as well as the cultural and social resources in which these new individuals will be socialized. These 'outputs' (individual lives, cultural and social knowledge) are supremely important since they ensure the reproduction of families and communities. Many who are involved in that work find it intrinsically valuable, since it expresses their commitment to the persons they care for, or indeed to the collective they support and are part of. This 'labour' then is just as much *Werk*-work as it is *praxis*. To argue that this work of care only serves the ends of preservation, has nothing to do with living well and is only about biological well-being, seems like a serious misdescription of it. If we generalize to other examples of work, the link Arendt establishes between what she considers genuine action and freedom, to the exclusion of labour and *Werk*-work, continues to be problematic. In many cases, individuals want to be recognized for their achievements in their particular work, in their workplace, their family or their local community. More broadly, many workers want to be recognized for the contribution they make to society. These demands of recognition testify to the capacity to set ends through the very act of working and, in endorsing those ends and how they have realized them, to stand up as a responsible individual among others, the definition of individual freedom and full individuality for Arendt, which she attaches exclusively to *praxis*. Also, against the idea that the instrumental, functional mindset attached to *poiesis* is antithetical to genuine social bonds, there is ample evidence, as we will show at length in Chapter 12, that significant social bonds, notably forms of real solidarity, are found in work, and indeed more broadly, that the division of labour is the basis of the political community (most recently Honneth 2023, see Chapter 14). If all of this is the case, then it is not self-evident at all that poietic activities are ontologically averse to freedom. As Marx said in the famous passage on the realms of freedom and of necessity, 'there can be freedom in this sphere'; indeed rather than a dichotomous distinction, this passage explicitly suggests that full freedom requires an articulation of poietic and praxis-actions. This is precisely the sense of Márkus' excursus through an original interpretation of Marx: the full meaning of production for Marx, he argues, is precisely to combine poietic and practical logics, each of which is equally required for a human society in which each individual can flourish (Márkus 2011, 49–50).

How unstable the distinction between *praxis* and *poiesis* is and how fragile a basis it provides for a hierarchy of actions that would then translate into a rejection of the central importance of work, is confirmed by the fact that major social philosophers who are directly inspired by Aristotle have in fact counted work as an eminent form of 'practice', that is, a form of action to which important 'goods' can be attached, which are then part of a 'good life'. This is the case with Andrea Veltman's account of 'meaningful work', which adopts precisely an Aristotelian approach that demonstrates all the 'goods' attached to it (Veltman 2016). An influential account of work as a form of 'praxis' had been developed earlier by Alasdair Macintyre, who, in one of his early texts, even made the point that 'we ought to eat in order to work' (1979, 44). This wilful inversion of the ancient motto whereby those who don't work cannot expect to eat, points to MacIntyre's influential conception of practice, as a cooperative activity constituted by internal goods, the realization of which allows individuals to develop their own virtues and around which a particular tradition and community can define itself as community of value (2007, 187). This rich concept of practice, for which work is a paradigm example, has been taken up not just in political philosophy (Breen 2019) but also by a number of scholars in management studies and business ethics (in particular by Ron Beadle, for instance 2012 and 2019, also Sinnicks 2021), as a guide for critical descriptions and for alternative thinking regarding the organization of formal work. Even though MacIntyre's critical description of modernity follows the classical pattern of tracing the withering of genuine practice and the destruction of value-based communities to the spread of utility thinking, a paradigm example of a practice for him is still an occupation, a job considered from the point of view not just of the types of skill and knowledge it involves, but also the broader human goods it pursues and the rich forms of interaction it harbours as a result of the pursuit of those goods. Farming for example is a typical example of practice (187). MacIntyre explicitly bemoans the fact that Aristotle was blind to the virtues that a community of professionals could develop and embody (159). In some of its historical forms, work might be mainly seen as a just kind of *poiesis*, an activity undergone purely for the sake of ends external to it, typically the production of use-values. And yet if it is organically integrated into a broader tradition, as part of the infrastructure that provides this tradition with its necessary material support, then the instrumentality inherent in this productive practice is transcended so to speak, and it benefits from being integrated into that world as one of its essential elements. Precisely these two possible characters of work, that it can by itself define a social tradition and be understood as a *praxis* (an activity entailing its own internal goods), or that it might be an essential element in a more general form of *praxis*, these two characters are destroyed in the transformation of work in modern conditions:

> The kind of work done by the vast majority of the inhabitants of the modern world cannot be understood in terms of the nature of a practice with goods internal to itself, and for very good reason. One of the key moments in the creation of modernity occurs when production moves outside the household. So long as production work occurs within the structure of households, it is easy and right to understand that work as part of the sustaining of the community of the household and of those wider forms of community which the household in turn sustains. As, and to the extent that, work moves outside the household and is put to the service of impersonal capital, the realm of work tends to become separated from everything but the service of biological survival and the reproduction of the labour force, one the one hand, and that of institutionalized acquisitiveness, on the other. Pleonexia, a vice in the Aristotelian scheme, is now the driving force of modern productive work. The means-end relationships embodied for the most part in such work—on a production line for example—are necessarily external to the goods which those who work seek; such work too has consequently been expelled from the realm of practices with goods internal to themselves. And correspondingly practices have in turn been removed to the margins of social and cultural life.
>
> (2007, 226)

As this citation shows, the centrality of work is a thesis to be rejected first because the time when work becomes central (for individuals and communities) is also the time when most work becomes pure *poiesis*, can no longer be seen as a practice or as an element of a practice. Secondly and even more concerningly, this transformation of work into pure *poiesis* combined with the reality that work has become central in individual and social life is in fact the root cause behind the elimination of practices from the core of social and cultural life. MacIntyre sees the increasing importance of consumption, particularly aesthetic consumption, as a direct outcome of the rise of instrumental thinking and more precisely of thinking and acting in instrumental terms only. The modern individual no longer organizes her life around the active pursuit of goods that will sustain a particular community and allow herself to grow as a self. Instead, the detached individual defines herself through what she can possess and enjoy. Beyond these pathological traits, however, the view of work as genuine practice remains as a guideline for reforming workplaces and the possibility of meaningful work. Indeed, in a more recent book, MacIntyre again makes work a paradigmatic example of an activity that can be an example of true practice in which agents cooperate for the realization of a common good, or of an activity where the ends are external to the activity and the agents only engage in it for individual, utilitarian ends (2016, 131–132). In these analyses, the blanket rejection of contemporary work is significantly qualified. He makes room for the possibility of meaningful work even in modern industrial labour, as for example among Japanese factory carmakers.

We can see in one of the most eminent post-Aristotelian accounts then that the problem with the centrality of work is not work per se, or the fact that work *as such* raises 'totalitarian claims', but the shape of work in modern society. Once again, the argument against work is reduced to empirical features of modern work, but it doesn't affect work itself. Indeed, as we saw with Schiller and MacIntyre, the Aristotelian tradition can in fact help to establish a counter-image to contrast with pathological forms of contemporary work. This positive image of work relates to individual self-realization and flourishing, the quality of social relations and the shape of the community. This confirms that a critique of modern society insisting on the pathologies affecting psyches, social bonds and political practices cannot be coherently grounded on an ontological separation ranking different types of action, but instead must establish more specifically how the conditions in which actions are performed, in particular work, lead to such pathologies. To attribute modern pathologies to intrinsic features of types of action is illegitimate. As MacIntyre makes the case, and as the second part of the book will attempt to show, countervailing images of non-pathological individual development, social solidarity and democratic politics in fact require a grounding in the individual and social experiences of work.

However, from our brief exploration of the complex field of Aristotelian objections three challenges remain, namely the challenge *from play*, the challenge *from leisure* and the challenge *from festivals*.

The challenge from play is that it might well be the case that some activities are significant, perhaps even indispensable for individual self-development and the nurturing of significant social bonds, but why should they take the form of work? Why can't they be play activities? The point about poietic actions having praxis dimensions might apply just as much to activities engaged in as play as opposed to work activities. One key difference between the two is the relationship to necessity. In play, the necessity built into the following of rules, the rules of the game, is freely accepted. This is what Danaher, citing Bernard Suit, refers to as the 'lusory attitude' (2019a, 232), freely accepting to play by the rules as a condition of play. In work by contrast, necessity is imposed from the outside. As we saw, the Greeks had a deep sensitivity for all the aspects of *Ananke* surrounding work, which made it intrinsically inimical to freedom for them. In Schiller, a key aspect of the play-drive is precisely that it liberates human beings from the 'earnestness' of material and moral obligations. The 'idleness and indifference' of the Greek gods are perfect representations of the play drive for him precisely for that reason. The Greek gods were 'preserved from the bonds inseparable from every purpose, every duty, every care' (131), that is, the kinds of heteronomy that work imposes on mortals. In play necessity becomes 'light weight' (130) whereas it is a heavy burden in work. To answer this challenge, we will need to show that it is precisely the facing of necessity that gives work the kind of material and normative weight that makes it a privileged conduit for individual self-development and solidary social bonds. As Marx said in the *Grundrisse* passage already quoted, 'really free working, e.g. composing, is at the same time precisely the most damned seriousness, the most intense exertion' (1973, 611). Chapter 13 will try to show why play cannot provide what work does in this respect.

The challenge from leisure is also about freedom and necessity but this time points to the beyond of work, that sphere of existence, where humans 'do whatever they wish to do'.

In response to this challenge, one confusion must first be clarified. To claim that work is central is not to say that no other forms of doing or being matter. It is just to say that work has such a deep impact on individual development and the life of the collective that it is 'centrally' important in several senses. The second part of the book articulates many different ways in which work is 'central', from simply being a significant form of experience, to being an indispensable condition of key human and collective goods. But asserting the centrality of work in no way denies the importance of other modes of being and acting. At the same time though, an argument will be mounted to show that it is in fact in facing the necessities built into work that full development of capacities, and a strong social bond can be developed. It is also crucial to remember that work in this book is not limited to paid employment and denotes activities engaged in to fulfil needs that are part of social reproduction. In that expanded sense, many activities that are examples of leisure activities (what Marx calls 'really free working' or 'higher activity') are forms of work on this expanded definition.

Another response will be made to the leisure challenge, based once again on the idea of necessity. As the last chapter will argue, philosophers tend to take too lightly the necessity to which work responds, and theytend to take work for granted. They assume the material and social world is a given, without acknowledging all the work that is required to produce and reproduce that world, from the food needed daily to feed all its human and non-human animals, to the complex infrastructures, material and symbolic, that need to be maintained for that lifeworld to continue to operate. The sheer mass of work that is needed for collectives and their individuals to be reproduced daily means that a lot of work is simply necessary. This is not quite the realm of necessity of which Marx speaks in Volume III of *Capital*, since this reproduction of the lifeworld involves activities that can be paradigm examples of 'free' action, like intellectual or artistic or scientific work. The necessity here is just the sheer necessity of social reproduction in its broadest sense, the sense that will be defended and illustrated in Chapter 10, which translates into a massive necessity to work. Once the myriad needs of individuals and their collective are acknowledged, the notion that machines will one day be able to fulfil all those needs appears highly dubious (Chapter 7). When this necessity to work and the demands it makes on collectives is acknowledged, the demand for leisure becomes highly conditional. Undeniably being in a condition where one does as one wishes is probably something to be desired. And yet by necessity it has to be limited.

When leisure means more than just 'doing as one wishes', and instead denotes *skhole*, that is, activities that are intrinsically valuable, another issue arises. Often the opposition between leisure and work overlaps with the distinction between classes of people, between those who have the capacities to truly engage in intrinsically valuable activities, as opposed to the people whose leisure would be meaningless, and for whom therefore the best kind of action is restricted *poiesis*. This is one of the most entrenched prejudices in Western thought, underpinning the separation between liberal and servile arts (Kimball 2010). This separation of humanity into the leisurely and the working classes is explicitly maintained in Pieper's account for instance, as his appeal to leisure as a sphere to be rescued is explicitly formulated in reference to 'intellectual workers' and their ontological difference from other workers (39–45). It transpires underneath Arendt's division of the three ontological classes of action. Given that labour and *Werk*-work are necessities, and given the finiteness of human time, the only way to ensure genuine action continues to be possible is if those who are most able to engage in it do so, while those who don't have those capacities, support the free (Canovan 1978). Admittedly, the appeal to leisure is not necessarily elitist. Some leisure scholars, like Hunnicutt (Hunnicutt 1988, 2013), recall that the demand for leisure has been a key working-class demand. They can refer to Marx who also endorsed the time for 'idleness or for the performance of activities which are (...) not directly productive (as e.g., war, affairs of state) or for the development of human abilities and social potentialities (art, etc., science) which have no directly practical purpose' (Marx 1988, 190). But the appeal to leisure can easily take on elitist traits, especially if the necessity to work is acknowledged. Then, an unsaid assumption is often that some need to work so that others who are capable of it, or who deserve it based on their wealth or power, can indulge in truly valuable leisure. Inegalitarian assumptions regarding individual abilities continue to be almost universally accepted in contemporary political philosophy (Gomberg 2007), even by otherwise progressive authors, even if they uphold equality as a key norm in other aspects. Against these elitist assumptions, Chapter 14 will argue that the only valid appeal to leisure is if it is distributed fairly among all, which means that all who can have to take on their share of necessary work.

The third and final challenge, the challenge from festivals is the most difficult to address. We will turn to it in the Conclusion. Here, the point will be to show that detachment, contemplation and the search for transcendence must not be thought of in abstract opposition to work considerations. In the meantime, another major tradition of thought arraigning the pathological nature of modern work needs to be examined, namely the many authors inspired by the writings of Friedrich Nietzsche.

6
Nihilistic Work

This chapter reviews the different types of arguments that have been formulated against the centrality of work by authors influenced by the thought of Friedrich Nietzsche.

The influence of Nietzsche's writings on later denunciations of work is significant, but it stems from his general approach and major themes in his thinking rather than his own pronouncements on work. Typical in this respect is Kathi Weeks' creative utilization of the themes of *ressentiment*, the overman, and the eternal return to articulate a mode of utopian thinking that is equally critical of the status quo and affirmative of emancipatory potentials in the present (Weeks 2011, 198–203). Nietzchean ideas exercise additional indirect influence on contemporary debates about work through major thinkers inspired by Nietzsche who employ his ideas in their own arguments against work. The first such strand is the complex case of Martin Heidegger. The second is the philosophical scene in France in the middle of the twentieth century, where both Nietzsche and Heidegger were the main sources of inspiration. Because Nietzsche influenced the work debates in this peculiar way, through his general approach and via later authors indebted to him, his critical statements on modern work are only briefly studied at the start of this chapter. Readers interested in a more comprehensive coverage can refer to the Nietzsche page in the onwork.edu.au repository and the OnWork newsletter post that was published in relation to it ('Nietzschean work' at onwork.substack.com; see also Sedgwick 2007; Roberts 2019). The bulk of the chapter is taken up by a discussion of the two strands of post-Nietzschean philosophy just mentioned. The chapter ends, as did previous ones, by reviewing the objections that will need to be taken up in the second part of the book. As is so often the case, both Nietzsche's and Heidegger's writings contain material that suggests a positive conception of work that responds to some of the objections that emerge from those writings.

The Case for Work. Jean-Philippe Deranty, Oxford University Press. © Jean-Philippe Deranty (2024).
DOI: 10.1093/oso/9780192887146.003.0007

6.1 The Nihilism of Modern Work

Modern work is for Nietzsche an eminent expression of 'slavish morality', the moral code he thinks became prominent in Western culture to justify the attempt by the many to reign in and replace older, more 'noble' attitudes to life, namely, those attitudes that do not shield us from the vicissitudes of life, including inequalities of rank and power. The third Book of the *Genealogy of Morals* thus presents a sarcastic description of the modern work ethic and its praise of 'the blessing of work' as a training to 'alleviate an existence of suffering'. Many of the traits highlighted by Nietzsche—'absolute regularity, punctilious and unthinking obedience, a mode of life fixed once and for all, fully occupied time' (Nietzsche 1989 [1887], 134–135)—directly anticipate later critical characterizations, notably Weber's, even if the historical narratives differ. Nietzsche exerted a direct influence on Weber (Solms-Laubach 2007). In *The Wanderer and his Shadow* (1880), Nietzsche castigates the 'anonymous and impersonal slavery' of work in the overall division of labour (Nietzsche 1987 [1880] §288). The abstraction of the modern economic system applies universal measuring and equivalence, even to human beings. The 'ability to make promises' is directly related to this transformation of individual personality into an expected quantity one can literally 'count on' and who can in turn apply calculability to their own life (Sedgwick 2007, 62). The mastery of the machine over the individual worker materially enforces the disappearance of the individual in the anonymous proletarian masses, which parallels the anonymity of citizens in mass democracy.

Other critical remarks reprieve the Greek trope pitting utilitarian, efficiency-driven *poiesis* against a *praxis* that seeks to achieve inherently valuable ends. In *The Gay Science*, for instance, Nietzsche highlights the effect of the work ethic on everyday cultural practices in a manner directly foreshadowing Adorno's *Minima Moralia*:

> Even now one is ashamed of resting, and prolonged reflection almost gives people a bad conscience. One thinks with a watch in one's hand, even as one eats one's midday meal while reading the latest news of the stock market; one lives as if one always 'might miss out on something'. 'Rather do anything than nothing': this principle, too, is merely a string to throttle all culture and good taste. Just as all forms are visibly perishing by the haste of the workers, the feeling for form itself, the ear and eye for the melody of movements are also perishing. The proof of this may be found in the universal demand for gross obviousness in all those situations in which human beings wish to be honest with one another for once—in their associations with friends, women, relatives, children, teachers, pupils, leaders, and

> princes: One no longer has time or energy for ceremonies, for being obliging in an indirect way, for *esprit* in conversation, and for any *otium* at all. Living in a constant chase after gain compels people to expend their spirit to the point of exhaustion in continual pretense and overreaching and anticipating others. Virtue has come to consist of doing something in less time than someone else. Hours in which honesty is permitted have become rare, and when they arrive one is tired and does not only want to 'let oneself go' but actually wishes to stretch out as long and wide and ungainly as one happens to be.
>
> **(Nietzsche 2001 [1882], 259)**

The Nietzschean take on the 'atrophy of praxis' applies in particular to art and aesthetic contemplation. Nietzsche proposes that the 'end of art' might be provoked by the rise of work as central value: 'We possess the conscience of an industrious age: and this conscience does not permit us to bestow our best hours and mornings on art, however grand and worthy this art may be. To us art counts as a leisure, a recreational activity: we devote to it the remnants of our time and energies' (Nietzsche 1996 [1878] §177, 350).

As can be expected from a classically trained scholar, Nietzsche also bemoans the withering of intellectual contemplation and genuine thinking as a result of the demands of the industrial system on bodies and minds: 'time for thinking and quietness in thinking are lacking, one no longer ponders deviant views: one contents oneself with hating them. With the tremendous acceleration of life mind and eye have become accustomed to seeing or judging partially or inaccurately, and everyone is like the traveller who gets to know a land and its people from a railway' (Nietzsche 1996 [1878], 131).

In general terms, work participates in the general descent into nihilism, the devaluing of all values, leading humanity to a state where it eventually wills nothing:

> It is clear, what I combat is economic optimism: as if increasing expenditure of everybody must necessarily involve the increasing welfare of everybody. The opposite seems to me to be the case: expenditure of everybody amounts to a collective loss: man is diminished—so one no longer knows what aim this tremendous process has served. An aim? a new aim?—that is what humanity needs.
>
> **(Nietzsche 1968 [1901], §866, 464)**

And in the *Genealogy of Morals* (1989 [1887], 276): 'life is made sick by this dehumanized and mechanical grinding of gears, the "impersonality" of the labourer, the false economy of the "division of labor". The aim is lost, genuine culture—and the means, the modem traffic with science, barbarized'.

A number of similar passages critical of industrial society and its work ethic can be found throughout Nietzsche's work. They are not numerous, and they are not the reason why he exerted a particular influence on later debates about work. These passages add to the general case against work, we might say, but they hardly define a specifically Nietzschean strand of work criticism. Such a strand exists, however, first of all because of Nietzsche's influence on Heidegger, and the importance in turn of that philosopher for later thinkers who were themselves critical of the centrality of work.

6.2 The Heidegger Case

Heidegger's impact on work debates is particularly tangled. On the one hand, his writings on technology remain a major source of inspiration for scholars criticizing modern productivism. These writings are directly connected to Heidegger's reading of Nietzsche in the late 1930s and the early 1940s, his own interpretation of nihilism and of its possible overcoming, the devaluing of all values and the need for revaluation. From this point of view, the centrality of work appears like a deadly symptom associated with the worst aspects of modernity, its inherent tendency to reify all beings, and with it potentially to destroy everything (including itself) in the process. On the other hand, Heidegger is also one of the main figures in the overall prosecution of work, this time not for his own criticisms of work, but rather for the exemplary nature of those writings that immediately preceded the essays on technology, in which he translated what he thought was 'the inner truth and greatness' of National-Socialism in his own philosophical idiom (Heidegger 2014 [1935], 222). These texts present a fascistic philosophy of work and because of Heidegger's stature and subsequent influence, they encapsulate in a particularly striking manner what the centrality of work meant at one moment in the twentieth century: namely, it was one of the main pillars of totalitarian politics, a motto that was directly implicated in the worst atrocities committed during that century. Heidegger and his writings become a major argument in the prosecution of work through *guilt by association*, that is, as exemplars of what propounding the centrality of work led to in the twentieth century. Read in this context, the horrendous irony of the inscription at the gates of several concentration camps, 'Work makes you free', can be read as an irretrievable indictment of work in modernity. We first review this latter aspect of Heidegger's place in debates on work and the kinds of arguments against work that arise from his implication with Nazi politics and ideology. We then consider the technology writings.

6.2.1 Work's Guilt by Association

To many who are aware of the horrors of modern history, upholding the centrality of work today is deeply problematic because of the historical echoes it conjures up. The centrality of work was claimed in emphatic fashion as one of the main pillars in national socialist ideology. Two authors directly influenced by Nietzsche, Ernst Jünger, and Martin Heidegger were active participants in this episode. Even though both of them were marginalized early on by the Nazi regime, their texts of the early 1930s are exemplary documents to witness the nefarious implications that can be entailed in modern work.

It is worthwhile briefly reviewing the description of work in Jünger's *The Worker* (*Der Arbeiter*), first because of the influence of that book on Heidegger and, second, because the book is itself a vivid formulation of the potential fascistic implications of celebrations of work.

In *The Worker*, Jünger makes work the cypher of the new times. The conceptual structure he ascribes to it is supposed to capture the characteristic features of all the trends—scientific, technological, cultural, economic, political, aesthetic, and ethical—that make up the new world order emerging from the First World War. On this view, the *Bürger*, the 'bourgeois', is the figure which embodies the essence of the long century starting with the French Revolution that ended in the trenches in 1914. The 'worker' embodies the principle of the new era after the collapse of that world. This is a Jüngerian vision of the overman, in which industrialized work is the concrete manifestation of the will to power. Through work, power can deploy its effects free from the constrictions and channels the nihilistic, bourgeois age imposed on it. This is power in an 'elemental' sense, the manifestation of life's unbound energy beyond the confines of moral codes and institutions. The total mobilization of science, technology, economics, and of social and individual forces during the First World War for the purpose of the enemy's destruction so exceeded the capacities of bourgeois institutions and mentalities that the latter had to collapse under the pressure. Following this collapse, nothing stands in the way of the full deployment of elemental power 'beyond good and evil' and the march of modern technology, the direct manifestation of this will to power, is unstoppable. Technology extends its influence in all the corners of the world (Jünger 2017 [1932], 148), alters and homogenizes landscapes and natural environments, reshapes cities in their planning and in their buildings, and intervenes in every aspect of everyday life. It makes its way into the intimacy of psyches and interpersonal relationships (Jünger 2017 [1932], 157), moulds individual bodies, alters the expressions on human faces, and modes of behaviour (Jünger 2017 [1932], 76). Even rest and hobbies take on work-like features and machinic dimensions:

> The workplace is unlimited, just as the working day spans twenty-four hours. The counterpart to work is neither some kind of rest nor is it leisure; rather from this perspective there is no situation that cannot be grasped as work. To give a practical example: the manner in which people now busy themselves with leisure. Leisure either bears, like sports, an entirely undisclosed work-character, or it represents—like entertainment, technical festivities, or country trips—a playfully coloured counterweight to work, but is in no way thereby the opposite to work itself.
>
> **(Jünger 2017 [1932], 56)**

Work here is used in its primary, physical sense, as the application of force that changes the shape of an object. The conceptual terms that capture the effects of such work are 'stamping and imprinting', *Stempel* and *Prägung* (Jünger 2017 [1932], 18), and 'modelling'. This explains why the concept of *Gestalt* (form) appears in the book's sub-title, adjacent to 'domination', and specifies the latter's meaning. New forms arise from forceful interventions on all kinds of objects and matter, including the human being. Work is also characterized as the application of a seal onto external material, or the branding of materials by a will's affirmation. The concept is both metaphysical and aesthetic, including in its application to the political, as state-power is conceived as a moulding of an entire collective life: 'the same power which the art of state power [*Staatskunst*] represents through domination is manifested in art through form-making (*Gestaltung*)' (Jünger 2017 [1932], 232). In the bourgeois world, the collective took the form of 'society', a disparate, formless collection of separate individuals. In the world ruled by work, the collective has the shape of the State, where the whole stamps its will onto its parts as a manifestation of its power.

The three interrelated concepts of work, domination, and form come together in the notion which for Jünger encapsulates the ontological originality of modernity, namely 'total mobilization'. The term has a functional meaning, the involvement of all the parts in the singular form that gives them their respective meaning ('*totale Mobilisierung*'). It also has a dynamic sense, as 'total mobile-making' ('*totale Mobilmachung*'), the uprooting of all elements and entities from their established places and relationships so they can be mobilized into the creation of higher shapes. The register is also martial of course. Total war, as Jünger made clear in his writings before *Der Arbeiter* and as he repeats it in the text, is for him the paradigm example of work as totalizing process of form-giving. But as we just saw, the totalitarian reach of power through work is also explicitly political. When Jünger uses the term 'total', he does just mean that nothing escapes the will to power in its drive to 'shape' and 'give form'. It is not just that the 'work character' of the new world is 'total' (Jünger 2017 [1932], 54), produces a 'total world-picture' (79), spread through space as a 'total space' (Jünger 2017 [1932], 92), that is, homogenizes space as technologies of creation and destruction are used in industrial ways and erase all differences. The book is also totalitarian in the common sense of the term. 'Total mobilization' means among other things that 'the form of the worker mobilizes the entire population without distinction' (Jünger 2017 [1932], 94). From this, there emerges a 'total obligation' for every individual to fit into the institutions and the processes that concretely express such mobilization. This total obligation replaces the old, bourgeois individual rights (Jünger 2017 [1932], 63) and has its counterpart in the right of the state to mobilize all sectors of society in a 'total effort' of the collective: 'This total effort is nothing other than work in the highest sense, that is: the representation of the form of the worker' (Jünger 2017 [1932], 130). Concretely, this means 'total work mobilization', in other words, 'comprehensive', 'compulsory work service', which extends 'not only to the contingent capable of bearing arms, but to the total population and its means' (Jünger 2017 [1932], 185).

Adapting another Nietzschean thematic strand, that of 'training and disciplining' (*Zucht*), grand predictions are made about the individuals and the nation that will be true to the challenges and promises of the age of work. Jünger foresees the emergence of a new 'primordial race' (*Urrasse*). This 'breed' will require a new type of 'leader' ('*Führer*'), one that will be 'the first soldier and the first worker' (Jünger 2017 [1932], 6) and assert the right of his nation to total domination. When this occurs, 'statesmanship and rule become possible in the greatest style, that is: world dominion will be possible' (Jünger 2017 [1932], 96). The now obsolete parliamentary systems with their decrepit bills of rights and lifeless constitutions will be replaced by a 'work democracy'. Already now, he claims: 'the will to total dictatorship recognizes itself as the will to total mobilization in the mirror of a new order' (Jünger 2017 [1932], 25).

Werner Hamacher, whose text 'Working through Working' is one of the key philosophical studies of this strand of work literature (Hamacher 1996), saw in Junger's *Der Arbeiter* the 'proto-fascist manifesto par excellence'. Hamacher came to his conclusion through comparative textual analysis of the texts by Jünger and Heidegger in the 1930s and the conception of work propounded in Adolf Hitler's 1925 infamous autobiography and his speeches of that period. It is worthwhile turning briefly to Heidegger's own writings now, so that the full force of the guilt by association argument is fully visible.

Historical evidence (Ott 1988; Martin 1989; Faye 2009, 2012; Wolin 2022) documents in incontrovertible fashion Heidegger's gradual and increasingly enthusiastic embrace, well before Hitler's accession to power, of the Nazi movement, an embrace that turned to determined action when he became rector of Freiburg University in 1933. His vocal support for the Nazi cause was widely acknowledged in the German public at the time, notably because of his publications in Nazi-friendly publications. This embrace of national socialism was clear to see in the public texts and speeches of the early 1930s, which were republished by Richard Wolin in *The Heidegger Controversy* (Wolin 1993). Three features are striking about these texts: first, Heidegger's unconditional 'following' (a crucial concept of national-socialist political theory) of the movement and its 'leader'; second, his attempt to give a metaphysical interpretation of the events in Germany, as the overcoming of European nihilism and the special destiny of the German people in this world-turning event; and third, consistent with the first two, a constant merging of day-to-day, tactical, political, and even administrative considerations with grand pronouncements about the past and the future of human civilization, mimicking the grandiose style of Nietzsche's latest texts, bar their wit and irony. These features of Heidegger's writing at the time can also be found in contemporaneous lecture courses, whose English translations have become available in the last decade or so (Heidegger 2009, 2010, 2013, 2014).

Consistent with this dedication to Nazi ideology and politics, Heidegger propounded a conception of work that took centre stage in his thinking during those years, and which was deeply indebted to Jünger, *The Worker* in particular. As volume 30 of the *Gesamtausgabe* documents, Heidegger engaged with Jünger's thought throughout his life. In the early 1930s, this engagement was nourished by a view of him as a visionary who had seen through the new spirit of the age, and indeed had lived this truth in his own flesh through his heroic deeds on the Western front, as related in Jünger's war writings, notably *Storms of Steel* (Zimmerman 1990). Even then, however, some differences already existed in the writers' reference to Nietzschean tropes. What distinguished Heidegger's account of nihilism and the assertion of the will to power then was the emphasis on the special destiny of the German people. Jünger's own stance was of course hyper-nationalistic, but it was of a more straightforward, patriotic hue. There is one passage in *The Worker* where the rise of 'the age of the worker' is tied to a special, 'German' sense of freedom (Jünger 2017 [1932], 7), but this is an exception. In contrast, from 1932 onwards, Heidegger tied his own narrative of the final stage in European nihilism and its overcoming in the Nazi revolution much more explicitly and in much more grandiloquent terms (if that is possible) to the role that the German people was supposed to play in the grand arc of Western culture. It is this focus on the alleged special destiny of the German *Volk* that makes Heidegger's views at the time, and in particular his view of work, chime significantly with national-socialist discourse.

As we learn from historians (Brückner 1988; Schatz and Woeldike 2001; Buggeln and Wildt 2014; Konitzer and Palme 2016; Lelle 2016, 2019, 2022; Axster and Lelle 2018), the national socialists' vision of work was directly articulated to their general racist and antisemitic vision of 'nationalism' as the defence of the community of those who share the same 'earth and blood', and of 'socialism' as service to the collective. The inclusion of work in the party's name was deeply meaningful. 'German work' (*Deutsche Arbeit*) in such a context denotes one of the main forms of active dedication to the *Volk*, next to the preparedness for sacrifice, under the authority of the State led by its leader. This is an organicist vision of collective work: each individual is to discharge their duty in an officially 'one class' state that nonetheless distinguishes people based on their rank and professional affiliation. This duty to dedicate oneself to service for the community has a more precise, normative dimension linked to the belief in the racial superiority of the Germans. Service to the German people on this view contributes more specifically to asserting the latter's supremacy and defending it against enemies. German supremacy reflects back on German work in turn, as its work ethic, the dedication to performance (*Leistung*) and 'beautiful work' (*schöne Arbeit*) are themselves expressions of racial and cultural preeminence. Instituting a *Leistungsgemeinschaft*, a community of performance based on the natural hierarchy of abilities, was a centrepiece of Nazi policy and became concretely institutionalized with the instauration of the 'compulsory labour service' (*Arbeitsdienstpflicht*) in 1935. As Nikolas Lelle notes (2016), Hitler explicitly viewed the swastika as both an antisemitic and a work symbol, the 'symbol of the victory of the Arian people', equivalent with the 'victory of the thought of creative work, which has always been antisemitic and always will be'.

Consistent with this normativity of the Nazi conception of work was a maniacal suspicion towards 'un-German' attitudes to work. These included first of all those who tried to 'shirk work', the *Arbeitsscheu*. They also included those refusing the principle of innate ability in performance and of a natural hierarchy of ranks (unionists, Marxists, and even liberals). The worst breach of genuine work ethic, however, was a form of 'anti-work', denoting economic activities viewed as perversions of true service to the *Volk*. These perverted forms of work, typically described as selfish, frenetic, speculation-oriented forms of activity, were associated precisely with people that had no attachment to any *Grund und Boden*, to any soil and ground whatsoever. All of these racist, eugenist, antisemitic, and anti-egalitarian aspects of the Nazi conception of work were acted out through concrete labour policies as the regime quickly intensified its terrorist methods. The view of work as a central plank in the new, racially purified German community played a direct part in the planning, first to exclude, and ultimately to destroy, those who were construed as a threat to the German people's essence and destiny. As we know, internment camps were also work camps and a number of them (Dachau, Auschwitz, and Theresienstadt for instance) welcomed the new prisoners with a motto that appealed directly to work as the supreme norm and the ultimate threat.

Heidegger's texts of the 1930s all demonstrate his willingness to echo and implement this vision of 'German work', including the rhetoric used by Nazi propagandists and Hitler himself. There is no need for our purposes in this book to study these documents at length. Interested readers can refer to secondary literature and to the onwork.edu.au repository, where many of these passages have been entered. The most discussed of these texts is the inaugural lecture Heidegger pronounced as new rector of the University of Freiburg, titled 'The Self-Assertion of the German University'. In it, he renounced classical academic freedom in the name of the true 'spirit' of the German *Volk* that German universities were tasked with bringing to light. This was the historical 'mission' of the German people, to 'submit to the power of the beginning of [its] spiritual-historical existence' (Wolin 1993, 31), that is, to recover the message from the Greek past as a future task and contemplate 'what reveals itself in its unfathomable inalterability', over against 'the entire might of the concealedness of what is' (ibid.). The rector exhorted students to enrol in the 'labour service' (*Arbeitsdienst*), which he instituted in his university a year before it became a nationwide policy. Another important text that can be singled out is a speech from January 1934 delivered in the largest lecture hall of the university to six hundred unemployed men who benefited from the newly introduced labour service programme (Wolin 1993, 55–60) This text rehearses most of the tropes of the national-socialist vision of work but also presents Heidegger's constantly repeated theme at the time, the unity of work and knowledge. What he called the 'spiritual' dimension of work was the knowledge of 'where one's place in the *Volk* is' and what the *Volk*'s own work consists of, which demands total dedication to the state and its leader. Rather than citing more of these well-known documents, a particularly illustrative passage from a 1934 summer lecture can be referenced instead, in which Heidegger provides his own interpretation of 'socialism' as work to carry out the mission of the historical people:

> The *Volk* is neither that spongy and jelly-like sentimentalism, as how it is today offered around often in a prosy manner, nor is the State only the present shut down form of organization, as it were, of a society. The State is only insofar and as long as the carrying out of the will of rule happens, which originates from mission and mandate and, conversely, becomes labour and work. The human being, the Volk, time, his-tory, being, the State-those are no abstracted concepts as objects for definition exercises, but the essential relationship is always an historical one, however, that means, self-deciding that futurally-has been. All overcoming of the genuine and non-genuine tradition must [go] in the crucible of the critique of historical resoluteness. That applies last but not least to the title that shall characterize the formation of our historical being, of "socialism." It means no mere changing of the economic mentality; it does not mean a dreary egalitarianism and glorification of that which is inadequate. It does not mean the random pursuit of an aimless common welfare, but it means the care about the standards and the essential-jointure of our historical being, and it wills, therefore, the hierarchy according to occupation and work, it wills the untouchable honor of every labor, it wills the unconditionality of service as the fundamental relationship with the inevitability of being. The questioning concerning our self-being originates from the essence of historical being as futurality, as care.
>
> **(Heidegger 2009, 136)**

While explicit racist and antisemitic elements are not obviously present in this passage, it is now well documented that they are part of Heidegger's thinking. This has become particularly visible after the publication of the *Black Notebooks*, in which less cryptic statements, notably against the Jews, are to be found. But experts also point to many other properly philosophical texts across his entire oeuvre, in which the denunciation of modern metaphysics connects with traditional antisemitic tropes (Faye 2009, 2012; Polt 2014, 2019; Wolin 2022). It is beyond doubt that Heidegger's antisemitism is part of the grand narrative of the forgetting of Being and its concealment under the totality of beings, "the very danger that he tasks the German people" with reversing in its 'mission' to return to the hidden truth of the 'Greek beginning'. In the text above, the 'overcoming of non-genuine tradition' might well be a veiled reference not just to the necessity to combat bad philosophy (the metaphysical tradition, liberalism, and universalism) with the right one (the historicality of *Dasein* and Being) but also a call to combat the effects of this bad metaphysical outlook on German society. 'Historical resoluteness' in this case is linked to an aspect of 'German work', which is to root out those elements in German society that prevent it from achieving its 'mission and mandate'. The narrative of the history of Being and of its concealment by subjectivistic and productivist metaphysics is consistently blended by Heidegger, not just in the texts of the early 1930s but throughout his work, with the tropes circulating at the time, which had also made their way into the Nazi conception of 'German work'. This blending defined Heidegger's own version of 'redemptive antisemitism' propounded by other German intellectuals with Nazi leanings, such as Carl Schmitt, a conspiratorial vision of Jewish influence tacked onto grandiose views of Western civilization that ended up justifying mass murder. This is confirmed by the explicit pronouncements in the *Black Notebooks*, but also in other passages characterizing Jewish people as 'the principle of destruction' (in a note from 1942, see Wolin 2022, 17) and 'a human type whose world-historical goal is the uprooting of all beings from Being' (Wolin 2022, 30). Against this background, the cryptic call in another 1934 lecture, to 'expose the enemy to the light' and 'prepare the attack looking far ahead with the goal of total annihilation' (Heidegger 2001, 73) makes it evident that Heidegger was much closer to Nazi thinking than his defenders are prepared to admit, including in the most criminal aspects of Nazi ideology. As the passage above makes clear, for Heidegger in the 1930s 'labour and work' are an intrinsic part of the historical mission of the German people that the national-socialist revolution was to help fulfil.

In the first part of his seminal text 'Working through Working', Werner Hamacher argued that the centrality of work in European fascism was more than just a historically localized episode. That work was a central component in the Nazi worldview in fact pointed to an inherently fascistic core in the belief in the centrality of work in modernity as a whole. Hamacher justified his claim conceptually by highlighting overlapping themes in Hitler's, Jünger's, and Heidegger's statements on work, pointing out that in all three cases, it was an activity characterized by the fantasies of 'mere integration, assimilation, appropriation, self-assertion, and self-production and not also alteration ("*Veranderung*")', in other words the fantasy of autarkic self-creation that expels its other and refuses to be othered by its relation to what it is not. This analysis chimes in with that of other social theorists who argue along similar lines that fascism reveals something essential about modernity and is not merely a historical aberration. The project of a rationally planned and industrially carried out extermination of entire groups of people points to a form of promethean hubris, the mad attempt to totally shape human destiny and the human community, a dystopian dream in which work is a decisive plank (Bauman 1989). Jünger's totalitarian conception of culture and politics based on the metaphysics of 'the worker' is a paradigmatic illustration of this. In Heidegger's vision in the 1930s, work also plays a central role, as both an enabling and a discriminating element, a 'crucible' for the community embarked in an epic struggle with external and internal enemies in its epochal mission. From this point of view, the texts and the personal actions of intellectuals like Jünger and Heidegger can easily be brought forward as having exemplary value. They can be read as eminently illustrative documents revealing the pathological nature of the centrality of work in modernity.

6.2.2 Heidegger on Machination

The startling paradox of Heidegger's oeuvre for debates on work is that it can be used to mount a case against work from two contradictory perspectives: from a perspective critical of him that sees in his writings of the 1930s an exemplary expression of 'the fascism of work' (Hamacher), that is, of the mortiferous fantasy of self-institution typical of modernity, or instead from a perspective inspired by his later work, which itself provides arguments denouncing that very stance and its destructive ideology of total control.

One easy way out of the contradiction is to ignore the first set of texts, and all the incriminating evidence that has now become public showing Heidegger's enthusiastic embrace of national socialism. Many scholars continue to refer to single texts in a decontextualized way, notably the conferences on technology, and their famous critique of 'enframing', even though it is now established that he never renounced his rabid antisemitism, and that he tampered with some of these later texts, as did editors of the *Gesamtausgabe*, to remove incriminating passages (Wolin 2022). One can also attempt to compartimentalize periods of Heidegger's life, separating the years in which he was implicated in Nazi politics from subsequent years, or separating the man from the philosopher. The problem with these stances is not just that the line between the person and the philosopher is very tenuous indeed. Heidegger himself thought of and presented his own person as playing a decisive role in the history of being. And deep thematic continuities have been highlighted throughout his work, which become particularly visible after the publication of the *Black Notebooks*, making the separation between the early 1930s and the later years dubious. For all these reasons, some scholars today express deep scepticism towards his thinking and advocate its rejection as a genuinely valuable philosophy (Faye 2009, 2012). Others, like Richard Polt or indeed Werner Hamacher (in the 'parerga' to his 1996 article), navigate a difficult line: they fully acknowledge the moral and political failings of Heidegger yet continue to insist on the philosophical value, despite all this, of his later work. For the purposes of the project in this book, even though the evidence of Heidegger's sustained proximity with paranoid reactionary thinking renders his philosophy difficult to take seriously any more, we do need to consider the second perspective on work highlighted above, because many scholars writing on work have cited and continue to cite these texts, including scholars like Polt who do not ignore his dark sides.

In the trajectory that led him from an endorsement of work as a central component in the German community's realization of its 'mission and mandate' in the 1930s to a critical theory of modern technology, the turning point for Heidegger occurred around his confrontation with Nietzsche. Nietzsche's late development of the theme of 'will to power', notably in the late notes gathered under an eponymous title, provided the conceptual vocabulary for Jünger in his depiction of 'the age of the worker' (see a direct quotation in Jünger 2017 [1932], 42). For him, as we saw, the will to power liberated from romantic, liberal, and bourgeois strictures finally found its face, its bodies, and its agency in the new industrial worker, including in his shape as a soldier in the trenches. In the early 1930s, Heidegger largely followed this positive, time-diagnostic understanding of the will to power. This comes through in the self-assertion text and the other private texts and public declarations from those years. The language of will and power also permeates the 1933–1934 lectures and there are echoes still in subsequent lectures, notably in the first lectures on Nietzsche. In those lectures, Heidegger maintains the focus on struggle (*Kampf*) as the moment of decision where essential truths are up for grabs (see for instance Heidegger 1991, 158). Heidegger's interpretation appears to still endorse the idea that the overcoming of nihilism is made possible by a 'resolute', 'decisive' embrace of a fight to the death with enemies to allow the advent of the people's essence.

Within a few years, however, in the *Beiträge* and *Besinnung* (respectively volumes 65 and 66 and of the *Gesamtausgabe*) and in lecture courses on Nietzsche during the 1940s, Heidegger's appraisal of Nietzsche, Jünger, the will to power, and associated themes shifted significantly (see Polt 2019). Will to power, willing, and power as separate concepts are interpreted now as the last of the metaphysical notions, no longer as categories enabling a passage beyond nihilism (see for instance Heidegger 1991, vol. 2, 205). Jünger's 'age of the worker' is read as a naïve embrace of a phenomenon that is much more a problem than a source of hope for humanity's destiny. His account of *Gestalt* as the creative, formative, 'stamping' action of *Macht* is transformed into the critical notion of *Gestell*, 'enframing' as the term is famously translated in the 1949 lectures on 'The Question concerning Technology'. The critique of Nietzsche's and Jünger's positive accounts of *Macht* as the principle for a post-bourgeois ethics and politics is reflected in the neologism of '*Machenschaft*', which names the productivist streak in the covering-over of Being. On this new narrative, the history of Being is characterized by an increasing veiling of its true source, and under the rise of subjectivism, an increasing tendency to reduce Being to beings that can be manipulated, shaped, and reshaped, according to human needs. Production (*poiesis*) and technical rationality (*techne*) become the overwhelming stances humans gradually take towards the world. Nature itself is viewed as that which 'makes itself'. At the end of the long historical arc of the unfolding of metaphysics, modernity is the age of the full implementation of this vision of Being as making. These lectures published in his lifetime have influenced many scholars critical of the productivism of modern, industrial society (for instance Foltz 1995; Bok 2014; Storey 2015).

The neologism *Machenschaft*, obviously based on the German verb for 'making' (*machen*), which English translators render by 'machination', denotes precisely the poietic, technological dimensions of the covering over of being:

> the name machination [*Machenschaft*] should immediately refer to *making* [Machen] (ποίησις, τέχνη), which we assuredly know as a human activity. This latter, however, is itself possible precisely only on the grounds of an interpretation of beings in which their makeability comes to the fore, so much so that constancy and presence become the specific determinations of beingness. The fact that *something makes itself by itself* and consequently is makeable in a corresponding operation: the *making itself by itself* is the interpretation of φύσις carried out in terms of τέχνη and its outlook on things, in such a way that now already the emphasis falls on the makeable and the self-making (cf. the relation between ἰδέα and τέχνη), which is called, in brief, machination. . . . The medieval concept of *actus* already covers over the primordial Greek essence of the interpretation of beingness. Connected to this is the fact that the machinational now thrusts itself forward more clearly and that, through the coming into play of both the Judeo-Christian thought of creation and the corresponding representation of God, *ens* becomes *ens creatum*. . . . The cause–effect connection comes to dominate everything (God as *causa sui*). That is an essential deviation from φύσις and is at the same time the transition to the emergence of *machination* as the essence of beingness in modern thought. The mechanistic *and* the biologistic modes of thinking are always only consequences of the concealed machinational interpretation of beings.
>
> **(Heidegger 1999, 100)**

This passage retraces in a few words the long historical narratives Heidegger presents in many other texts from then on. Entailed in this narrative are critiques of Nietzsche and Jünger, as well as self-criticisms for having followed them earlier on. This 'turn' in Heidegger's thinking leads to a comprehensive critical theory of industrial modernity that appeals to many. On this reading, modernity appears as an utterly nihilistic epoch that is destructive of nature as well as of humanity. Crucially, the spread of meaninglessness and destructiveness characteristic of modernity is referred to the reductive, poietic attitude to beings, which considers them solely from the point of view of what can be made of them and with them, including what can be made of humans and with humans. In this context, work points to a general, reifying, and in the end destructive attitude to the world. As such, it is directly implicated in modernity's worst pathologies.

In the volume of notes covering the years 1936–1946 (volume 7 of the first *Gesamtausgabe*), published under the title 'Overcoming of Metaphysics', this indictment of work as the concrete manifestation of '*Machenschaft*' is formulated explicitly:

> The fact that man as *animal rationale*, here meant in the sense of the working being, must wander through the desert of the earth's desolation could be a sign that metaphysics occurs in virtue of Being, and the overcoming of metaphysics occurs as the incorporation of Being. For labor (cf. Ernst Junger, *Der Arbeiter*, 1932) is now reaching the metaphysical rank of the unconditional objectification of everything present which is active in the will to will. If this is so, we may not presume to stand outside of metaphysics. Collapse and desolation find their adequate occurrence in the fact that metaphysical man, the *animal rationale*, gets fixed as the laboring animal.
>
> This rigidification confirms the most extreme blindness to the oblivion of Being. But man wills himself as the volunteer of the will to will, for which all truth becomes that error which it needs in order to be able to guarantee for itself the illusion that the will to will can will nothing other than empty nothingness, in the face of which it asserts itself without being able to know its own completed nullity. Before Being can occur in its primal truth, Being as the will must be broken, the world must be forced to collapse and the earth must be driven to desolation, and man to mere labor. Only after this decline does the abrupt dwelling of the Origin take place for a long span of time. In the decline, everything, that is, beings in the whole of the truth of metaphysics, approaches its end. The decline has already taken place. The consequences of this occurrence are the events of world history in this century. They are merely the course of what has already ended. Its course is ordered historico-technologically in the sense of the last stage of metaphysics [...] The laboring

> animal is left to the giddy whirl of its products so that it may tear itself to pieces and annihilate itself in empty nothingness.
>
> (Heidegger 2003, 86)

The appeal of prophetic texts like this, and of the philosophical framework that supports them, is obvious. The late Heidegger seems to capture fundamental concerns about the environment and to propose a consistent metaphysical explanation of their causes. Today one could easily retrieve such a text as predicting the collapse of civilization as a result of climate change, itself the outcome of the hyper-productivism of modern, industrial society. Work, in this narrative, is the symptom and the cause of decline, collapse, and desolation that the philosopher sees as 'already taking place'. As this text says, work is not just deleterious as a value behind productivism, extractivism, and capitalistic greed, which lead to the destruction of environments. More deeply, Heidegger's critique of nihilism suggests work is the ultimate absurdity, the final stage in meaninglessness, because it is a mode of 'revealing' beings, of creating a 'clearing', which in fact reveals nothing, 'clears' a space for nothing, since work can only ever receive its meaning from something else, some goal or end for the sake of which it is performed. Power by itself, the sheer exercise of power, willing for the sake of willing, all of which are metaphysical concepts behind the ascendancy of work in modernity, are meaningless by themselves. When the human being has become 'the worker', as Jünger argued, they have regressed to animality, since they live their lives merely for the sake of it, without being receptive to any transcendent meaning. We see here themes emerge from the Aristotelian tradition we encountered in the previous part.

6.3 French Heideggerians

Heidegger exerted a tremendous influence on post-war philosophy and on post-war French philosophy in particular. It is worthwhile dwelling briefly on that particular reception of Heidegger, for which Nietzsche was also a major reference, as several original thematic threads arise from it, adding new arguments against work.

As it became clear that Heidegger had been a convinced defender of the national-socialist project, instead of this suggesting that a different way of doing philosophy would therefore have to be adopted, the involvement of the thought of Being with moral and political collapse paradoxically became another reason to continue reading him. The logic behind this commitment to Heidegger as a guiding light for contemporary philosophy became quite convoluted. The very entanglement of the thoughts of Being and of nihilism with the 'metaphysical' project one aimed to overcome made these thoughts indispensable, precisely because they came the closest to civilizational catastrophe (see paradigmatically Derrida 1989). This paradoxical assumption is one of the defining features of the philosophical scene in France after phenomenology lost its hegemonic standing and a new generation came to the fore. In this philosophical scene, work is a notion, which, on the whole, is negatively loaded (Deranty 2016). Following the Nietzschean and Heideggerian indictments that were highlighted in the preceding sections, work is seen by French philosophers in that scene as one of the main symptoms of the deleterious metaphysics of modernity. However, they add original dimensions to the idea of a nihilistic, productivist metaphysics, which in turn translate into new arguments against work.

One of the reasons behind this originality stems from the role played by the writings of Georges Bataille for many of these thinkers. Like many philosophers of the mid-twentieth century, Bataille's ethical and political claims are grounded in arguments of philosophical anthropology, blending readings of recent anthropology, sociology and biology with conceptual tropes, which in Bataille's case are borrowed from an idiosyncratic reading of Hegel and Nietzsche. The model of the human Bataille proposes (notably in Bataille 1988) depicts humanity as a species caught between two tendencies.On the one hand, there is the quasi-animalistic reproduction of both individual and social life, which demands a rational organization of production and of the circulation of material and symbolic utilities. In this mode, humanity is the calculating species. Humanity, however, is also caught up in a larger scheme, the 'general economy' of life itself, which demands not the rational saving of resources, but rather the expenditure, the loss without counterpart, of excess energy. Only by giving in to this logic, or at least attempting to retrieve its possibility in a rationalized, industrial age where this tendency has become nearly impossible to fulfil, can humanity do justice to its capacity for transcendence:

> human life cannot in any way be limited to the closed systems assigned to it by reasonable conceptions. The immense travail of recklessness, discharge and upheaval that constitutes life could be expressed by stating that life starts only with the deficit of these systems; at least what it allows in the way of order and reserve has meaning only from the moment when the ordered and reserved forces liberate and lose themselves for ends that cannot be subordinated to anything one can account

> for. It is only by such insubordination—even if it is impoverished—that the human race ceases to be isolated in the unconditional splendour of material things.
>
> **(Bataille 1997 [text from 1933], 180)**

In this notion of a 'travail of recklessness' appears the theme of *an 'other' of work*, or of *another form of work*, a form of work that would not follow the instrumental logic of the best means for chosen ends but instead would be pure expenditure of energy for its own sake. This theme of an other of work or of another kind of work is one of the major emphases from the French tradition. In line with the other critical narratives we studied in previous chapters, modern conditions for Bataille are the times when calculating rationality has triumphed, and the logic of excess that is the logic of life itself, which manifested itself in agonistic rivalry, in struggles to the death and in acts of excess, including non-calculating generosity, now only expresses itself in petty form, in the shameful enjoyment of one's wealth, the debasing of what was noble, a rancorous attitude towards ostentation, or indeed making one's utilitarian work the centre of one's life (Bataille 1997, 31). Authentic life by contrast is one that is pure expenditure, work that serves no end, consumption that is unconcerned with the work that went into making the products it devours. Bataille calls it 'sovereign life', to indicate that it is life lived untethered to the heteronomy of instrumental, interested action. The authentic community is the community of sovereign individuals who have rejected the values of the work society. The long extract below is worth citing in full, as it gives a new twist, from a perspective informed by (a certain reading of) Hegel and Nietzsche, to the denunciation we encountered already of work as *poiesis*, as unfree and inauthentic human life, and indeed to the distinction between the realm of necessity and the realm of freedom:

> What distinguishes sovereignty is the consumption of wealth, as against labour and servitude, which produce wealth without consuming it. The sovereign individual consumes and doesn't labour, whereas at the antipodes of sovereignty the slave and the man without means labour and reduce their consumption to the necessities, to the products without which they could neither subsist nor labour. In theory, a man compelled to work consumes the products without which production would not be possible, while the sovereign consumes rather the surplus of production. The sovereign, if he is not imaginary, truly enjoys the products of this world—beyond his needs. His sovereignty resides in this. Let us say that the sovereign (or the sovereign life) begins when, with the necessities ensured, the possibility of life opens up without limit. Conversely, we may call sovereign the

> enjoyment of possibilities that utility doesn't justify (utility being that whose end is productive activity). Life beyond utility is the domain of sovereignty. We may say, in other words, that it is servile to consider duration first, to employ the present time for the sake of the future, which is what we do when we work. The worker produces the machine bolt with a view to the moment when this bolt will itself be used to assemble the automobile, which another will enjoy in a sovereign fashion, in contemplative drives. The worker does not personally have in view the sovereign pleasure of the future car owner, but this pleasure will justify the payment that the factory owner anticipates, which authorizes him to give a wage to the worker without waiting. The worker turns the bolt in order to obtain this wage. In principle, the wage will enable him to meet his needs. Thus, in no way does he escape the circle of constraint. He works in order to eat, and he eats in order to work. We don't see the sovereign moment arrive, when nothing counts but the moment itself. What is sovereign in fact is to enjoy the present time without having anything else in view but this present time.
>
> **(Bataille 1997 [1953], 315)**

One term for this other of work that sovereign life engages in is *play*:

> To consciousness—and to the seriousness of death, which is its initial content—[the sovereign individual] opposes a playful impulse that proves stronger in him than the considerations that govern work. The individual affirmation is ponderous; it is the basis for reflection and the unhappy gravity of human life: it is essentially the negation of play. Sovereign affirmation is based only on the play of unconsidered sentiments, as are the impulses of rivalry, of prestige, the rebelliousness and intolerance toward the prohibition that has death and killing as its object. What the sovereign takes seriously is not the death of the individual, it is others: to the fact of surviving personally he prefers the prestige that will no longer add to his stature if he dies, and will continue to count only so long as others count [...] In the midst of all the others, he is not work that is performed but rather play.
>
> **(Bataille 1997, 317–319)**

For leading French Heideggerians, such as Nancy, Derrida, and Blanchot, and today the Italian philosopher Agamben, the figure of Bataille represents a major inspiration. Each in their own way draws particular themes from his writings to develop a conception of the community that explicitly rejects the centrality of work. The core idea that is retained from Bataille is the emphasis on the experience of limits, the limits of the self, of the self within itself, and the limits between self and other, which in different ways are a condition for a genuine articulation of selfhood and community, for what Bataille calls the conditions of 'sovereignty'. The focus on approaching and experiencing the limits of self, the focus on separation from others and of the self from itself are interpreted ethically and politically by Bataille's successors. In an ethical sense, from the experience of radical separation between self and other flows a form of absolute recognition of the necessity of the other's presence and hence an absolute duty towards the other. Politically, the notion of a sovereign self, once applied to a multitude of beings, leads to the idea of a plurality of radically separated selves. This is the idea for instance behind Nancy's ontological scheme of the 'being-singular-plural', as the proper image of the collective (Nancy 2000).

These thinkers combine the thoughts of sovereignty, of limit and separation, with the Heideggerian narrative of the forgetting to Being to articulate idiosyncratic critical theories of modernity. The conception of a collective as a plurality of radically separated selves can be related for instance to the idea of ontological difference (the difference between Being and beings) and its collapse, or its cover-up, in modern worldviews. The tendency in Western metaphysics to collapse the difference between Being and beings translates into the attempt constantly repeated in modern history to define collectives in reference to some kind of 'immanence', thinking for instance that the collective should be grounded in some feature (national, ethnic, or human essence on some Marxist accounts) that would be internal to all its members, and which the collective would express and be responsible for fulfilling. Such dreams of immanence, such reduction of the Being of the collective to a feature commonly shared by the beings making it up, can only end in severe pathologies since the community is based upon an erasure of constitutive differences. In such frameworks, the Nazi fantasy of a 'self-instituting' community, or the establishment of a society that would realize human nature in Soviet communism (see Blanchot 2015, 81) are two archetypical examples of the dangers lurking in such understandings.

Work in these narratives is more than just productive activity engaged in for the fulfilment of needs, though, as we saw, Bataille and the French philosophers inspired by him do not deny this aspect of social reality (see in particular the section on work in Lévinas' *Totality and Infinity*, 152–174). Beyond the mundane concept of work as productive activity, work becomes a metaphysical principle pointing to the idea of immanence itself as being a kind of 'work', a form of ontological work as it were, whereby a substance would realize itself, make itself 'operative', 'operate' on itself, to realize the essence implied within itself.

Two dualisms directly linked to the problematic centrality of work in modernity arise from such accounts. The first is between subjects viewed as particulars belonging in a universal in some essentially defined way (in a relation of immanence between particular and collective), which then would have to be 'produced' or 'worked upon' (for instance in a theory of socialization) to match their essence, as opposed to individuals viewed singularly, each as a finite yet absolute given, representing a version of the Bataillian sovereign. These singularities can still live a collective life, but as a plurality of sovereign individuals. This passage from Nancy captures this idea well:

> Singularity perhaps does not *proceed* from anything. It is not a work resulting from an operation. There is no process of 'singularisation,' and singularity is neither extracted, nor produced, nor derived. Its birth does not take place *from out of* or as an *effect of:* on the contrary, it provides the measure according to which *birth,* as such, is neither a production nor a self-positioning, the measure according to which the infinite birth of finitude is not a process that emerges from a ground [*fond*] or from a fund [*fonds*] of some kind.
>
> (Nancy 2000, 27)

The second dualism concerns the community and opposes two models of it. The first model is an 'operative' one, conceiving the community as the outcome of work, not just the work of individuals and the division of labour, but more fundamentally the work of the collective on itself to produce itself. Such a conception of the community as resulting from its own 'self-production' and 'self-institution' is implied every time social and civic bonds are thought of as realizing (or having to realize) some truth or value or essence immanent to the collective: a national narrative, an ethnic identity, a cultural exceptionalism. By contrast, the genuinely 'sovereign' community arises not from the realization of some essence or truth or value but is simply given in the being-together of the radically separated singularities. That community must then be called 'inoperative', in the sense that there is no work of that community within itself or upon itself that would make it occur. What the plural singularities share in this community, rather than some imaginary value that would define its specific immanence, is precisely their shared separation. The next two passages from Nancy's *Inoperative Community* capture well those themes shared (with significant variations between authors of course) across this philosophical landscape, in which Nietzsche and Heidegger provide two fundamental layers of reference:

> community cannot arise from the domain of work. One does not produce it, one experiences or one is constituted by it as the experience of finitude. Community understood as a work or through its works would presuppose that the

common being, as such be objectifiable and producible (in sites, persons, buildings, discourses, institutions, symbols: in short, in subjects). Products derived from operations of this kind, however grandiose they might seek to be and sometimes manage to be, have no more communitarian existence than the plaster busts of Marianne [the symbol of the French Republic—JPD). Community necessarily takes place in what Blanchot has called 'unworking' [*désoeuvrement*) referring to that which, before or beyond the work, withdraws from the work, and which no longer having to do either with production or with completion, encounters interruption, fragmentation, suspension. Community is made of the interruption of singularities, or of the suspension that singular beings are. Community is not the work of singular beings, nor can it claim them as its works, just as communication is not a work. Or being an operation of singular beings, for community is simply their being-their being suspended upon its limit.

(Nancy 1986, 31)

And in this other passage, the danger of 'immanence' is explicitly spelt out:

Community is given to us with being and as being, well in advance of all our projects, desires, and undertakings. At bottom, it is impossible for us to lose community. A society may be as little communitarian as possible; it could not happen that in the social desert there would not be, however slight, even inaccessible, some community. We cannot not compear. Only the fascist masses tend to annihilate community in the delirium of an incarnated communion. Symmetrically, the concentration camp—and the extermination camp, the camp of exterminating concentration—is in essence the will to destroy community. But even in the camp itself, undoubtedly, community never entirely ceases to resist this will. Community is in a sense resistance itself: namely, resistance to immanence. Consequently, community is transcendence: but 'transcendence,' which no longer has any 'sacred' meaning, signifying precisely a resistance to immanence (resistance to the communion of everyone or to the exclusive passion of one or several: to all the forms and all the violences of subjectivity). Community is given to us-or we are given and abandoned to the community: a gift to be renewed and communicated, it is not a work to be done or produced.

(Nancy 1986, 35)

The features characteristic of this philosophical scene should be clear by now: an ontological mode of argumentation inherited from Heidegger; a heightened sense for the absoluteness of ethical demands following civilizational collapse; and a distrust towards traditional forms of politics, as mass movements ended up in totalitarian systems in which humanity was radically maimed and denied. Despite the singularity of this philosophical scene, some strong thematic overlaps also exist with other traditions we studied already, for instance in setting up an opposition between a realm of necessity associated with work, and the realm of freedom beyond work. Two further thematic threads can be briefly highlighted, which contribute to the originality of these approaches.

The first is the link that is established between work and the theme of 'the death of the other'. That theme finds its inspiration in three main references: idiosyncratic readings of Hegel, and in particular of the struggle for recognition; Heidegger's definition of *Dasein* in *Being and Time* as 'being-towards-death' and his argument that no one can die for me just as I cannot die for the other; and Bataille's own focus on death as the paradigm experience of limits. Acknowledging the possibility of the death of the other, both as a possibility to conjure up and as potential loss in the face of which nothing can be done, is conceived as the fundamental source of the ethical relationship (Lévinas 1979, 179; Blanchot 1988 [1983], 21). When they think about work, this notion of the death of the other is directly implicated.

Two fundamental attitudes based on two ways of dealing with death are opposed. On the one hand, in a world in which the logic of work dominates, where the social order is wholly organized with a view to realizing some end that is posited as immanent to society, the death of the other is considered either as a natural event, without any ethical significance, or indeed as normal sacrifice in the realization of the essence, or finally, for all those that get in the way of the realization of society's essence, as something that needs to be rationally planned and executed. Work in that scenario takes on the trait of a 'work of death'. As Blanchot writes in reference to Nazi and Soviet concentration camps: 'work, death: equivalents' (2014, 81). By contrast, in the 'inoperative' or 'unavowable' community, that is the community that is based merely on the primitive, ontological fact of being-together and not on any work trying to produce communality, the death of the other is itself a structuring condition: in facing the death of the other, each faces the other's and their own finitude, everyone shares in separation, we are all united in what separates us. In this community, some work is needed of course, but it is not the 'operations' of work, or indeed the work of society upon itself, that secures the life in common. What is central in a community that rejects all attempts at securing some form of immanent bond, is not work.

The other original emphasis from this tradition is the idea we already encountered with Hamacher of 'the other of work' and of 'another work'. All the leading philosophers in this tradition develop germane notions around similar intuitions: '*désoeuvrement*' in Blanchot; the 'inoperative', 'unworking' community for Nancy; Derrida's emphasis on the '*parergon*', on what lies 'next to' and 'beyond' the main work, the *ergon*, and yet is essential to it; Deleuze's insistence on Bartleby's 'I would prefer not to'; Agamben's ethics of 'impotence', of 'means without ends' and pure potentiality that does not have its truth in actualization; Rancière's focus in his later work on 'pathos', on not doing anything as a paradoxical mode of resistance. These notions and emphases of course are each time different. But they all emerge from the concerns we listed: rejecting the immanence of self-producing community, the community of those who belong (through natality, race, productive worthiness, human essence), which inevitably identifies all those beings who don't belong, to whom therefore harsh treatment is inherently justified. Translated in epochal terms, this is a rejection of the societal logics that led to totalitarianism in its different forms. In ethical and political terms, this translates into their different attempts to make room for difference without it being ontologically tied to identity. From all these concerns, the centrality of work is misplaced, indeed represents one of the main tropes through which the pathological metaphysics of modernity has concretely manifested itself. In this reference to 'another of work', however, another emphasis is also included. This is the idea of a different kind of being and doing, which even implies a paradoxical kind of work, namely, an active, dynamic, potentially even productive acknowledgement of being with and sharing the world with others, suggesting precisely the kind of community without immanence that we have been looking at. The paradigm example of this other work for all these thinkers is literature, or rather writing (again with significant differences between their approaches of course), understood as inscriptions for all to see of what unites beyond essential bonds. This 'other work' is also active in the sense of active resistance, in that it actively avoids and seeks to deconstruct, 'unwork', all death-carrying forms of immanence. This notion of the other of work or of another work is therefore a different notion than what is traditionally understood as leisure. It can imply the idea of letting others be and letting everyone 'do as one wishes', but it is different from living the 'ludic life' (Danaher). This strand of contemporary philosophy propounds an ideal of non-economic activity, even of non-economic work that continues to inspire post-work theorists: we find its influence in Kathi Weeks' *The Problem with Work*; and it is the central reference for James Chamberlain in his *Undoing Work* as well as Pfannebecker and Smith's *Work Want Work*.

6.4 Non-nihilistic Work

Let us review the arguments against the centrality of work we have encountered in this chapter. We saw Nietzsche formulate a number of objections to the modern organization of work: a classical bemoaning of the loss of '*otium*', the ability to enjoy genuine leisure; his own version of the 'atrophy of praxis', that is, the increased inability to do things for their own sake, which reverberated in the approach to art for instance. More generally, the modern work ethic participated for him in the general nihilism of modern European culture. How can this Nietzschean case against work be responded to?

For the objections that conceptually match those that draw on classical Greek tropes, the preliminary answers provided at the end of the last chapter also apply, namely that negative aspects of the contemporary economic organization, for instance the kinds of dispositions a particular organization of work favours in individuals, or how it influences aesthetic practices, are not arguments against work as such. Further, the demand for leisure is a valid one, but it doesn't justify overlooking the demands necessity places on us, individually and collectively. The final chapter of the book explores this dimension at length.

In fact, another line of response in the previous chapter also applies in the case of Nietzsche. Beyond his fairly standard denunciations of the modern work ethic, one can find in his writings a positive account of work, one that focuses no longer on empirical traits of work in modernity, but rather, as MacIntyre does from his Aristotelian perspective, and as this book also does in the approach to work it proposes, by considering specific features of work as a kind of activity.

Section 288 of *Human, All Too Human* thus rehearses the classical contrast between industrial and pre-industrial, artisanal work, propounding an unexpected Nietzschean version of luddism:

> To what extent the machine abases us.—The machine is impersonal, it deprives the piece of work of its pride, of the individual goodness and faultiness that adheres to all work not done by a machine—that is to say, of its little bit of humanity. In earlier times all purchasing from artisans was a bestowing of a distinction on individuals, and the things with which we surrounded ourselves were the insignia of these distinctions: household furniture and clothing thus became symbols of mutual esteem and personal solidarity, whereas we now seem to live in the midst of nothing but an anonymous and impersonal slavery.—We must not purchase the alleviation of work at too high a price.
>
> **(Nietzsche 1996 [1878], 383)**

Nietzsche's point is clear: what makes modern work bad is what it takes away from what work meant in the past, namely 'mutual esteem' through reciprocal recognition of one's contributions to others' lives and, on that basis, 'solidarity'. Nietzsche's conclusion is striking: 'we must not purchase the alleviation of work at too high a price'. In other words, there can be intrinsic goods attached to work, which disappear with mechanized work.

A section from *The Gay Science* develops the classical contrast between *praxis* and *poiesis* and turns it on its head, proposing a conception of work as an end in itself:

> Seeking work for the sake of wages—in this, nearly all people in civilized countries are alike; to all of them, work is just a means and not itself the end, which is why they are unrefined in their choice of work, provided it yields an ample reward. Now there are rare individuals who would rather perish than work without taking pleasure in their work: they are choosy, hard to please, and have no use for ample rewards if the work is not itself the reward of rewards. To this rare breed belong artists and contemplative men of all kinds, but also men of leisure who spend their lives hunting, travelling, in love affairs, or on adventures. All of them want work and misery as long as it is joined with pleasure, and the heaviest, hardest work, if need be.
>
> **(Nietzsche 2001 [1882], 108)**

Here, work itself is not the issue, but rather work that is undertaken in conditions of heteronomy. Work that is self-chosen, even if it is 'the hardest' can become the most necessary activity.

As the citation above indicates, artistic practice and artists are the prime examples of genuine work for Nietzsche. His writings contain many passages in which craftmanship, dedication to one's work and to one's oeuvre (*Werk*) are lauded without hesitation. Artistic creation and artistic life matter most particularly because they are privileged methods to undertake the arduous task of 'self-overcoming' that is the basis for a truly ethical attitude. Self-overcoming entails work on the self, the goal of which is effacement of the self before their works, their *Werk*. This is in direct contrast to his twentieth-century heirs, many of whom, as we saw, emphasize the impossibility or the absence of work, and search for an other of work. To cite just one passage:

> Our slow periods.—This is how all artists and people of 'works' feel, the motherly human type: at every division of their lives, which are always divided by a work, they believe that they have reached their goal; they would always patiently

> accept death with the feeling, 'now we are ripe for it.' This is not the expression of weariness—rather of a certain autumnal sunniness and mildness that the work itself, the fact that the work has become ripe. always leaves behind in the author. Then the tempo of life slows down and becomes thick like honey—even to the point of long fermata, of the faith in the long fermata.
>
> **(Nietzsche 2001 [1882], 240)**

In the last writings, work is associated with the will to power. The notion takes on naturalistic dimensions, denoting directed energy expenditure as life forces interact with their environment and manifest their liveliness through the creation of new forms, notably by confronting other life forces and by seeking to bend them in their struggle for self-assertion. Nietzsche sometimes toys with language from thermodynamics but continues to give the concept of work his own specific emphases, namely the antagonistic, form-shaping, and form-creating features of life interacting with other life forces in the environment. The passage below illustrates these aspects well in a critical discussion of Darwin. The work that all life processes consist of should not be seen as 'adaptation' to the pressures of the environment, he argues in this note (see also already in the *Genealogy*, 1989 [1887], 78–79), but the other way around, as struggling with, and taking from, the environment that is assertion of organic life itself:

> The influence of 'external circumstances' is overestimated by Darwin to a ridiculous extent: the essential thing in the life process is precisely the tremendous shaping, form-creating force working from within which utilizes and exploits 'external circumstances'. The new forms molded from within are not formed with an end in view; but in the struggle of the parts a new form is not left long without being related to a partial usefulness and then, according to its use, develops itself more and more completely.
>
> **(Nietzsche 1968 [1901], 344)**

The shaping power of life forces, in other words their physical capacity to 'work', is identified across life dimensions. The process is for instance ascribed to psyches, where it designates the struggle between drives.In the case of 'noble' souls who wilfully engage in internal wars, the term singles out the original ground of their capacity for superior creation. Nietzsche thus speaks of 'this uncanny, dreadfully joyous labor of a soul voluntarily at odds with itself that makes itself suffer out of joy in making suffer', which is 'the womb of all ideal and imaginative phenomena', and 'brings to light an abundance of strange new beauty and affirmation, and perhaps beauty itself'

(1989, 87–88). In a later passage in *Will to Power*, the idea of psychic work is used in a literal sense:

> Why is all activity, even that of a sense, associated with pleasure? Because before it an obstacle, a burden existed? Or rather because all doing is an overcoming, a becoming master, and increases the feeling of power?—Pleasure in thinking.—Ultimately, it is not only the feeling of power, but the pleasure in creating and in the thing created; for all activity enters our consciousness as consciousness of a 'work'.
>
> **(Nietzsche 1968, 349)**

The concept of work can therefore have entirely positive senses for Nietzsche. In the late passage below, this translates into a paradoxical, Nietzschean form of socialism, not too dissimilar from the vision of Oscar Wilde at the same time, where the slavery of wage labour is replaced by an egalitarian aristocracy of work, and work is whatever activity each individual selects to develop their own powers to the full:

> Workers should learn to feel like soldiers. An honorarium, an income, but no pay! No relation between payment and achievement! But the individual, each according to his kind, should be so placed that he can achieve the highest that lies in his power. The workers shall live one day as the bourgeois do now—but above them, distinguished by their freedom from wants, the higher caste: that is to say, poorer and simpler, but in possession of power.
>
> **(Nietzsche 1968, 399)**

In this passage once more, the distinction is not between *praxis* and *poiesis*, but between free *poiesis* as creation and as expression of a free individuality and unfree *poiesis*, such as the one undertaken in wage and slave work.

In the notes gathered in *Will to Power*, the naturalistic sense of work is mobilized to continue to denounce the life-denying efforts of 'ascetic' ideals, which attempt to deal with the suffering involved in life's existence by turning away from it. Work is part of the reality of existence that strong souls are able to embrace and to will (*Will to Power*, §130, 224). Typically, the redemptive and creative gestures of the Overman, who inherits all of the human past and launches humanity onto a new, post-nihilistic path, is consistently described as Zarathustra's 'work' (Nietzsche 2006 [1883–1885/1888], 7, 11). Zarathustra performs his destiny as a self working on itself, producing a *Werk* that overcomes the old self and produces a new one. In the process, through his example and his followers, Zarathustra opens the door for changing human history: 'My suffering and my pity—what do they matter! Do I strive for happiness? I strive for my work!' (2006 [1883–1885/1888], 266).

For Nietzsche then it is not work as such that is the issue. Indeed, the overcoming of nihilism requires its own forms of work. In many passages, Nietzsche seems squarely at odds with his twentieth and twenty-first century followers, who see work as an ontological factor in modernity's pathologies.

6.5 Is Work Inherently Fascistic?

If we now turn to the objections to the centrality of work arising from the complex scene of post-Nietzschean philosophy succinctly presented above, they seem to boil down to the following four points. First, the fact, compounded by the exemplary cases of Jünger and Heidegger, that at a crucial juncture in European history, work was directly implicated in industrial war, mass extermination, and the thorough negation of individual and public freedoms. Is it possible after Auschwitz to claim that 'work makes you free', as the second part of this book attempts to do? A second objection is that not only did fascism make work central, in fact there is an inherent fascism in work, meaning that the assertion of the centrality of work is directly related to the attempt to think of the human community as a collective that should 'self-institute' and be 'self-produced', which translates into the exclusion of all those who don't fit in: foreigners, and all those deemed unable to contribute in a correct way. Third, as work becomes central, all beings, including humans, are reduced to measures of utility. The centrality of work leads to an entirely reified world, which ends up in self-destruction, as humanity treats itself instrumentally and destroys its environment. And fourth, genuine forms of subjectivity, intersubjectivity and collective life are premised on forms of being and doing that actively counter the reifying, 'fascistic' logic of work, notably by making room for the finitude and mortality of others, and letting beings be.

How can such powerful objections be responded to?

Let us consider the first two worries together first. Undeniably, the organization of work can play a decisive functional role in totalitarian regimes. Christophe Dejours, who is the main proponent today of the centrality of work, has shown this clearly in reference to Nazi concentration camps (Dejours 1998, chapter 8). A purely technical, instrumental focus on one's actions can shut people off from ethical obligations towards others. Genocidal crimes in the twentieth century were often abetted by people just trying to do their jobs as best they could (Arendt 1963, 73). Dispositions enabling the reproduction of totalitarian organizations, like unquestioned deference to authority, uncritical work zeal, and the blind following of charismatic leaders, are easily cultivated in hierarchical work organizations, sometimes deliberately so. This is precisely what Heidegger was trying to encourage and cultivate among students in favour of the Nazi revolution and its leader in his public interventions in the 1930s. Furthermore, work's fundamental function is to reproduce social systems. A totalitarian regime requires its own social reproduction. Even at that basic level, work is implicated in totalitarianism. All of this is true. And yet, that work was mobilized to entrench totalitarian organizations does not mean that work is inherently fascistic. Holding that work is central is precisely to hold that it is not neutral with respect to ethical and political concerns, and that it plays a major part in the normative nature of social systems. The last chapters of the book outline the many ways in which this is the case. But this ethical and political significance of work can vary widely. In other circumstances, work can also be the foundation for solidarity, for the development of prosocial, other-directed dispositions, and for democratic politics. There is a circular logic at play here (Deranty and Renault 2022) between the general ethical and political culture of a community and the ethical and political cultures in its work spheres: the ethical and political nature of the spheres of work is obviously impacted by the normative quality of social relations outside work but work also plays distinct roles in shaping this overall normative culture. The point here, though, is that the overall normative effect of these social logics is undecided. Work is not inherently democratic, nor is it inherently fascistic. Work itself is normatively ambivalent, but through the circular logic just intimated, as the last chapters of the book will attempt to demonstrate, it is functionally decisive (or 'central') for the normative quality of social relations, the mode of collective organization, and via these collective frames, the kinds of individual virtues and dispositions that are favoured or hampered in particular historical settings. Work can make you free or it can make you a slave, it can help build democratic lives or foster intolerance and even murderous regimes and individuals who collaborate in them—it is up to each society at every moment of its history to decide how this plays out.

This emphasis on the normative ambivalence of work, then, objects to the generic rejection of work many post-war Heideggerians have supported on ontological grounds, on the grounds namely that it is implicated in an 'immanentist' vision of communities which allegedly translates in a necessary way in the fantasy of a community in charge of itself, which then necessarily leads to the exclusion and potentially the extermination of those who are deemed to not fit in. Beyond the intrinsic ambivalence of work, it can also be reminded (and Chapter 13 will extend on this at length) that it is a fact of human life, not a fantasy, that lifeworlds have to be reproduced, which is what work activities ensure. In this sense, human societies do have to 'self-produce' and 'self-institute', because no one else is going to do it for them. From this point of view, the concepts of production, reproduction, institution, cannot be inherently suspect. They designate necessary features of human life. As we saw, Lévinas fully acknowledged this, as did Nietzsche (and Marx) before him. Once this is acknowledged, the last chapters of the book will show that the specific challenges built into these activities of social reproduction have some intrinsic feature which *can* make of them, not just conduits of individual self-development in a technical sense (the learning and mastery of different skills, which can be ethically ambivalent), but also conduits of moral and democratic self-development. In other words, in good circumstances, the experience of work can promote the acknowledgement of others in their differences rather than contributing to closing them off from the community. Against the Greek prejudice in favour of '*theoria*' which demotes '*techne*' as being a limited, 'narrow-minded', merely technical form of rationality, it will be shown that the rationality mobilized in work can have a liberating effect. To name just two key arguments briefly here: this is because, first of all, competence and workmanship are modes of doing that can attract recognition independent of any other individual feature, racial, sexual, or otherwise. Social prejudices of course can always and indeed often do act as filters in the actual recognition and rewards of performances, but these biased forms of judgement are not intrinsic to work. They are cultural representations that are imported into work from outside of work. Work itself, the technical activity of producing an outcome in response to another's need, only asks to be judged on technical criteria. There is an inherently democratic and egalitarian logic in this. Chapter 11, on the long history of work, will document how this egalitarian logic in fact was already at play even in premodern settings otherwise marked by highly hierarchical social structures. And secondly, the experience of work is the experience of necessity, in particular of the necessary dependence of each on everyone else. Inegalitarian societies hide this interdependency by naturalizing occupations and ideologically justifying that some work for others without reciprocity. But the dependence of each on every other one is just as much an ontological fact as the co-appearance in Being post-war Heideggerians refer to in order to ground plurality. And such co-dependence in needs also has a logic of solidarity built into it, well captured in the old motto reprised by Marx, that each should contribute according to their abilities, and each should receive according to their needs.

By contrast, the 'singular plurality' that French Heideggerians appeal to might be founded on a basic ontological fact, the fact that the world appears to all singularly and in their plurality. But how is this plurality materially reproduced, we want to ask? Doesn't human history show that the social bond that has united communities of singular plurals has consistently been based on exclusionary logics? The 'logic of work' based on merely technical concerns and rooted in shared necessity does not by itself invite such biases. Indeed, this technical logic is arguably a solidaristic logic, since it aims at the reciprocal fulfilment of needs. It becomes exclusionary when cultural biases enter into its organization. The mere appeal to the ontological fact of being-together, then, is not sufficient by itself to safeguard against exclusion and discrimination. Believing that just naming being-together as ontological fact is sufficient to ensure its potential in every historical instance is to give too much political and ethical force to ontology. Conversely, acknowledging the necessity of social reproduction, which is ensured by work, by itself does not entail giving in to exclusionary biases in any necessary way.

The third and fourth worries, about work as reifying attitude and alternative modes of being in the world, can be addressed with the help of Heidegger himself. Another great paradox about him is that, just like Nietzsche, other writings by him, some chronologically very close to his most dubious passages, can be used to make an altogether different case about work. In these passages, in opposition to the idea that work is directly implicated in the concealment of being, some forms of work are taken as paradigm examples of human activity through which a 'clearing' occurs, that is, a space within which genuinely meaningful connections with environments and beings within them are made possible. This side of Heidegger has been famously picked up by Hubert Dreyfus and scholars working on skill and expertise, notably following Dreyfus' influential reading of *Being and Time* (1995, 2014). The discussion of a workshop in chapter 3 of Division I of *Being and Time* is the paradigm case of a place in which the human person finds herself inserted into a multi-layered network of meanings that give direction and purpose to her activities, to the objects, persons and world surrounding her, and in the end help her to anchor herself in the world. In the workshop:

> The work produced refers not only to the 'towards-which' of its usability and the 'whereof' of which it consists: under simple craft conditions it also has an assignment to the person who is to use it or wear it. The work is cut to his figure; he 'is' there along with it as the work emerges... . Thus along with the work, we encounter not only entities ready-to-hand but also entities with Dasein's kind of Being—entities for which, in their concern, the product becomes ready-to-hand;

> and together with these we encounter the world in which wearers and users live, which is at the same time ours.... Our concernful absorption in whatever work-world lies closest to us, has a function of discovering; and it is essential to this function that, depending upon the way in which we are absorbed, those entities within-the-world which are brought along in the work and with it (that is to say, in the assignments or references which are constitutive for it) remain discoverable in varying degrees of explicitness and with a varying circumspective penetration.
>
> **(Heidegger 1962, 100)**

The passage is reminiscent of the extract from *Human, all too Human* cited above in which traditional craftwork is described as a way for individuals to meaningfully insert themselves in their social world. Beyond this social dimension, the passage also intimates that work activities can be the point at which the world can be disclosed for further 'circumspective' attention, in other words, become the starting point for genuine knowledge. We explore this idea of the 'transcendental' function of work, the way it can ground us in reality because it forces us to face it, in Section 13.2.3. Heidegger repeats similar analyses a few years later, notably in the 1934 seminar on logic already quoted. This text is typical of the great ambiguity of Heidegger as a philosopher. While in this lecture course Heidegger clearly attempts to align his philosophical reflections with national-socialist ideology, underneath the *Völkisch* tropes, the echoes of Nazi slogans (the reference to 'joy') and antisemitic insinuations, can be found a remarkable description of work as 'clearing', in which the 'being of beings', and our being in their midst, are disclosed:

> In work and through it beings first become manifest to us in their determinate regions, and as worker the human being is transported into the manifestness of beings and their jointure. This transporting is nothing supplementary, grafted onto the I, but this transporting belongs to the essence of our being. This transportedness into things belongs to our constitution. For that reason, one is correct in saying that unemployment is not only the privation of a merit, but it is a mental shattering-not because the lack of work thrusts the human being back to the individualized isolated I, but because the lack of work leaves empty the being-transported into things. Because work carries out the relation to beings, therefore unemployment is an emptying of this relation to being. The relation remains, to be sure, but it is unfulfilled. This unfulfilled relation is the ground of the desolation of the one who is without work. In this desolation, the relation of the human being to the whole of beings is as lively as ever, but as pain. Therefore, unemployment is impotent being-exposed. Work is correspondingly a transporting into the jointures and forms of the

> beings that surround us. That is why the enjoyment of one's work is so important. It is not a mood that only accompanies our work; it is no addition to work, but joy as fundamental mood is the ground of genuine labor, which in its execution first makes human beings capable of existence. In labor as the present in the sense of making-present, the making-presence of beings happens.
>
> **(Heidegger 2009 [1934 summer course], 127)**

If work can be a 'clearing' in this way, then once again the reification of all beings that is diagnosed as the pathology of modern metaphysics is no longer attached to work as such. There are no features of work as a kind of activity (along the lines defined in the Introduction) that would make it essentially reifying of all it connects with. Indeed, as Heidegger suggests here, some forms of work (but certainly not all) might in fact be apt to disclose to us features of entities around us, and their manifold possible and actual interactions among each other and with us. If that is the case, we can acknowledge the importance of other modes of being and acting beside working (work's centrality is not synonymous with exclusivity), but this acknowledgement need not be expressed in terms of an antagonism between types of action. In other words, it might be important for people to have the time and resources to engage in 'inoperative' forms of action and experience, but this does not have to mean that it is those non-work actions and experiences only that make up the true community. Indeed, if the necessity of work is acknowledged, it might well be the case, as the last part of the book argues, that work keeps its priority from a social and political point of view.

7
The Imminent Obsolescence of Work

The long first part of this book, which includes the first six chapters, has reviewed arguments that target contemporary work of course, but are also premised on background narratives viewing work as a problematic creation of capitalist modernity. With this chapter, we move to a new family of objections to the centrality of work, where the historical reference is the present and the near future states of work. The line of objections we investigate in this chapter centres on empirical scenarios predicting that, as a matter of fact, work is going to become increasingly obsolete as machines and automated processes are able to replace human workers in their activities. If more and more work is performed by machines, then very obviously it can no longer be held to be central to human life. Indeed, one of the pathologies of late modernity is to hold on to the centrality of work as a value for individual existence and the institutions that ensure social inclusion, welfare, and citizenship, at a time when there is less and less work available. This apparent absurdity was already the starting point of André Gorz's reflections in his books of the 1980s. Many contemporary post-work theorists continue to base their reflections on the empirical assumption about work's imminent obsolescence and the absurdity of maintaining the centrality of work in such a context.

To investigate the case against work from this perspective, we begin by recalling older accounts that provide relevant historical and conceptual context: first, popular predictions at the end of the nineteenth century that already envisioned the end of work; and second, the complex discussion of automation by Marx in his mature writings. In reviewing these older accounts, we emphasize the ambivalent message they conveyed about the impact of automation on the value and even about the availability of work in the future. As we will see, they did not advocate or indeed predict 'the end of work'. In the final part of the chapter (Section 7.3), we review recent discussions of automation and show that the jury is still out on whether the current wave of innovation will make work increasingly rare and potentially obsolete.

The Case for Work. Jean-Philippe Deranty, Oxford University Press. © Jean-Philippe Deranty (2024).
DOI: 10.1093/oso/9780192887146.003.0008

7.1 Early Predictions

Towards the end of the nineteenth century (but an early instantiation is Etzler 1842, see Granter 2009, 9–30), following repeated waves of technological ruptures and the momentous social disruptions they had triggered, new imaginaries crystallized in industrializing nations. This was captured in flourishing socialist literary production: in pamphlets and journalistic pieces that accompanied activist politics (Paul Lafargue's *Right to Be Lazy* (2012 [1883]) is typical in this regard); in theoretical essays denouncing capitalism and detailing the outlines of a new society (Marx and Engels' work of course, but also the many writers who attempted to propagate popular versions of socialism, for instance Gronlund's *Cooperative Commonwealth*); and a new genre of fiction, of which Edward Bellamy's 1888 *Looking Backward: 2000–1887* was the most renowned at the time. Bellamy's novel and the date of its publication are watersheds, pointing to the moment in modern culture when the tremendous productive power of applied science and industry forced the European imagination to anticipate what the 'future of work', and society as a whole, might become. 1888, to recall, is the year in which Nietzsche produced his last books. Socialist utopias, such as the one depicted by Bellamy in his novel, thus offered countervailing diagnoses and answers to the crisis in modern culture.

Bellamy's novel tells the story of Julian West, a young man from Boston, who falls into a deep, hypnosis-induced slumber, and wakes up 113 years later to discover that in the year 2000 the United States has become a socialist utopia. Among the main topics explored in the story is the reorganization of work and its drastic reduction thanks to automation. With technical progress, people can retire at forty-five and welfare and basic needs are freely provided for all, as are education and culture. Bellamy's novel was a bestseller, one of John Dewey's favourite books right until the 1930s. It was the main source of inspiration for labour organizers and socialists throughout the English-speaking world and inspired its own political movement. The novel triggered a famous response by William Morris who in his 1890 *News from Nowhere* depicted an alternative vision of future society, one in which machinic progress would alleviate arduous and boring work and thereby enable a return to work in its authentic form, as an activity continuous with art, such that artisanal craftsmanship could become realized as the ideal of work. Another eloquent contribution to these socialist imaginings in the late nineteenth century was by Oscar Wilde in his 1891 essay 'The Soul of Man under Socialism'. The following passage perfectly captures a prominent mood of late-nineteenth-century industrial century:

> Up to the present, man has been, to a certain extent, the slave of machinery, and there is something tragic in the fact that as soon as man had invented a machine to do his work he began to starve. This, however, is, of course, the result of our property system and our system of competition. One man owns a machine which does the work of five hundred men. Five hundred men are, in consequence, thrown out of employment, and, having no work to do, become hungry and take to thieving. The one man secures the produce of the machine and keeps it and has five hundred times as much as he should have, and probably, which is of much more importance, a great deal more than he really wants. Were that machine the property of all, everyone would benefit by it. It would be an immense advantage to the community. All unintellectual labour, all monotonous, dull labour, all labour that deals with dreadful things, and involves unpleasant conditions, must be done by machinery. Machinery must work for us in coal mines, and do all sanitary services, and be the stoker of steamers, and clean the streets, and run messages on wet days, and do anything that is tedious or distressing. At present machinery competes against man. Under proper conditions machinery will serve man. There is no doubt at all that this is the future of machinery, and just as trees grow while the country gentleman is asleep, so while Humanity will be amusing itself, or enjoying cultivated leisure – which, and not labour, is the aim of man – or making beautiful things, or reading beautiful things, or simply contemplating the world with admiration and delight, machinery will be doing all the necessary and unpleasant work.
>
> **(Wilde 2001 [1891], 170)**

Wilde's vision in this text reflects insights that circulated widely at the time, which already announced many of the themes reprised today by post-work theorists who are equally fascinated by the powers of automated production and their potential effects on social organization. Then as now, thinkers highlighted the ambivalence of automation. On its current trend, it appears to lead to greater enslavement and impoverishment for many, but under a different political organization it could become an instrument of liberation. The hope of a life of leisure, of finally reaching the 'realm of freedom' and leaving behind the 'realm of necessity', thus seems to be in view.

It is important to be mindful of how far narratives about 'the end of work' and the trust in automation's capacity to deliver a form of 'luxury communism' stretch back, for two main reasons. First, returning to the origins of narratives about the end of work makes it clear that such narratives have been repeated in every new generation ever since: Keynes' 'Letter to My Grandchildren' and Russell's *Praise of Idleness* were published in 1930 and 1935; Arendt's 1957 *Human Condition* captured the angsts about automation in the immediate post-war era, in response notably the ground-breaking writings of George Friedmann, culminating in his 1955 *Industrial Society* (Smith 2017). The Commission on Automation and Technological Change convened by the US President Johnson in 1964 (Bell 1973, 249) is a symbolic date marking a new wave of questioning. Gorz's writings in the early 1980s are under the spell of the first wave of computerization in industry. Aronowitz and Di Fazio's *Jobless Future* (1994), Aronowitz and Cutler's *Postwork* (1998) and Jeremy Rifkin's *End of Work* (1995), are typical end-of-century doom scenarios (Strangleman 2007 for a review of late 1990s 'end of work' sociology). In the last ten years, of course, predictions about technological unemployment at the hand of automation have been expressed by scholars from all kinds of perspectives (Srnicek and Williams 2015; Susskind and Susskind 2015; Bastani 2018; Susskind 2020; Danaher 2021). There is a sobering point in this reminder: at every one of these stages, the future demise of work at the hand of automation was predicted and in every single case the decades that followed belied the predictions. There were major issues in the functioning of labour markets and the situation of work for many, for sure. But never an 'end of work'. The reasons behind these failed predictions are instructive: in some cases, it was economic and technological factors that were overlooked, but in Keynes' and Russell's case, even more simply, the extraneous historical circumstance of a world war. There is a basic but powerful lesson in this: human history is unpredictable because so many factors are involved in determining its course. The capacity of some machines to replicate some forms of human work is just one of them. By itself it is not sufficient to warrant predictions about the shape of economies into the future. Today, any scenario about the demise of work that does not take into account the likely impacts of climate change has to be inherently flawed. It might well be that climate remediation or a potential forced deglobalization would require the creation of all kinds of new jobs, or at least still require a lot of work, much of which might not be achievable or economically viable if outsourced to automated processes and machines.

Furthermore, as the reference to William Morris reminds us, what is anticipated in many past predictions is the end of stultifying, dangerous, and dirty work, of 'useless toil' (Morris 1993 [1884]), but not the end of work per se. Oscar Wilde once again provides an excellent illustration of this point. While he articulated the hope that machines would liberate humans from the slavery of toil, he also contrasted this with chosen work. Indeed, work is a central category in his defence of an individualist, libertarian type of socialism, since it is through work, defined in a broad sense as 'the sphere of activity that is really congenial to (people), and gives them pleasure', that individuality can be both fully developed and fully express itself. When such conditions are in place, we have a social organization where everyone can be their true self by doing their chosen work:

> he who would lead a Christlike life is he who is perfectly and absolutely himself. He may be a great poet, or a great man of science; or a young student at a University, or one who watches sheep upon a moor; or a maker of dramas, like Shakespeare, or a thinker about God, like Spinoza; or a child who plays in a garden, or a fisherman who throws his net into the sea. It does not matter what he is, as long as he *realises* the perfection of the soul that is within him [emphasis JPD].
>
> **(Wilde 2001 [1891], 166)**

7.2 Marx on Automation

Within the tradition that finds the promise of some form of 'luxury communism' beyond the immiseration and work intensification caused by capitalist automation, Marx's earlier reflections in the 1857 'Fragment on Machines' in the *Grundrisse* and in the 'machinery' chapter in volume one of *Capital* (Marx 1991 [1867], 492–640) are particularly significant.

These texts present a clear conceptual delineation of automation as a specific threshold in the organization of production. According to Marx, automation occurs when three conditions are met: when the 'motive power' providing energy to the whole process is itself 'self-acting', in other words, is itself a machine; when the different machines involved in the production process are 'articulated' like organs in a body, which ensures continuity across the different stages of production; and when human intervention is needed only in a 'supplementary' way, that is, when it is the machines doing the actual working on the object of labour (*Capital*, 500–503; *Grundrisse*, 692). Once such a technical system is in place, the next stage is when machines are themselves produced by the means of machines (*Capital*, 506). When this threshold has been reached, 'the total process is examined objectively' (*Capital*, 501) rather than subjectively. This means that the relevant reference points in the formal organization of the labour process are the machines, whereas in earlier periods, as in the age of manufacture, it was still the human agents. As a result,

> it is the machine which possesses skill and strength in place of the worker, is itself the virtuoso, with a soul of its own in the mechanical laws acting through it. The worker's activity, reduced to a mere abstraction of activity, is determined and regulated on all sides by the movement of the machinery, and not the opposite.
>
> **(1973 [1857], 692)**

This technical description of automated production process, in contrast to earlier modes of production, grounds the second key feature of these texts, namely the impact of automation on the content of work activities. While there are many orders of magnitude separating the complexity of earlier industrial machines and contemporary robotic processes guided by arcane algorithms fed on gigantic neural networks, it is striking that the main effects noted by Marx are also to be found in the contemporary world of work: prolongation of the working day; enslavement of the worker to the work process and the machine; intensification of work; deskilling and hollowing out of individual activities which become insignificant in comparison with the complex overall technical process; increased surveillance and compliance.

However, while 'a section of the working class is rendered superfluous by machinery', in fact the effects of automation on employment are far from homogeneous. In *Capital*, Marx highlights that the impact of automation on employment is uneven (1991 [1867], 570–572). He lists a number of countervailing economic factors and thereby directly anticipates arguments raised today in debates on the future of work, as we'll see in the final section of this chapter. Automation creates new needs, which require new occupations. Marx already has a version of the 'multiplier effect': increased productivity in particular parts of the economy leads to demand for work in sectors not yet automated, as the automated sectors require more services. More productivity in the production of raw material leads to increased employment in sectors using it, provided they are not fully automated. An increase in productivity makes it easier to refine the technical division of labour even further, to specialize production on subparts of larger products, which can increase employment. More products to be exchanged world-wide leads to the need to increase distribution world-wide. Finally, as Gorz also argued, the explosion in productivity combined with the appropriation of the surplus product by the privileged classes (owners and elite workers) means that the latter can devolve much of their domestic work to classes of servants, or indeed draw on new professions to indulge in their newly created luxurious tastes. For all these reasons, there is no linear correlation between automation and technological unemployment.

The machinery chapter in *Capital* focuses on present and short-term impacts of automation, while the *Grundrisse* passage anticipates long-term prospects. Indeed, the *Grundrisse* predict in striking manner what the ultimate effect of automation might be, namely a self-undermining of the capitalist system at its own hands. The original tenor of this passage explains why it has continuously attracted the attention of radical political theorists, from Italian autonomists to current public intellectuals seeking in Marx a guide for understanding the path society might take with the spread of automation (Mason 2015; Karakilic 2022).

Marx's core assumption in the 'Fragment on Machines' is that a full expansion of automation across all sectors of production would have a revolutionary effect on economic and hence on social organization. This is for simple reasons: when production is automated across the board, the key factor of production is, first of all, technology and the scientific knowledge that makes technology possible and, secondly, the rational organization of labour, both at the macro- and micro-levels. He writes:

> to the degree that large industry develops, the creation of real wealth comes to depend less on labour time and on the amount of labour employed than on the power of the agencies set in motion during labour time, whose 'powerful effectiveness' is itself in turn out of all proportion to the direct labour time spent on their production, but depends rather on the general state of science and on the progress of technology, or the application of this science to production.
>
> **(1973 [1857], 704)**

Marx thus already had in view what late-twentieth-century sociologists would term 'knowledge society', 'information society', or 'cognitive capitalism'. The problem with this shift to knowledge as the core factor of production, however, is that it robs the capitalist economic system of its own foundation, which is the exploitation of living labour. Capitalism strives feverishly to reduce the part of human labour in production through automation. Competition between capitalists demands it for reasons inherent in the competitive market system, such as the constant search for more productivity, the reduction of production prices, and first-mover advantage. Automation is also a way to control labour when it begins to organize and resist exploitation. But the source of surplus value is living labour, not constant capital. Machines do not create surplus-value, they merely pass their value to the products. It is workers who use the machines that create extra value. When machines replace workers, sources of profit disappear with human labour at the same time. Capitalism is therefore 'the moving contradiction, in that it presses to reduce labour time to a minimum while it posits labour time as sole measure and source of wealth' (1973 [1857], 706). Capital 'works towards its own dissolution' by spearheading automation (1973 [1857], 700).

This view at the horizon of fully automated capitalist production is highly stylized. In his critique of end-of-work theorists, Caffentzis highlights how in later texts Marx outlined many 'countervailing factors', which allow the capitalist class to resist this self-induced downfall, by constantly innovating in the compression of what human labour remains and discovering or, if needs be, inventing new avenues for profit (Caffentzis 1999). Yet the *Grundrisse* passage remains highly valuable for our concerns because of what it reveals about Marx' vision of automation's full impact on human work.

What is the outcome of this contradiction capitalism imposes upon itself? One logical outcome would seem to be social collapse as capitalism necessarily leads to mass unemployment. This is the scenario predicted by many, including by Gorza few decades ago. In the *Grundrisse*, however, Marx presents a different scenario. As automation spreads and productivity skyrockets, the labour time necessary for the creation of capitalistic wealth, in other words surplus labour, diminishes accordingly. More and more effort can therefore be spent by more and more people, not on working for immediate needs, but rather to develop and invent new knowledge, some of which in turn further improves the technological and organizational factors making up 'fixed capital', that non-labour part of capital which increasingly takes charge of production. A similar effect arises also from the position of workers in automated labour processes: the more the process is autonomously activated, the more the worker 'comes to relate to it as watchman and regulator' (1973 [1857], 705). Again, this liberates an increasing number of minds to study the ways to improve production, but also understanding of how humans interact and cooperate. At some point, a threshold is reached where the contradiction identified above comes to a crisis: the capitalist system has in effect obliterated the very condition of its own reproduction as a system, namely human work. But the outcome of this crisis is not social collapse: instead, the gigantic progress in productive and organizational techniques has liberated time for the many and enabled them to develop their own capacities, both cognitive and social. As a result,

> The surplus labour of the mass has ceased to be the condition for the development of general wealth, just as the non-labour of the few, for the development of the general powers of the human head. With that, production based on exchange value breaks down, and the direct, material production process is stripped of the form of penury and antithesis. The free development of individualities, and hence not

> the reduction of necessary labour time so as to posit surplus labour, but rather the general reduction of the necessary labour of society to a minimum, which then corresponds to the artistic, scientific etc. development of the individuals in the time set free, and with the means created, for all of them…. The development of fixed capital indicates to what degree general social knowledge has become a direct force of production, and to what degree, hence, the conditions of the process of social life itself have come under the control of the general intellect and been transformed in accordance with it. To what degree the powers of social production have been produced, not only in the form of knowledge, but also as immediate organs of social practice, of the real life process.
>
> **(1973 [1857], 706)**

This looks a lot like 'fully automated luxury communism', in which work is no longer needed. We seem to have here an early vision of post-work society. The reference to artistic and scientific development in free time seems to mobilize the classical tropes studied in Chapter 4 of this volume, of leisure opposed to toil, *praxis* to *poiesis*. The end of 'penury and antithesis' seems to coincide with a society where individuals can realize all their potential beyond the strictures of work, or indeed 'do as they wish'.

The end of the fragment, however, shows that work in fact still features centrally in Marx's vision in 1857. Automation, he writes, 'will redound to the benefit of emancipated labour, and is the condition of its emancipation', not its demise. The following passage explains why this is so:

> The saving of labour time [is] equal to an increase of free time, i.e. time for the full development of the individual, *which in turn reacts back upon* the productive power of labour as itself the greatest productive power. From the standpoint of the direct production process it can be regarded as the production of *fixed capital*, this fixed capital being man himself.
>
> **(1973 [1857], 711—emphasis JPD)**

Free time enables full development of the individual and this 'reacts back upon the productive power of labour': the development of intellectual and creative capacities leads to greater scientific and technical knowledge and better social coordination. Since it is now human knowledge that propels production, human labour remains 'the greatest productive power' but in a new sense and in a new shape. The 'fixed capital' which is now automated (the intelligent machine system) is equally the fully developed human being since the automated machines are products of the 'general intellect', itself the collective expression of human knowledge. A virtuous circle has thus been created. With the reduction of labour time, we have more intelligent individuals creating a more intelligent social organization in which there is a lot of free time to develop intelligence and reap its benefits. But since the conditions for this free development of each and of all together are the fully developed forces of production now taking the shape of intelligent, automated machines, it is also the case that 'the full human being' ('man himself') is a product not just of free time, but of the entire productive process, which includes the new labour process. Both free time and labour time require each other: free time is the condition for the new form of labour time (machine labour), but free time is not to be opposed to labour time since it enters directly into labour time in the form of higher knowledge. Consequently, automation will indeed destroy work in its present form, but this will not lead to a society without or beyond work. Instead, the new society spawned by full automation will be one based on a new, 'emancipated' form of work.

The end of the passage presents another argument to maintain the centrality of labour time even when time has been freed from surplus labour. As in many other passages, Marx applies Hegelian tropes to make the point that without discipline and exercise to develop and apply them, knowledge and practical abilities remain abstract. The individual with a lot of free time still requires work because work is the condition to develop their capacities, as work provides opportunities for exercise, practice, and the discipline attached to them:

> It goes without saying that direct labour time itself cannot remain in the abstract antithesis to free time in which it appears from the perspective of bourgeois economy. Free time—which is both idle time and time for higher activity—has naturally transformed its possessor into a different subject, and he then enters into the direct production process as this different subject. This process is then both discipline, as regards the human being in the process of becoming; and, at the same time, practice [*Ausübung*], experimental science, materially creative and objectifying science, as regards the human being who has become, in whose head exists the accumulated knowledge of society. For both [the worker in the process of becoming emancipated and the one who has become emancipated, JPD], in so far as labour requires practical use of the hands and free bodily movement, as in agriculture, at the same time *exercise*.
>
> **(1973 [1857], 712; the last expression in English in the German original, JPD)**

Labour time remains essential to free time as it provides the opportunities to actualize the development of capacities made possible during free time, through the opportunity for 'discipline' and 'practice'. There is no *becoming* emancipated without the discipline provided by work and there is no *being* emancipated without it either, since emancipation is premised on higher forms of knowledge which need to be applied and put into practice. This applied side concerns the subjects who acquire higher knowledge, but it is also true of knowledge itself, since there can be no progress in theoretical sciences without practical application and no application without 'exercise'. These arguments do not erase the distinction between 'direct labour process' and 'free time', or between productive activity and 'higher activity'. Rather, both sides are necessary to each other. Without 'higher activity', which produces science and technology as well as the self-knowledge of the individuals as social individuals, there can be no emancipated labour. But without labour, there can no 'higher activity' since knowledge needs the discipline of exercise to be actualized through application. A famous earlier passage had already formulated this idea:

> Capital's ceaseless striving towards the general form of wealth drives labour beyond the limits of its natural paltriness and thus creates the material elements for the development of the rich individuality which is as all-sided in its production as in its consumption, and whose labour also therefore appears no longer as labour, but as the full development of activity itself.
>
> **(1973 [1857], 325)**

This vision of the fully developed individuals emerging from large-scale industry remains valid in *Capital*. It is precisely at the end of the machinery chapter that Marx envisions

> the individual human being who is absolutely available for the different kinds of labour required of them [...] the totally developed individual, for whom the different social functions are different modes of activity they take up in turn.
>
> **(1991 [1867], 618)**

The ultimate goal, in *Capital* as much as in the *Grundrisse*, remains 'the abolition of the old division of labour'. As we just saw, however, this does not equate with the abolition of labour but rather with a new era of emancipated labour. The fragment on machines in fact does not point to a society beyond work, but instead envisages an emancipation *of* work, and work remaining a central factor in individual and social life, even at a higher technological stage.

7.3 Spectres of Automation

As said above, earlier predictions of an end of human work, including the most influential passages in Marx's work, have a sobering effect. They immediately suggest a large dose of scepticism towards the latest anticipations (incisively formulated by Wajcman 2017). This is so, first on factual grounds, as transformations brought by innovation historically have not translated into a diminution of the need for work overall, and secondly, as early socialist writings suggest that emancipation from capitalist work could be accompanied by new, emancipated work, not emancipation from all work (see also Benanav 2022).

Despite this long history of failed predictions regarding the end of work, many analysts today argue that this time 'things are different', that the 'end of work' or at least a massive impact of machines on employment is in sight this time. Such predictions are routinely made in the press and in popular publications, but mostly speculate on the basis of anecdotal evidence of the latest technological breakthrough. More substantive evidence, with reference to verified employment trends, economic arguments and the actual capacities of new technologies, is provided by technology experts (Gruetzemacher et al. 2020; Gruetzemacher et al. 2021), labour economists and management theorists (Brynjolfsson and McAfee 2011, 2014; Frey and Osborn 2017; Chessell 2018), 'futurists' (Ford 2015, 2021), and scholars with expertise both in an academic field and in new technologies, such as legal scholars Richard and Daniel Susskind (Susskind and Susskind 2015; Susskind 2020). These predictions focus on the impact of rapid and exponential progress in robotics, AI, and computer science and information technology. These are supposed to make possible a tremendous expansion in the computerization of industrial processes, leveraging the power of big data in all sectors of the economy, including in the sector that today employs most workers, namely services. The end of work is near, then, in a basic empirical sense. In the future, these analysts argue, there will be less and less work to be performed by humans simply because increasingly sophisticated machines and robots fed by huge amounts of information and coordinated via sophisticated automated networks will be able to carry out tasks so far performed by humans more efficiently and with greater economic productivity.

First, there is simply the immense progress made by robotics in recent years. The tremendous range in size and adaptability of the latest robots means an increasing number of tasks can now be mechanically completed in all dimensions, from the nano- and the microscopic to the outright cyclopean. Robots take on toilsome work in heavy industries such as mining and construction, precision work in the automobile industry, and perform high precision interventions in human surgery. Exponential progress in recent years in data gathering, coding, and in programme architectures means that the power of artificial intelligence can be integrated with robotic and machinic processes and further improve technical efficiency and economies of investment. Integrated with artificial intelligence, machines can take on interpersonal tasks in the service sectors, for instance in the food and retail industries. They can increasingly interpret, 'understand', replicate, and respond to emotional and social cues. Artificial intelligence can be used across networks, with relevant data being constantly updated and shared in real-time across multiple machines. This has the effect of replacing human agents not just in one post, but across a number of associated jobs, for instance, with the integration of big data and electronic surveillance in security screening at airports and in sensitive buildings. With constant progress in data storage, calculation, and analytical power, new techniques in artificial intelligence such as deep learning, artificial neural networks, and genetic algorithms mean that big data can be deployed to replicate, match, and outperform human intelligence and human skills in activities, which until recently were deemed unattainable to machinic processes, such as scientific research, artistic creation, and complex writing. Jobs that until recently appeared immune to automation become accessible to machines. An increasing number of tasks in medicine, management, the financial sector, the legal and the educational sectors, creative industries, are now open to increased invasion by machinic processes. When one considers the performances of the latest machines and algorithms, the acceleration in innovation, the integration and cumulative effects spurning digital technologies and robotics together, it is difficult to resist the conclusion that no human work is immune to automation in the near to middle term.

Many economists, historians, business scholars, and executives, however, resist the conclusion that we are on a path towards mass technological unemployment (Deranty and Corbin 2024). Large surveys of employers and business analysts present contrasting evidence. For instance, via a questionnaire involving 3000 companies, Bughin (2020) concludes that labour redistribution will occur. Global accounting firms, banks, and business consultancy groups are often adamant regarding the potential for AI to increase productivity overall and thereby to finally reverse the well-established trend in sluggish productivity growth over the last decades (for instance Purdy and Daugherty 2016; Saniee et al. 2017 who predict labour productivity increases by up to 40% in 2035). Gillham et al. (2018) in a PWC report estimated that global GDP would increase by 14% by 2030, an equivalent of up to $15.7 trillion. A 2020 McKinsey report evaluates the annual value increase of AI in the banking industry at $1 trillion, or 15.4% of sales. All geographical regions of the global economy are said to benefit. As we will discuss below, economic theory predicts that increase in productivity and value creation historically results in employment. Concurrently, international institutions so far report the absence of a significant impact on job markets (Georgieff and Milanez 2021 and Lane and Saint-Martin 2021 for the OECD). The ILO has published many reports on the future of work, which tend to be cautiously optimistic (for instance ILO 2018). A 2018 study by the World Economic Forum (2018) predicted that automation will result in a net increase of 58 million jobs, with a total 133 million new roles created and 75 million current workers displaced. In a recent OECD paper, Squicciarini and Staccioli (2022) study the impact of natural language processing techniques on specific occupations and find no significant effect on employment. A study by Acemoglu, Autor, Hazell, and Restrepo (2020) concludes no significant effect yet in the last decade at the occupation or industry level in the United States. This is a targeted empirical confirmation of Autor's more general conclusions in the early 2010s, in which this leading labour economist cautioned against overly pessimistic conclusions about technological unemployment (Autor and Handel 2013; Autor 2015; see Celentano 2019).

The standard approach to discuss the likelihood of technological unemployment is by labour economists who devise methods to extrapolate the replaceability of human work for particular tasks and deduce from it the impact on occupations and industries more generally. Methodological disagreements between experts can lead to wildly different predictions. For instance, Frey and Osborne's method, which led to their widely cited predictions of 47% of jobs under threat in the United States in the next two decades, was refuted by Arntz et al. (2016, 2019), which resulted in much lower outcomes (around 9% across the OECD, with a high of 12% in Austria and a low of 6% in South Korea). In another noteworthy approach, Princeton computer expert Edward Felten and his colleagues have developed a model for how computerization and specific AI functions can affect the activities making up particular occupations, which also lands on more measured conclusions (Felten et al. 2019, 2021). Evidence from economic history indicates that, to date, new technologies have consistently created new jobs, both directly and indirectly (David 1990). In an important review of the literature, which combines a historical approach with a task-focused one, Ekkehardt et al. (2019) conclude that AI in fact is likely to play out in ways different from previous waves by increasing productivity and potentially creating more inclusive growth, provided correct educational measures are taken in countries that are part of globalized labour chains.

At the heart of those more measured assessments are arguments from mainstream economic theory. In many cases, automation brings with it a 'productivity effect', as increased productivity in one sector raises labour demand in other sectors. As Smith (2020, 134) explains, 'the automation of one industry means higher demand for labour in other industries like the production of machines, the cultivation, extraction, or processing of raw materials, and the building of infrastructure like ports and highways'. The productivity effect can have a number of other ripple effects. Among the many economists who have studied this, the most influential are Acemoglu, Autor, and Restrepo, and the authors they have collaborated with. In their contribution to *The Economics of Artificial Intelligence* (Agrawal et al. 2019, 197–236), Acemoglu and Restrepo summarize in plain terms the economic mechanisms associated with the productivity effect. First, a rise in the demand for labour follows automatically from economic growth triggered by innovation. In theory, the demand for labour can be witnessed even in sectors where automation occurred. Second, demand for labour can increase because automation triggers increased demand for capital. Third, automation can deepen existing automation, which increases productivity without substituting labour (since it is machines that are improved in this case). And fourthly, and most importantly, AI automation creates new tasks. The creation of new tasks is a key component of the labour economists' arguments against mass technological unemployment. The phenomenon has been thoroughly evidenced by Acemoglu, Autor, and Restrepo's research over more than two decades of publications.

Another significant macro-economic aspect of innovation has been highlighted by Autor in his 2015 paper in reference to Michael Kremer's famous O-ring theory (1993), which explains how different task-fulfilling agents in the chain of production (including human and non-human agents) impact on each other's value and on the overall value produced, so that decrease or increase in value produced by one of them impacts on the value produced by the others. As a result of it, 'when automation or computerization makes some steps in a work process more reliable, cheaper, or faster, this increases the value of the remaining human links in the production chain' (Autor 2015, 6). This is compounded by the fact that in many cases, machine work requires human work as its support or complement and does not fully substitute it (Ebben 2020).

Another economic side effect of innovation well evidenced in economic history and theory is the 'multiplier effect'. Increased productivity and increased value as a result of innovation in industrial and manufacturing sectors leads to increased demand in service occupations connected to them. Services can even include manufacturing industries servicing automated factories. In a study involving Frey, this effect was shown to be particularly prevalent in developing countries (Berger et al. 2017). Based on all these reasons, leading economic historian Joel Mokyr (Mokyr 2018) is resolutely optimistic about AI's potential to restart growth. In response to the objection that productivity increases are not observed in statistics today, Brynjolfsson et al. (2019) argue that technological innovation suffers from an 'implementation lag' and accurate measurements of the impact of AI on productivity are yet to be known.

Finally, a number of Marxist authors show that the logic of capitalism dictates that work is a long way from becoming obsolete as a result of automation. The absence of technological unemployment is nothing to celebrate, as it coincides with higher levels of precarious work, underemployment, and exploitation. But for this chapter, the key point is scepticism towards general technological unemployment.

Drawing on an argument in Cohen's classical reconstruction of historical materialism (Cohen 2000 [1978]), Barbara Nieswandt (2022) shows that private property in the means of production and the profit motive, two structural features of capitalist economies, make it unlikely that AI-based automation will lead to massive job losses. Strict property rules mean that technological innovation is exclusively owned, applied, and the outcomes of its productivity-raising potentials captured by private owners. The profit motive means that the deployment of technologies in a capitalist context is guided solely by the search for profit. The combination of these two factors means that technological innovation in a capitalist economy serves to increase output in order to increase profit. Other alternatives cannot be countenanced given the rules of the capitalist game. This is true not just of the altruistic alternative that would mobilize technology to reduce working hours, but even of the possibility of using productivity to reduce the wage bill while keeping production constant. Given the other tools capitalists possess to ensure exploitation of workers, the search for profit is better served by increasing output than job churn.

Another argument draws on readings of Marx, which emphasize class antagonism as a decisive factor in the organization of capitalist production, including in its adoption of technological innovation. A major use of technology in this context is to bypass labour forces when they are organized and are in a position to push back effectively against capital imperatives (Marx 1991 [1867], 562; Mueller 2021). In contrast, when the capacity of labour to organize is weakened, the need to shift work to capital to bypass labour is a lot less pressing (Fleming 2019). This is compounded by the cheap cost of labour, also an effect of weakened labour protections. When human labour is relatively cheap, there is no incentive for capital to invest in and deploy expensive technologies. Surplus-value can be extracted just as well from human workers (Dinnerstein and Pitts 2021). Furthermore, in the current phase of capitalism, it is shareholder value that matters, not productivity. This means that if shareholder value can be ensured through other means than investment in technology, which entails a significant threat of sunk costs, this is what is likely to happen. With the sophistication of financial tools and the protection ensured by promiscuous taxation schemes nationally and internationally, there is no pressing incentive for many industries to invest in technology. Even if the previous arguments did not obtain, the current economic context and its ideological underpinning in fact does not incentivize massive deployment of job-replacing technologies.

Yet another argument concentrates on the differential impact of productivity across sectors (Benanav 2022). Overcapacity in manufacturing and agriculture leads to an exodus of workers towards service and care sectors, where productivity can only be achieved through wage suppression and depreciation of working conditions. Once again, the outcome is an explosion of employment in new sectors and a return to older forms of work relations. These new occupations come with low wages, precarious working conditions and tenure, and uncertain hours. But there is no massive job churn. Robots and automated processes might well be technically capable of replacing many, most, or at some point all humans in these service occupations, but there is no economic rationale for doing so.

In response to all these economic arguments, based either in Marxist political economy or in mainstream economic theories, proponents of the mass technological unemployment thesis can point to the seismic dimensions of technological rupture we are currently living through. Automation, notably AI-based processes, is progressing at an accelerating speed, is achieving results and is beginning to outcompete humans in areas nobody predicted just a few years ago. This time, it looks as though things truly are different. Analyses of the impact of innovation on employment that might have been true until a few years ago would then be obsolete.

Some extra arguments can be raised, however, to complicate the issue. First, there is a mismatch between arguments for mass unemployment based on technological considerations, and sceptical reservations based on economic considerations. Economic arguments do not deny the reality of technological progress but point out that we cannot directly infer from what a single machine is capable of achieving in a laboratory context to whether it makes economic sense for this kind of machine to be massively deployed by employers in the real economy. Economic theory and economic history point out not just the unknown of new tasks and new jobs that might arise from the current round of innovation, based on what we know of the past. They also point out the factors potentially constraining mass deployment of technology, namely whether it actually makes economic sense to do so. As said, it might be the case that in many situations, human labour will remain cheaper than complex machinery.

Other limitations to mass deployment of technology can be highlighted. First, many jobs are in reality more difficult to perform, or involve more tasks, or involve more complex interconnections between different parts of the work process, than is assumed when predictions about replacement by machines are made based on matching machine capabilities and generic descriptions of human skills (Ebben 2020). This insight is comforted by the psychodynamic analysis of work, which inspires key arguments in the second part of the book. As the psychodynamics of work evidences at length (Dejours 2006, 2009, 2015), in many cases tasks can only be effectively performed if workers add their own input to the formal instructions defining the task and how it is supposed to be achieved. This added input is needed because formal instructions can never pre-empt all the obstacles that get in the way of task fulfilment: unhelpful managerial commands (which might be too vague or generic, too strict for changing situations, might entail contradictory prescriptions, and so on); frictions between coworkers or between teams; issues with machines and automatic processes (including gaps between theoretical machine capabilities and actual delivery on the job); all the possible mismatches between managerial and customer expectations and worker's delivery; and many other possible contingencies. In the reality of work situations, workers standardly need to adapt to changing situations, interpret rules, creatively circumvent unforeseen challenges, alter protocols, just so that the task is actually completed. This adaptability demanded of many workers relies on human ingenuity, often on the capacity for creative thinking, lateral thinking, interpersonal skills. In highly controlled environments, it makes sense to match human skills generically defined (as they are in studies in labour economics) with machine capabilities. But real workplaces are very different from labs: in many cases, sometimes even for tasks that might appear very simple to an observer, it is in fact a whole array of different skills, including on the spot capacity to innovate, that is needed from the human worker.

This technical argument is comforted by a critical point about the assumptions that are made when defining efficient fulfilment of tasks. As De Stefano makes the case (2020, 10), a purely analytical definition of tasks might overlook hidden costs to automation, leading to suboptimal efficiency overall. This is the case for instance when work schedules are run in a purely automated way and result in increased casualization and precarious conditions, which affect performance in turn.

There are also issues when generalizing from one national context to another, as differences in the structures of the national economy, the policy context, the legal framework, the education system, cultural attitudes to technology and work, even geography, mean that AI impacts work differently in different economies (Clifton et al. 2020).

Finally, there are external material conditions underpinning the deployment of AI which cannot be taken for granted. Computational power supported by adequate hardware (notably quality micro-conductors), and energy availability (Hwang 2018), are non-trivial conditions of automated systems, notably the data centres supporting AI. These need to be considered when calculating the likelihood of human tasks and jobs being replicated in the real world. Geopolitical troubles, economic or resource limitations might well slow down or hamper AI deployment simply because material support is lacking. In a world prone to climate crisis, which might lead in many countries to severe water restrictions (when water is required for cooling systems), the environmental impact of AI might constrain its deployment, at least if sustainability becomes a serious parameter in economic activity. The conclusion from all these considerations is that, despite the impressive developments in AI and the spread of automation in many economic sectors, it is still impossible to tell at this stage whether this time things really are going to be different. There might well be serious shocks to many industries and sectors of production, it might well be the case that automation will be a major disruptor with significant social repercussions, affecting the lives of many. Labour economists who are sceptical of automation's power to cause mass unemployment like Autor have well highlighted the risk of polarization in wages and working conditions. But for our purposes in this chapter, the key point is that it is far from established that these disruptions will be the mass unemployment that many predict, notably post-work theorists who use this as an argument for their scenarios of social organization 'beyond work'. The ability of every generation under accelerated industrialization to imagine the ways automation might impact lives—and the visceral experience many have had of being displaced by newly automated workplaces—do not line up with expert analyses of the relation between work and automation, which show (in varying ways) that automation changes work rather than making it obsolete. In any case, as Cynthia Estlund shows emphatically (2021), even if there will be less work to distribute in the future, it might still be the case that the 'goods' of work and the centrality of work need to be retained, which means that, rather than welcoming or attempting to accelerate the shift 'post work', we should instead think on how to reorganize it, so that it can be meaningful to all. The next chapter considers objections that question this very possibility, arguing from the point of view of social and political theory.

8
The Social and Political Irrelevance of Work

The first six chapters of the book considered arguments against the centrality of work premised on accounts of the character of work in past historical moments. The previous chapter initiated a temporal shift, considering arguments based on work in the present and the future. This chapter pursues this temporal shift. Its focus is on theoretical misgivings about the centrality of work in present and future conditions from the points of view of social and political theory. The first section reviews arguments from classics of post-war political sociology that coined the term 'post-industrialism' to describe changes in the economic, social, and political organization of rich countries in the 1970s. 'Post-industrialism' entailed the demise of work as a culturally, socially, and politically central institution. The second section reviews objections from the theoretical side of sociology, arguing against the very idea of an institution and form of experience being 'central' in modern life. The third section considers philosophical objections against the perfectionism that seems to be entailed in the idea of work being central to individual and social life. In contrast with previous chapters, the objections presented here will only be responded to in the second part of the book.

8.1 Post-industrialism

The 'post-industrial' designation dates back from the 1980s, when a group of leading European sociologists attempted to describe a new regime of social-economic organization in industrialized nations. In this new regime, they argued, work was set to lose its significance in three related ways: in political terms, as the key vector in the structuring of political conflict and political organization; in social terms, as an institution around which a large section of the population develops a sense of shared social, cultural and moral identity; and in cultural terms, with the demise of work as the central value of modern capitalist society. Gorz's writings of the 1980s overlap substantially with this

The Case for Work. Jean-Philippe Deranty, Oxford University Press. © Jean-Philippe Deranty (2024).
DOI: 10.1093/oso/9780192887146.003.0009

sociological literature. To present the constellation of themes surrounding the post-industrial heading, an apt guide is Shaun Wilson's *Struggle over Work* (Wilson 2004), chapter 2 in particular, whose lead we follow in this section (see another good summary in Granter 2009, 135–164).

Alain Touraine's diagnosis regarding the political obsolescence of work was a natural conclusion of his focus on the 'new social movements' of the late 1970s and early 1980s. The theoretical crux of Touraine's argument was that in every historical constellation of objective social determinants and corresponding conditions of social action, particular types of political agents more eminently capture, in their organization, mode of action, and the objectives they pursue, the potentialities and points of tension that the social situation harbours. In industrialist society, a clear site of conflict was the capitalist firm, where class interests were visibly at odds. Those interests concerned mainly the organization of production and issues of redistribution. Mass production was in a process of rationalization and gradual expansion, which meant that workers could still refer to older modes of working and of organizing to denounce their new working conditions. As a result of these conditions, labour-based parties and the union movement could mobilize massively and represent, sociologically, culturally, and politically, one of the main actors involved in the political conflict structuring that societal type. Post-industrial society refers to a new mode of economic organization in which production and consumption rely increasingly on information and symbolic goods and bureaucratic agencies play an increasingly significant role. As a result, the sites and the objects of political conflict are displaced away from the firm and become more diverse. The new social movements no longer aim to represent the collective interests of a particular class but rather to challenge the very organization of society at various points. The conservative consensus that underpinned the old industrial conflicts is ruptured in favour of new social and cultural demands, typically represented by the feminist, anti-nuclear, and environmental movements. In this renewed political scene, the old labour movement becomes out of touch. Its cultural and political obsolescence is rooted in the disappearance of homogeneous class consciousness as the working class is fragmented between diverse socio-professional groups and the global working class expands with the emergence of new industrialized nations. The labour movement becomes a marginal figure, engaging in defensive status struggles and being relegated to a satellite role in the larger political realm.

Claus Offe's diagnosis of the disorganization of capitalism in the 1980s (Offe 1985) overlapped with Touraine's conclusions about the obsolescence of the labour movement as a relevant political actor in the new configuration of post-industrial society. The two sociologists diverged on many points in their overall appraisals of the societal changes coinciding with the demise of the Fordist mode of production. However, one key agreement among them was the view that the new structure of the economy led to a 'disaggregation of interests within the workforce' (Wilson 2004, 53), in other words, a divergence between working populations over their respective interests. For Offe, this was due in no small part to endemically high levels of unemployment, as he thought that the disappearance of industrial jobs would not be compensated by the creation of new service sector jobs. This argument anticipated current diagnoses about looming mass unemployment, a key argument in a number of post-work proposals, by more than forty years. Offe also identified the increase in precariousness and marginalization as key factors in the fragmenting of interests among the working populations and the shattering of class consciousness.

According to Offe, the demise of class solidarity was paralleled by a weakening of the union movement, due first to a decrease in members as a result of aggressive policies on the part of employer groups, relayed and institutionalized by states rapidly embracing neoliberal thinking. This was coupled, he argued, with the damaging effects of a structural paradox in union action, namely, the risk inherent in using formal power, that playing an active role in legislation and decision-making comes at the cost of the power to mobilize. As Wilson shows, this explanation of labour demobilization entailed a significant cultural dimension. Offe argued that the demise of the union movement was underpinned by a demise in the work ethic, a demise that had its roots in the implausibility of attaching moral responsibility to employment as the main vehicle for social and political integration, when these activities are increasingly precarious (Wilson 2004, 64). The upshot of Offe's vision was comparable to Touraine's: the labour movement had become a marginal figure in the political contests of the new capitalistic configuration. Work is no longer central in politics, either as a principle defining specific interests around which a mass political movement could rally, or as the basis for an organized movement, or as a cultural value. This is precisely what Habermas had in view when he talked of an 'exhaustion of utopian energies' (Habermas 1994).

As time has passed, these analyses might seem dated and lacking in relevance for contemporary debates. But is the social-economic-political situation we are in now radically different from what it was forty years ago, or is it just the outcome of an intensification of trends that were already identified then? One might well argue that the economic trends that appeared in the early 1980s have intensified and transmogrified but have not changed in nature, and in any case, have not changed the place of work in modern politics. Globalization and automation have further eroded the industrial base in Western nations, and this process is now also beginning to affect countries that sought to catch up with industrialized countries in the last decades of the twentieth century. What we have then is deindustrialization across the board, making old-style proletarian mottoes even more obsolete. Information- and data-based production and consumption have exploded, but early sociologists already identified the first waves of computerization and raised concerns about the individualization of work that came with them, translating into an increased difficulty in mobilizing workers. They also expressed scepticism about the goal of full employment in such a context. The first signs of work precariousness noted then have only intensified in recent years and arguably coincide with a rise in the 'disaggregation of interests' across nations and indeed across global value chains. The conclusions that sociological analyses of the 1980s drew about the place of work in contemporary society thus appear to chime in eerily with contemporary post-work diagnoses. This is no surprise for readers of contemporary post-work theory given the seminal role Gorz's writings play in it and since his reflections were rooted in 1980s social theory.

Such long-term validity of old sociological analyses might be viewed as another way to confirm the scepticism towards work's centrality. Forty years ago, post-work theorists might say, clear-sighted analysts could already see that the composition, organization, and value platform of the labour movement could no longer provide a valid progressive political direction for the new times. It was already evident then, and is confirmed even more so today, that a unified class consciousness cannot be found among the fragmented experiences of all the different kinds of populations experiencing the precariat condition. Despite frequent attempts at rekindling it, the weakening of the union movement has gone on unabated. Already then, the aim of full employment was a mistaken political goal, something that seems to be starkly confirmed today by the threat of mass unemployment as a result of automation. The dramatic rise in the level of risk associated with environmental degradation makes the aim of full employment even more ill-advised, given the nefarious effects of many kinds of jobs in today's economic organization. The old sociologists had already made this point (Offe 1996, 23–24, 208–209), as of course had Gorz. The temporal bridge linking earlier post-industrial social theory to contemporary post-work theory finds another confirmation in the widespread embrace of a universal basic income as one of the more apt political goals that progressives and democrats should pursue. Offe was one of the founders of the Basic Income European Network. Already then, in 1986, the value of work appeared obsolete. Why persist in keeping it alive today?

As we will see in the next section, these sociological descriptions of work's loss of relevance find an echo at the theoretical level in conceptual doubts about using the notion of 'centrality' in relation to complex social systems.

8.2 A Category Error

A founding assumption of modern social theory is captured by the notion of differentiation (see Eisenstadt 1964, 376 for a clear summary). The notion denotes an evolutionary, comparative, and functional approach to how human societies are supposed to develop over long periods of time. It is premised on the idea that a human collective maintains itself in existence, 'reproduces' itself, by ensuring that a number of key functions are satisfied, such as access to essential resources for food and technological production, the organization of collective power, the socialization of younger generations via the sharing and developing of common knowledges, beliefs, and values, a system of punishments for infringements to collective rules, and so on. Society engages in a process of 'differentiation' when those functions are no longer fulfilled through practices embedded in the overall way of life but rather by practices that take place within specialized institutions (a legal system, a system for making decisions affecting the collective, and so on), each institutional sphere being dedicated to the delivery of a particular function. This institutional division of labour induces other processes of social differentiation: different functions are taken up by different subgroups within society (for instance, a warring class or a peasant class); each separate institutional sphere develops its own internal rules, its own 'culture' and ethics, its own criteria of successful or illicit action, its own process of recruitment; different social roles become distinguished from each other (warrior, priest, king, slave), each with its own value system, typical psychological profiles, sets of knowledges and skills. Classically, 'differentiation' is supposed to make sense of the 'evolution' of human society, from an early type where the only social division is by gender, to other types of social organization where different forms of ascription (by gender, by kin, by class, by wealth, by birth) regulate the apportioning of individuals to increasingly separate institutional spheres. Beyond the many substantial variations in narratives and the categorical and explanatory frameworks they devised, all the great founders of sociology and many later sociologists following in their footsteps have embraced a vision of modern society as the final outcome of a manifold process of differentiation. Indeed, for the founders of sociology as a distinct discipline, one of the initial motivations was precisely to describe and explain key aspects of social differentiation, to understand the laws of social change, characterize broad patterns of social evolution, and inquire into the consequences of social differentiation for modern individuals.

This baseline assumption of social theory and of sociology entails a simple and powerful objection to the idea of the centrality of work. Since each function is necessary for social reproduction, it does not seem to make sense to select one function in particular (work), as being 'central' over against the others.

This conclusion deriving from the fundamental assumption of social differentiation appears to be explicitly envisaged by the founding figures of sociology. Max Weber's theory of rationalization in systems of action leads precisely to his vision of a vast process of differentiation: capitalistic firms become separated from households, the State separates itself from society, the legal system becomes increasingly formalized and separates from older, more encompassing moral systems. These institutional differentiations are linked to the emergence of distinct 'value spheres' (science and technology, art and literature, law and morality) out of the encompassing metaphysical worldviews embedded in the main religions, notably monotheistic faiths. Each one of those value spheres obeys its own logic, follows its 'own law-like process of rationalization' (*Eigengesetzlichkeit*). Habermas' reconstruction of Weber's theory of societal rationalization in volume one of the *Theory of Communicative Action* provides a synthetic summary of this grand historical, comparative narrative (Habermas 1984, 143–272). In such a summary, the leading methodological attitude is precisely to seek out and emphasize the multiple processes of 'differentiation' between institutional complexes, between fundamental values, between attitudes toward the world, indeed between different kinds of world (social, objective, subjective). The upshot of such an analysis is the plurality of significant reference systems for individuals.

It is in one of Georg Simmel's first books, published in 1890, titled precisely *On Social Differentiation*, that the category of 'centre' in the analysis of modern society is explicitly rejected. The book studies the evolving dynamics between individuality and group belonging from a long-historical perspective. Over the course of human history, Simmel intends to show, an increasing number of idiosyncratic features constitutive of individual selves are gradually enabled to manifest themselves. In that sense, individuality broadens in its scope and autonomy increases. This widening of subjectivity is supposed to be tied to the weakening of the bonds linking individuals to their primary groups, the kin or the clan. As these bonds loosen, new 'social circles' emerge in which the individual can find a new home, for instance, their profession, associations outside of work, and so on. These social circles in turn allow selves to define themselves in new ways and expand the scope of subjective identity. Differentiation in this scenario occurs at all levels: more groups appear as a result of functional differentiation between institutions; large groups fragment under the pressure of specialization; and individuals themselves become 'differentiated', first in an external sense, as each individual has increasingly more opportunities to connect with other groups corresponding to her or his own idiosyncratic traits, and internally as well, as increasing aspects of their person find institutional anchor points in the social world. The key aspect of this narrative for our interests is when Simmel stresses that in complex societies, many of the social circles to which an individual belongs are not 'concentric', that is, do not all refer to one overarching point or value or set of interests that would cohere and dominate the others. One might pursue particular interests in one's profession and an entirely different set in one's hobbies, or one's family values might not match the normative references of professional life. Instead of being concentric, Simmel's key metaphor states, the circles 'cross each other'. This 'crossing of the social circles' is different for every individual, because every individual belongs only to the groups to which they have an affinity, and these affinities, being individual, are different for everyone. Indeed, the individual's subjectivity can be defined as an individual's own idiosyncratic 'crossing of social circles' (Simmel 1989, 241). Not only are there no 'centres' for anyone in particular (only an intersection of circles), but there are also no centres in general.

The reflections of social theorists in the middle of the twentieth century—for instance, Talcott Parsons or Niklas Luhmann, to name two of the most influential ones—aimed to systematize these earlier analyses of different units, levels, and spheres making up society and the different mechanisms linking them as the grammar to explain social differentiation and evolution. Parsons, for instance, argued that every instance of social action (individual action undertaken in reference to others, within a common frame of reference) is the result of three subsystems, the personality, cultural, and social systems (Parsons 1991 [1951]; Münch 1982), being combined each time in a specific way. Separate processes need to be delineated to explain how such interpenetrations are possible: notably, how cultural values take on social reality through institutionalization and how internalization processes enculturate personalities. Parsons pursued the analysis of these social mechanisms by constantly revising and refining his categorical vocabulary. In the final and most famous refinement of his modelling (Parsons and Bales 1953) encapsulated in the AGIL schema, Parsons identified four fundamental sets of problems any system of action faces: the problems of adaptation, goal selection, integration of different units of action, and of latency of the overall system of action.

In such a detailed, multi-level, and multi-perspectival analytical framework, the category of 'centre' appears to reduce the complexity of the social world to a simple figure with one, or possibly only a few, significant institutional spheres. This seems to represent a serious loss of analytical acumen and accuracy. Concretely, in their everyday life, individuals accomplish many different kinds of social action, and each mobilizes the three fundamental subsystems in a specific way, involving each time different institutional complexes, each with its own sets of knowledges, skills, norms, and values. Neither from the point of view of the institutional world, nor from the point of view of individual experience does the category of 'centre' seem adequate. Given the complexity of modern social systems and the multifold institutional attachments of modern individuals, how would one decide which dimensions are 'central'? Methodologically, the application of the AGIL schema explicitly belies the search for a 'centre': adaptation is ensured by economic institutions; goal setting by political institutions; integration by legal institutions; and latency by kinship and cultural and religious institutions. Such a model expressly forbids one to claim that economic institutions (where work would naturally be placed) would somehow be 'central'. It may be that in particular historical situations, economic norms and values 'colonize' the other subsystems and repress these subsystems' own norms and values, as Habermas argues is the case in capitalist societies. But that is an empirical fact, indeed a pathology of modern capitalism. In analytical terms, it makes no sense to predetermine that one subsystem and the cultural values and personality traits associated with it take precedence over the others, as a matter of theoretical decision. When Parsons talks of a 'structural core', in *The Social System*, for instance, he does this precisely to denote a plurality of institutions, namely, those institutions that are 'directly constitutive of the patterning of social relationships themselves through the definition of the statuses and roles of the parties to the interactive process' (Parsons 1951, 33). These institutions that form the structural core of the social system are themselves 'differentiated both for different roles within the same social system and for different social systems'.

In fact, if any institutional sphere can be called 'central' in a modern setting, it is instead the state, in the sense that its legislative, administrative, and executive functions exert the most influence relatively speaking on other social interactions and individual choices. This emphasis on the modern state as the centre of social life through its unmatched power to influence the frame of reference for all social actions is particularly visible in theories of modernization and development in the 1960s (Eisenstadt 1964, 377; 1970). Once again, the usage refers back to the founders of the discipline. Durkheim already characterized the state as the 'centre' of the social system based on an analogy with the brain as the 'centre' of the nervous system (Durkheim 1986, 40). In the *Philosophy of Money*, Simmel used the centre metaphor also to designate the 'central power of the group', in other words, the institutional realm through which collective rules are decided and enforced (Simmel 2004 [1907], 184). But even if the state is the most important institution on these accounts, the other worries about the very category of 'centrality' remain. The state can be called the 'centre' of life only in a loose, metaphorical sense.

It is worth emphasizing again that, as we saw in Simmel's early conception of 'non-concentric' 'social circles', the objection to the category of 'centrality' in the context of classical social theories applies as much to individuals as it does to institutions. This goes to the heart of the theoretical aims of classical sociology and its mid-twentieth-century heirs. One of the puzzles these scholars wanted to solve is the paradox of the parallel increase in individual autonomy (for instance regarding choice of partner or profession) at the same time as social systems grow in complexity. That modern individuals are 'plural' is a basic assumption in this field (Lahire 2011).

This objection from social theory, which targets the adequacy of the 'centrality' category for modern contexts and questions the validity of applying it to work in any case, adds theoretical weight to the sociological studies we reviewed in the previous section, which showed empirically the loss of significance of work in post-industrial society. Given the continuity we highlighted with contemporary post-work theory, social theory's analytical arguments also add weight to contemporary post-work worries about the continuing reference to work as a central component for individuals, society, and politics. What links all these approaches is the shared view that the centrality of work is not a fact about human life but a pathology of modern society, as one particular institutional complex with its own set of values and demands has been made central to the detriment of the other aspects of social life. Habermas' metaphor of the 'colonization of lifeworlds' (Habermas 1984) is an apt and striking formulation of this pathological character of the centrality of work, underpinned by his own model of social theory, which draws substantially on the classics. What classical social theory highlights is that continuing to defend the centrality of work today is not only erroneous on ethical and political grounds but also on theoretical, conceptual ones: not only *should* work not be so central, given all the harms that are associated with its centrality, given how unrealistic the promise of full employment is, but work in fact *is* not central, if we take seriously the complex structure of modern, 'differentiated' lifeworlds. Work can only become central in a pathological situation in which the rationality of modernity (differentiation) is denied.

We find this connection between theoretical and empirical concerns about work's centrality raised explicitly in Axel Honneth's recent book on socialism (Honneth 2017). A key argument Honneth raises in criticism of the nineteenth-century founders of socialism in his effort to establish a more valid, contemporary version is precisely their fixation on economic relations as the central area of social life. For the early socialists, Honneth argues, economic relations were the sole place of interest in their denunciation of injustice and equally the place from which they thought a transformation of society could occur. All the theoretical mistakes and political shortcomings of the movement in its traditional form, he argues, stem precisely from not acknowledging functional differentiation as a key feature of modern society. The founding fathers of socialism were convinced that in the future the integration of all social spheres would be determined solely by the requirements of industrial production. They did so despite the fact that their liberal counterparts and their intellectual opponents had begun to highlight the socio-political consequences—arising by the late eighteenth century at the latest—of the differentiation of society into various social spheres, which came increasingly to be analysed with reference to their respective functions (Honneth 2017, 78–79). This erroneous analysis of modern society's development led to the categorical mistake consisting in making 'central' a particular institution, and particular forms of social action and social relations, which are in fact just one type among others:

> Just like pre-modern social theorists, socialists from Saint-Simon to Marx conceived of the functioning of societies as being vertically directed by a *central authority*. The only difference is that this authority was not represented by the state, but by the economy. It would have been far more insightful from the perspective of social theory to criticize the capitalist relations of the time for not permitting the various independent spheres of action the freedom to follow their own respective social logic—which was the freedom that representatives of liberalism originally accorded to these spheres. It would have been possible, therefore, to affirm the tendency towards functional differentiation and demand that e.g. love

> and democracy be excepted from economic imperatives. At the same time, socialists could have expressed their skepticism about the possibilities for establishing this separation under capitalist economic conditions.
>
> **(Honneth 2017, 81—emphasis JPD)**

This recent critique of the socialist tradition thematizes a methodological thread that has been present in Honneth's work from the beginning and is at the heart of his own proposal to make recognition the main operative concept in critical theory (see Deranty 2009a for a detailed reconstruction of this journey). As is well-known, the tradition of critical theory Honneth situates himself in is that of the 'Frankfurt School' (1991). In that tradition, a famous desideratum is that critique should be 'immanent', that is to say, the critique of social phenomena should not rely on norms external to the description of society, such as an independently defined conception of justice, freedom, or equality. This demand for immanent as opposed to externally grounded criticism is justified on complex theoretical and methodological grounds that need not be rehearsed here. Ultimately the justification is practical: if society is to be transformed so that its pathologies are addressed and injustice and unfreedom are rectified, this will have to occur on the basis of intellectual, moral, and material forces already be present in existing social reality. A major implication of this demand for immanent criticism, then, is that the categories used to describe the organization of society should also make it possible to highlight the normative leverage with which to criticize society and with which pathologies and injustices could be addressed. The model of course is Marx's 'critique of political economy', which simultaneously describes bourgeois society, unveils its unjust and pathological structures, and suggests how these will be overcome. This program of immanent criticism, however, was not properly realized by Marx, Honneth has argued in many texts leading to the *Struggle for Recognition*, precisely because Marx made social labour this central category carrying the load of social theory and social criticism simultaneously (see for instance 1995a). In fact, Honneth reads the whole first generation of Frankfurt School theorists critically, precisely because they remained indebted to Marx's methodological centralization of work (Honneth 1991). In making 'social labour' the central operating concept, Adorno and Horkheimer repeated Marx's own mistake of reducing the whole gamut of social interactions to just the social relations implied in the 'metabolism of society with nature'. This was wrong descriptively, for the image of society implied in it, for the description of the full gamut of capitalist pathologies and injustices, and for the image of emancipation that such a conception logically entails. This Honnethian critique of the paradigm of social labour is a vivid illustration of the force that a critique of the idea of 'centrality' can have from the perspective of twentieth-century social theory.

8.3 Normative Objections

The sociological and social-theoretical objections to the centrality of work reviewed in the first two sections are echoed by discussions in contemporary moral and political philosophy, with the specific set of assumptions and interests that are characteristic of that disciplinary area. From the point of view of contemporary moral and political philosophy, the thesis of the centrality of work sounds like a paradigm example of a perfectionist statement. Perfectionism is the approach that defines the right ethical and political conduct as that which helps to realize what is good for human beings and that defines this good as the perfecting of characteristic human capacities. The *locus classicus* is Aristotle's *Nichomachean Ethics*, in which *eudaimonia*, 'happiness' or fully 'doing well', the ultimate good, is identified with virtue, and virtue in turn consists in human agents exercising their human capacities at their best, under the command of the distinctive human capacity for rational deliberation. Stating that work is, or ought to be central, appears to be identifying a good for human beings, 'working', and by stating that it is 'central', seems to place this good at the pinnacle of a 'perfect' human life, for individuals and collectives alike. Marx is classically read as taking a perfectionist stance in many of his passages on work, both to condemn how capitalistically organized work prevents humans from realizing this central good and thereby humanity's 'essence' and appealing to it for his vision of emancipated society. This would be a society where that central good would be fully realized for each and every person, typically involving creative, cooperative, multi-sided activity (Arneson 1987).

Perfectionism has met with many criticisms over the last five decades, since Rawls began to identify it under this term and first rejected it (Rawls 1999, 285–292). The most well-known opponents are philosophers defending some version of political liberalism, who worry about the 'illiberal' assumptions and implications of a perfectionist stance in politics. But critiques of perfectionism have also been formulated from other quarters of normative philosophy, including by analytical Marxists and a leading egalitarian welfare theorist like Richard Arneson. In the context of the debates around perfectionism, four issues (at least) can be identified with the thesis of the centrality of work. These issues are connected to the sociological and social-theoretical worries presented in the first two sections, since key assumptions underpinning the criticisms of perfectionism concern the structure of contemporary polities and to what extent strong prescriptions about a value such as work can be rightfully formulated in this historical context.

The first issue relates to a key aspect of the goods making up a good life overall, namely, the '*internal pluralism*' among these goods, the idea that there are 'several distinct, intrinsically valuable elements that can be combined in a single, reasonably unified picture of a good human life' (Nussbaum 2011, 9; see also Arneson 2000, 48–49). So-called 'objective lists' of human goods emphasize and theorize the plurality and irreducibility of these goods (for instance Parfit 1984, 499; Scanlon 1998, 124–125; Nussbaum 2012). On what grounds could work be declared 'central' by comparison with other 'goods' humans seek to achieve in their overall search for well-being? There are tensions among the goods, some (like physical integrity) might be necessary conditions while others might accept varying degrees of accomplishment. But the whole point of the list is that all the goods that can be identified as aspects of a good human life matter. Why would work be more important than friendship, love, knowledge, or the enjoyment of beauty in the overall assessment of a life that is fully human?

Indeed, a point raised by Richard Arneson in his seminal article on meaningful work and market socialism (1987) also clearly highlights the internal pluralism that applies to work itself as a generic term. Arneson lists all the different kinds of goods that individuals might attach to work. This includes seventeen different possible features an individual might find attractive in work, for instance, to name just the first three for illustration, a wage, knowledge or contribution (1987, 528–529). If work can mean so many things to different people, this in itself makes it impossible to speak of work as a single, generic good. Depending on the individuals, it is particular features of work that matter more, and some might matter less or not at all. That makes it difficult to claim that work is central in a general sense.

Such a list of all the different goods that different individuals might attach to work raises a second issue which becomes particularly visible if we consider that, outside of Marxist theories, no contemporary 'objective list' of the goods making up well-being mentions work as a good as such. A reason for this might well be that work is *an instrumental activity*, but the goods making up a good life are intrinsically valued. And so, the goods that work enables one to achieve might well enter into an overall picture of a good life, but not work itself. Work might well, in good circumstances, enable the exercise of 'rational activity' and 'the development of one's abilities' (Parfit 1984), or be a key avenue for realizing some 'achievement' (Scanlon 1998; Rice 2013), but it is the latter that are the intrinsic goods, not work. 'Human nature' perfectionism, which ties the goods to be perfected to characteristic features of being human has the same issue. We know that the young Marx made work the essential feature of the species in his 1844 manuscripts, but as we saw in Chapter 3, many Marxists argue that this is not what should be kept from Marx. And as Will Kymlicka observes (2002, 193), citing Mary Midgley, it is a conceptual mistake to conclude from work as an anthropological *differentia specifica* to its alleged normative preeminence. Such preeminence can only be demonstrated through normative argument, but it is hard to see what argument could be mounted to favour work, if it was an intrinsic good at all, over other goods. As Kymlicka writes 'the issue is not whether unalienated labour is a good, but whether it is an overriding good, a good which is necessary to any decent life, and which outweighs in value all competing goods. I see no reason to think unalienated labour is such a good' (2002, 192). Thomas Hurka, probably the most trenchant defender in contemporary philosophy of human nature perfectionism does not list work among the goods whose aggregation is said to constitute the good life for human beings (Hurka 1993).

Kymlicka's well-known rejection of non-alienated work as a principle of justice, which is based on his rejection of Marxist perfectionism, alerts us to the *epistemic* dimension of the problem. This connects with the worries we encountered already as an implication of Foucauldian arguments in Chapter 4, or indeed as a consequence of the historicist worry in the very first chapter. The rejection of essentialist and ethnocentric views can be given an anti-perfectionist formulation: on what empirical or conceptual grounds precisely could work be singled out as the single most important good, or one of the most important goods, which it would need to be if it were 'central'? What kind of justification could be provided for this view? The epistemic burden associated with proving this thesis seems far too heavy to carry, indeed impossible to cash out.

Finally, the most glaring issue with the thesis of the centrality of work in the context of debates on perfectionism is raised by the fact of *external pluralism*. This is the assumption that individuals are entitled to hold their own conceptions of the good, provided these conceptions are, in Rawls' seminal characterization, 'reasonable', that is, conceptions of the good life that include values and norms allowing their holders to engage with others in fair social cooperation, notably as they each recognize each other's basic liberties as well as their own right to hold their own conception of the good, however these might depart from their own. There is therefore an inevitable and irreducible pluralism between conceptions of the good, this one 'external'. Such value pluralism is a historical fact and a fundamental normative principle in the organization of modern societies. Recognizing, entrenching, and developing the consequences of this fundamental demand for religious and cultural toleration is of course the founding principle of political liberalism. Such a principle translates into a strict political rule that the state cannot favour any particular conception of the good over others in its constitution and in the development and application of its policies. The state must remain ethically neutral, lest it fails to treat some of its citizens with the respect and the dignity they are owed. How this principle applies to work is obvious: understood in perfectionist terms, the centrality of work is one conception of the good that some are fully entitled to hold. Indeed, many people as a matter of fact take work to be a central component of what makes life a good life. But it would be 'illiberal', an unjustified encroachment on individual freedom and a mark of deep disrespect towards those not holding this view, to impose it on everyone. A clear formulation of this consequence is made by Kymlicka in his *Contemporary Political Philosophy*, in his critical assessment of the many Marxist conceptions that place unalienated production at the centre of the just society:

> there are many values that may compete with unalienated production [...] Some people will view productive labour as 'life's prime want', but others will not. A prohibition on alienated labour, therefore, would unfairly privilege some people over others.
>
> **(2002, 193)**

Some might choose to work in alienated conditions, Kymlicka points out, because the benefits they might draw from it (notably a wage) would enable them to realize other goods, and they have a right not to count work as an essential part of their own vision of the good life. Not only must we refrain from saying that work is central because that would disregard the irreducible internal pluralism between goods and because of the epistemic impossibility of demonstrating it. On political grounds also, asserting the centrality of work as a normative principle would be unjust. It would breach the neutrality of the state and the respect we owe to all since it would favour a particular conception of the good over others.

Arneson arrives at a similar conclusion but through an argument based on the very logic of perfectionism. Precisely because there is an internal pluralism between the different constituent features of the good life, a consistent perfectionist politics (which Arneson does not think is the right way to think about politics) must seek a translation of it through institutionally secured external pluralism, that is, by ensuring that state actions refrain from privileging some conceptions of the good over others:

> Given the great number and variety of the human goods that could enter into a life that ranks high by perfectionist criteria, in practical terms perfectionism will endorse policies that are very close to the stance of state neutrality with respect to meaningful work.
>
> **(Arneson 1987, 526)**

As in Kymlicka's case, the point about internal pluralism leads to a demand for institutionally enshrined external pluralism. This explains why, despite the prevalence of work as a central concern and value in the socialist tradition, Arneson argued in 1987 that socialist justice would not be realized by enforcing meaningful work for all. He has since rejected this conclusion (in Arneson 2009), but the reasons stated in his initial 1987 piece continue to be enlightening as one of the strong 'cases against work'. The anti-perfectionist stance of 1987 made it clear that socialist justice should be concerned with ensuring the satisfaction of preferences for all, which would be best served by a market organized on socialist principles. Arneson's conclusion outlined both normative and efficiency-based concerns that would prevent even a socialist political program from making work politically central. This is significant: It is not just political liberals that worry about the political implications of the thesis of the centrality of work but political philosophers with socialist aims as well.

The ideas of state neutrality, toleration, and of respect for alternative conceptions of the good are clear worries about the political implications of the centrality of work. It is worth briefly reviewing one instantiation of this worry, both because it is a famous one that articulates the rejection of the centrality of work on political grounds in particularly sophisticated and detailed fashion, and because it does so by emphasizing a conceptual point that will be at the heart of the argument in favour of work in the second part of the book. This is the book by Philippe Van Parijs, published in 1995, *Real Freedom for All.*

This conceptual point just alluded to comes into view if we recall that the book's protracted argument in favour of universal basic income began in a critical confrontation with Rawls which highlighted the latter's ambivalent attitude to work. One of the key points of criticism following the first publication of the *Theory of Justice* targeted the nexus between fair distribution of primary goods and individual attitudes to work. The Difference Principle, critics emphasized (Musgrave 1974), seemed to favour individuals who chose not to work or not to work to their full capacity. This, the critics argued, could be construed as a breach of the neutrality principle in favour of idlers. Rawls conceded the point and changed the formulation of his Difference Principle as a result, adding leisure among the primary goods (Rawls 1974). He did this because he wanted to avoid what was for him an unwelcome, unintended consequence of the principle's application. His sensitivity to the criticism highlighted a key assumption underlying his conception of the just social order. Rawls did not mean to favour 'idlers', people who deliberately choose to work little or not at all (prefiguring the people interviewed by David Frayne in *The Refusal of Work*), not only because this would be a breach of the neutrality principle but also because it would contradict a baseline assumption regarding the well-ordered society, namely that the latter relies on a principle of active cooperation and reciprocal contribution through work. For Rawls, this principle of reciprocity constituted a fundamental social-theoretical assumption regarding the well-ordered society he tried to model. As such it contributes to the legitimate claims citizens are entitled to make on social wealth. Social welfare is owed to individuals on the basis of their contribution to the social order in accordance with their talent. This strongly held view of reciprocity led him to famously argue that 'those who surf all day off Malibu must find a way to support themselves and would not be entitled to public fund' (Rawls 1988).

In his 1991 article, 'Why Surfers Should Be Fed: The Liberal Case for an Unconditional Basic Income' and in a much more extensive manner in *Real Freedom for All*, Van Parijs questioned Rawls' altering of the difference principle precisely because of the privileging of work it revealed. Such a privileging, he argued, contradicts the principles of state neutrality and value pluralism, since it unduly favours one particular conception of the good, the individual commitment to work, over alternative conceptions favouring leisure or even outright idleness. The 1995 book developed the argument much further, using a sophisticated combination of normative and neo-classical economic arguments to defend the right of 'idlers' (people voluntarily choosing not to work, or to work less than they could) to have their own vision of the good supported by the state. This, the book aimed to show, would best be achieved, on both normative and efficiency considerations, through a universal basic income financed at the highest level possible.

Several aspects of Van Parijs' argument pushed the rejection of the centrality of work on political grounds into new territories, formulating conclusions that were directly antagonistic to intuitions linking justice to productive, reciprocal contribution. First, there was the central 'external assets argument'. Given the principles of value pluralism and state neutrality, which prohibit favouring one conception of the good over others, individuals who choose not to work have a rightful claim to an equal share of the wealth created by those who work, since they were fully entitled in the first place to choose not to work. Since work is only one individual preference among others, it has no special claim on the sharing of social wealth, whatever one's actual contribution to it. This is a direct rebuttal of the principle of reciprocity.

A second, even more counter-intuitive argument was the idea of 'employment rents'. In the grand calculation of endowments that needs to occur to ensure fair and optimal calculation of the basic income, the goods that matter are not just external endowments, that is, assets measured in prices, and internal endowments, 'talents' of all kinds (or their absence), which must be added to the mix to compensate for undeserved differentials in abilities, but also jobs. Jobs in a world where unemployment is economically detrimental are themselves 'assets'. Indeed, Van Parijs argues, for reasons explained by contemporary wage theory, these rare assets in fact attract higher income than they normally would in an ideal, 'Walrasian' market, that is, a market where prices (and wages) perfectly reflect the equilibrium of supply and demand. Since they are precious resources, that is, assets that in an economically non-perfect world are in greater demand than can be provided, and since those who enjoy these jobs receive a surplus income (an income that is higher than what those who are not in the job would accept), they need to be considered as taxable assets, the rent of which those without work are entitled to given the previous external assets argument. Work, in the form of waged work, becomes 'central' in this case, but in a very specific sense, to the extent, namely, that it is a privilege that those who don't share in have a rightful claim against (1995, 109). Those who choose not to work, the voluntarily unemployed, in fact do others (the employed and the involuntarily unemployed) a service because they 'give up their share of that asset and thereby leave more of it for others', and therefore, on anti-perfectionist grounds, they 'should not be deprived of a fair share of its value' (ibid.). In consequence, precisely because they choose not to work, 'idlers' in fact should receive a portion of the tax on work, a rent justified by the fact that it is a valuable asset to others. In fact, it is this tax on work that is to fund a UBI at a higher level than would otherwise be possible.

In yet another paradoxical conclusion, a '*job-sharing* strategy, say through a compulsory reduction in maximum working time, is bound to perform worse than basic income as a strategy against unemployment, from a real-libertarian standpoint' (Van Parijs 1995, 109). Beyond issues of practicability, making jobs central in policies that are specifically targeted at unemployment is counter-productive by comparison with the basic income, because it lowers the tax base that would otherwise be distributed, which in turn unjustly deprives those who choose not to work from the extra income they would otherwise get in a context without working time reduction.

Finally, Van Parijs doubles-down on the paradox when he argues that his basic income scheme will make it easier to choose work for the sake of it, in relative independence of the income generated by it:

> the higher the grant, the easier it is to create one's own job by becoming self-employed, to work part-time or to accept a lower wage in order to get a job that has a non-pecuniary feature (including training opportunities that improve future pecuniary prospects) to which one attaches particular importance. … With a high basic income, it can safely be predicted that all those who wish to perform paid work will actually do so (abstracting from search periods), whether as waged or self-employed workers.
>
> **(1995, 126)**

In other words, the best way to ensure work as a chosen good becomes realistically attainable for many peoplewithout penalising those who prefer leisure or idleness is to renounce the centrality of work as a goal of public policy altogether and instead adopt a scheme which, at first sight, replaces the need for all work (since it covers basic needs). Gorz had argued in similar fashion a decade or so earlier when he moved himself from a platform of working time reduction to the universal basic income idea (Gorz 1999, 83).

The sophistication and paradoxical nature of Van Parijs' book make it a tremendous challenge, even a provocation, for defenders of work as a central pillar of a just polity. As we saw, the book specifically challenges the idea of reciprocity, the old principle according to which 'if a man shall not work, he shall not eat' (Paul in 2 Thessalonians 3:10), which Rawls had reformulated using a more contemporary, American type of 'idlers'. Following the book, a rich debate was reignited regarding the normative merits of the principle of reciprocity (see Widerquist 2006 for a list of the main authors involved, which includes most of the leading contemporary political philosophers). To affirm or reject the value of reciprocity in the theory of justice, contemporary political philosophers proceed by attempting to establish the ground, nature, and extent of claims each individual is entitled to raise against others and against the collective. Is claiming a share of wealth to which one has not contributed 'parasitic' on those who have? Is it a form of exploitation of those who work by those who refuse to? Or is it those who have the chance to own external assets (independent wealth and formal employment) who in fact benefit from an unfair advantage, meaning that those who are not-employed (voluntarily or not) deserve a compensation, in the form of a share of the surplus the workers produce? These are the kinds of questions considered in these debates. What remains largely unthematized is just what we noted earlier on about the exact status of the notion of reciprocal contribution in Rawls. The principle serves not just normative purposes, as the justification for individual claims to a share in social wealth. It is also a descriptive, 'ontological' assumption, an assumption expressed from the point of view of social theory, not of value theory, about the role of work in the very existence and 'reproduction' of society, and this in two fundamental senses: first, in the basic, material sense that work is needed for society to be reproduced; and second, that the sharing of work among participants, captured in the concept of 'cooperation', grounds a social bond whose normative force is not well captured by the grammar of claims one may rightfully raise against others. Reciprocity through active contribution creates a form of solidarity which translates into the rights and duties that constitute reciprocal support through co-participation in social life. This is an entirely different approach from the one taken in contemporary political philosophy, which focuses on the question of who is entitled to what share of wealth redistribution on the basis of individually owned property. The second part of the book (Section 12.4 in particular) develops this alternative approach and does so with Rawls as one of its main references.

From this point of view, the deeply paradoxical nature of Van Parijs' real-libertarian rejection of the work ethic reserves one final surprise. One of the key insights behind his idea of taxing the 'employment rent' (sharing the wealth created by those who work among all) is that it in fact redresses one of the major injustices of the current system, which is that most of the wealth, status, and power goes to those who have achieved good positions in formal employment, to the detriment of those who have not: those in jobs considered 'low-skilled', those who cannot find work, those whose work is not recognized as such because it is not engaged in for a wage (many types of care work), those who need to do 'double shifts' in order to earn a wage at the same time as they look after dependents (see the conclusion of the 1991 article for a lucid statement of this insight). Van Parij's fundamental aim with the UBI is to allow each and every person to be granted the material means, the 'real freedom', to achieve their individual life goals. But a secondary aim is also to ensure fair compensation for all the kinds of work that are actually performed in the reproduction of society but go unrecognized and unrewarded in the current structure of market economies. Paradoxically, this very insight overlaps with one of the key intuitions at the heart of the positive case for work.

As the Introduction explained, to respond to the objections against the centrality of work presented in this chapter requires drawing on substantive arguments that can only be presented and justified in full much later in the book. Therefore, we will have to wait until the right moment comes to pick them up again. With this chapter, the first part of the book, which canvassed the 'case against work' by critically reconstructing its main theoretical sources, comes to a close. The next chapter dedicated to feminist perspectives on work provides the hinge that connects the two parts of the book and that will take us to the partwhere the 'case for work' is made in its own terms.

PART II
THE CASE FOR WORK

9 Feminism's Ambivalent Attitude to Work

This chapter considers the extensive treatment work has received in feminist writings through successive generations (Ferguson 2019 for a lucid presentation of key moments). By the vague term 'feminist writings' is meant theoretical enquiries in any field (including in the natural sciences) that have feminist concerns as part of their core theoretical (methodological, conceptual, historical, empirical) assumptions.

Many of the injustices and harms suffered by women throughout history, in the most diverse social and cultural contexts, have been linked to aspects of work, whether some of the most tedious or arduous tasks were overwhelmingly reserved for women or their social contributions were not valued and recognized, or they were excluded from the opportunity to participate in work and thereby receive full social and political recognition. Empirically, therefore, work is a highly problematic category from a feminist point of view, as it has been and remains a form of experience, framed by social and economic institutions and underpinned by cultural representations, through which female disadvantage has been consistently expressed and entrenched. Many feminist texts can be cited in the case against work. At the same time though, feminist writers throughout the generations have been sensitive to the distinction that needs to be made between, on the one hand, the negative traits of work as it is organized in their society, and on the other the positive contributions work can make to women's lives, including in their striving for emancipation. Many feminist texts provide strong vindications of the general argument much of this book relies upon, which invites us to distinguish between the factual organization of work and what work could bring to individuals and communities if it was organized differently.

Among the many theoretical innovations brought about by feminist theorizing, one is particularly important for this book. This is the importance a particular strand of feminist theory has given to issues of reproduction, both sexual and social reproduction, not only as key topics to study in their own rights, but also as suggesting a specific perspective from which to consider

The Case for Work. Jean-Philippe Deranty, Oxford University Press. © Jean-Philippe Deranty (2024).
DOI: 10.1093/oso/9780192887146.003.0010

culture and society. The case for work that is developed after this chapter attempts to take up this inspiration from feminist theorizing. The second part of the book relies on the extension of the feminist concern for social reproduction that is already suggested by major feminist scholars and makes an extended concept of reproduction the foundation for the case for work it puts forward.

For these two sets of reasons, feminist writings on work thus provide the hinge allowing us to move from the case against work to the case for work.

The issue of manageability, that is, the difficulty in finding a manageable way to deal with all the relevant literatures, is even more acute in this chapter than in the previous ones. Feminist perspectives and feminist concerns on significant social problems, like the centrality of work, mobilize knowledge and conceptual discussions that stem from many disciplinary perspectives, involving both social and natural sciences: from biology and evolutionary theory, history, anthropology, sociology, and politics, and of course philosophy. Since the 1970s, feminist scholarship in all these areas has grown considerably. In order to chart a walkable path across such mountains of relevant scholarship, the chapter restricts itself to two simple tasks. First, to illustrate, by reference to a few important feminist authors, the key ambivalence about work noted above: that is, empirical condemnation of how work participates in women's oppression, which is countervailed by the promissory potential many feminist thinkers have found in work. And second, why the focus on reproduction is essential to theories of human society.

9.1 The Origins of Female Oppression

In every generation, feminist scholars must struggle anew against attempts to naturalize gender inequality, that is, to interpret natural-scientific data and the apparent implications of natural-scientific methods in a way that is supposed to causally explain, and thus implicitly justify, the disadvantaged status of women as a group by comparison with men. In every new generation, a similar pattern can be observed. Characteristic features indicating some type of dimorphism between the sexes are highlighted and a narrative deriving from these noted differences then purports to explain how they causally lead to the minority status of women. Historical examples of such characteristic differences have been physical strength, gonadal difference (egg versus sperm), child-bearing capacity, hormonal differences (men as angry warriors, women as empathetic and weak), neuronal difference (male versus female brains). Recent narratives draw on Darwin's theories of sexual selection. Arguments are mounted to show how the pressure to maximize reproductive fitness applies differentially to bodies dimorphically distinguished, and how these differential logics causally produce female subordination. For instance, to take a characteristic example, in Symond's 1979 *Evolution of Sexuality*, the different reproductive logics followed by human males and females are explained in reference to differences in their gametes: females having fewer, larger gametes, is assumed to lead to a more selective approach in choice of mate, while the smaller, more multitudinous gametes of men are supposed to lead them to attempt to inseminate as many females as possible, and to enter into competition with other men, notably for the control of resources. In turn, the time devoted to intra-male competition is supposed to require of males that they seek to control female sexuality to ensure paternity of their offspring (Liesen 2007 for a lucid, critical summary from the perspective of feminist evolutionary theorists). Work is implicated in all these narratives because the generic social division arising from sex-based differences overlaps with the sexual division of labour. For instance, differences in physical strength or the necessities attached to child-bearing and child-rearing are supposed to explain differential productive activities, notably the fact that big-game hunting is reserved for men and gathering and small-game hunting for women.

Feminist scholars have different strategies at their disposal to counter the naturalizing effects of such approaches. They can question the dimorphism from which conclusions about social status are drawn. Cordelia Fine for instance has convincingly shown that there was little scientific evidence that gender differences are rooted in the neuronal body (Fine 2010) or the hormonal body (Fine 2017). They can question the inferences leading from dimorphic differences to conclusions about social activities, as when anthropologists problematize the assumptions behind 'man the hunter' hypothesis, regarding for instance the physical limitations allegedly preventing women from engaging in game hunting (Quinn 1977; Mukhopadhay and Higgins 1988). A third strategy, which we briefly review in this section because it puts work at the centre, consists in mounting counter-narratives of how differences in biology should be interpreted in social terms. We will look at three important feminist scholars across three generations, who have provided their own narrative of the origins of women's oppression and have made work a central element in them. These narratives offer the first illustration of the ambivalent status of work in feminist thinking.

As an eminent representative of American first-wave feminism, Charlotte Perkins Gilman's writings, notably *Women and Economics* (1898) and *The Home* (1910) are notable for the place they reserve to work. Gilman is one of the strong, early feminist voices to make women's emancipation fundamentally dependent on overcoming the sexed division of labour as it is organized in her time, which dictates that man is destined by his biology to be active in the labour market while women are naturally destined to be secluded in the home and to have their activities restricted to the roles of housewife, housemaid, or prostitute. Female emancipation, Gilman argues in her books and in her public advocacy, means not just full political participation through the vote, but also and in fact primarily, full participation in social production, outside the stultifying atmosphere of 'the home'. What is particularly significant for our concerns in this book, is that these classical arguments are grounded, typically for her time, in a counter-narrative about the evolutionary origins of the sexual division of labour. One major claim arising from her alternative Darwinian story about the early origins of the division of labour is that '*woman was the first worker*' (1910, 104). By this, Gilman means that really productive work, the invention of useful crafts and tools that helped the species to survive was done by women, while men's typical activities, like war-mongering or shamanism, were productively useless.

Her argument is based on speculations about natural selection, and not sexual selection. Motherhood in an evolutionary perspective is synonymous with the complete dedication of the female to the survival and well-being of the offspring. In turn, this deeply ingrained urge to care, which is characteristic of female beings, translates into the search to find the best ways to protect and nourish. The root of human inventiveness and ingenuity, therefore, is in fact to be found in the female concern for the preservation of the species:

> Maternal energy is the force through which have come into the world both love and industry. It is through the tireless activity of this desire, the mother's wish to serve the young, that she began the first of the arts and crafts whereby we live. (…) Maternal energy, working externally through our elaborate organism, is the source of productive industry, the main current of social life.
>
> **(1898, 129)**

We find here an early expression of a trope that appears regularly in feminist writing, that there is something specific about early female work that made it more worthwhile than what were typically male activities. This line of speculation continues until today, for instance in debates in anthropology about gathering and small-game hunting, as activities typically undertaken by women in hunter-gatherer societies, and whether they bring in more calories than big-game hunting, the activity reserved almost universally for men. A famous debate in the field is whether big-game hunting in fact has anything to do with providing food and is not instead a form of social signalling rather than a productive activity (Hawkes 1990, to cite only her first article on the topic).

A *locus classicus* of second-wave feminism in which work appears centrally in the narrative about the origins of women's oppression is the first two chapters of Beauvoir's *Second Sex*. Work plays an essential part in what she sees as 'the key to the whole mystery' of how women became subjugated by men early on in human history. Because of her biology, Beavoir argues, woman has to take on the largest share of the biological tasks involved in reproducing the species. But what truly characterizes the human species from her existentialist perspective is 'transcendence', the ability to posit human ends not found in the given, which provide meaning to it and transform life from a mere biological phenomenon to something that has value. Because they are less encumbered by the biological constraints of sexual reproduction, men have more opportunity to dedicate themselves to activities that express and realize this capacity for transcendence. Biology therefore unfairly favours and unfairly penalizes each one of the two genders in the realization of the human being's ontological destiny. Both genders share in the striving for transcendence, but only one of them is in a position to dedicate themselves to it fully. As he is able freely to assert himself as transcendence, and thereby to claim the full ontological status of human beings, man is the one who is in a position to define the other gender as Other. Woman becomes the Other of man because her role in reproduction prevents her from fully asserting herself as existential freedom.

Work plays the central role in Beauvoir's speculative narrative, because it is the qualitative difference between the work that women and men typically did early on that explains how the superiority of men over women became socially established. Women's work was either animalistic in kind ('breast-feeding are not activities but animal functions') or as domestic work to which women were condemned because of child care and weaker physiology, mere drudgery, 'locking her into repetition and immanence' and producing nothing new or valuable, just as Hannah Arendt would analyse labour a decade or so later (see Veltman 2010 for the parallels). Only men's work was true to human being's ontology, which is 'to posit ends and project paths to them'. *Homo faber* was male, Beauvoir stipulates in her reversal of the 'women as first worker' thesis, and this, just as equally as its importance for the material subsistence of the species, matters for the latter's ontological destiny. In a clear, early rendition of the 'man the hunter' trope, she explains and justifies that hunting was always socially favoured over gathering and child care, and that 'throughout humanity, superiority has been granted not to the sex that gives birth but to the one that kills' (68–69). In subsequent history, men entrenched their initial superiority through institutions, laws, myths, and rationalizing stories, but this superiority was established in the different works the two genders performed.

As Beauvoir notes, however, what appears as a curse in one mode of social organization becomes a merely contingent factor in another, if the biological facts about childbirth and breastfeeding can be alleviated through technical progress and a social reorganization of reproduction becomes concretely possible. The more women can be liberated from the burdens associated with the biological necessities of species reproduction, the more their objective social situation allows them to achieve status equality with men, notably as they can embrace forms of work that genuinely allow them to posit their own ends and 'project paths to them', as well as giving them financial independence. While work was directly implicated in the emergence of female oppression in the early stages of the sex-based division of labour, it becomes one of the vectors of emancipation in modern times, as women's enslavement to sexual reproduction can be neutralized:

> When she is productive, active, she regains her transcendence; in her projects she concretely affirms her status as subject; in connection with the aims she pursues, with the money, and the rights she takes possession of, she makes trial of and senses her responsibility. Many women are aware of these advantages, even among those in very modest positions. I heard a charwoman declare, while scrubbing the stone floor of a hotel lobby: 'I never asked anybody for anything; I succeeded all by myself.' She was as proud of her self-sufficiency as a Rockefeller.
> **(Beauvoir 2010, 641)**

Simone de Beauvoir does not make work the sole, or even the principal vector of female emancipation. In a move that anticipates later radical feminist views, she notes that gainful employment is at best a steppingstone for a true challenge to patriarchal rule (2010, 641). However, even though *The Second Sex* ends with a qualification about the role of paid employment in women's emancipation, it remains the case that work as activity of production, as material implementation of life projects (both individual and collective), is for Beauvoir the concrete expression of the human capacity for transcendence, what she and the other French existentialists understood by '*praxis*' (Deranty 2016). We saw all the problems that are entailed in Arendt's description of labour activities and her strict separation between labour and work. Beauvoir's traditionalist picture of the early human community then raises critical questions: wasn't much of the work men traditionally did also an answer to biological demands and were they not themselves steeped in repetition and drudgery? Conversely, why couldn't activities of care and activities performed in the home also be described, *qua* activities, as being themselves productive and creative?

This latter conceptual move is precisely the theoretical gesture performed by Maria Mies in her own historical reconstruction of the origins of women's oppression, notably in 'Social Origins of the Sexual Division of Labour', which forms the second chapter of her influential *Patriarchy and Accumulation on a World Scale*. Like de Beauvoir, Mies underpins her historicist, materialist approach with a naturalistic layer, by integrating biological dimensions to explain the differential social treatment of the sexes via the division of labour (1986, 52 for a clear statement). In her case, however, child-bearing, nursing, and child-rearing are reinterpreted as factors making of women 'the first workers', echoing Charlotte Gilman's earlier attempt to link reproductive tasks to an original concept of work, by emphasizing the productive and creative dimensions entailed in reproduction. While Gilman emphasized ingenuity and inventiveness, however, which made women the first industrious gender, the first inventors and engineers as it were, Mies finds the productive aspects of women's work already in their biological, reproductive capacities:

> women can experience their whole body as productive, not only their hands or their heads. Out of their body they produce new children as well as the first food for these children. It is of crucial importance for our subject that women's activity in producing children and milk is understood as truly human, that is, conscious, social activity. Women appropriated their own nature, their capacity to give birth and to produce milk in the same way as men appropriated their own bodily nature, in the sense that their hands and head, etc., acquired skills through work and reflection to make and handle tools. In this sense, the activity of women in bearing and rearing children has to be understood as work.
>
> (1986, 53)

Not only do child-bearing and child-rearing count as work, in the sense in which Marx defines it in a famous early passage of *Capital*, that is, as the introduction to the book also recalled, as intentional, technical action aiming to produce outcomes destined to satisfy human needs (Mies 1986, 50; Marx 1991 [1867], 173). In fact, childbearing, nursing, and rearing are the primordial meanings of work for her, historically and even conceptually. Producing children through one's own body and producing food for children out of one's own body represent the paradigmatic examples of work, if the definition of human work is that it is *production of life*, both in the sense that it reproduces life and it produces for life.

From this primordial sense of work as production of life, which is rooted in the individual's own life, Mies extends her argument to encompass external nature and more mediated modes of 'production'. First, she suggests, in a line of argument that announces her later work in ecofeminism, women's whole-body involvement in their labour favours a profound knowledge of their own nature, and by extension, through introspective analogy, of generative processes in external nature as well (1986, 54). Based on this knowledge of self and external nature, and in a further extension of the idea of women's work as productive of life, Mies then brings forward the other key notion of *subsistence work*. The concept at first has a historical meaning. Referencing anthropological research, Mies argues that women's specific relation to self and to nature would have made them the inventors of agricultural tools, such as the digging stick and the hoe. As gatherers and then as the first cultivators, women were the ones on whom the species relied essentially in its early days to survive. The survival of humankind for Mies was due much more to 'woman-the-gatherer' than to 'man-the-hunter'.

> Women's productivity is the precondition of all other human productivity, not only in the sense that they are always the producers of new men and women, but also in the sense that the first social division of labour, that between female gatherers (later also cultivators) and predominantly male hunters, could take place only on the basis of a developed female productivity. Female productivity consisted, above all, in the ability to provide the daily subsistence, the guarantee of survival, for the members of the clan or band. Women necessarily had to secure the 'daily bread', not only for themselves and their children, but also for the men if they had no luck on their hunting expeditions, because hunting is an 'economy of risk'.
>
> **(1986, 55)**

What explains the origins of oppression of women by men are tragic consequences of the initial sexual division of labour. Mies contends that women's work is characterized by a continuous extension of their productive capacities, obeying a logic of internal growth that is respectful of life: from childbirth to child feeding, to rearing, to 'growing and making grow', to social cooperation. Men's work, by contrast, is grounded in bodily experiences and object-relations that are not intrinsically productive, but rather treat the environment and the beings in it, including the other sex, as otherness to appropriate, control, and as the case may be, to destroy. While women's intrinsic attitude to work is inherently productive and creative, men's attitude to work is aggressive and destructive. This duality in dealing with otherness is reflected in the tools men specialize in, namely weapons, tools of destruction and of control by the threat of death. This duality in fundamental 'object-relations' becomes entrenched to the detriment of women as a group with the rise of agriculture. Cautiously following Elisabeth Fisher (Fisher 1979), Mies argues that it was the mastery of techniques of breeding, combined with the monopoly over the uses of lethal weapons, which transformed human society, from a stage where productive female work could sustain symbolic male activities in relative harmony, to one where male economic activity became the systematic and ruthless extraction of goods and values from women's bodies and women's activities (Mies 1986, 63). Once this structure of subjugation was in place, institutions and cultural ideologies developed to keep women in their place, as the subjected 'other' of men, to be used for their specific benefits (Mies 1986, 67).

Knowledge about the early history of humanity has been significantly revised and updated since the publication of Maria Mies' classic. It is likely that specialists in early human history find this chapter of *Patriarchy and Accumulation on a World Scale* outdated today, in its speculations about the first inventions, the structures of early societies or the scale and structure of the oppression suffered by women with the invention of agriculture. However, even though Mies' reconstruction might be contradicted by new knowledge in many of its details, its emphasis on the material aspects of early human work, in particular on the essential contribution of women's work in the long early history of humanity, remains thought-provoking for reflections on work. This general lesson that can still be drawn from Mies' chapter is confirmed if we return to Gerda Lerner's classic history of patriarchy, which was published in the same year (Lerner 1986) and which mobilizes an even larger amount of archaeological and anthropological information available at the time. The first two chapters of Lerner's book overlap with Mies' general point that childbearing, nursing, and rearing tasks, far from preventing women from working, would have created instead a material context in which, not only did women perform essential work for the human collective, but they would have developed their own knowledge of the natural environment, and would have been the ones most likely to invent and perfect key artefacts at the beginning of technological evolution, such as carrying, digging, and grinding tools.

However factually erroneous these historical accounts might have become, what matters for this book is the fundamental concerns animating them. In these retrospective enquiries, work has an intrinsically ambivalent role. It is directly implicated in the emergence of women's oppression, through the asymmetries made possible by the sexual division of labour. And yet, productive, creative, other-sustaining activities are essential aspects that come to light in these speculative narratives. Not only do they account for the specificity of women's experiences, but they also emphasize the intrinsic value of women's work, for themselves and for the human community. As they emphasize the material and technical aspects of women's work, they also suggest how work can become a powerful leverage for the emancipation of women. Most importantly, in the course of reconstructing the origins of women's oppression, these accounts formulate a rich concept of work, which highlights its specific features and its essential nature for human survival and flourishing. This ambivalence towards work and this conceptual lesson that can be drawn from feminist enquiries can be witnessed again in enquiries about modern society and the modern forms of female oppression.

9.2 Work and the Modern Oppression of Women

The history of feminist scholarship is riven with tensions and open conflicts, not just because of theoretical and methodological disagreements, which are natural in any area of enquiry, but also because of the practical dimension of feminist perspectives. Since feminist enquiries aim to denounce and address different forms of women's oppression, they are intimately tied to particular contexts and the different groups involved in them, notably the group of women in those contexts. As a result, there is an unavoidable tension between the general claims that any theory aims to produce and the particularity of contexts. Concretely, this has meant that general claims generated by one group of women to denounce their own oppression have often been viewed as inadequate by other groups of women living in different, and sometimes even in the same, contexts. The silver lining of this conflict-ridden history is that feminism, unlike few other perspectives in the contemporary humanities and human sciences, enables us to see the connections between different aspects of modernity, which otherwise might be studied separately. The rich diversity of feminist enquiries unveils the dark side of modernity and shows the connections between different aspects of women's experiences, where work each time is a central component. These dark aspects of modernity include colonization and imperial domination, new forms of racial oppression, including new forms of slavery, and new forms of exploitation and social domination, linked to capitalist industrialization.

Historically, it is the latter set of issues that have been predominant in feminist scholarship (however, see Freedman 2017 for an anthology including voices from around the world, not just Western feminism). The emergence of industrial capitalism in a few countries in Western Europe was accompanied by a restructuring of gender relations and of the social, political, and economic place reserved for women. Modern capitalism functions on the basis of a redefinition of the relationship between those who 'take work' and those who 'give work' (to use the German phrases), namely a generalization of the wage relation. The wage relation, as we saw in Chapters 2 and 3, rationalizes the way in which 'living labour' is made available and utilized so as to maximize the new means of production. As such the wage relation is a constitutive dimension of the gigantic shift that takes place once the production of value for exchange on commodity markets overtakes the initial function of work, which is the production of value for direct use. One key aspect of the wage relation and of production for exchange is the new carving up of social reality it entails, between a formal realm of production on the one hand, and a private realm of reproduction on the other. This separation between social and economic spheres is paralleled by a separation between genders that is both real and taps into a deep social imaginary: men do the 'real work' for the formal economy, while women are relegated in the home to do domestic and care activities (see the lucid, seminal formulation by Benton 1969, and Illich 1980 who coins the term 'shadow work'). Men's work is viewed as real both because it is the one creating and being remunerated with abstract value (profit and wage) and it is supposed to be truly arduous and creative, while women's work is supposed to be simply an extension of natural tendencies and performed out of love, and thus is not real work. The underlying premise is that both kinds of activities naturally complement each other in the family unit. To this separation between types of activities within the family (real work versus activities based on natural propensity) is attached a strict separation between social and political rights and duties: full legal autonomy, rights of political participation, and later on right to social welfare for the 'active' gender; minority status, no right to political participation, and welfare accessed through the husband for the 'passive' one (see Deranty 2000 for an early expression of this view in Hegel, as well as his implicit problematization of it).

The first waves of feminism were especially sensitive to this phenomenon. As we saw, it is the starting point of Charlotte Gilman's reflections. It features centrally in Beauvoir's depiction of contemporary women's oppression. It is a key feature in 'liberal' feminism. It is the central issue in Betty Friedan's *Feminine Mystique* (1963), for instance. It is a key concern in Catharine Mackinnon's version of radical feminism (Mackinnon 1989) or in Carole Pateman's celebrated *Sexual Contract*.

This modern separation of a sphere of production from a sphere of reproduction and its attendant sexual division of labour, has been the source of injustice and suffering for women both in the home and outside the home. As women were relegated to housework and the work of care under the pretense of natural predisposition, activities linked to house and care work became devalued or even invisibilized, including a large part of that work that is arguably repetitive and unfulfilling. That this work would be done, and would be done by women, was just taken for granted. As this work attracts no wage, and wage and money are the eminent forms of social valuation in contemporary society, the gender attached to house and care work became structurally disadvantaged on labour markets. As a result, throughout modern history, in all kinds of geographical contexts, it is women who have had to bear the larger share of low-paid, precarious, and part-time work. Even when they were able to enter secure and symbolically valued work, the stigma of being woman entering the manly world of real production created all kinds of material and symbolic obstacles, from promotion to pay inequality. Conversely, when some professions attracted a high proportion of women, this invariably meant symbolic and material devaluation. 'Feminization' in work has meant occupations taking on features of work conditions that are typical of what women have encountered, irrespective of the gender of the worker: that is, precariousness in all aspects of employment and work activity.

If by work is meant waged work as it has historically been organized in the last two hundred years of modern capitalism, then it is beyond doubt that work has been responsible for countless forms of injustice and suffering for women. Asserting the centrality of work in this specific sense is therefore highly dubious. However, as we will now see, modern feminist scholarship is far from rejecting work in a blanket fashion.

9.3 Domestic Work and Social Reproduction

Feminist thinking underwent a substantial surge during the radical decade of the 1970s. Feminist demands were one of the most prominent voices in the waves of protests against established forms of inequality that swept through societies at the time. The central theoretical approach shared among many protest groups, including feminist ones, was Marxism. Famously however, the 'marriage of Marxism and feminism' never really took place then (Hartmann 1979; Arruzza 2013). Many tense debates opposed Marxist feminists and feminists using other approaches, and tensions were also high between Marxist, socialist, and materialist feminists (see Gimenez 2000 for a useful discussion of the different terms). More recently, these old debates and Marxist ideas have been revisited again in Social Reproduction Theory (Bhattacharya 2017; Mezzadri 2019). For this book's interest, these old debates and their recent reprisal are highly significant. Kathi Weeks' seminal book is substantially inspired by the writings of the theorists and activists involved in the Wages for Housework movement, one of the key movements of that period. More generally, these discussions highlight precisely what this chapter aims to emphasize, namely, the great ambivalence of work from a feminist perspective, and as a key insight arising from this scholarship, the deep conceptual lesson that can be learnt from it.

A large part of the debate between Marxist and non-Marxist feminists, and indeed among materialist feminists themselves, revolves around the correct characterization of the relationship between capitalist exploitation and patriarchal domination. Beyond their disagreements, Marxist feminists all agree that women as a group are exploited in a specific way under capitalism. The ambivalence towards work comes from the fact that it is particularly important for them to highlight that women do work in the full sense of the term and that this work is important for society and for their family, indeed that it is essential. It is from these reflections that the notion of social reproduction has emerged as a key concept in social analysis. Reconstructing the detail of these debates would far outstretch the scope of this book (see Bryson 2003 and Mezzadri 2019 for lucid conceptual reconstructions). Instead, taking our lead from a lucid conceptual reconstruction by Mackinnon (1989, 60–81), from a non-Marxist, radical feminist perspective, a number of key theses formulated by some of the leading feminist thinkers can be highlighted, which show the ambivalent role of work in their thinking.

Let us begin with the negative aspects. A blatant form of injustice suffered by women in modern times is that most of them work and yet, for significant periods of time, receive no income for their work when the latter is performed in the home, and a lesser wage than men when that work is performed outside of the home. A large part of the discussions in the 1970s focused on domestic work and questioned how Marx's theory of surplus value and the law of value should be applied to best characterize it and the form of exploitation it entails. At the heart of these debates was the relationship between women's unpaid domestic work and the wage earned by men, the 'breadwinner' in a typical family setting (dalla Costa and James 1972; James 1973; Federici 1995). A key lesson from Marx's critique of modern political economy is that the wage is an essential element in the ideological obfuscation and economic exploitation experienced by workers. On the surface, the wage is the amount of money returned by the capitalist owner for an equivalent amount of value-producing labour provided by the worker. In reality, the worker receives only a portion of the value that the use of his labour-power has produced. The wage allows the worker to reproduce his labour-power, but the capitalist pockets the surplus-value created by the worker, based on the fact that it is he who owns the means of production. All the work that is performed in the home serves to 'reproduce' labour-power. To put it more concretely, among other things (notably the caring of children, the sick and the old) domestic work enables the wage workers to return to the factory every day having been fed, clothed, and with all their needs (including emotional and sexual ones) fulfilled. How does this domestic work relate to the core relationship between capitalist and worker and more specifically, how does it relate to the mediating element between them, the wage? Since the wage covers the reproduction of labour-power, does the man's wage entail as one of its constitutive parts also the work performed at home by women, given that, as noted, the latter is essential to reproduction? In this case domestic work is indirectly rewarded through the man's wage. Or does the breadwinner's wage in fact only cover the consumption of commodities for reproduction, leaving all the extra work performed at home by the woman unpaid? Such unpaid work is an essential element of the capitalist economy since it reproduces the factor that creates value (labour-power). Given that this domestic work is unpaid, does this mean that it increases surplus value, since a part of the worker's reproduction is taken care of without being included in the man's wage, and the wage is deducted from overall value but in this case only covers part of reproduction's expenses? And if that is the case, if unpaid women's work helps to increase surplus-value, then capitalism has a direct economic interest, beside ideological preferences, for keeping women in the home and having them reproduce labour-power for free (Gardiner 1979).

If women's work in the home is unpaid yet contributes to surplus-value, then we have a classic case of exploitation: a legal title and an institutional set-up (marriage and the single breadwinner family model) justifies what is in fact a swindle, namely work that creates value but receives no retribution for it. Is that all there is to women's exploitation? Another productive Marxist category that could be used to analyse women's situation is that of 'primitive accumulation'. In that case, we would look at women's exploitation as the outcome of a long historical process seeking to dispossess, devaluate and domesticate women, notably through violent interventions on their bodies (Federici 2004).

Or women's exploitation could be analysed as occurring via a 'mode of production' specific to gender relations, next to capitalistic exploitation which occurs via commodity production. That other mode of production would be patriarchal in the historical sense of an arbitrary power exercised by the *pater familias* on dependent members of the family (Delphy 1984, notably 'The Main Enemy' [1970]). From this point of view, modern societies present an odd combination of two modes of production, one centred on the wage relation, and the other harking back to much older times (see also Bennholdt-Thomsen 1988; and Bennett 2007, chapter 3, on similarities between medieval and modern work for women). In such a patriarchal mode of production, work is defined not by the technical and economic constraints operating in the competitive market economy, but by the arbitrary decisions of the family head. In formal terms, this kind of exploitation is akin to a relationship of slavery: How much is expected of women in terms of work effort, how much she will receive for herself in return, none of this is specified in a formal contract, except in highly exceptional circumstances. The amount of work fulfilled, the ways in which it is fulfilled (with more or less help, for instance regarding the availability of appliances), the objects of the work, all the features defining work, its ease or irksomeness, varies from woman to woman depending on the benevolence of her master, even if cultural norms place limits on this variability.

Another salient feature of domestic work (Mies 1988) is that in many circumstances, in countries in the Global South in particular, this work involves not just caring for the other family members, but also the production of goods, either for consumption by the family or indeed for sale on the market. In those cases, the unpaid work of women directly produces value without full retribution for it. When the housewife is also a wage-worker, she combines exploitation outside and exploitation inside the home. In many situations, this work from home that sells its outputs outside the home is informal work, which is characterized by low or no pay, potentially terrible working conditions and overall precariousness (Mezzadri 2020).

A lot of the time, the work performed by women in a domestic setting is not recognized as work, or at least as valuable work. The lack of economic reward matches the symbolic denial of recognition. In a society where money is the preeminent mode of social mediation, non-salaried activities become obscured from view. What is in fact essential work, the reproduction of lives, is not validated as such. Furthermore, many parts of domestic work seem to be mere drudgery. The more interesting work is often reserved for men, both inside and outside the home, with women taking on the tedious tasks. Here, exploitation takes on another meaning: it signals the forced assigning of one gender to the more menial parts of labour processes, both within and outside the homes. This form of exploitation has a distributive dimension: why should one gender in particular have to do the more tedious tasks?

Given all these aspects of exploitation, the thesis of the centrality of work seems untenable. Indeed, a key demand emerging from the feminist activists linked to Italian autonomism was the 'refusal of work'. If society's main institutions (home, school, university, factory) are under the sway of the logic of value-extraction, if society at large is akin to a 'social factory' fulfilling the functions required by capitalism, then only an overcoming of that logic as a whole can be the proper response to alienation and exploitation. The rejection of domestic work therefore should not be, as in first-wave feminism, to achieve full inclusion in formal work, but rather rejection of domestic work as part of the rejection of all (capitalistic) work (see Berg 2014 for a more recent formulation, critical of materialist feminist). Hence the famous statement from the Wages for Housework writers: 'Slavery to an assembly line is not liberation from slavery to a kitchen sink' (dalla Costa and James 1972, 48).

However, as Chapter 3 has shown, the autonomist refusal of work is refusal of capitalistically organized work, of work for the sake of abstract value. It is not refusal of work *tout court*. Indeed, a key operative category in autonomism is 'living labour', which denotes both individual productive life forces, and the capacity of socialized individuals to bring together their individual resources as a multitude to create a collective lifeworld. As we saw, the image of emancipated work in autonomist thinking, which was translated into a positive concept of biopolitics, appears not by positing a utopian antithesis of existing work beyond the system, but rather as liberation of the life forces, both individual and community-building, which capitalism oppresses and capitalizes on. The essential role of labour in the reproduction and development of individual and collective life is demonstrated in the same movement as the theory of its domination and exploitation unfolds.

The same logic operates in materialist feminist analyses and in more recent social reproduction theory. Just as they highlight the many ways in which gendered work is devalued, exploited, coerced, invisibilized, and so on, the force of these critical analyses rests precisely on the fact that they simultaneously show how much this work is in fact 'real work', that is, entails technical knowledges and skills and is intrinsically productive, productive namely of all the many elements that are required for human lives to be reproduced 'daily and generationally' (very clearly in Laslett and Brenner 1989). As such, all this 'reproductive' work, which is also literally productive (of human lives, human relations, and the human collective), has value, first in the simple sense that it matters a lot. In fact, it is essential work since it is the work that ensures that the individual lives making up society are created and recreated in all of their dimensions; physically, emotionally, socially, and culturally. And it has value in the economic sense, in an explicit way when it is work that produces for markets outside the home, or because it is work that is necessary for capitalistic functioning (through the reproduction of labour-power), which capital externalizes onto families and women without fully paying for its costs.

The great ambivalence of work in materialist feminist writings is thus that work is the main vector of women's oppression in modern settings, and yet the analyses demonstrating this show at the same time how essential women's work is, for individual lives, for families and for the communities in which individual lives unfold. This work of reproduction is itself ambiguous in its outputs: it reproduces individual lives that will have to conform to capitalist settings. As such it contributes to the reproduction of the system. At the same time, however, it is work that produces human beings, human relations and the collective. The aspects of that work that warrant criticism, the fact that tedious tasks, or tasks that are the least valued, are often reserved for women, do not speak against the importance of women's work and the importance of work for women, but rather demand that the injustice entailed in the gendered division of labour be corrected. Once again, the injustice is all the more serious if work matters to the people performing it and for the outputs it produces. Beyond this ambivalent status of work in materialist feminist writings, a key conceptual lesson emerges from reading them.

9.4 Social Reproduction: Generalizing the Concept

For debates on the centrality of work, the focus on reproduction we owe to feminist scholarship is invaluable (Bakker 2007 is very useful for showing how extensive the concept is in some of its historical references). By lifting the veil on large sections of society where decisive work is performed and yet is taken for granted, what is brought into view more generally is the fundamental role of the work of each and everyone in the lives of every individual and of the collective as a whole. The feminist focus on women's work suggests a holistic vision of society, issuing a basic but fundamental insight of social ontology about what it takes for a social organization to allow individuals and the collective as such to be sustained over time, to 'reproduce' themselves. Once the veil is lifted on all the work women do, we realize that, beside the specific activities that are directly involved in the creation of profits and the receipt of wages, there is in fact a much larger continent of activities going on, which are necessary for the reproduction of individual and collective lives (Daniels 1987, from a non-Marxist perspective, highlights this well). The generalizing insight of social ontology, then, is that all this work of reproduction is needed not just for the production of abstract value, but much more fundamentally, for the production and reproduction of individual lives and of the collective life in which individuals live.

Paradoxically, such an insight was made possible by Marx and Engels already, precisely when they introduced the concept of reproduction next to that of production. This a paradoxical effect of Marx and Engels' reflections, since, as many Marxist feminists have shown, they undeniably failed to fully do justice to the significance of 'reproductive' work and did not consider the injustices linked to the gendered division of labour. Even in their failings, however, Marx and Engels' introduction of the concept of social reproduction makes it possible to consider in one synoptic view all the different types of activities that are involved in the 'reproduction' of individual lives and the collective in which these individual lives unfold. Once such a perspective is adopted, the work that women until very recently were exclusively in charge of doing (domestic work, housework, care work) is just one (large and significant section) of all the other activities that help to create, recreate and in the best of cases, aid in flourishing, individual and collective lives. This perspective then presents society as a whole and society in all of its specific structures and institutions as the outcome of both activities of 'production' and 'reproduction'.

Such an insight is not just 'ontological' or descriptive, but also entails intrinsic normative dimensions. It immediately encourages us to study the relationships between types of activities, what each brings specifically to the collective, how these different outputs are ranked culturally, what social and material rewards they attract, how these activities are organized and how such organization takes into account the needs and capacities of those who fulfil them, These are typically the questions feminists raise in relation to women's condition in contemporary society, but these questions are relevant generally for all individuals and all groups, notably in their interactions with each other. The feminist focus on social reproduction entails a decisive insight of social ontology and critical social theory about human societies.

When we consider human society in this way, as the outcome of individual and aggregated activities of work, the conceptual boundary between production and reproduction becomes very blurry. This is another insight that generalizes points raised by many feminist scholars when they insist that reproductive work is 'real work', both in the sense that it produces value (however contested the meaning of that concept) and is intrinsically productive. The fundamental intuition driving the case for work in the second part of this book relies on this idea. Ultimately, all (actually useful) work is both productive and reproductive at the same time. Every work activity produces an outcome, one that should fulfil a need. If it doesn't, then it is bullshit work or unproductive or unsustainable work. The notion of being productive is intrinsically normative. And in being productive of a useful outcome, work participates in the reproduction of individual and collective life and is thus reproductive in that sense.

These meanings of production and reproduction do not match their use in Marx and in Marxist feminism or indeed more generally in contemporary social and political theory, where production denotes work that makes material outputs which are either useful (use values) or commodifiable (entail exchange value), and reproduction denotes work that creates and recreates human lives. However, the expanded sense of social reproduction this book's argument proposes should be intuitively easy to accept. Indeed, as we will now see, it is in fact suggested by Marx and Engels themselves.

In chapter 23 of volume one of *Capital*, Marx introduced the notion of social reproduction through an analysis of the 'simple reproduction' of the capitalist economy. By introducing this term, he meant at first simply to add a set of diachronic factors to his overall analysis of how capital, once created through the extraction of surplus values, is accumulated. This refers to an apparently trivial aspect of all human societies, which is however crucial for political economy, namely that

> a society can no more cease to produce than it can cease to consume. When viewed, therefore, as a connected whole, and in the constant flux of its incessant renewal, *every social process of production is at the same time a process of reproduction*.
>
> **(Marx 1991 [1867], 711—emphasis JPD)**

Marx introduced the notion of reproduction in this short chapter with the aim of emphasizing the temporal aspects of capitalist self-reproduction and what they entail for capitalist exploitation. His aim was to show how 'by means of nothing but the continuity of the process, by simple reproduction, the characteristic result of capitalist production (becomes) a result which is constantly renewed and perpetuated' (716). The cyclical nature of capitalist value extraction ensures that all the main characteristics of that mode of production, notably the very particular relation of domination linking capitalist and worker, become entrenched over time. Marx needed to make this point at the start of this new section in the first volume of *Capital*, because it underpins the processes of accumulation this part, part seven, is dedicated to.

As he does this, however, Marx inadvertently opens up the perspective that will prove so crucial for feminist concerns. Considering the form of social organization that capitalism needs to be in order to be able to constantly 'renew and perpetuate itself' forces the political economist to analyse more precisely how one of the structural factors underpinning the entire capitalist mode of production is itself reproduced, namely labour-power. And this, in turn, means asking how the labourers themselves, whose labour-power is purchased by the capitalist and exploited to produce surplus-value, are reproduced. To explain the simple reproduction of capitalism, political economy then needs to consider precisely how 'the incessant reproduction, the perpetuation of the worker' is ensured, as it is 'the absolutely necessary condition for capitalist production' (716). Simple reproduction, which meant initially just the reproduction of the system as such, now also entails social reproduction, the reproduction of the individual lives whose living labour can be exploited, and in turn the analysis of the social setups that support those lives. An analysis that started at the general macro-economic level and relied upon a basic point of social ontology, thus translates naturally into more specific questions that arise as soon as you need to know how the lives of the workers whose work underpins the whole system are reproduced, each one of them individually, and across the generations. The work of Louis Althusser in the 1970s, of which the most well-known exemplar is his text on 'Ideological State Apparatus', aimed precisely to perform this extension anew, from the economic self-sustenance of the system to its sociological, cultural, and even psychological conditions (Althusser 2011).

One of the first questions that arises from this new perspective is of a distributive character. Life reproduction means the consumption of resources, which in turn, in a money-mediated society, means income. How do the functional positions of capitalist and worker translate into the distributive modalities by which the classes access their means of subsistence? (712) Beyond this economic question, however, many other questions arise, simply because the reproduction of human lives and of a human collective over time entails so many other dimensions. It is at this point that Marx's concept of reproduction becomes such a powerful analytical tool for feminist concerns since it leads directly to asking how in modern society individual lives and the collectives that support them are actually reproduced, who takes responsibility for it, in all of the aspects that this involves. As soon as that question is raised, light is cast on the sexual division of labour and the cultural order of recognition that accompanies it, since different genders take on different roles, and are rewarded symbolically and materially in different ways, for these roles. Then it becomes clear how the work of one gender who clearly takes on more of the work of reproduction, in the restricted sense of the term (as reproduction of lives separate from production work), is functionally indispensable for capitalism, and is thus exploited in specific ways. Suddenly, apparently non-economic, seemingly natural activities of child-bearing, child-birth, child-rearing, emotional care, socialization, and enculturation, become key functional factors of capitalism, which means that capital must have a direct interest in organizing and exploiting them in specific ways.

The key insight for this book's argument is that, as soon as society is considered in this way, the diversity of work tasks involved in such reproduction comes into view. Considering from a functional perspective how 'the capitalist produces the worker as wage-labourer' leads to asking sociologically under what exact conditions 'new workers are brought into existence' (717), which then directly invites a consideration of the work of sexual labour and the maintenance of kinship structures. It leads one to ask how 'muscles, nerves, bones and brains of existing workers are reproduced', in other words who does the work of providing subsistence and caring, both who produces the goods that make possible this work of feeding, but also the work of preparing food for consumption and physically and emotionally caring. Included in this perspective is 'at the same time the transmission and accumulation of skills from one generation to another' (719). This denotes the socialization and education of the young. Once the generational dimension is introduced, it is not just the young who are of concern, but also the old, the sick, the incapacitated: what happens to individuals when they are not able to bring their labour-power to the market for commodity production? Who looks after them? This is a particularly pointed question to ask in a system whose sole interest in individuals is their capacity to be engaged in activities through which surplus-value can be created, a system therefore that has no interest in all the individuals who, for some reason, cannot engage in those activities, including the ones who have to take on the activities of reproduction. The inherent contradiction of capitalism from the point of view of social reproduction, that it is a system that relies on the reproduction of its main force, the workers, and at the same time structurally undermines the very people who ensure such reproduction, becomes immediately visible once you follow the thread of social reproduction under capitalist conditions (see in particular Vogel 1983). All these different aspects of 'social reproduction' have been taken up as central areas of enquiry by materialist feminists. As we can see, however, these aspects also point to a generalized sense of reproduction, as the work involved in the reproduction of individual and social lives, a meaning that is already suggested by Marx himself, in the central chapter introducing the concept.

Engels' *Origin of the Family* made a decisive contribution along the same lines. Drawing on Marx's forays into pre-capitalist modes of production, Engels broadened the focus of the social reproduction perspective, by adding a historical dimension to the analysis of capitalism's essential functional conditions:

> According to the materialistic conception, the determining factor in history is, in the final instance, *the production and reproduction of immediate life*. But this itself is of a two-fold character. On the one side, the production of the means of subsistence, of food, clothing and shelter and the tools necessary for that production; on the other side, the production of human beings themselves, the propagation of the species. The social organization under which the people of a particular historical epoch and a particular country live is determined by *both kinds of production*: by the stage of development of labour on the one hand and of the family on the other.
>
> **(Engels 2010, 54)**

This text explicitly acknowledges sexual and social reproduction as intrinsic forms of 'production', namely as the 'production of human beings'. The phrase he uses, 'production of immediate life', can only denote what is classically understood by 'reproductive work', that is, the creation of human beings and the work of sustaining them qua living beings. This much-commented passage thus unequivocally names 'reproductive work' as a form of production (Munro 2019 emphasizes this point). The production of durable goods and the production of human beings are both equally necessary for 'the production and reproduction' of life.

Engels' patriarchal bias comes out straight away when he inconsistently restricts the concept of *Arbeit* to the production of durable goods ('the development of labour') and does not extend it to work in the home, even though he has just argued that both kinds are both productive and reproductive from the point of view of society. This echoes the passage in the chapter of *Capital* that was just cited, in which Marx referred to 'the workers' drives for self-preservation and propagation' (1991 [1867], 718) to explain how workers reproduce their lives, thus failing to see reproduction as work. In a number of other texts, it is clear that he viewed the family unit as a pre-economic, naturally given condition of economic organization (Vogel 1983, 65). Despite the openings just cited, when it came to actual analysis of political economy, Marx and Engels restricted production to just the manufacturing of food and objects, or indeed, in a blatant anachronistic move, to the production of commodities even in precapitalist societies (Nicholson 1999). They projected the division between economic and private, non-economic sphere, into the history of human societies. But these mistakes, which are ironically based on them sharing a key plank of an ideology they were dedicated to criticizing, does not alter the value of the general insight they formulated, which was developed and amplified by feminist thinkers. There is nothing in the concept of a 'mode of production of material life conditions' (Marx 2000, 425) that dictates that we should restrict the view to the work producing physical objects and food. It is Marx and Engels themselves who invite us to include the activities of sexual reproduction, care, and socialization in the tasks required for the reproduction of society and of the individual lives it harbours (Munro 2018).

In the final two sections, we verify the ambivalence of work for feminist writers and the conceptual significance of the idea of reproduction, by briefly considering the importance of work in Black feminist writings and in two key feminist authors in conclusion.

9.5 Colonization and Slavery

As was remarked at the outset, an invaluable lesson from the history of feminism has been to highlight how different forms of oppression in different contexts have been connected to each other, as parts of the web of capitalist organization spreading across the globe. In particular, major feminist studies have emphasized how the process of housewifization in a few rich countries has been structurally connected with other forms of oppression associated with colonization and imperial domination. One of the most brutal dimensions of this has been the modern experiences of slavery.

In this area again, the literature is immense. One body of work that highlights in particularly lucid form the many threads connecting at times distant aspects of the complex network of capitalist exploitation, including colonization and imperial domination, is the recent body of writings by Nancy Fraser (Fraser 2014, 2017, 2022; Fraser and Jaeggi 2018). Fraser's starting point is the historical division operated under capitalist economic organization, between the sphere in which surplus-value is created, and the other social spheres, notably the family, the public realm and non-human environments. The logic of capitalist organization is to force these other spheres to transform so they become enabling conditions of profit-driven economic activity. These other spheres, however, have their own internal logic and requirements. Fraser thus reframes the idea of contradictions and crisis-tendencies of the capitalist system in terms of boundary conflicts between the economic and other social spheres. In particular, Fraser is one of the most trenchant analysts of the conflict inherent in capitalism, between its reliance on the reproduction of labour-power necessary for value creation, and its constant attempt to shift the cost of reproduction onto families and reproductive workers, which leads to ever-renewed 'crises of care'. Fraser's contribution has also been to emphasize the changing historical dynamics of these conflicts of reproduction. She suggests modern capitalism can be divided into four different regimes (mercantile, liberal, state-managed, and neoliberal), in which the relations and boundary conflicts between social spheres are redrawn each time. Citing the extensive work in feminist and post-colonial studies in recent years, Fraser also includes the key distinction between core and periphery. While in the most industrialized countries surplus has classically been extracted through the exploitation mechanisms analysed by Marx, in the periphery, more direct forms of expropriation, that is of coercive extraction of labour-power and resources, occur.

All these social-theoretical distinctions make it possible for her to show the differential impact of changes in the organization of capital on women's experiences. While in the centres of capitalism women were progressively excluded from labour markets during the nineteenth century, Fraser follows Maria Mies in arguing that colonization and the forced economic restructuring of colonized economies had a very different impact elsewhere. As she writes, 'far from creating housewives in the Global South, capitalism's advent turned some women into enslaved breeders and beasts of burden and others into rural farmers living separately from husbands employed in urban wage work, while leaving still others in communities based on extended kinship' (Fraser and Jaeggi 2018, 88). Following decolonization, the new, fully globalized shape of neoliberal capitalism has seen a dramatic rise in poorly paid, largely unprotected forms of employment, in the informal sectors of the global economy and in the export-processing zones, for example in the *maquiladoras* at the border between the United States and Mexico. In these new sectors of the global economy, the lack of legal protection and the extremely low rates of pay affect women disproportionately. It is hundreds of millions of women today who are forced into hard labour and are subjected to systemic threats of physical and emotional violence, including sexual abuse.

An extreme form of hardship resulting from the global reorganizations of work has been the experience of slavery, notably as it has been documented and theorized by Black Marxists, Black feminists, and Black historians for the United States. Referring to this work as well as historical scholarship on other parts of the world, Fraser highlights that the establishment of racialized markers separating populations both within and outside core nations has been an intrinsic aspect of modern capitalism. Legally framed exploitation was reserved for the populations at the core and required some payment for reproduction costs. The direct grabbing of labour-power and of natural resources through methods of 'expropriation' by contrast allowed capitalists to acquire essential resources without having to pay for them, or for far less than they would have at the core. Nineteenth-century slavery, and after the abolition of slavery, forms of extreme economic subjection (in the sharecropping system for instance) in the United States are paradigm examples of expropriation.

Strikingly, however, many scholars who have written on Black women in the United States, and in particular many Black feminists, have shown that, even though Black women endured many forms of physical and social oppression in their experiences of work throughout modern American history, work at the same time had a special place in their lives (see eminently Dill 1979; Collins 2000, 45–69; Harley et al. 2002). Professional work allowed many women to assert their identity and their worth against racist and sexist prejudices (Shaw 1996). Work, paid and unpaid, allowed them to actively support family and community, a key value for many African-American people (Jones 1985). For many, work organizations provided the social and material context from which to formulate demands for rights and equality (Guy-Sheftall 1995, 9–15). An important strand in Black feminist writing identifies the unique conditions of work for Black women, as a key factor in their social positioning in American society (Brewer 1993), notably in contrast with the situation of Black men and white women.

One of the most famous texts highlighting the central role of work in the lives of African-American women is the 'reflections on the Black woman's role in the community of slaves', written by Angela Davis during the year she spent in prison (Davis 1972). Davis mobilized the Hegelian scheme of the master-slave dialectic to demonstrate that the experiences of work Black women were subjected to during slavery, while they were soul- and body-destroying, were also crucibles from which they were able to assert their autonomy, both in relation to their masters and in their own community. The context of slavery, Davis contended, made housework an entirely different experience for black women. The home of slave families was a place where some minimal degree of autonomy could be exerted in contrast with outside work. Work in the home for women, rather than being a sign of social relegation and subjection, took on the opposite meaning of autonomy, fight for survival, and in the context of extremely oppressive conditions, even of resistance (Davis 1972, 87). Stressing the continuity between activities of survival from the home and activities of overt resistance outside, Davis recounts the historical record of rebellion by slaves against their subjection, in which women played a direct part. In outside work, the sharing of harsh conditions had an equalizing effect. In subjecting women to the violence of slave work, oppression ironically 'released her from the chains of the myth of femininity', of being the weaker sex, incapable of genuine independence. These experiences of the community-building power of domestic work, of being equal to men under oppression and of sharing their acts of defiance and later on their struggles for emancipation, made women the centre of Black resistance to racial and capitalist oppression: 'She would be prepared to ascend to the same levels of resistance which were accessible to her men' (Davis 1972, 89).

9.6 Feminist Representations of Emancipated Work

Davis's text illustrates the ambivalence of work for feminist scholars in the starkest possible terms, referring as it does to some of the most alienating and oppressive conditions of work in modern history, and finding in these experiences precisely the conditions for individual and collective assertion of resilience and autonomy. Many other feminist scholars have also found in work a form of activity and of social experience that could serve women's emancipation. As we saw in the previous section, a more general lesson can be learnt from this to make the case for work. To conclude this chapter, we briefly focus on two leading feminist thinkers who have explicitly drawn this generalizing conclusion themselves.

In *Feminist Theory: From Margin to Center* (1984, 98), bell hooks rejects the liberal motto that 'work liberates women'. This motto, she argues, is wrong, empirically and politically: it ignores the fact that many women, in particular Black women, had always worked; that the problem for them was not to enter the workforce but to work in employment that was well-paid and that was not drudgery; and that the white, middle-class motto of liberation through work, because it spoke only of a specific minority of women, alienated poor, working-class, and Black women from the feminist movement.

This critique of the 'liberation through work' motto, however, does not amount to a rejection of work. On the contrary, the conclusion hooks draws from her critical analysis is that a different work agenda should be held by the feminist movement: one that stresses the need for full economic self-sufficiency through well-paid jobs for everyone, rather than access to high career positions to match powerful men (hooks 1984, 99). Indeed, beyond the issue of self-sufficiency, a more fundamental concern is the value of work as such, as an individual activity serving social needs. There is an intrinsic, liberating power in work, hooks argues, independently of the economic security it might provide. Economic security could be achieved through other modes of social organization. But the values inscribed in work as an individual contribution to society are intrinsic and as such should be upheld for all women. Indeed, recognizing this intrinsic value of work would imply recognition of the fact that women have always worked, and done essential work, as the main agents of social reproduction (hooks 1984, 102). At the heart of the feminist project, therefore, should be a 're-thinking the nature of work': 'By attributing value to all the work women do, whether paid or unpaid, feminist activists would provide alternative self-concepts and self-definitions for women' (hooks 1984, 102).

The conclusion to her chapter is an explicit case for the communal and personal value of work, even of work that is socially devalued:

> Re-thinking the nature of work is essential for the feminist movement in the United States. As part of that re-thinking, women must learn to value work.... Women, like other exploited and oppressed groups in this society, often have negative attitudes towards work in general and the work they do in particular. They tend to devalue the work they do because they have been taught to judge its significance solely in terms of exchange value. Receiving low wages or no wages is seen as synonymous with personal failure, lack of success, inferiority. Like other exploited groups, women internalize the powerful's definition of themselves and the powerful's estimation of the value of their labor. They do not develop an attitude towards work that sees it as an expression of dignity, discipline, creativity, etc.

In *Passionate Politics* (2000), hooks returned to the goods of work for women. Even before economic self-sufficiency, which in neoliberal capitalism is often not ensured by formal employment, the first good of work is psychological and existential, because work both allows and forces you to participate in 'something larger than oneself'. Work outside the home provides 'increased self-esteem and positive participation in community' (2000, 50). Once again, she surmises that a comprehensive feminist platform therefore must encompass a major effort to 'rethink work', so that everyone is in a position 'to live fully and well', by 'doing work which enhances self-esteem and self-respect while being paid a living wage', including for those whose chosen work is to stay at home and raise children (2000, 52).

This call for feminists to rethink work because of the crucial goods that properly valued work entails for women was also expressed in the conclusion of Maria Mies' *Patriarchy, Accumulation on a World Scale*, which was published in the same year as hook's *Feminist Theory*. As we saw, Mies' perspective is that of 'subsistence'. This leads to a vision of work as being first and foremost the activity of social reproduction, a conception that cites literally Marx and Engels' characterizations of work as 'production and reproduction of immediate life':

> A feminist concept of labour has to be oriented towards the *production of life* as the goal of work and not the production of *things and of wealth* (...). The *production of immediate life* in all its aspects must be the core concept for the development of a feminist concept of work.
>
> **(Mies 1986, 216)**

Such a conception of work is both critical and constructive and is materialistic in its own way. It asks that we consider all the activities performed in society, from the point of view of exactly how they contribute to the reproduction of lives. This immediately highlights the absurdity of the capitalistic system, which values activities whose outputs are often irrelevant or even destructive of individual minds and bodies, communal bonds, and their environments. It highlights the arbitrariness of current identifications and rankings of genuinely valuable social activities. Looking at all activities performed in society from the point of view of how they help reproduce life immediately makes us reconsider and correct their actual value for 'subsistence', whether they are waged or unwaged, performed within formal markets or not. The radical transformation in the vision of what work is, and which work activities matter from the point of view of social reproduction, obviously has significant implications for how society ought to be re-organized to ensure real equality between all members:

> From this changed concept (of labour) will follow a change of work, of work organization, of the sexual division of labour, of the products, of the relation between work and non-work, of the division between manual and mental work, of the relation between human beings and nature, of the relation to our bodies.
>
> **(Mies 1986, 212)**

It is difficult to assert the political and social centrality of work more forcefully and more clearly than Maria Mies does in this passage. Simply asking how individual and collective lives are to be sustained, as a matter of fact, and who is in charge of that work, immediately undercuts the social organization based on the maximization of profit, as well as the entrenched asymmetries in the cultural evaluation of contributions.

The alternative political vision guiding Mies' critical analysis of patriarchal capitalism in the end echoes the one proposed by André Gorz in his latest writings (Gorz 1999, 72–78; 2018). In her conception of authentic work and of emancipation through reorganized work, work is no longer a burdensome activity engaged in for an income or for profit, an activity that is purely utilitarian and separated from other activities. As part of the web of social life, work in this vision is integrated with the other modes of being and acting that link each person to others and to the world. Maternal labour, the eminent form of reproductive work, provides a paradigm example of such links for her. But in bearing, birthing and bringing up a child, heteronomy, boredom, suffering as well as enjoyment, self-fulfilment and happiness are conjoined. This ambivalence is the ultimate lesson to be learnt from social reproduction work. Work has to be done, is a necessity accompanied by all kinds of tedious and even deleterious impositions, but it is at the same time the path to self-expression, self-realization and in cooperation, the basis of human collectives, from households to local communities to entire societies. The following passage from the book's conclusion ties all these themes together:

> The same unity of work as a burden *and* work as enjoyment can be found among peasants whose production is not yet totally subsumed under commodity production and the compulsions of the market. The peasants who have to work from dawn to dusk during the harvesting season, for instance, feel the burden of work more than anybody else in their bodies and in their muscles. But in spite of the hardship of this work, it is never only 'a curse'. I remember the times of haymaking or harvesting on our small subsistence farm in my childhood as times of extreme labour intensity for everybody -mother, children, father-and as times of the greatest excitement, enjoyment, social interaction. I found the same phenomenon among poor peasant and agricultural labourer women in India during the season of rice transplantation. Although in this case the work had to be done for an exploiting landlord, the combination of work and enjoyment, of labour and leisure was still there.
>
> **(Mies 1986, 216)**

Strikingly, even in her ecofeminist writings, where one might expect that the rejection of capitalist productivism would extend to the concept of work in general, this positive vision of authentic work based on the perspective from subsistence is maintained, as 'life-producing and life-preserving work', which is the 'necessary precondition for survival' (Mies and Shiva 2014 [1993], 298).

The next chapter expands on all these ideas and attempts to detail the main features of the revised conception of work, which follows the feminist lead and simply defines it as the activity of social reproduction.

10
The Work of Social Reproduction

The previous chapter opened the conceptual perspective, from which 'the case for work' can now begin to be made. This short chapter considers what this perspective entails for the characterization of work. To do this, the idea of work as encompassing the activities of social reproduction is connected with the initial sketch presented in the introduction. In the last section, the chapter considers criticisms that might be raised against the definition of work resulting from this combination.

As the reader might recall, the initial definition of (human) work presented it as an activity with four characteristic features. In turn, it is the impact of those features on human psyches, bodies and relationships that are supposed to explain why and in what sense work might be called 'central' or constitutively important for individuals and communities. These features were: first that work designates activities that have an instrumental character. Work activities are engaged in with a view to achieving something beyond what is being done. Second, work activities obey technical constraints and are evaluated according to technical standards. Third, they are social in a number of senses. The technical dimension is intrinsically cultural and intermeshes with important values of the society in which work is conducted. Work activities often have someone else as the addressee of the work gesture. This stems from the fact that human beings are particularly dependent on their co-generous peers for their survival and well-being, including regarding the many conditions that need to be in place for other work activities to be performed. Finally, and crucially, a fourth feature of work activities that is not sufficiently highlighted is that they are performed under strong constraints, they are under the sway of several kinds of 'necessities', the first of which is simply the fact that, in the social set up in which they occur, the activities of work have to be performed, that a lot of work is something 'someone has to do'. How does such an initial characterization of work relate to the idea of the work of 'social reproduction'?

The Case for Work. Jean-Philippe Deranty, Oxford University Press. © Jean-Philippe Deranty (2024).
DOI: 10.1093/oso/9780192887146.003.0011

10.1 The Work of Social Reproduction

From feminist theorising, we retrieved two core notions and with them the viewpoints onto society they denote, namely the notions of 'subsistence' and 'reproduction'. From the perspective of what it takes to ensure subsistence and reproduction, the many activities of work that sustain society become particularly visible. Work from this perspective designates the set of activities that are necessary to secure the production and reproduction of the life of humans in their society. But the introduction began with Hegel's basic definition of work as fulfilment of needs. Linking needs fulfilment to reproduction might raise objections. When feminist thinkers focus on the tasks of social reproduction, the activities they have in mind do not encompass all that is entailed in the idea of needs that work would fulfil. Some of those needs might be expensive ones, that is, the needs of individuals who happen to require luxurious goods to feel contented. Or they might be 'false needs', needs superimposed upon subjectivities by an oppressive social order (Cutts 2019 for a lucid analysis of the classical discussion by Marcuse (2002 (1964, 7–9)). Surely that's not what social reproduction is about, a critic might say. The notion of social reproduction points to work that is essential but is not recognized. And work in social reproduction theory is positively connoted. But saying work is the fulfilment of needs includes unnecessary and even alienating needs.

We consider expensive tastes and false needs in a section of the last chapter (14.2). For the purpose of this present chapter, the key point is that even though it may be the case that some needs are superfluous or alienating, this does not alter the fact that human beings need a great many things in order to survive, ensure their well-being and possibly thrive, and the majority of the resources that allow them to achieve those states can only be brought about by actions that are goal-driven, that abide by technical and cultural standards, and that rely in some way on the actions of others around them. Furthermore, most of the time humans undertake these actions because they have to, not really because they want to, in other words, under the sway of some necessity. These actions are what we mean by work.

Another concern might be that, just as the concept of needs is a famously slippery one, so is the concept of life. What exactly is meant by 'production and reproduction of human life'? What kind of life is that? Correlative to the extension of the concept of social reproduction, the notion of life here simply indicates all the features of what makes a truly human life, including biological, psychological, cultural, social, and political conditions. Life here simply means all that is involved in humans living as they do, what makes up the human life-form (Ikaheimo 2022), in all the dimensions that this encompasses. As will now be emphasized, work is required in all these dimensions.

Yet another problem with linking work to social reproduction (in an extended sense) is that often work is unnecessary, does not even fulfil any needs, typically in the case of 'bullshit jobs', jobs with no meaning or content. And a lot of work of course is destructive of life, in all kinds of ways and to all kinds of degrees, including all the work that is spent in a mode of economic production that is rapidly destroying the environment sustaining human life. But tying the definition of work to social reproduction helps precisely to adjudicate between 'good' and 'bad' work. As a matter of fact, a lot of work is needed for social reproduction but of course not all work is for social reproduction. Ideally though, that is what work ought to be. This is precisely the political significance of the organization of work, to which Chapter 14 is dedicated. Saying that work denotes the activities that produce the outputs necessary for social reproduction therefore is not meant to exhaust all the possible examples of work, but rather to emphasize the prevalence and importance of work for human life. This is important because work is consistently taken for granted in social and political theory (a point subtly made from a sociological perspective by Lynne Pettinger 2019), and also because looking at work in this way helps to better see some of its distinctive features, notably why it is 'central' in different ways.

An important point to emphasize in this respect is that social reproduction is not just the production and reproduction of individual lives, but also the production and reproduction of the collective life of which the individuals are part. What is meant by collective life? There is no need to enter complex discussions of social ontology to give intuitive content to this notion. By collective life is meant the collective aspect of individual lives. These are the supra-individual social and material infrastructures that are necessary for the reproduction of individual lives. This bundle of supra-individual infrastructures might be generically called 'collective life' since it is more than just supra-individual organizations: these infrastructures all touch the lives of the individuals and are, as it were, 'lived' by them, in the sense that individual engage with them through the living of their lives. These infrastructures include the system of values, shared histories and beliefs, which bind a collective together through broad frames of meaning. It includes the system of social norms, which enable 'unsociable sociable' individuals to live together, from rules of politeness to specific social roles to legal norms. It includes the system of political decision-making, through which the collective shapes its own life as a collective. And it also includes the material infrastructures without which, first, none of those other systems would function, and second, without which individual work would not be possible. For individual lives to be reproduced, schools, tribunals, parliaments, but also mills, dams, electricity, and internet grids need to be 'produced and reproduced'. Collective life relies on the work of individuals to be produced and reproduced. Reciprocally, because of the extreme social dependency of the human animal, which is not just social and cultural, but also includes material, technical interdependency, individual lives directly depend on collective life, and indeed on the work that is specifically dedicated to producing and reproducing collective life (building schools, dams, and tribunals, making sure they function well enough, and so on). Social reproduction on the enlarged concept advocated here includes all those dimensions: the work of individuals to produce and reproduce their own individual lives, the lives of particular others and the life of the collective, and the work of the collective to produce and reproduce individual lives.

Highlighting this dialectic allows us to see a point of difference between the definition of work used in this book (based on earlier work, see notably Deranty 2015 and 2022) and the conception Axel Honneth has recently presented (2023, notably at 139–148). Honneth also uses an extensive sense of social reproduction and defines work as the activities necessary for it. He defines this necessity as the set of all the things society values, which, because they are part of the collective life form, society agrees require work and effort to produce and reproduce. The underlying thought then is that since work is about social reproduction, it is social by definition. Honneth uses the phrase 'social labour' to emphasize the point, but his demonstration makes this added adjective redundant. His argument helps to demarcate work, which seeks to produce and reproduce socially valued things, from private activities undertaken not on the basis of socially significant values, but for personal reasons. The problem with adding this redundant adjective 'social' to work is that it blurs the dialectic between the individual and the collective we just emphasized. It makes all forms of work social, whereas some types of work, even though they are of course socially framed (culturally, technically, legally, and so on), are for the reproduction of individual lives, while others specifically aim to produce and reproduce collective infrastructures. We might say that all work is indeed social simply because human individuals are intrinsically social animals, but not all work has social aims.

To return to the core features of our concept of work, one final trait to emphasize is that the idea of a work of social reproduction has a strong *dynamic* connotation: it is about producing and reproducing in a concrete sense; it implies that efforts have to be made, techniques employed, physical, cognitive and affective energy spent, in order for the reproduction of life to be achieved. The fundamental intuition at the heart of this book is the significance, both for individual psyches and bodies and for collective organization, of these goal-driven, technically framed efforts that are required for there to be a society of individuals, that is, for there to be individuals who can continue to live human lives as well as a collective of these individuals which, as a collective, is a necessary framework for their survival and in the best cases, their thriving.

This intuition can be found in many writers in the history of social and political philosophy. Indeed, it is at the heart of Gorz's vision of full individual and collective autonomy, pointing not to a society 'beyond work', but a society beyond waged work, where activities of production can finally be engaged in full autonomy (Bowring 2002 as a later expansion of the model). We remember Engels' strong words: the 'production and reproduction of immediate life', he wrote at the start of the *Origins of the Family*, is 'the determining factor in history' (Engels 2010 [1884], 54). Rawls' theory of justice is premised on this core vision of what a human collective relies upon. His name for society, as a 'cooperative scheme' (1996, 18), implies the work that is entailed in sustaining this scheme:

> society is … a more or less complete and self-sufficient scheme of cooperation, making room within itself for all the necessities and activities of life, from birth until death… It produces and reproduces itself and its institutions and culture over generations and there is no time at which it is expected to wind up its affairs.

The passage insists well on the necessity aspect of social reproduction: the necessity to work to maintain the conditions allowing for all the necessities of life, for each individual and across the generations, never abates. We should not expect that our 'affairs' could ever 'wind up'.

This idea that the work of social reproduction never ceases was already captured in the thought experiment Marx expressed in the letter we cited in the introduction:

> Every child knows a nation which ceased to work, I will not say for a year, but even for a few weeks, would perish. Every child knows, too, that the masses of products corresponding to the different needs require different and quantitatively determined masses of the total labour of society. That this necessity of the distribution of social labor in definite proportions cannot possibly be done away with by a particular form of social production but can only change the mode of its appearance, is self-evident. No natural laws can be done away with. What can change

> in historically different circumstances is only the form in which these laws assert themselves.

The text adds the dimension of allocation and distribution of work tasks, showing that the notion of social reproduction immediately raises questions of justice and fairness. We explore these questions in the next chapters. For now, what matters is this bedrock idea: individual life and the collective in which individuals live, which they sustain, and which sustains them, should not be taken as givens. In order for this collective and individuals to exist at all, and to maintain their existence over time, all kinds of tasks have to be fulfilled. Work is the set of activities that ensure this.

10.2 So Much Work

To view social reproduction as the outcome of 'total social labour' requires that one generalizes the 'needs' and the 'products' Marx refers to in the passage above. Given the complexity and diversity of human needs, a lot more than food, clothing, and shelter is needed to ensure the 'production and reproduction of immediate life'. Since work is defined as the instrumental activity that aims to support individual and collective life under all of their aspects, work is required in all kinds of spheres. Going through these different conditions and spheres is useful, as it shines a light on the sheer amount of work that goes on at any moment in a human collective, and because it provides elements that allow us to respond to objections.

As was just mentioned, even for the production of goods destined for direct consumption by individuals (food, clothing, shelter), some infrastructures are required which only the collective, or at least a part of it, more than just a few single individuals in any case, can create and maintain: the roads to transport goods; the clearing of land for gardens; bridges; dams; electricity grids, nuclear plants, data centres, and so on.

Under a generalized concept of social reproduction, however, the same point applies to all those aspects that concern the collective's key functions in ensuring the production and reproduction of individual lives. Given that these functions are necessary for the production and reproduction of individual and collective life, some work is specifically required by them.

The most basic function a collective has to secure is maintaining itself in existence against external threats. Each citizen has to dedicate some of their time to defending the city, as in the Greek polis, or every member of a clan in hunter-gatherer societies, or specialist soldiers are employed to do so. Whether it is done by every social member or a specific class, defending the collective is a type of work, as Plato already explicitly described it (Plato 2013, 57): it is a goal-driven activity that has its own techniques, and it is very obviously engaged in for the reproduction of collective life. There are also functions that demand to be secured when the collective reaches a certain level of complexity, typically when state institutions emerge. This refers to what social theorists call the administrative system. When separate institutions exist, they require their own forms of material reproduction. This is achieved through taxation, which allows a redistribution of social wealth and an allocation to parts of the social whole that are not directly productive of wealth. Taxation relies on individuals who collect, count, manage the goods and the money raised. These individuals are engaged in a particular kind of work, with its own standards, goals, and so on. Or to name another central aspect of the administration of collective life: very early on in human history, social interactions were regulated by rules that became formalized and the object of a special sphere, the sphere of law and justice. Maintaining the knowledge of laws alive, upholding and applying them, are all essential to the reproduction of collective life once it is organized according to such laws, and this in turn necessitates a specific kind of work.

Of course, collective life sustains individual lives not just by providing the conditions for the production of goods (through the division of labour and material infrastructures), or by fulfilling administrative functions maintaining the collective together as a form of organization. Just as importantly, individual human lives rely on the collective because human beings are intrinsically social beings whose very being depends on relations with others and is even constituted by them to an extent. This points to two other fundamental aspects of social reproduction: sociality and culture.

Human beings organize their lives through complex systems that involve different types of social relations: in particular, relations of kinship, relations of obligation (gifts, debts, promises, bonds of different kinds) and relations of power and authority. In taking their place and taking part in these interactions, individuals gain a particular social status and develop their identity. Status and identity are crucial to a human life, as much as food and shelter. Given the extreme social dependency of the human animal, status and identity are typically examples of 'goods' that are equally individual and social: individuals need these goods but can only develop them through interactions with others, and these interactions both enact and depend upon the supra-individual normative framework in which these norms underpinning identity, status positions, positions of power and kinship relations are defined for each and every one. Beyond the social representations crystallizing into specific norms defining status and rank and thereby impacting on identity, human collectives also rely on fundamental representations, beliefs, values, which make up the collective 'imaginary', the cultural glue binding the collective together (Godelier 2007). Throughout most of human history, these worldviews were articulated around myths and religions, which systematize and justify the core beliefs and values of the collective. All these social and cultural aspects of human life are interwoven, such that, for instance, social interactions performatively reinforcing gender, are governed and justified by fundamental values enshrined in the collective's worldviews. Furthermore, these social and cultural aspects of the collective frame of existence also intermesh with the organizational and technical spheres. They specify who works for whom, they influence, beyond purely technical considerations, how work is organized concretely in space and time, which occupations are valued, and which attract social contempt, who gets which allocation of total social labour, and so on. If work is the set of activities ensuring the reproduction of individual and collective life and given that such social reproduction involves the rich and complex social and cultural spheres just mentioned, then there is work to be done in all of these spheres as well. There is specifically social work, which serves to reproduce and maintain the normative infrastructure regulating interactions. And there is specifically cultural work, to cultivate, preserve, and pass on knowledge in this generation and the next. This involves notably and crucially the collective's language. Finally, every human society adds aesthetic dimensions to its social and cultural collective life. Aesthetic functions change significantly in their organization and ontology across time and cultures (Deranty and Olson 2019). In many societies, aesthetic production and reproduction is one part, sometimes a crucial part, of cultural reproduction, and more specifically, of cultural reproduction in its most fundamental layer, that is, regarding the representation of myths and of core religious beliefs. Aesthetic production and reproduction involves its own form of work, as part of the reproduction of the collective.

The point of listing some of the main 'functions' and 'systems' making up a human collective is to emphasize the enormous amount of work that goes on for the production and reproduction of individual and collective life. Before we study in the next chapters what makes work 'central', it is important to see clearly what the implication is of defining work as the technical activities that ensure the reproduction of the human life-form. This implication is simple: it takes a lot of work, much-varied work, work by many people, work involving many different aspects of human life, to ensure the reproduction of 'immediate life' from one day to the next and into the next generation.

10.3 Which Activity Is Not Work?

This vision of work based on a maximum extension of the notion of social reproduction seeks to avoid the regrettable limitation of work to just the production of material goods and technical objects, like tools, machines, and weapons. In doing so, however, we run up against the objection that the extension goes too far and that generalizing in this way makes it difficult to say with any clarity whether an activity qualifies as work or not. There are several ways of articulating this difficulty.

One way is to point out that there are activities that directly help in social reproduction, but that the agents might not want to describe as work. This might be the case in particular if in the society under consideration, the activity is not called work, but is considered an intrinsic part of a social obligation, and it is the relation of obligation that matters, not the activities of producing goods attached to it. In modern society, care work is a tricky case from this point of view. On the one hand, we want to make sure that our conception of work encompasses care activities. At the same time, it might well be the case that, without necessarily being victims of a naturalizing ideology, some parents care for their children, or someone cares for a sick or an old person, not thinking of it as work but precisely as care. If asked, they might not call it work. Should we still call it work if they don't? We consider this objection based on the difference between first- and third-person perspectives in the next chapter. As we try to show there, it seems justified to describe as work activities that fit the definition proposed, even if the people performing them would not.

Another problem with the extension of work to all activities of social reproduction is that this label seems to apply to so many types of action that have some relevance to individual or collective life that the term might encompass too many different kinds of action. If we consider that in many societies religious beliefs are among the most important aspects of social reproduction, then are we also saying, based on our definition, that rituals, ceremonies, sacrifices, all the different ways in which religious peoples exercise and transmit, 'reproduce' their beliefs, should be called work? Or if we include the transmission of language and cultural knowledge in the elements of social reproduction, should we then say that when spectators attended a tragedy in fifth century Athens, BCE, and thereby enjoyed a creative 'reproduction' of their founding stories and myths, and of their own language, going to the theatre therefore was work for them? That would seem to stretch the category in implausible ways, but is it not implied by the extended view of social reproduction?

This sceptical remark can be fleshed out using arguments from the debates around universal basic income, as the point is well articulated there that social reproduction relies on actions of different kinds, not just goal-directed, productive activities. If social reproduction entails many kinds of action, then defining work as the activity of social reproduction is too vague and clear criteria are required to demarcate work activities from other 'reproductive' ones. But what are those criteria? In their adoption of a post-work position to model the integration of animals in society, Donaldson and Kymlicka (2019) provide a lucid summary of these discussions and elaborate a generalized notion of 'passive contributions' that is particularly relevant. Social reproduction, they argue, should be conceived in a 'post-productivist' manner (Fitzpatrick 2004 as a direct reference), that is, as something that is only partly, perhaps not even predominantly, reliant on work activities. As they point out, social life is reproduced daily in all sorts of ways. Some of the key activities contributing to social reproduction are activities that sustain the moral fabric, such as behaving with courtesy, civility, tolerance, respect for the law, displaying concern towards others. These activities do not seek to produce a useful output. Other examples come to mind, whereby living our everyday lives *de facto* reproduces features of the lifeworld. Simply speaking my language helps to ensure my linguistic community continues to exist. Celebrating collective memories, recounting shared stories, reproduces the past between friends and family, and the past of the community at large. It helps to keep knowledges, values, norms alive. These are all activities that help 'reproduce' social life, and yet they are not examples of work, on any plausible definition of it, and in particular on the definition provided so far. Mentioning 'activities of social reproduction' therefore does not help to define work. Saying that work involves activities of social reproduction seems too vague and too broad.

But the claim that many kinds of action other than work ensure social reproduction needs to be severely qualified. Undeniably, many different forms of action contribute in their own way to the reproduction of individual and collective life. But only work 'produces and reproduces' human life, on any plausible meaning of 'produce', which surely must include the dynamic element noted earlier. Stopping at a red light, displaying basic courtesy, speaking my native language 'reproduces' society only in ways that might be called accessory, or by accident. These actions might enact sociality but they don't produce it in a strict sense. Many of these contributions may be called 'passive' precisely because it takes a lot of direct effort and technical attention to actually, materially reproduce a society and the lives of the individuals in it. Indeed, many passively reproductive activities, like obeying the law, exercising restraint in public space, in fact only have reproductive power in a negative sense, to the extent that they entail refraining from doing something that would harm individual or social life. They don't actually create any 'goods' or fulfil any needs. Social reproduction itself needs to be produced and reproduced, whereas non-work activities of social reproduction only contribute to it accessorily. The examples taken by Fitzpatrick in his 'post-productivist' model of social democracy are instructive: the reproductive powers of care and of the environments are themselves dependent on work, and he says this explicitly. Care is impotent if it does not involve the gestures, performed in the right way, which are to produce it. To consider the environment as an element of social reproduction, that is, as a large non-human reality that sustains and is impacted by human activities, work interactions with it need to be counted. Some of those work interactions might well destroy it, but the point of calling it the environment is that it is the humans' environment. As such, there is a lot of work being performed that makes it a human environment and not all of it destroys it as a whole or the beings in it. Some of that work in fact allows that holistic reality to be remediated and for some of the non-human beings in it to flourish.

In conclusion, and to further substantiate the conception of work as the productive, needs-fulfilling actions ensuring social reproduction, *the production of reproduction* as we call it here, two germane definitions of work by leading social scientists can be summoned, which highlight different dimensions of it. The first is by Charles and Chris Tilly (1998, 22), who define (human) work as efforts that add use value to goods or services others can lay claim to. This helps to emphasize the 'outcome'-oriented and 'other-directed' aspects of work. Work supports the production and reproduction of individual and collective life by producing stuff (goods and services) that is valued by others as being useful to them (whether or not they are right about it).

We might also cite the rich conceptual analysis proposed by Sandra Wallman in her introduction to a special issue of *Current Anthropology* on the social anthropology of work. There she defined work as:

> the performance of necessary tasks, and the production of necessary values – moral as well as economic. The task of meeting obligations, securing identity, status and structure, are as fundamental to livelihood as bread and shelter. On this basis, work may be defined as the production, management and conversion of the resources necessary to livelihood.
>
> **(Walman 1980, 302)**

Wallman uses 'livelihood' in a generic sense, to denote all the conditions that need to be met for individual human lives to be reproduced in a given society. She emphasizes 'necessity' as a defining feature of work tasks. Work tasks ensuring 'livelihood' are necessary as they provide the goods that are deemed necessary in a particular society for human lives to be reproduced. These include basic biological needs, but also social and cultural conditions, enabling individuals to acquire the kinds of identities, social standings, and forms of personal meaning, which are necessary for material, social, and psychological survival and indeed for flourishing at that time and in that space. The organization of the producing, exchanging, and consuming of resources to sustain 'livelihood' is guided by the relative values placed on those goods, which includes personal viewpoints. Beyond the narrow definition of economics in modernity, work is an economic activity in a more fundamental sense, in the sense namely, that it is about the production for exchange and use of values, which in many cases can hardly be represented by money. Rather, those values reflect the preference system of the society and the individuals in it, in which different resources are used to secure livelihood.

The productive dimension of work, what makes it the necessary condition of reproduction and what distinguishes it from other kinds of activity, is emphasized in the reference to 'resources' as what work tasks 'produce, manage and convert'. The material processes of production, management, and conversion of resources deliver the outputs necessary for livelihood. Since all dimensions of livelihood are concerned, the resources on which work operates are themselves manifold and comprise much more than just the narrow list of resources in classical economic theory. Besides capital, land, and labour, the list also includes symbolic resources, of a cognitive type, like information, and of a normative type, like cultural norms; and psychological or existential resources, such as a sense of life's meaning, linked to the structure of time, and identity. The 'effort' dimension is discussed by Wallman in reference to the most basic definition of work which stems from physics, and which continues to apply in human work, as energy transfer that changes the direction or the shape of an object. This basic, physical dimension of human work was well identified by Marx (see Chapter 3, Section 3.5), as the 'physiological' layer of all work, but also in his well-known use of the new chemical concept of 'metabolism', which denotes a form of organic work. Wallman highlights this feature as well, to describe the material, creative dimension of the production, management, and conversion of resources. Human work requires the expenditure of physical, emotional, and intellectual energy, which are mobilized with the view to changing something in the world in order to create some value, in the basic sense of something that is *of value* for someone. Those parts of the world being worked on can be of all ontological kinds: an elemental piece from nature (a tree branch, a mass of marble, a clump of clay or coal); an organized process (think about the expression 'pushing paper' to describe administrative work, which literally refers to the definition from physics); some physiological or psychological features of another human being (operating on them if they are sick; washing them if they can't do it for themselves; talking to them in a way that will calm down their anxiety). Whether it creates new ones, or manages or transforms existing ones, work expends resources so as to demonstrate its efficaciousness and produce its outputs. Work is thus energy transfer in manifold ways: it consumes human energy to establish energy transfers in the material and social worlds. All work is toil in this sense, exertion, causing heat, friction, and some degree of exhaustion for the subject engaged in it. In turn, it introduces exertion, heat, tension, friction, changes of shape or structure, to parts of the world, including in other human subjects. All work is thermodynamic, we might say, as a form of energy transfer that changes interactions between systems (Vatin 1993; Suzman 2022, 27–38).

Once we keep in view these outcome-driven, use-related, value-driven, other-dependent, energy-hungry, dimensions of work, the worry about an all-too-encompassing notion disappears. No other kind of action has all of these features. And as these features characterize work and make it the productive activity that it is, work is the only kind of action that can materially ensure the production of social reproduction.

How does this apply to the two counter-examples above? If we think about it in light of the features just mentioned, it might be the case that, in some circumstances, a religious ritual is in fact a form of work. It is work for the priests to begin with since their ritual activities enact the function they fulfil for the collective, the valuable outcomes they produce for it. But even for the worshippers there might be some form of work involved. It all depends on the context, on their intentions and beliefs, and on the significance of the ritual in that culture. If singing, reciting, dancing, sharing in a sacrifice, and enduring the boredom of a long ceremony, are the ways by which each individual contributes to the collective recreation of stories and myths that provide sources of meaning, which go on to frame other life actions and life experiences, then these active parts of the ritual are a form of work. Indeed, 'liturgy' in Greek is literally a form of '*ergon*', 'work for the public'. In the case of the theatre, the playwright, the actors, and the musicians, as well as all the people who manage the theatre building, build the props, and so on (the point of listing all these people is again to bring to attention just how much work is involved in every nook and cranny of social life), all obviously work. But do the spectators work as religious worshippers might in some historical contexts? What is it spectators actively do that would bring value to others and to the collective? Consumption, enjoyment, being entertained are not forms of work. They are conditions for there to be creative works, but they don't create anything themselves. In some historical contexts, however, it is quite plausible that active participation by the audience would be an intrinsic part of the performance's overall effect, notably if key societal values and stories are being represented and recreated in the performance. Indeed, in contemporary art, active participation by audiences is often an intrinsic part of the 'work of art'. In some contexts, then, there is indeed work performed by the spectators. The key in these examples is to focus on the features that were highlighted: what is it that is actually being done in each case? Is it done with purpose? How does it produce use for someone, an output with value? How does this contribute to individual and collective life? The reasons why we might object to calling such practices work stem from the strong separation operated in modernity between the formal sphere of work and other spheres of life. But if work is just the activity that ensures the material production of social reproduction, then it is present throughout all spheres. Indeed, it is what enlivens and activates those spheres, as the creative, productive part in human action. In the next chapter, we consider the long historical reality of this aspect of human existence.

11
The Long History of Work

The previous chapter established the concept of work with which the 'case for work' can now be made, in the second part of the book. Each chapter in this part aims to achieve two main goals. The first is to rebut the objections that remain after the critical review conducted in the first part. As we saw, many of the arguments and references that seem to add up to a strong case against work in fact do not sustain critical scrutiny. Some of the most important thinkers that are taken to show the nefarious nature of work, on empirical, conceptual, or methodological grounds, in fact can be read in ways that highlight the importance of work for subjects and communities. Many points raised in contemporary anti- and post-work writings that are inspired by these references turn out to be empirically or conceptually problematic. However, even after parsing the case against work in this critical way, many objections remain, which the next chapters attempt to answer, drawing on the basic perspective of social ontology presented in the previous chapter. As these rejoinders unfold, this perspective from social reproduction becomes richer and gradually enables the other main goal in this second part to be realized, namely, to make the case of work not just in negative fashion, but also positively, by presenting a new, comprehensive picture of how work is central to self and society.

In this chapter, we return to objections based on the alleged historical uniqueness of modernity's relationship to work (see Deranty 2015 for an early exploration). As we saw, such objections are often cast by citing evidence from historical and anthropological scholarship, as well as the authoritative names of Marx, Weber, and Foucault. Many theorists who criticize the centrality of work make the point that the notion of 'work' is a 'late invention' coinciding with the advent of capitalist modernity, that other human societies did not consider themselves, the world around them, and the role of individuals in the collective, through the prism of productive activity, wealth creation, and the contributions of individuals to that wealth, and that this unique modern obsession with work is one of the main sources of the injustices and pathologies prevalent in modern societies, from alienation, exploitation, and disciplining to the destruction of natural environments.

The Case for Work. Jean-Philippe Deranty, Oxford University Press. © Jean-Philippe Deranty (2024).
DOI: 10.1093/oso/9780192887146.003.0012

Here we consider in particular the *historical contingency* objection, which states that the centrality of work is associated with a social arrangement that is based on a set of values that arose at a particular time and whose time is now gone; the *ethnocentric* objection, which states that it is a mistake to project our concern for work into cultures in which other values have primacy; and the *nominalist* challenge, which refers to the great variability with which human societies have depicted different kinds of activities, to deny that there is a homogeneous notion of work that would be valid across times and across cultures. We respond to these objections by considering a wealth of anthropological and historical evidence. By centrality of work is meant here simply, following Wallman, that work impacts significantly on the identity and social standing of individuals, and that it is a major axis in the organization of society. On the basis of all the evidence considered, we show that work has been central in many human societies besides modern, industrial ones.

11.1 Work in Garden Societies

To find our bearings in the overwhelming wealth of potential references, let us pick up again the thread that ran through Chapter 1, taking our lead from Dominique Méda's 1995 book on work as a disappearing value. In that first chapter, we abstained from questioning the analysis of anthropological and historical scholarship that launched Méda's reflections, as we just began our journey through arguments against the centrality of work. What we refrained from saying then was that the sources Méda cites lend themselves to entirely different conclusions from the ones she draws. All the passages she quotes already indicate a point that becomes increasingly obvious the further we delve into the classics these quotes are taken from, and even more so when we consult other studies in social anthropology: namely that other human societies might not have been 'structured by work' in the way modern societies are but work was a very important institution in them as well and represented a major form of experience for individuals living in them.

This becomes apparent already if we return to the main reference used by Méda, Bronislaw Malinowski's 2014 [1922] *Argonauts of the Western Pacific*, a famous study of Trobriand society in Papua New Guinea and a foundational book of social anthropology (Malinowski 2014 [1922]). Malinowski has been subjected to much criticism by following generations of anthropologists, notably by some of his most famous students (Firth 2002[1957]). Other leading anthropologists, like Annette Weiner, have been more measured in their criticism of him, but still corrected his interpretations of key aspects of Trobriander life, notably on gender relations and sexuality (Weiner, 1977, 1988). Despite these reservations, however, those parts of his book that describe the material culture, the organization of labour and the ways of working of Trobriander people remain authoritative.

Méda uses a few chosen passages at the start of Malinowski's classic in her attempt to demonstrate that work is a modern invention and that in pre-modern cultures it did not exist as a separate social representation, it did not underpin the organization of society and it was not a significant form of individual experience. Yet Malinowski's long descriptions of Trobriand economics, including the passages cited by Méda, show the opposite. Indeed, Méda's general thesis is contradicted by her own analyses of those passages, which illustrate the rich texture of work in Trobriand society, both as an institution and as a form of experience. In these analyses, her stark claim that work became experienced as such only in modernity is diluted into the more modest claim that pre-modern people did not experience work separately from the encompassing social relations to which it was attached. As she develops this alternative set of claims, the features of Trobriander work she highlights, which aim to show that work was for them an inherently social and cultural activity, not a purely instrumental, individualistic one, look remarkably like features that could also apply *mutatis mutandis* to modern work, if only one does not restrict oneself to the narrow, neo-classical definition of work used in contemporary economic theory, where it is merely a disutility that rational agents accept to undergo in order to achieve their individual preferences. Debunking this model of work in anthropological research was an explicit methodological aim of Malinowski's study (2014 [1922], 63–65), along with the other false assumption that pre-modern people worked as little as possible. Indeed, Malinowski's rejection of a neo-classical approach in cultural analysis is general and therefore includes modern society. He states emphatically that the 'rationalistic conception of self-interest' is preposterous for 'man', in other words, for human beings in general. When Malinowski writes that the Trobriand example provides '*one* instance' (he emphasizes the word) that falsifies the assumptions about human work built into neo-classical economic theory, he clearly implies that this is an extra reason, beyond the intrinsic interest in their culture, to study them. But Méda's claim that Trobrianders did not experience work as such is premised on just this narrow conception of work the study she cites explicitly rejected.

Instead of adopting such a narrow vision of work, which conflates the formal definition from economic theory and the experiences people, including modern ones, make of it, let us return to what Malinowski's classic actually teaches us.

Section 4 of chapter 2, which includes the first methodological discussion of economic anthropology we just mentioned, begins with these words:

> Half of the natives' working life is spent in the garden, and around it centres perhaps more than half of his interests and ambitions.
>
> **(Malinowski 2014 [1922], 61)**

This directly contradicts the claim repeated by so many contemporary social and political theorists, that 'work only takes up a small part of the time and the interests of the people considered' (Méda 1995, 33). Malinowski specifically mentions the individuals' 'interests and ambitions'. He has no trouble assigning individual motivations and forms of experience to Trobrianders in relation to their working activities. As all the sections on Trobriand economics demonstrate, and as Weiner's studies also establish albeit with a different interpretive lens, the representations and practices of work in that society have a major influence on the intentions, perceptions, and actions of each individual *qua* individual, and they matter as a result of the features of work itself, not just because work activities are part of other social logics (such as kinship obligations and deference to power).

That work matters a lot for the Trobrianders is confirmed by Malinowski's repeated statement that work efforts are in many ways 'an end in themselves' for them (2014 [1922], 63). The first sense in which this is true is in the commitment to work efforts. Trobrianders can 'work hard, and work systematically, with endurance and purpose' (2014 [1922], 63). There is specific social prestige in working hard, with an explicit name to denote it:

> A good garden worker in the Trobriands derives a direct prestige from the amount of labour he can do, and the size of garden he can till. The title *tokwaybagula*, which means 'good' or 'efficient gardener,' is bestowed with discrimination, and borne with pride. Several of my friends, renowned as *tokwaybagula*, would boast to me how long they worked, how much ground they tilled, and would compare their efforts with those of less efficient men. When the labour, some of which is done communally, is being actually carried out, a good deal of competition goes on. Men vie with one another in their speed, in their thoroughness, and in the weights they can lift, when bringing big poles to the garden, or in carrying away the harvested yams.
>
> **(2014 [1922], 64)**

There is also social prestige attached to working well, in being a 'good gardener' not just as someone who can toil, but who also masters gardening techniques:

> Each man's harvest is exhibited for criticism in his own plot, and parties of natives walk about from garden to garden, admiring, comparing and praising the best results.

A similar social valuing of workmanship applies to other crafts, such as jewel-making (184–185), and most especially to building canoes (124).

Working hard and working well are thus intrinsic values in Trobriand society, but they also serve extrinsic purposes, namely the creation of large surpluses and of the most beautiful specimens. Quantity and quality of production before contact with the West (when surpluses became exported) was for social competition: social recognition was directly attached to success as a gardener (2014 [1922], 64). For the rich and powerful, social authority was demonstrated through the largest harvest (produced by others).

Key aspects of this dual, intrinsic, and extrinsic worth of work for the Trobrianders are its 'aesthetic' dimensions. Aesthetic attention to gardening work serves first of all technical and instrumental purposes. Tidy gardens, in a tropical setting especially, are a necessity for optimal production. As we just saw, Trobriand gardeners worked hard to maximize output both in absolute quantity and in the quality of individual products. Another aspect is linked to social standing, no longer in the meritocratic sense of excelling over others, but in the sense of basic moral standards to uphold. A clean garden is expected of any self-respecting person: 'No self-respecting man would dream of omitting to do this' (2014 [1922], 62).

Yet another important aspect of the aesthetics of gardening work is its essential magical surroundings:

> Another, and perhaps the most interesting example of non-utilitarian work is afforded by the big, prismatic erections called *kamkokola*, which serve ornamental and magical purposes, but have nothing to do with the growth of plants.
>
> **(2014 [1922], 62)**

Work in canoe-building shows the same multiplicity of meanings. The canoes of Trobrianders are feats of shipbuilding technique, taking them safely on the *Kula*, the voyages across surrounding islands to visit partners and perform the gits and counter-gifts that cement alliances, signal status, and entrench social power. Canoes of course also allow them to fish. A beautiful canoe for the Trobrianders is thus first of all a well-built, efficient equipment. But canoes are also beautiful artefacts in which the makers and the owners take great pride, which onlookers gather to admire, notably on the sacred day of their launch (2014 [1922], 158). And the fabrication of canoes is surrounded at every one of its stages, all the way to the launching into the sea, with magical practices.

So Trobrianders worked a lot, worked hard, strived to work well, some of them were able to create what the rest of society considered beautiful and therefore precious artefacts which were highly valued. They knew they would receive social recognition for all of these things. If they were powerful, they would depend on the work of others for the display and the cementing of their power through large and impressive work outputs. If they were of lesser standing, they would engage in social competition with others through their work efforts. They would be judged negatively for lesser forms of work, for producing less and for producing unremarkable specimens. Given all of this, what other conclusion can we draw, but that work must have mattered a lot to Trobriand people? They spent a lot of their time and energy in work, they learnt most of their manual skills and much of their natural knowledge through work. A large part of their social standing was directly dependent on their work performances. To use Wallman's conceptual language, essential sources of livelihood for the Trobrianders, notably identity and status, were directly dependent on their work. Malinowski knew what he was saying then when he referred to the Trobrianders' 'interests and ambitions' surrounding their garden work.

Méda argues that this does not show the importance of work for Trobrianders because, as Malinowski describes it, work was part of social obligations that determined its material organization and its meaning, based on kinship (most of the work products were due to the sister's family) and dependence (labour was owed to important men and to chiefs). However, rather than interpreting the overarching social order governing work efforts to mean that work does not matter by itself, since it is social obligations that provide the true incentive for individuals, an alternative conclusion might be drawn: when strong obligations define social life, and these obligations are cashed out to a large extent (there are other ways to show deference to authority and other ways to interact with kin) in obligations to work and to distribute the products of work in specific ways, then work de facto matters a lot. We can apply here the material, 'productive' argument from the previous chapter. Work is the activity that literally realizes the obligations. It does not exhaust their cultural meanings, but it gives them reality, at least to a large extent (other gestures can do that as well). Such reasoning applies especially to the *Kula*, a most important institution in Trobriand society. Deciding to depart on a *Kula* directly translates into a lot of work (building new canoes to begin with). Being a significant part of the most significant institution, work for the *Kula* surely must have mattered a lot to the Trobrianders.

A similar point can be made regarding magical beliefs and practices. Given how significant the *Kula* institution was, no wonder that work for the *Kula*, the building of canoes, was surrounded by sacred cultural practices, to ensure the technical excellence of the ship, speed in particular, to exorcise against evil spirits, and generally to beseech success in the new expedition. Similarly, garden work was also surrounded by complex magical rites, performed by specialist magicians. What conclusion should we draw from this, about the significance of work activities? One might say that their religious and magical surrounding means that their primary meaning was social and symbolic for the individuals, and for the collective that they above all else served to ensure the reproduction of the social order by adherence to rites and key beliefs, in which case work did not matter qua work. Or we might conclude instead that work mattered a lot precisely because it was the direct object of some of that culture's most important beliefs and was at the centre of deeply significant ritual practices. It was the canoes and the gardens themselves, worked upon by the people and enabling the work of people, which were the direct objects of sacred deference.

The same point can be made from a different angle. Next to the ritual activities surrounding gifts and counter-gifts involved in *Kula* exchanges, important trading occurred at the same time, where objects and materials that could not be produced at home were acquired, such as adze-axes or clay pots. Malinowski shows that departing for the *Kula* was not just symbolic, not just about maintaining social alliances and establishing status, but was also a directly economic endeavour, in the standard sense of the term, with much trade and barter being undertaken. Similarly, while work on canoes was surrounded by magical practices, it was also engaged in through a well-oiled division of labour and required oversight and directing by building experts (2014 [1922], 167–177). In other words, the fact that work was surrounded by magical beliefs and ritual practices did not make it less work, if by work we mean productive, technical activity. Activities that had strong social and symbolic importance like the *Kula* had work as a central component, with all the technical dimensions of it in full knowledge and display to all involved. Malinowski makes this point explicitly when he shows how for the Trobrianders there was a 'cooperation between labour and magic' in the production of sound and beautiful canoes (126): both were required and the technical aspects of good workmanship, notably from the experts, were recognized in their own right.

We can refer here to another classic of social anthropology where just this point regarding the 'interlocking' of religious beliefs and productive action is emphasized. This is the series of theoretical observations Raymond Firth, one of Malinowski's most famous students, added in the introduction to the second edition of *The Work of the Gods in Tikopia* (Firth 1967). The book describes in minute detail the complex ritual programme that the community of this small Polynesian community used to engage in twice a year over six-week periods, in order to resacralize its canoes and temples, initiate the planting and undertake the harvesting of yam, perform important memorial rites, and manufacture the yearly provision of turmeric, a substance of high material and symbolic value. A complex schedule of six weeks of ritual activities thus prepared and supported the 'work of the monsoon' and the 'work of trade-wind' (Firth 1967, 34–37). Firth makes the following observation:

> A striking feature of the conduct of the Work of the Gods was the intricate intermingling of esoteric and exoteric features in it. This occurred in several ways. Ritual and economic activity were linked together in the very construction of the whole cycle since one manifest intent of the ritual was the promotion and sanctification of the economic process. Work and rite tended therefore to alternate, each as it were supporting and leading to the performance of the other.
>
> **(Firth 1967, 11)**

In fact, not only did rite 'promote and sanctify' work, but ritual practice was also considered by the people of Tikopia as being itself a form of work because of the high demand in time and energy it made on them. Therefore, they used the same word, '*fekau*', for the activities demanded by the rituals and for profane labour. This interlocking of sacred and profane activity was consummated, Firth notes, in the fact that the outputs of ritual activity, once they had been offered to the gods, could then serve immediately for human consumption. The 'work of the gods', we might say, was seen by the people of Tikopia as true work for them, including in the rewards of work.

To conclude what we learn from a full reading of Malinowski's classical study, far from being an activity 'half-way between effort and play' (Méda 1995, 34), by which Méda means that work for these 'pre-modern' people did not matter as such, and the truly important aspects of social reproduction for them involved symbolic action and concerned the respect of tradition, in fact work for the Trobrianders had many, highly significant and explicit dimensions *as* work, that is, as toilsome, productive, technically guided activity. It consumed a lot of their time and energy; individuals demonstratively engaged in it to show their commitment and their expertise; social status was directly related to this commitment to their work ethic; it required the learning of specific knowledges and skills, which thus constituted a large part of each person's cognitive resources; it was an integral, explicitly identified part of the most important activities through which society was reproduced, including in its symbolic structure.

Comparable evidence regarding the many ways in which work matters to individuals in horticultural societies can be garnered from another key reference cited by Méda, namely the writings of Philippe Descola prior to his monumental *Beyond Nature and Culture* (Descola 1994, 1996). In these books is clearly outlined the significance of work for Achuar people, despite the fact that, as he analyses it in his more recent magnum opus, their imaginary and the ontology on which their world view is premised are utterly different from the Western one.

On Descola's observations, Achuar men worked on average five hours per day, and women six (1994, 357). This is significantly more than the figure of 'twenty hours a week' that is often quoted about preindustrial societies, following Sahlins. These figures include hours spent in hunting and gardening activities, as well as domestic work. Descola's calculations are based on the classical distinction between production and reproduction. On an expanded conception of work, which includes for instance the care of children and their education (see the discussion in Descola 1994, 355), or the specific social obligations women have to fulfil, for instance when the family receives external visitors, the five or six hours of work per day underestimates how much the Achuar work.

For both sexes, social status is directly tied to work achievements, in gardening for women and in hunting for men: 'It is highly unlikely that a good hunter would be warried to a bad gardener and vice-versa' (1994, 374). Unlike the Trobrianders, the Achuar do not have a special term to designate a good worker. However, Descola explains that there is an implicit representation of it, which we can 'deduce from its opposite', the *naki*, the 'lazy person'. This representation points to the work ethic specific to Achuar culture:

> Laziness is clearly defined by the Achuar as the mediocre fulfilling of obligations that befall everyone: a man is lazy if he seldom goes hunting and if he clears small parcels of land; a woman is lazy is she does not look well after her garden and does not make a lot of manioc beer. Laziness confers a devalued social status, maybe even the only status that is explicitly devalued in such a society that is otherwise

> extremely egalitarian. When one has the bad luck of being married to someone who is publicly recognised as being lazy, one is perfectly entitled to abandon them, since they have not fulfilled their normal role in the necessary complementarity of productive tasks.
>
> (1994, 369)

Once again, work efforts, both in relation to their quantitative and qualitative aspects, have a direct and explicit social value. From Descola's descriptions, it is clear that this value is publicly acknowledged.

Descola's descriptions give an insight into what work activities might have meant for the Achuar people he visited in relation to their identity. He describes in moving pages the importance of gardens for Achuar women, where they spend the longest part of their days (1994, 1996, 198–264). It is their 'world', the only space that belongs to them individually, a space intimately linked to all the major experiences of their personal lives, where they give birth and express their grief when a loved one has been lost. It is the space where they establish their standing, both in the eyes of their spouse and within the broader community, by demonstrating their ability to toil and to produce plentiful and beautiful gardens. As with the Trobrianders, garden work is driven not just by productive considerations (although these matter a lot), but also aesthetic ones, not only creating well-tended gardens, but also experimenting with new varieties and promoting as great a diversity of plants as possible, growing even plants that play no role in consumption. This aesthetics of garden work is not just a form of social competition, there is also intrinsic pleasure in witnessing a beautiful garden. Work therefore represents a major part in the lives of Achuar women: it occupies most of their time, it defines the space that belongs to them and where they have some of the most formative experiences of their lives, it is the basis of their developed knowledge of the natural world, it is the way by which they establish their reputation in the eyes of their closed ones and the broader group, it gives back to them and to others an image of themselves.

Descola's reports even provide an insight into the intimate, affective dimensions of Achuar work. As with the Trobrianders, the horticultural work of Achuar women combines botanical knowledge and technical know-how, two areas in which Achuar women excel, with magical work, the work necessary to ensure beneficent spirits will help in promoting plant growth, and maleficent spirits are kept at bay (1994, 191–220). A crucial component of magical practices in Achuar culture is the interpretation of dreams. For the hunters dreams are an irreplaceable part of hunting, dictating the times of the hunt and presaging its success (1994, 324–330; 1996, 122–140). For both genders, it is not just social standing but even the innermost life of individuals, through their personal dream worlds, which have so much importance in their culture, which are directly associated with the duties and the challenges they face as workers.

11.2 The Myth of Early Leisure Societies

Another important strand of social anthropology to consider is the research on hunter-gatherer societies that has been conducted since the late 1960s. Following a paradigm-setting conference held in Chicago in 1966, and the eponymous publication in 1968 of *Man the Hunter* (Lee and DeVore 1968; see the account in Suzman 2022, 125–145), a new approach emerged, challenging the traditional picture of hunter-gatherers as people whose primitive techniques and mode of economic production barely enabled them to achieve subsistence level, and who as a result were not in a material position to enter the path of cultural evolution. Following this paradigm shift, hunter-gatherers were presented by many anthropologists as people who had the wisdom to limit their wants and were thereby able to achieve true 'affluence' with minimal amounts of work, as all their socially defined needs were easily fulfilled. With far less work to do than modern citizens, they had much more time to dedicate to socializing, leisure activities, and sheer idleness. Their lack of interest in accumulation was connected to the absence of wealth disparities, which meant they were able to enjoy egalitarian and free social relations, with no established forms of authority or hierarchy, notably among the genders. Having no interest in constantly expanding production for the sake of accumulation, hunter-gatherers also had a much lighter footprint on their environment. The hunter-gatherer mode of human organization was thus presented as the polar opposite, functionally and normatively, of modern society, with the contrast turning largely around the place of work in individual lives and the social imaginary (see the introduction in Gowdy 1998). Given that humanity has lived in this foraging mode of economic organization for the largest part of its history, modern, industrial society in contrast, which is barely two hundred years old, has nearly exhausted all natural resources and contains many injustices and pathological traits, appears as a dystopian heir to a much more balanced way of living individually and collectively.

Outside the disciplines of ethnology and anthropology, it is without a doubt the texts by Marshall Sahlins, notably his *Stone Age Economics* (Sahlins 1998 [1972]) and 'The Original Affluent Society' (originally 1974, reprinted in Gowdy 1998, 5–42) that had the most profound impact across the other humanities and social sciences in promoting this vision. It is unsurprisingly to him that Méda turned when she asserted that 'work occupies only a small part of the time and interest of the people considered'. Sahlins' startling claim that hunter-gatherers only worked on average a maximum of twenty hours a week is often referenced by social and political theorists to gesture towards an anthropological backdrop which is supposed to show the contingency and pathology of modern society's relation to work. Given the role this reference to hunter-gatherer societies has played and continues to play in debates on work, it is useful to briefly survey two strands of arguments that dispel the myth of early human societies being affluent, leisure societies.

First, many anthropologists, including anthropologists who studied the hunter-gatherer societies on which Sahlins based his claims, have raised serious doubts about the image of them that has been crafted so that they could appear as a foil to modern, work-based society (see Lucassen 2021, 38–41 for a historical criticism). Kaplan 2000 is particularly useful for his comprehensive summary of these sceptical arguments (see also Kurtz 1994 for the debate on the San Bushmen more specifically, and more recently Hawkes, O'Connell, Blurton Jones 2018). Serious methodological doubts about the studies used by Sahlins make the evidence they provide highly unreliable and undermine the strong conclusions he drew on their basis. Considering the whole range of activities that people in some of the societies studied actually spent in ensuring their material livelihood leads to hours per week that are more than double the famous twenty-hour figure. Studies of societies in similar geographies have returned triple the numbers of hours worked (for instance Hawkes and O'Connell 1981 for the Alyawarra in Australia). The claim that hunter-gatherers chose to not engage in technological development because they wisely limited their wants and refused to enter a cultural path that would have required more work, is belied by their practice when they come into contact with modern technology and modern foods, which are standardly keenly adopted by them. The claim that hunter-gatherer societies are the original 'affluent' ones is belied by medical and biophysical evidence, such as the high negative impact of low-energy and low-quality nutrition on infant and adolescent growth, the high rate of infant mortality and the very early age of adult mortality. Individuals interviewed by anthropologists testify how much the uncertainty about food availability and indeed the experience of hunger, affected them physically and psychologically. In many cases, idleness was not a free choice but was enforced upon people, because of the harshness of the climate or the lack of easily accessible food sources, which meant subsistence efforts only brought negative returns. In short, the counter-image to work-centred modern society that societies of foragers are supposed to present is highly problematic on factual grounds.

Beyond the sceptical doubts expressed by many specialist anthropologists about the 'original affluent society' thesis, even more significant for our purposes is a second strand of evidence about foraging societies, which shows that, as is the case of horticulturalist people, work in fact played a major role in them. Richard Lee's classic book on the !Kung San of Botswana is a precious resource in this context. The chapter on hunting shows how centrally important the activity is to the San Bushmen. From the age of nine, as genders begin to be differentiated, boys start to learn their skills. Studying animal tracks, watching men preparing for the hunt and returning from it, listening to endless stories of hunting expeditions, is 'a major pastime of the older boys' (Lee 1979, 236). Adulthood is reached only when one has killed a mature antelope by poisoned arrow. 'If these conditions are met, the first buck ceremony is held, an extremely important milestone in the life of a hunter' (238). The difficulty in killing these animals means that young men might not reach formal adulthood until they are thirty years of age. Ceremonies for the first male and the first female animals killed involve specific cuts and tattoos: 'the resulting tattoos, which are permanent, announce to the world the young hunter's new status' (238). This new status makes the young man a much better prospect for marriage. A hunter's career goes on until he dies. Because Bushmen are fiercely egalitarian, a number of strategies are in place to downplay hunting success, but there is still high social recognition attached to it. Given the importance of hunting in men's lives, it is their main topic of conversation. Even though meat provides only a third of nutritional energy, it is a great cause of celebration for the group when it is brought back to camp. As in many other cultures (the Achuar for instance), hunting is preceded by magical rituals.

When we read Lee's first-hand descriptions of the hunting world of !Kung San men, it seems difficult to avoid the conclusion that much of their identity turns around their work. Hunting is their main occupation from their childhood to their death. It is what inspires and guides their knowledge of the natural world. Most of their skills and craftmanship revolve around hunting and the fabrication and care of the tools for hunting. Apart from what we might call 'political' mechanisms that grant individual rights of leadership (from marriage, inheritance, or personal qualities), social status, which is literally etched on their bodies, is defined to a large extent by their expertise as a hunter. It is through hunting that men contribute mostly to the subsistence of family and the larger group. It does not seem far-fetched to say that, even if they have a lot of idle time (but one aspect of controversies in the last decade has turned on the validity of previous time calculations), for !Kung San men, their work is central to their identity and structures a large part of their inner and public lives.

More evidence about the multi-dimensional importance of work in hunter-gatherer cultures can be found in ethnographic accounts spanning the planet (Kelly 1995 for a synoptic survey of hunter-gatherer scholarship and the wide diversity in hunter-gatherer cultures). For reasons of space, only three representative cases are mentioned, from regions of the globe far apart from each other, each highlighting specific forms of individual and collective significance of work.

In *Labor's Lot. The Power, History and Culture of Aboriginal Action* (1994), Elizabeth Povinelli showed the distinct way in which Belyuen people of far North Australia conceive of hunting and gathering activities: namely, as reciprocal interactions between the work of mythical ancestors and their own interventions on the land. Ritual practices and the keeping alive of mythical knowledge are the media through which ancestors' and present human actions combine. Hunting and gathering as a result do a lot more than bring necessary calories for them: they help maintain the land itself; and given its significance for the people living on it, they in turn help to maintain the latter's identity. In this conception, economic action is indissolubly linked to cultural, and in the context of colonial land rights disputes, political dimensions. Povinelli demonstrated how a trans-substantiation conception of human action's efficacy underpins this holistic conception of work:

> Rather than congealing in objects made or gotten, in the short run Aboriginal labor is seen to penetrate them, in a way analogous to how sound passes through the ears and air areas.... In the long run, people who live and labor in an area (and who are thereby seen to be 'stuck' in it) permeate the region with their words and sweat. When they die, they are embodied at the site; their spirit/self resides there.... Thus hunting's cultural production unfolds through time in a process that includes human hunting action, mythic reaction, and eventual mythic transformation.
>
> **(1993, 152–153)**

In this social imaginary of work, working activities are the material way to realize the connection of living humans to the land and the mythical ancestors, a connection that forms the baseline structure of personal and collective identity. Working activities in this case are indissolubly reproductive of physiological and symbolic livelihood.

In *Drama and Power in a Hunting Society* (1982), Anne Chapman described the way of life of the now-extinct Selknam of Tierra del Fuego at the Southern tip of the American continent. She cites Carlos Gallardo's Los Onas: 'the hunt occupies most of their time and they give themselves to it with body and soul, with an unextinguishable ardour, and with real and very intense passion, as it is the greatest pleasure of their existence' (Chapman 1982, 22). Chapter 2 outlined what was that society's socio-economic structure. Chapman organized the description by identifying different status positions. The first was that of 'expert artisan' (*haalchin*), which designated individuals who excelled in activities all individuals were expected to perform. This recognition of expert skill included both genders, such as a woman expert at making clothing or baskets, or men particularly good at making bows or arrowheads. Being a proficient hunter, and more specifically a skilful archer, brought special recognition, as did being a good cormorant hunter, as this style of hunting was particularly dangerous. For each one of those special skills, particular names distinguished the individuals and were used publicly to acknowledge their superiority. High status in hunting translated into success in marital union (1982, 41).

Chapman's presentation is particularly instructive in presenting religious statuses as part of the socio-economic structure, linking forms of social distinction to the particular activities select individuals were able to perform for others and for the group as a whole. For the Selkman, essential functions in social reproduction were fulfilled by the shamans who interceded with and controlled supernatural forces, sages who were responsible for maintaining knowledge of the tradition and for name-giving, and prophets, who were even more revered than shamans and sages.

At the other end of the continent, we learn about the Inupiak nation in the Alaska in studies by Ernest Burch (Burch 2006). Here again, social distinction stems to a large extent from excellence in valued activities everyone is expected to engage in. Burch cites Simpson on how one becomes a leading man:

> '*umialgich* were family heads who acquired positions of unusual influence in the community by being more thrifty and intelligent, better traders, and usually better hunters, as well as physically stronger and more daring' than everyone else. But there were also experts in particular activities (*atangich*) who took charge of operations when particular group tasks required efficient management and expert direction. These temporary 'bosses' received their social distinction from collective acknowledgement of their higher skills.
>
> (2006, 68)

In summary, the ethnographic record shows that in many cultures, there are distinct words for different aspects of work and for important occupations, linked to the ways in which people imagine their place in the world, what the world is made of, and how humans interact with the world and the entities within it. In many cases, indigenous cultures had a strong work ethic where the values of hard work, good work, and beautiful work largely determined personal standing within the family and the broader group. For all involved in the group, whatever their social ranking, learning the knowledges and skills required by that society's specific 'mode of production' occupied a large portion of individuals' time and defined their identity to a large extent. It formed a large part of their education, and in many cultures, the work of subsistence in fact was a true 'occupation', in the sense that it defined the person's main interests, how she viewed herself, the interests she would share and discuss with others. There was often a robust link between the religious belief system and the system of occupations. A significant part of religious practices, both those performed by the collective and by individuals, had to do with efficient and successful outcomes in that occupation, or indeed success in the competition with other participants sharing that occupation.

Before we draw on this evidence to address the objections presented in the first chapter, we need to take a short detour through pre-modern Western societies, as historicist objections also refer to those examples in asserting the uniqueness of work's centrality in modernity.

11.3 Cultural Histories of Pre-modern Work

As we saw in the first chapter, references to 'pre-modern' modes of social organization, notably the ancient Greek and Roman worlds, are consistently mobilized in contemporary social and political theory, to highlight how historically unique the modern belief in work's centrality is. However historical scholarship has moved on significantly from the famous interpretations provided by Finley, Polanyi, and Veyne. The great historians had a lasting influence on the vision of work in pre-modern societies. They seemed to have definitively established that ancient societies did not conceptualize economic action as a separate sphere, and correspondingly had no general concept of work. As a result, the conclusion went, their economic organizations and activities should not be analysed with the categories defining the modern economic outlook, that is, in terms of efficiency, productivity, value creation, innovation, and so on. Instead, ancient societies should be viewed through the lens of what truly mattered to them and in terms of the principles that actually organized their social world, including productive activities, that is, the hierarchy of social statuses. Within these hierarchical worldviews, working activities were universally despised, as signalling dependency and lack of freedom.

Recent historical scholarship has questioned these assumptions and significantly enriched knowledge about the ancient worlds of work. Specialists of global history (Lucassen 2006, 2021; Lucassen et al. 2008; Komlosy 2018) show the significance of institutions and experiences of work in societies across the world, much earlier than the late eighteenth century, when work is supposed to have been 'invented'. Economic historians of antiquity have disproved the received view that the absence of a separate notion of economic action was reflected in the fact that ancient economies remained stagnant for long periods of time (Bresson 2016). Empirical enquiries in economic history have been underpinned by methodological discussions, which are particularly relevant for this book. The central question has been whether historians and social theorists are entitled to use analytical categories that are alien to the worldview underpinning the society they study, in particular, whether the analytical categories of Marxist, neo-institutionalist or neo-classical models can be meaningfully applied to ancient economies. For contemporary economic historians, the answer has been a resounding yes. Economic realities have objective dimensions that can be identified and measured through the formal concepts and methods of economic theory (for instance, amounts of outputs produced in different sectors of production, demographic trends, how labour is allocated, labour productivity, rates of innovation, and so on), and one is entitled to using such concepts to describe any economic organization and its evolutions over time. We will return to this point in the next section, to counter the nominalist challenge. As an outcome of these discussions, many economic historians of the ancient world have adopted a neo-institutionalist approach, which focuses on the way in which institutional realities (types of labour contracts, the different forms of slavery, the organization of markets, and so on) established particular structures of positive and negative incentives that guided the behaviours of social actors. This approach allows historians to apply formal economic analysis, while making room for the influence of mentalities, values, and social perceptions on the agents' decisions and behaviour (Scheidel et al. 2007). The conclusions reached in these recent debates show practical ways to combine descriptions 'from the outside' that provide invaluable information on the organizational features of a distant society (in this case pre-industrial Western nations), with an internal approach that is hermeneutically sensitive to the motivations and values of the actors, 'from the inside'.

These neo-institutionalist studies in ancient economics have been complemented by a new wave of cultural histories of work, which provide fresh insights into the institutions and experiences of work in antiquity. Two recent collections (Verboven and Laes 2016 and Ephraim Lytle 2019) provide particularly informative entry points into this vast literature. This recent scholarship shows how rich and varied experiences of work were in Western antiquity, how much work mattered for many people on an individual level, and how much institutions and representations of work mattered in social organizations. In light of this recent scholarship, the historical assumptions about pre-modern work that continue to underpin discussions on work in contemporary social and political theory appear severely outdated (typically Honneth 2023, 21).

A point consistently made by historians of work in the ancient world is the stark disconnect between the canonical texts that are often used as the single source of information on ancient work (classical passages in the works of Xenophon, Plato, Aristotle, Seneca, and Cicero), and the social and economic reality at the time, which contemporary economic and cultural history unveils. Such a disconnect stems from the fact that the texts of the canon often reflect the prejudices and ideological biases of Athenian and Roman elites and their attempt to justify their domination over working populations. It is a mistake, however, to read these texts as though they were representative of mentalities across ancient societies and accurately inform about the real place of work in them. Upper classes had a direct, social-political interest in assigning lower status to working classes, so as 'to marginalize moral threats to the socio-political order' (Bond 2016, 241). In order to quell discontent and assert their domination, upper classes sought to impose a narrative that justified their position, by linking work to morally degraded activities and identifying workers as naturally inferior beings. However, this elite view was far being universally shared. Its ideological character appears already in the fact that most men of the upper classes, who might have publicly lauded the life of *skhole* and *otium*, the importance of leisure for a truly accomplished life, were also businessmen, wholesalers, owners of large agricultural properties, as Cicero himself recommended (1991, 59), or indeed spent a large part of their time performing cultic duties or political office functions (Verboven and Laes 2016, 3). Sarah Bond also makes the point that the evaluation of craft and of commercial activities was very different in the centre of power compared to towns near ports and on the busiest trading roads, like Philippi in Macedonia (Bond 2016, 132).

One significant aspect of this divide between elite views and the complex tapestry of social reality concerns the equation of work with heteronomy and dependence, a feature, which, as we saw, many modern social and political philosophers have inherited from the ancient paradigm. Social historians warn about judging too quickly from literary, philosophical and other textual sources. Flohr (2016) makes the point in relation to legal statuses. Against the traditional view of the ancient economies as 'slave economies', he notes that slaves in fact did not make up the majority of the workforce, but probably peaked at 20% in Rome. But for the majority of free workers, as Flohr and Wilson also show (Wilson and Flohr 2016), there would have been a wide range of degrees of autonomy in work, which would have been negotiated in day-to-day interactions and would have depended on many factors, notably the material organization of each work process.

Against the view that work in the ancient world was uniformly considered a debasing activity, social historians note the many ways in which occupational identities mattered and could enjoy public recognition. In Imperial Rome, most professions were organized in formal associations, the *collegia* (Bresson 2016, 148–150). Their relationship to political authorities varied across history, and at particular times some of them had a high social standing, notably the *collegia* involved in valued public works (aqueducts, bridges, baths, temples). In recognition of their contribution to collective life, they were formally involved in ceremonies, like the inauguration of temples and monuments, had reserved seatings at the theatre, were allowed to bestow public honours on respected citizens. Public recognition was high in particular for the professions ensuring the reliability of the *annona*, the constant supply of food to the capital and the main cities. For their role in fulfilling the population's needs, the *collegia* could rightfully present themselves as being 'as much the pillars of society as political elites claimed to be' (Verboven 2016, 189).

This positive value of professional activity is reflected in the attitudes of individual workers to their occupations. Studies of the epigraphic record by Burford (1972), Joshel (1992), Lis and Soly (2016), Cupcea and Varda (2018) show the extent to which craftsmen, including in occupations attracting the lowest social consideration (shoemakers, even miners) and including slave workers, displayed pride in their professional activities via their epitaphs, and for exceptionally successful individuals, through paid dedications on altars and ornate decorations in tombs and funerary monuments. Public memory at the time was paramount to an individual's sense of self. To cite just one spectacular example, Lis and Soly mention:

> Roman baker and bread contractor Marcus Vergilius Eurysaces, who was probably a freedman. His tomb, dated ca. 50–20 BC, is remarkable not only because of its location—at the convergence of two roads just outside of Rome—and its vast size

> and the construction materials, but also and mainly for the friezes depicting all stages in the production process, from grinding wheat to baking bread.
>
> **(Lis and Soly 2016, 267)**

The fact that all stages of the work process are displayed on a rich tomb visible to all is highly significant. It shows that one could rightfully take pride in one's work, and that the activities of work were not intrinsically shameful. Superior workmanship and craftmanship were in fact highly valued. There was general appreciation for 'work well done' delivering beautiful artefacts and for the display of *ars*, the expert mastering of skills and technical knowledge (De Robertis 1971; Tran 2016; Faitini 2023). The positive valuation of *ars* was not restricted to manual crafts, but extended to all forms of activity where one could display expertise, like politics or philosophy. It included a reference to training and apprenticeship. All of these terms were positively connoted. Indeed, many literary passages addressed to elite audiences also expressed this general admiration for expert work producing admirable results.

The value of superior craftsmanship and the universal valuing of superior achievements were eminently displayed in the genre of *ekphrasis*, the literary description of admired works of art. The *locus classicus* is the passage in the *Iliad* where Hephaestus creates a shield for Achilles. Lytle notes that pictured on the shield is precisely the idealized image of what work can produce, a peaceful, bountiful landscape, contrasted with a city at war (Lytle 2019, 10). The status of *magister*, possessor of technical knowledge and know-how, was applied to the goddess Minerva herself, as patron of the arts and crafts. It is highly symbolic that Ulysses identifies himself to Penelope on his return to Ithaca by recounting how he carved their conjugal bed from the trunk of a tree and how he built his house around it (Sapirstein 2019). The most emblematic Greek hero was himself a master craftsman.

Antithetical to the aristocratic disdain towards dependent work and the degrading nature of physical effort, a popular competing trope was to mock the rich for their lack of fortitude and their incapacity to work hard (Lytle 2019). This reflected a prevalent work ethic, which dictated that virtue is demonstrated through *ponos* and *labor*, the capacity to engage in hard labour. As Lis and Soly write:

> The dominant myths, epic, lyric, tragedy, philosophy, and the acts of heroes and other role models indicate that making worthy efforts was regarded as a duty and a necessity throughout Classical Antiquity, not only because the Gods demanded efforts from everybody, but also and especially because the social value of such efforts was generally recognized. Idleness was harshly condemned in Homeric

> poetry. In his *Works and Days* Hesiod stated pithily: 'Work is no disgrace: it is idleness which is a disgrace.' His words were repeated centuries later as an adage or slogan, both by Pericles and by Socrates, by Demosthenes and by his adversary Demades. To quote Xenophon: 'The best men and dearest to the Gods are those who do their work well.... He who does nothing well is neither useful in any way nor dear to the Gods.'
>
> **(2016, 264)**

This positive evaluation of hard work and of good work, as service to the collective and the Gods and as the path to the virtuous life, was reflected in the veneration of Hercules. Leading philosophical schools, notably the Stoics and the Cynics, extolled the virtue of working life, which led to positive views even of wage work. All classes had a function to fulfil in social life, and every individual, whatever their standing, should avoid idleness. The Cynics even went so far as lauding the labour of the poor as 'it was associated not only with virtues such as honesty, moderation, and justice but also with inner freedom and self-fulfilment' (2016, 262).

There was thus a comprehensive ideal of work in antiquity, comprising a number of values, to which workers appealed in their attempt to assert their identity and contest elite contempt. This ideal defined a conception of the good life in which work played a central part, as an activity through which one could practice and demonstrate virtue and excellence. Besides the capacity to work hard and technical proficiency, these work-related values also included practical knowledge, service to the community, honesty in trading as a sign of a virtue, reverence for the gods, notably those to whom professional service was dedicated.

Another relevant strand of historical enquiry for this section concerns the European Middle Ages (see Garver 2019 for a recent overview). This scholarship is significant because it informs us about the place and meaning of work in European society directly preceding the time when work was supposed to have become central, coinciding with the rise of modern capitalism. It shows that the experiences of work and the establishment of work institutions structure individual and social development well before the eighteenth century.

Of particular interest for our purposes are the landmark studies by Jacques Le Goff (1980) and George Duby (1982) depicting the rise and the evolutions of the 'three orders' trope, an enduring representation of society, in which Christian monarchies were conceived as organizations united under the divinely ordained king and in which 'some pray, others fight, and still others work'. The scheme emerged as early as the ninth century. The historians document the way in which the understanding of 'those who work' changed over time, and how this shift expressed the growing importance taken by the world of work in medieval imaginaries. At first, 'those who work' were equated with the '*servus*' and '*agricolae*': enslaved and servile labour, toiling to support the two higher orders. The three-order scheme served initially as a justification for the exploitation of the majority, based on an ontology of inequality and hierarchy, with humanity seen as divided between different natures. '*Labor*' was equated with '*dolor*' (suffering) and '*sudor*', the sweat of toiling Adam and Eve. Marx still referred to this vision of work in a well-known passage of the *Grundrisse*: 'In the sweat of thy brow shalt thou labour! was Jehovah's curse on Adam' (Marx 1973 [1857]: 611). Already in its first appearances, however, the scheme implied reciprocal dependence and complementarity between the orders: 'on the function of each the work of the others rests, each in turn assisting all' (Duby, citing Adalbero of Laon 1982, 51).

By the end of the eleventh century, the ontological conception of unequal orders began to make way for a functional division. The servile nature of workers was gradually replaced by the new figure of the '*laboratores*' whose exemplary embodiments were individuals exercising social power through their occupations: wealthy individuals, craftsmen, rich peasants. The *laboratores* now enjoyed full social visibility, as important actors on whom the monarch relied to support the kingdom. Duby cites this passage from John of Salisbury's *Polycratus* (1159):

> then and then only will the health of the commonwealth be sound and flourishing when the higher members shield the lower, and the lower respond faithfully and fully in like measure to the just demands of their superiors, so that each and all are as it were members one of another by a sort of reciprocity, and each regards his own interest as best served by that which he knows to be most advantageous for the others.
>
> **(1982, 300)**

This gradual acknowledgement of 'those who labour' is reflected in the shifts in cultural representations. Le Goff shows how, from the twelfth century onwards, an actual 'theology of work' developed in Western Europe, in which the values connected to the world of work and the professions gradually infiltrated the imaginary underpinning of society, to the point where 'the world was subsequently conceived as a vast workplace on the analogy of the urban workplace in which various trades collaborated' (1980, 67). In the words of Gerhoh of Reichersberg (in his 1187 *Liber de Aedificio Dei*), the universe created by God is 'the great factory ..., a sort of universal workshop' (1980, 116). As a recognized contribution to the reproduction of Christian society, each person's work became a potential path to redemption. No trade was an obstacle to salvation, each had its Christian 'vocation'. All crafts belonged to the *familia Christi*, binding all good workers together. Indeed, as Le Goff notes, contrary to the humanist ranking of activities between liberal and mechanical arts, and their retrieval of the old dichotomy of *vita activa* and *vita contemplativa*, the mechanical arts were admitted early on in the representations of valuable activities. As was the case in the Roman world, the technical aspects of work, linked to the specific work cultures of trades and corporations, not just their economic weight, became positively acknowledged as elements contributing to the reproduction of the collective order. This religious elevation of work coinciding with its increased social and political visibility was particularly evident in the 'sermons *ad status*', that is, sermons directed at the lay constituency through its organization in professional bodies. The *corpus* of the world was no longer seen as being composed of orders defined in terms of differing natures, but of estates distinguished by their professions. Craft identity already became a significant part of people's self-understanding. Occupational and religious elements began to merge in the idea of individual 'vocation' (Le Goff 1980, 114; Faitini 2023, 116–121).

This sense that one's personal identity was tied to one's estate and vocation found a supportive institutional framework in dedicated professional associations from the thirteenth century onwards, the guilds. Over the next two centuries, guilds became key economic, social and political institutions. For their members, they represented an all-encompassing framework, which touched on all aspects of their lives. They organized the trade through legal and economic regulations, formalized training and the learning of skills, established networks for masters and entrepreneurs, ensured the transition of businesses after the owner's death (Stabel 2019). Beyond their economic role, medieval guilds offered their members mutual support and protection for all the accidents of life: they were the initial organizers of public hospitals and schools, provided loans and organized emergency funds for struggling members (Rosser 2015). The bonds uniting the members had explicit moral and religious expressions, well summed up in their self-understanding as 'fraternities'. They famously participated in religious ceremonies and public celebrations under their banner and in the corporation's dress code. Given the all-encompassing nature of life in a fraternity, a specialist historian can conclude that for many medieval craftsmen and industrial workers, 'it was work and membership in the guild that constituted the worker's identity' (Stabel 2019, 97).

This adds to all the evidence we found in anthropological research and ancient history, documenting the varied ways in which experiences of work and work organizations have mattered deeply to human individuals and human communities across time and in a wide variety of human cultures. The final section of the chapter will draw on this material to answer the historicist worries about the centrality of work, which operate in the background of many contemporary rejections of work.

11.4 Answering the Historicist Objections

Let us begin with semantics. As we have just seen, in many human societies that were not organized like modern, capitalist ones, a whole vocabulary existed to identify key aspects of work activities. There are terms to designate the physically arduous and persistent nature of labouring: *ponos* for the Greeks, *labor* for the Romans, *takat* among the Achuar (Descola 1994, 367–370), the *fekau* of people living in Tikopia. We focused on hunter-gatherers and horticultural societies, but we could have included evidence from pastoralist ones. For instance, based on his field work with the Tuaregs across the Sahara and Sahel regions of Northern Africa, Gerd Spittler (1990) has described the conception of work of the Kel Ewey of Niger, captured in the word *asshaghal*, which designates specifically activities that are both tiring and useful. In all cultures, there are nouns to designate useful tools and artefacts and verbs to designate particularly significant technical actions, like '*najana*' for the Achuar (Descola 1994, 373) for artisanal production. Even in societies with little technical specialization, social categories are used to distinguish important occupations, like shaman, or sage, or warrior, or priest. During initiation ceremonies among the Baruya people of Papua New Guinea (Godelier 1986 [1982]), some adolescents were singled out by the shaman as future 'great men' who were going to excel in particularly valued activities, protecting the community against its enemies or producing valuable commodities. They would become great warriors (*aoulatta*), shamans (*koulaka*), cassowary hunters (*kayareumala*), salt makers (*tsaimaye*). There was a specific category (*tannaka*) for gardeners who did not go to war and instead worked harder than others, with a larger workforce, to produce a surplus enabling the community to support its warriors and the wealth required for initiations. And of course, there were hundreds of specialized occupations in imperial Rome, including aquarium fishermen, 'nomenclators' remembering the names of constituents for politicians, or mirror carriers. Across the record, we find morally tinged terms that reflect the social estimation, positive or negative, of particular activities and of modes of working, like the Trobriander *tokwaybagula* for expert work, or the *basaunoi* of the Ancient Greeks. Surveying the cultural history of work and the ethnographic record we thus find ample evidence that modern society is not unique in thinking and naming activities of production and reproduction, the particular types of human effort that go into them, and the status that society attaches to individuals who engage in these technical efforts.

When it is claimed that other human societies 'do not have a concept of work', what is meant then is just that they do not have a modern concept of work, or a concept of modern work. They do not have one single term that would capture the array of associated meanings that the mindset typical of modernity classifies under 'work'. Such a remark, however, is not particularly enlightening. It just states the obvious, namely that different human societies think of themselves differently, and accordingly think of their work of reproduction and name that work, differently. As a matter of fact, though, human societies outside of modern, capitalistic ones, do have terms to designate what are *for them* the most salient aspects of the activities of social reproduction, beginning with what are for them striking features of such activities (usually denoting toil, unpleasantness, but also usefulness, or service) in contrast to other modes of action, as well as social categories, like the occupations specializing in particular activities. Countless examples show how much and in what varied ways work mattered to individuals and to collective self-representation in different cultures and at different times. It is not an ethnocentric projection, then, to talk about work and its importance in human society and for human individuals at large, whether they are modern or 'pre-modern', industrial or not, Western or non-Western. It is a mistake to try and find in other societies work categories that would match the modern ones. But it is not a mistake to study these societies' own world of work, and how and why work institutions and work experiences matter to them, as economic and cultural historians and anthropologists do.

These simple points were formulated in a decisive fashion by Philippe Descola himself, in *The Society of Nature*. This is particularly significant since his *Beyond Nature and Culture* makes a thorough, encyclopaedic case for the diversity and irreducibility of fundamental ontologies underpinning the wide variety of human cultures. From this later study, one could conclude to the uniqueness of Western modernity regarding the importance of work. In *The Society of Nature*, however, Descola had showed pre-emptively, as it were, that it is a mistake to infer an alleged unique nature of modernity's interest in work from the irreducible cultural differences separating human collectives across time and space. The Achuar have a unique way of viewing the world, the entities it harbours and their place in it. Their conceptualization of the activities they have to engage in to reproduce themselves are thus underpinned by an ontological grammar that is utterly different from the productivist ontology of the moderns. As Descola shows, they think of work as establishing a relationship with entities and in this way helping to realize the potentialities entailed in them. But Descola's analysis proves performatively that it is possible to describe the key categorical differences between ontologies. Based on this, it is also possible to take these differences into account and to compare conceptualizations of work. Taking into account their relational ontology, and the contrast with modern productivism, the anthropologist can make intelligible to non-Achuars, to some extent at least, how the Achuar view their modes of working. Ethnographic analysis turns into a hermeneutic of the Achuar world of work, which can pinpoint not only differences but also overlaps between these otherwise thoroughly different social imaginaries. It turns out that even though the Achuar do not have a concept that captures all the meanings associated with the modern term 'work', they have a word, '*takat*', the substantive form of the verb '*taka*', designating 'difficult physical activity that mobilises technical know-how and the mediation of a tool' (Descola 1994, 368), which encapsulates core meanings of modern work. The toil implied in the term makes it close to the Greek *ponos* and the Latin *labor*, but it is also used in a sexual sense, and in that meaning is close to the French verb '*besogner*'.

Having thus established the semantics of work in a horticultural society whose ontology is incommensurable with the western one, Descola can then formulate in elaborate terms the conclusion we expressed already in more basic terms. Namely, it is a mistake to conclude that, because such a culture does not view work as a separate sphere of activity by which society's wealth is produced, as the moderns (allegedly) do, therefore this society does not have any concept of work at all:

> is there not in every society a part of the system of representations which defines more or less explicitly the differentiated allocation of the labour power, the intensity and rhythm of energy expenditure, according to tasks, or the hierarchical valorisation accorded to each? For instance, there is no doubt that the Achuar have a precise idea of the quantity of effort required by productive techniques they practice. Such energetic expenditure is of course not conceptualised by them in the form of a quantifiable allocation of labour that would include the composition of the factors of production. But that does not mean either that the very concrete efforts by which the Achuar socialise particular portions of nature are represented by them as a game, or some vague way to commune with the universe. Therefore,

> it does not seem accurate to assert that work becomes an objective reality only in societies where it is perceived as specific category of social practice. Achuar labour is not alienated since its goals and the means to perform it are controlled by those who do it, but that does not mean that it is not work.
>
> (Descola 1994, 351)

This leads Descola to formulate a robust response to the methodological part of the ethnocentric objection:

> It is legitimate to criticise the indiscriminate projection of the categories of political economy into societies that have none of the institutions such categories are supposed to analyse. However, unless we condemn ourselves to solipsism, such salutary operation should not lead us to evacuate all analytical concepts from the social sciences, under the pretext that they are not construed as such in indigenous representations.
>
> (Descola 1994, 351)

Following Descola and anthropologists of work like Applebaum and Spittler, as well as the historians of work, notably historians of the Greco-Roman world who, as we saw, have dealt with this methodological conundrum extensively, when facing the issue of cultural variability, we are not condemned to oscillating endlessly between the seemingly contradictory stances of external, objective analysis and internal, cultural hermeneutics. It is in fact methodologically sound and indeed epistemically enlightening to treat the category of work at two different levels.

'Work' can be understood firstly as an analytical category that can be applied 'from the outside' to any human society, to study the way in which individual efforts are deployed there, using particular techniques, to fulfil needs and thereby reproduce individual lives and the community itself. From this perspective we can analyse how in that society individual efforts are distributed, notably along gender lines, how the efforts are technically mediated, collectively organized, socially evaluated, how the outputs of those activities are distributed, stored, appropriated, owned, how these divisions, organizations, and appropriations of work activities relate to religious beliefs and practices, and to power structures. This analytical and descriptive enquiry is just what anthropologists engage in when they study human societies, whether modern or 'pre-modern', industrial or pre-industrial, from the point of view of their social reproduction. For anthropologists, even those like Marshall Sahlins or Richard Lee who emphasize a radically different attitude to subsistence activities compared to non Western societies, the term and the concept of 'work' are not problematic. Anthropologists do not argue that the societies they study 'have no concept of work', or that 'work is a modern invention'. They debate with other anthropologists over the exact definition of economics in anthropology, whether we should take a 'substantivist' approach and delineate economic activities from other social actions, or a formalist approach, inspired by neoclassical economics, which defines economic action as a specific form of rationality, related to the choices individuals make in using limited means for competing ends. Whichever position economic anthropologists take in this debate, what is not at issue for them is that work is a pertinent category that can be applied to all human societies, since they all have to reproduce themselves (Spittler 2016). Similarly, economic historians today have no issue using the concept of work for ancient worlds and studying work organizations with the analytical tools of modern economic and organizational theories.

It is worth adding that it would seem odd to reject the use of generic categories such as kinship, religion, war, or art in the study of cultures other than one's own (see Descola 2021 for a comprehensive study of image-making practices across human cultures), on the basis that people in these cultures might not have a term to describe those social realities as modern usage does, or what they include under one such term does not overlap with ours. It is puzzling how social scientists who would not raise issues with categories such as religion or war quibble over the concept of work.

Besides the analytical use of the work category, the focus can also be put on the way in which activities of social reproduction are conceptualized and imagined in a particular society, what terms are used, involving which normative connotations, to describe and rank activities, occupations, experiential aspects of particular activities, categories of workers, and so on (Joyce 1987 as a good representative). Even though the conceptual features of the Achuar '*takat*' (an activity involving arduous effort and the use of tools and techniques) seem to overlap partly with a modern conception of work, Descola notes that the Achuar themselves used the Spanish term *trabajo* to describe the work they did when they were hired for petroleum companies, even though, from an external, analytical perspective, what they did for them would have been well described by these features (Descola 1994, 368). This is because *takat* for them is not an external reality that can be exchanged for something else, but an attribute of the person. Work for money therefore cannot be *takat*. But instead of seeing this as proof that the Achuar don't have a concept of work, it is more fruitful to note both that in fact they do have a term, which captures many of the senses of modern concepts of work, and also a different ontology which gives that term its own special sense, such that in order to say 'I work', it makes sense for them to say something like 'my work works on me'.

All human societies work, simply because they have to reproduce themselves. But different societies understand this work of self-reproduction differently. The two perspectives, the external, analytical, and the hermeneutic, descriptive one, are both legitimate. Together, they contest the claim that work is a modern invention, or that some societies have no concept of work.

The anthropological work of Descola and Spittler shows that a nominalist approach that rejects transcultural and transhistorical claims about work is methodologically pernicious and even self-contradictory. Such an approach forbids comparison across history and across cultures, yet comparisons are highly informative and have been used as a trusted method in the social sciences from the beginning. When Max Weber identified the Protestant work ethic, he tried to understand precisely what made the modern economic outlook different from previous ones. The uniqueness of the modern work ethic only appears in contrast to other ways of conceptualizing economic activity, notably against other Christian variants of the theories of creation, original sin and salvation. The same point can be formulated in terms of hermeneutics: a hermeneutically sensitive approach to another culture is not premised on the assumption that one just has to immerse oneself in that culture's indigenous categories to understand it, but rather that the bridge between one's own culture and the culture studied can be bridged if an effort is made to identify differences in representations. And without recourse to analytical categories defined independently of a culture's perspective, there is no way to conduct social-scientific analysis.

Following these reflections, the ontological part of the historicist objection evaporates as well. The question: 'does work exist if it is not experienced or thought?' is vacuous, since there can be no human society without work, and therefore no society without the experiencing, the conceiving and the naming of its activities. As Descola made the point emphatically, there has to be some representation of the different individual and social aspects of the experience linked to the necessity to work. The fact that these descriptions do not overlap between cultures is just a fact about cultural differences. If in one society the same word is used for hard work and for sexual activity, the conclusion that ought to be drawn from it is not that the society does not have a concept of work, but that its way of representing work draws on a way of conceiving the world, an ontology, that leads indigenous minds to associate work with sexual activities, as happens in the imaginaries of other indigenous people, as in the case of the French *besogner*. If a society uses the same term for material production and for the activity of shamans (Méda 1995, 32), we should not conclude from it that it does not have a concept of work, which would imply that only a narrow concept of material production for market exchange is a valid definition of work, but rather that in that society some physical and symbolic endeavours are placed on the same scale. Indeed, such conceptualization of socially reproductive activities that views the role of shaman as comparable to that of hunter is in fact more insightful than one that restricts work to the production of material goods or to having formal employment.

When social and political theorists argue that there are many human societies that 'don't have a concept of work', or that work was 'invented' in the late eighteenth century, they imply that modern people do have one such concept, that it is homogeneous and universally accepted and used in this homogeneous sense. But this is clearly not the case. The work category is very slippery for modern people because of the many varied meanings it can have. The conception of work that Smith and generations of economists after him used to establish political economy narrows the meaning of work in a way that is highly debatable. As a matter of fact, modern societies do not have a general concept of work either, given how polysemic the term is across different contexts, how unstable its definition, and how uncertain the boundaries between what counts as work or not. Indeed, the cultural variability among representations of activities of social reproduction extends among modern societies themselves. The vocabularies of work do not fully overlap between modern nations. Simple terms in one language, like the French *métier*, the German *Beruf*, the English *workmanship*, have connotations that their translated equivalents do not have and require long paraphrases to fully convey all their meanings. As was already pointed out in Chapter 2, there is no single, consistent work ethic across modern national cultures, each nation's history leads to specific emphases in negative and positive social understandings and expectations about work efforts.

Delving into historical and anthropological scholarship thus helps to rebut most of the objections stemming from the historicist worry. We consider the *realm of necessity* objection at length in the last chapter. The dialectical reward from conducting this survey is the substantive conclusions about the importance of work for human beings that emerged from it. In the next chapter, we focus on the many social dimensions of this importance.

12
The Social Centrality of Work

The previous chapter sought to allay the concerns that are raised from a historicist perspective. The last three chapters respond to the remaining objections and continue to use this as an opportunity to highlight key aspects of the centrality of work. Chapters 13 and 14 focus on the importance of work for individual people and on the political importance of work respectively, using the expanded concept of social reproduction. In the present chapter, we consider different ways in which work is central in a 'social' sense.

As we saw in Section 9.2, one major objection from sociology and social theory is that speaking of a 'centre' in complex societies with high degrees of functional and institutional differentiation is mistaken on factual and categorical grounds. Why would one particular social sphere, and the functions that are fulfilled in it, be more 'central' than other spheres and their own functions? On what grounds should we consider that one type of social experience, work, is more important to modern individuals than other experiences? Why should leisure activities that matter to individuals, or those moments when political decisions are made or national life is celebrated, be deemed less 'central'? On what grounds should professional identity trump other aspects of personal identity? Depending on one's point of view, other spheres could just as well be viewed to be more necessary for social reproduction, like the state, as the ultimate source of legitimate power, or the markets that allow individual actions and preferences to be optimally coordinated. And it might be true factually that work has become central for modern individuals, but as many argue, this centrality is a pathology. The chapter first responds to the categorical objection, before highlighting a number of different ways, seven to be exact, in which work can be shown to be 'socially' central. In each case, the term centrality means something different.

12.1 Problematic Metaphors

The objections from social theory and sociology rely on the assumption that modern social organizations are made up of different 'spheres' and

The Case for Work. Jean-Philippe Deranty, Oxford University Press. © Jean-Philippe Deranty (2024).
DOI: 10.1093/oso/9780192887146.003.0013

'subsystems'. As we saw in Section 8.2, social evolution, the shift from traditional to 'post-traditional' societies, is viewed as a process of 'rationalization', such that the different requirements for the reproduction of individual and communal life are fulfilled in functional spheres that become gradually differentiated from each other via increasingly detached institutional systems. Work on this model is just one 'sphere' among others, the sphere in which the material underpinnings of individual and collective life are secured, and given that modern societies are capitalist societies, the sphere where value is created for the purpose of exchange and profit. For the critics of the 'work society', whether of Marxist or feminist inspiration (like Kathi Weeks), and indeed those critics who adopt other normative presuppositions, it might be a fact in modern life that institutions of work have taken on a central place within complex social organizations, and that work dominates the intimate and social parts of individual's lives, but such centrality is problematic, for all the reasons post-work theorists highlight. To the normative objections raised against this 'pathology' of work in modernity, social theory adds a categorical one: not only is it wrong to make work central, but it is also conceptually mistaken because modern societies in fact have no centre, and modern individuals live in a plurality of circles, engage in social bonds that only partly overlap and are often not 'concentric'.

The perspective from generalized social reproduction very simply and thoroughly undercuts this categorical objection. The objection is premised on the idea of 'spheres' of social life, of separated 'subsystems', with work one sphere that takes on too much importance in relation to the others. But as soon as we consider society as something that needs to be 'reproduced', it becomes immediately clear that work is not a sphere of social life, or a subsystem in the sense in which social theory discusses it. Work is a sphere of social life only if just some work activities are considered as work, those in particular that are related to production for the market, and all the other activities of social reproduction are ignored. This simple point has been at the heart of feminist scholarship and its focus on social reproduction, as we saw in Chapter 10. The point that was raised initially out of concern for the work of care and domestic work can be generalized and extended to all other spheres. There is a lot more work being performed than just the activities that aim specifically at the production of goods needed for material subsistence (food, clothing, shelter, tools) or commodities to be sold on the market. Work has to be performed in every one of the spheres and subsystems that make up modern societies.

For example, one subsystem concerns social reproduction in the specific sense of the concerted efforts it takes to maintain the moral and cultural bonds that unite the different generations making up a community. A lot of work is required for this form of reproduction. It includes the work of socialization and education which is split between households and formal institutional settings. The professional part of that latter subsystem relies in particular on the work of educators, but also on the work of all the people who ensure schools are operational, in terms of infrastructures, finances, curriculum, and so on. As soon as we consider what it takes for this subsystem to fulfil its function, we realize just how much work goes into it. As with the work of immediate care, a lot of work in this subsystem is waged, but a lot of it is not, namely all the work performed by parents, community associations, and volunteers. Another example is the political system, with its own dedicated institutions. In many representative democracies, that part of the overall institutional set-up relies on the work of countless people, waged and unwaged, who sustain the party system through organizational and militant work, help elections run, disseminate ideas, organize debates, and so on. A third important subsystem is culture, which is reproduced by armies of professionals, creators, and administrators, who make old and new cultural resources available. An equally big army of non-waged individuals contribute purposefully to the reproduction of cultural knowledge, if only the parents who teach their children the language and the shared knowledge of the community. The social system as a whole relies on specific work of administration and maintenance at the different geographical levels of its territory; on the work of police enforcement; on the work of those who maintain material and technical infrastructures; of those who intervene in situations of crisis, to repair or avert further damage. We can multiply the examples. Work is needed everywhere, in every 'sphere' of society, in all of its systems and subsystems, to operate, sustain, and repair all the institutions involved in those systemic parts, which in turn are the conditions for the reproduction of individual and collective lives.

A Marxist critic might raise the objection that all of that work being performed in different parts of the social system to ensure the latter's reproduction does so to facilitate the valorization process, so that none of the subsystems escapes the overall framework of commodity production. This might seem to be an objection to the idea being formulated here, that a lot of work is not for subsistence or commodity production. But such an objection misses the point. Even if much of the work going on in different spheres of society is guided by capitalistic concerns (for instance in the ideological content of school curricula, or the values taught children in families), it remains the case that work is not a 'sphere', even on this view of society. The basic point is that work is performed in every sphere and cannot be called a sphere itself.

Every 'sphere' and 'subsystem', and the social system itself as whole, is maintained in existence and 'evolves', in the language of twentieth-century social theory, thanks to the goal-directed activities performed by a myriad of individuals who purposefully ensure they do their bit so the part of the overall system to which they contribute continues to function. The system as a whole and every sphere in it requires work, some of it waged, 'formal', some of it 'informal', volunteer, or unwaged. Work can be described as one 'sphere' of society only on the old untenable assumption that the only production that truly exists or matters is the production of material goods, or, on a Marxist variant, the production of commodities, or in a classical economic version, of goods to be exchanged on the market.

These different versions of the same obfuscation are entrenched by the uncritical use of two linguistic tropes, which continue to be used in many contemporary writings of social and political theory. The first problematic trope associates work with the '*economic sphere*', as if all use values produced by work activities were produced for exchange. In fact, a lot of work is performed to produce some value with no view to exchange, not just in care situations, but more broadly in all situations where the point is to just contribute to social reproduction in some way, say, in helping count votes on election night, tending a city garden, teaching an evening arts class. Workers in these examples might even engage in the work purely for the income they receive from it. From their point of view, work then is definitely an economic affair. But these work activities are neither the direct production of subsistence goods, nor the production of goods for exchange on the market, they are not part of the 'economic sphere' on the traditional sense of the term.

The second trope is the physiological metaphor of work as the '*metabolism of human society with nature*' (Marx 1988 [1861–1863], 40 as paradigm example). Marx's metaphor gave a definitive formulation to a vision of work that was widespread in the early stages of social theory when work was reflected upon in the context of newly arising industrial society. It became a widely accepted, rarely challenged definition of work in social theory henceforth (Honneth 2023 for a critical historical review).

Following the criticisms raised by feminist scholarship (Section 9.3), these two tropes can be safely jettisoned. Work is not a 'sphere' but a set of activities present in all social spheres; it is not restricted to economic activity. And while a lot of work consists in producing, shaping, and transforming natural resources to secure subsistence, a lot of other work fulfils needs and ensures social reproduction without directly 'interacting with' nature. Undoubtedly, as Section 10.3 said already, all work has a core thermodynamic aspect: by definition, all work is the application of some force (physical, symbolic, psychological) to effectuate some change in the world. Thereby all work involves energy transfers. Moreover, there are very few cases of work, maybe none, that do not rely indirectly at least on the use of some natural resources, at the very least the natural resources that are our bodies and our brains. All the different aspects of care for instance, which, in the traditional conception of 'social reproduction', are placed at the opposite end of the archetypal examples of 'metabolic' activities such as agriculture and mining, do require material support: objects to use that need to be manufactured, places where care is provided that need to be built, maintained, heated, and so on. But these 'conditions of labour' (Marx 1988 [1861–1863], 5) are not what is meant by 'metabolism of society with nature'. By this is meant appropriation and shaping of natural elements for the purpose of producing use values, notably as they are meant to be transformed into commodities. The metaphors of economic sphere and metabolism, while they are important for other purposes and in other contexts, play a major role in obfuscating work issues, by hiding the fact that work occurs in every sphere and is not limited to direct 'interactions with nature'.

12.2 Types of Social Action

If work is not a sphere but a particular kind of activity present in all spheres, then the burden of proof to defend the centrality of work rests with identifying what makes work activities particularly significant in comparison with other activities.

Here, we need to be precise about the question at issue. The claim is that work activities are 'central' in some specific way. This implies a comparative study of different types of action. We are looking at the significance and impact, for individual and collective life, of different kinds of action. In this chapter, we are pondering this significance and this impact from a 'social' point of view. What does such a social point of view entail?

We get some clarity if we consider the perspective from which actions are considered. Studying work as a type of 'social action' is different from studying types of action from a *first-person* perspective, looking at their significance for an individual from a phenomenological, psychological, or existential point of view. It is also different from a *'we'-perspective*, which looks at the significance of types of action when the collective reflects on its life as a collective, in a political form of reflexivity. Here the perspective is the *second-person perspective*, in the singular or the plural sense of 'Thou'. We are looking at individual and joint actions and what they mean for the relationships individuals have with each other, whether alter and ego interact with each other as two single Thous or as a larger plurality of Thous. Admittedly the maximum scope of the social perspective makes it also a 'we' question since it involves the collective as a whole. But the social here is considered from the 'horizontal' point of view of the bundle of relations between individuals, some of whom might know each other, but many of whom do not. This is not the social whole as the object of collective deliberation, as in politics. The perspective here is the one taken up in particular in social theory and theoretical sociology, with the early definition of social action by Max Weber the reference point (1978, 4 for the canonical passage): the ways in which individuals pursue their goals by taking into account the actions of others, and how the interactions thereby created produce aggregate, 'social' phenomena. In what sense is work 'central' as such a social action? Why would it be more 'central' than other types of social action?

Unlike first-person centrality and political centrality, which are studied in the next two chapters, here the meaning of centrality is more diffuse, or even defensive. The point in this chapter is to uphold the great significance of work activities among social actions, against the many ways in which this significance has been rejected or undervalued. It is undeniable that other types of action are also significant in the social life of individuals, for instance when there is a public argument about morally or politically difficult issues. But there has been a tendency in philosophy and in many approaches in the social sciences to treat work in a way that does not do justice to its social significance.

So, what are the different kinds of social action that need to be taken into consideration if we aim to comparatively highlight the significance of work? Philosophical literature on action is of little help to answer this question. Even though it is vast, spanning the entire tradition from Aristotle to complex debates in contemporary analytical philosophy, including non-Western traditions, it is difficult to find a thorough taxonomy of types of action. In the analytical tradition, action is of interest initially for metaphysical purposes: to explain the links between intentionality and effective intervention in the world, asking for instance whether intentions should be thought of as the causes of action and what the exact status of intentions as mental states is. It is a concern of metaphysics and philosophy of mind, even of logic when it intersects with models of rationality. Because of this orientation, much of the discussion in the philosophy of action is content with using the most banal acts performed in everyday life, like flipping a switch to turn on the light or turning left at the fork to get to Katmandu (examples in Davidson's canonical 1963 essay, 2002, 4 and 7), or taking a walk for an example of joint action. These lines of questioning mean that there is no attempt to distinguish between individual acts and social actions, or between different kinds of joint actions. Searle's seminal book of social ontology (1995) is a primary example: the passage on the maintenance of institutional facts (1995, 117–119) only mentions symbolic and linguistic acts and does not consider other forms of action that might be needed to support institutional realities over time. It certainly does not mention the fact that a lot of work is needed for the continued existence of institutional facts, including work on material aspects of the world.

Even philosophers who are concerned with action specifically for solving problems in practical philosophy look for features of action that are fundamental and shared by all kinds of action, without distinguishing between different types (typically Vogler 2002, who makes an instrumentalist conception of action the underlying structure of all forms of action). Even a philosopher like Christine Korsgaard who writes in the footsteps of Kant ends up erasing what appears to be a baseline distinction in his practical philosophy, between hypothetical and categorical imperatives, a distinction that seems to issue in a distinction between instrumental and moral action. Following Kant's distinction, work would be a most obvious illustration of technical, instrumental actions, which are based on a hypothetical assumption: *if* you want to achieve x, *then* you need to do y. Kant contrasts such actions based on hypothetical imperatives with moral action, which expresses a categorical command, requiring of us to will and do the right thing categorically, with no 'ifs' or 'buts' we might say. Korsgaard, however, argues that since the means are contained in the end (if you truly commit to achieving an end, you analytically commit to using the means to achieve it), the 'distinguishability' between types of action, in the end, is reducible to the general pattern of practical, normative rationality, with the categorical imperative expressing its ultimate rationality (Korsgaard 2008, 63).

Given that the established philosophical literature is of little help for our purposes, we need to return to the tradition of social theory, which was the reference point for the objection against the very category of centrality. A particularly useful thinker for our purposes remains Habermas, who drew extensively on the tradition of social theory to establish a taxonomy and characterization of different types of social action, notably in the *Theory of Communicative Action.*

The distinctions Habermas outlines in his rereading of Max Weber might be mentioned first, as they give a good indication of the types of social action under review (Weber 1978, 24–25; Habermas 1984, vol. 1, 279–286). These distinctions arise from the consideration of the different goals that can motivate an individual to act in the social world. The archetype is an agent who selects the appropriate means for their chosen ends by considering affordances and obstacles presented by objects and conditions in the external world, including by other agents. When they act in this way, actors engage in *purposive-rational action.* When the ends and means that an agent follows are informed by a substantive value framework (a strong ethic, religious or aesthetic principles), we have *value-rational action.* When the agent acts on the basis of their emotions, we have *affectual action.* And in *traditional action*, the actor simply follows traditional patterns of action.

This taxonomy is of interest to Habermas because the different types of action orientation it highlights point to different concepts of social action. Habermas thinks that Weber, in a manner similar to analytical philosophy, unduly restricts the concept of action to the type of conduct agents engage in when they seek to realize their goals from the point of view of instrumental rationality. As Weber himself states, action on this view is intrinsically 'oriented to success', where success just is the realization of the goals by the individuals. Habermas does not deny that such actions matter. However, other kinds of social action should not be viewed as 'lesser' types, or it should not be assumed that there is one archetype for all social actions, namely cognitive-instrumental action. The tradition of social theory itself provides other conceptions. Next to the instrumental, teleological focus, which informs for example the conception of action in neoclassical economics or rational choice theory, other social theorists, notably Durkheim and Parsons in his footsteps, have emphasized *normatively-mediated actions*, where the actions are promoted or prohibited in line with moral and cultural norms (Habermas 1984, vol. 1, 88–90). Erwin Goffman focused on *dramaturgical* and *expressive actions*, where the focus is on the manifestation of inner states by the doer (Habermas 1984, vol. 1, 91–94).

Habermas' key intervention was to outline these different viewpoints highlighted by the classics of social theory and reorganize them systematically in a new taxonomy. The basis for it is the distinction between two irreducible types of social action: one where the individual agents coordinate their actions with each other on a purely cognitive-instrumental basis, by considering each other *strategically*, each seeing the others as obstacles or promoters to their own ends; to be contrasted with *communication*, where individuals coordinate their actions by attempting to reach an agreement among each other. Next to actions whose rationality is measured in terms of *success* stand *communicative actions* that aim at reaching *understanding.* Adapting the various viewpoints of classical sociologists, and applying the well-known distinction between objective, social, and subjective world, Habermas delineates three sub-types of communicative action, where the focus each time is on one of the three worlds more particularly: social actions where the emphasis is on coming to an agreement over a particular state of affairs by establishing the truth regarding some its aspects; social actions in which the coordination between actors turns mainly on establishing the right conduct by reference to norms; and social actions where the emphasis is on the authenticity and truthfulness displayed by agents in front of other agents (Habermas 1984, vol. 1, 329). These pure types of communicative action, Habermas notes, are usually all at play in the complexity of everyday interactions.

Thanks to Habermas, then, and even if his taxonomy has been subjected to intense criticism from the moment the *Theory of Communicative Action* was published (see in particular Honneth and Joas 1991, more recently Breen 2012), we have here a rich set of distinctions to orient us in our enquiry. Where does work fit in such a taxonomy? Habermas' own answer to this question is ambiguous. This hesitation has been debated at length in critical social theory (McCarthy 1978; Honneth 1995a). These old debates remain instructive, in particularbecause Habermas' conceptual vocabulary can be mobilized afresh to highlight different ways in which work can be characterized as being central from a 'social' point of view.

Habermas clearly states that strategic (the instrumental approach to other agents) and communicative action are two distinctive, basic types of social action, not just two analytic perspectives on action (Habermas 1984, vol. 1, 286). This dichotomy is a structural feature of his thinking throughout his career, directly indebted to Arendt's famous contrast between labour, work, and action (see Breen 2007 for a thorough review of relevant passages). In the writings preceding the *Theory of Communicative Action*, work is the paradigm example of instrumental action (see for instance Habermas 1971, 91 or 1972, 176). As McCarthy showed (1978, 26), the strict separation of instrumental and communicative action is in fact untenable notably because the features that are characteristic of interaction apply also to work, the archetype of instrumental action. If, for the sake of argument, we take work in the classical sense of economic activity, bracketing out for a moment the issue we uncovered in this notion, even that type of work is bounded by legal and moral norms, not just by technical and efficiency considerations; it is based on discussions, notably between managers and planners, but also with other workers, to establish the most efficient and indeed the fair ways to organize it; it involves subjectivities, in terms of their knowledge, skills, and their very motivation to work, and indeed in terms of their expectations regarding work, concerning their well-being and their conceptions of the good. Correspondingly, work involves the different types of validity claims (reference to objective truth, normative correctness, subjective truthfulness) that characterize communicative action.

At times Habermas acknowledges the points raised by McCarthy, as in this passage:

> 'I do not deny that normally instrumental action is embedded in communicative action (productive activity is socially organized in general). But I see no reason why we should not adequately analyse a complex, i.e. dissect it into its parts'
>
> **(Habermas, cited in McCarthy 1978, 27).**

McCarthy references this acknowledgement to propose that the distinction between instrumental and communicative action does not contrast types of action, but rather aspects of complex social actions. Accordingly, one aspect that can be thematized in action is the rationality of the means–end nexus. Here we rely on empirical knowledge: whether the modes of action map on to actual states of the world (empirical truth) and whether the technical means are effective (pragmatic verification). In this 'instrumental' aspect of social action, analytical consistency is also a concern: whether the preference rules and decision procedures are applied consistently. But social action can also be considered from the aspect of normative expectations, the expectations agents have towards each other as well as the normative framework in which the action takes place. In some subsystems, one aspect of action predominates, typically the instrumental one in the economic sphere and in administrative institutions, while in other subsystems, typically families and the public sphere, it is communicative aspects that predominate or should predominate. In some circumstances, other aspects of communication are foregrounded, such as moral adequacy or expressivity.

A number of critical disciples have pointed out that Habermas consistently falls short of this solution, and that there is a tendency in his writing to interpret ontologically distinctions that should be merely analytical (Fraser 1985; Honneth 1991; Honneth and Joas 1991). This is particularly problematic in his famous diagnosis of the 'pathology' of modern societies involving a 'colonization of the lifeworld' by systemic mechanisms. The concept of lifeworld plays a major role in the second part of this chapter and the rest of the book. It is a term borrowed from Husserl (Husserl 1970 [1936]) that denotes society from the point of view of the 'participants', that is, the individuals as they interact with each other, attempt to coordinate their actions and avoid serious conflict, by relying on a thick layer of shared knowledges, beliefs, and norms (Habermas 1984, vol. 2, 113–152). On Habermas' grand, post-Weberian reconstruction of the 'rationalization' process that is synonymous with modernity, lifeworlds become increasingly 'rationalized' as they submit the cultural and normative glue holding social bonds together to rational scrutiny. As this process occurs, the potentials inherent in non-communicative types of action-coordination (money and power) are also released, which prove more efficient in the increasing complexity of economic and administrative systems. Rationalization in communicative processes (critical scrutiny on tradition and culture) thus unleashes rationalization at the instrumental level (increasing sophistication in coordination through money and administrative power). These forms of efficient, instrumental coordination have their institutional footholds in the lifeworld, in markets and the legal system in particular. But their non-communicative logic overflows into other institutional realms and spheres, as it were, and gradually seeps through the lifeworld. As a result, efficiency-based, anormative, purely analytical ways of thinking and acting gradually replace communicative modes of interaction. As his critical disciples have highlighted, this vision is premised on a dualistic approach to society: on this model, social integration, which involves normatively regulated interactions, is ensured by communicative action, while system integration, which focuses on material reproduction through industry and administration, relies on instrumental modes of thinking and acting. Despite Habermas' qualification and McCarthy's conciliatory attempt, the distinction between types of action remains at the level of the critical diagnosis and is duplicated by a distinction between separate spheres of action. Accordingly, lifeworld and system are not just two ways to look at society but correspond to separate spheres, and these separate spheres function on the basis of the distinctive logics of communicative versus instrumental action. Work on this model is explicitly located in the systems part of the analysis, and obeys only instrumental logics of empirical validity, analytical consistency, and efficiency calculation. But, as we saw, work is not a sphere, and as his critical disciples, Nancy Fraser in particular from a feminist perspective, pointed out a long time ago, work actions, even purely economic ones, are too complex to be reduced to instrumental action.

These hesitations notwithstanding, Habermas' approach remains seminal for our purposes. The model of complex action proposed by McCarthy, based on the distinction between different aspects of action, provides a clear structure to describe how social and technical dimensions are intertwined in work.

In particular, it highlights how deeply work is involved in social reproduction, how much social interactions are necessary for work and to what extent work is itself a major form of social interaction. Once the complexity of work as social action thus becomes apparent, different modalities of work's social centrality can be outlined, as we now proceed to show.

12.3 The Work of Communicative Action

Communication is a second-order kind of action according to Habermas' definition: it is a collective action that helps to coordinate individual actions, 'an interpersonal relation that is effective for coordination, that orders scopes of action and sequences of interaction' (Habermas 1984, vol. 1, 296). This quote shows the two levels clearly: through communication, agents seek to achieve understanding among each other, and that understanding is about what each is to do and what they will do together. To use one of Habermas' examples: accepting an order from someone is itself an action, but that action in turn implies performing the actions that are conveyed through the order. One type of individual action that can be coordinated in this way is productive action, work. On this model, it makes sense to say that instrumental action is 'embedded in' communicative action: there can be collective discussion, agreement, and disagreement, over how to organize production, who should do what and how, how the outputs should be distributed. But productive action itself on this model can still be viewed as a different kind of action, a 'cognitive-instrumental' as opposed to a communicative one.

From what we have seen in the previous section, however, and from the point of view of the realistic, encompassing consideration of work this book puts forward, this view needs to be problematized and a more intimate mixing of communicative and instrumental dimensions in work actions highlighted. If we do that, it becomes clear what it is in work that makes it socially central. Two key claims capture this mixture of instrumentality and communication in work activities: first, that work is to a large extent constituted by communicative action, not just 'bounded' by it; and second, that communicative action relies on work in a number of ways.

Let us begin with the first claim: a lot of work is not just embedded in, bounded by, discursive and normative interactions, but in most cases, is constituted by them.

All work has a technical dimension: there are proven methods to achieve particular outcomes in all types of work, involving particular tools, weapons, machines, processes, procedures, how to use them, how to organize the work process for individual workers and collectives, and so on. It is a mistake, however, to think that technique obeys only 'cognitive-instrumental' considerations. For example, a rich school of history and anthropology of technique in France has convincingly highlighted the fact that 'technology is a human science' (Haudricourt 1987; Sigaut 1999; a seminal reference is Leroi-Gourhan 1943, 1945), that is, that it is part and parcel of the social world, including in its symbolic and cultural dimensions, and needs to be studied within this broad context. Productive techniques are not just governed by empirical and utilitarian concerns. They are governed also by social norms and cultural values which do not just frame the technical processes, but influence them directly, in their very unfolding. Decisive insights were provided by Marcel Mauss in his seminal studies on the 'techniques of the body' (Mauss 1973 [1936]; Sigaut 2002), in which the sociologist highlighted how deeply cultural norms impacted even the most basic ways to utilize the human body in everyday life actions (in walking, swimming, digging trenches in the First World War, and so on).

Mauss defined technical acts as 'efficacious traditional actions' (Mauss 1973 [1936]. 75). This definition is a direct inspiration for the conception of work presented in the introduction (notably following Dejours 2018, see Deranty 2009). Every term matters here. First, a technical act is an act performed intentionally, one that is engaged in specifically with the view to producing a particular effect. It aims to be efficacious. Beyond cultural relativism, the French tradition of anthropology and history of techniques highlights the realist, material elements in technical use that cross over between cultural contexts: if one wants to grind grain, make an adze axe, or construct a canoe, there just are more efficient ways to use the human hand and the human body generally to gather, shape and activate material resources. And different elements and natural resources also have their own objective constraints on technical uses. Some woods are just better than others to make bows and arrows. From this point of view, it is true that the cognitive-instrumental logic has its own momentum. At the same time though, technical action is not just constrained by material elements but is also 'traditional', in two different senses: first in the sense that techniques have to be learnt, passed on from expert and teacher to learner and novice, from one generation to another, which is what Mauss emphasized especially. And second, as Sigaut stressed (1990), in the sense that an efficacious act that is entirely new in a given social context will likely not be received as such, will most likely be rejected as transgressive of some norms, and its efficacy not even acknowledged. The very efficaciousness of instrumental action relies on social validation. As ethnographic studies demonstrate at length, technical action is both cultural and moral. It is based and draws on particular beliefs, values, shared understandings of self, the collective, and the world. For instance, the ways gardening and hunting are organized in the Achuar society studied by Descola rely directly on their specific ontology, their conception of what plants are, how humans interact with animal beings, and so on. And technical action is guided by norms, shared ways of defining the right and the wrong, the good and the bad. All technical actions, even in contemporary contexts, are subject to social taboos, prescriptions of all kinds that define the work process itself in its very unfolding. These are not mere 'boundary conditions' but constitutive of technical acts since this normative and cultural constitution of technical action applies to the work process itself (how things are done), to the distribution of the agents in the process (who does what), and the distribution of the work outputs (who gets what).

That work actions are constituted communicatively (in Habermas' sense) is verified by the fact that the three dimensions of social interaction Habermas shows are mobilized in communicative action, that is, social bonds, cultural resources, and personality features (Habermas 1984, vol. 2, 137) are also directly present in the actual unfolding of work actions. When agents organize a work process, engage in it, and distribute its outputs, these three dimensions are involved. This is clearly seen when employees object to a manager's command in reference to societal norms, or because the command undermines key relationships in a working group, or because it violates what are deemed constitutive dimensions of subjective well-being. The social, cultural, and psychological dimensions at the heart of work actions thus make most work a type of communicative action, that is, a coordination of individual actions that considers the imperatives of technique, but relies intrinsically on minimal forms of solidarity, on cultural knowledge, and on distinctive personality features.

Let us now look at the second key claim: communicative action itself relies on particular types of work. Habermas shows that communicative action mobilizes symbolic and psychological resources that are developed in connection with the lifeworld to which the agents belong: cultural knowledge, which helps them come to an understanding in the collective interpretation of states of affairs; social knowledge, which stabilizes the membership of each individual in the group and secures the latter's cohesion; and the psychological competences of agents needed for social interaction, which are acquired through socialization. When individuals engage in communicative action, by drawing on these symbolic, normative, and psychological resources, they simultaneously reproduce them: 'interactions woven in the fabric of everyday communicative practice constitute the medium through which culture, society and self get reproduced' (Habermas 1984, vol. 2, 138). Habermas thus hands to communicative action the task of reproducing the lifeworld under the three aspects of cultural reproduction, social integration, and socialization.

What Habermas fails to emphasize is that a large part of what allows each of those three dimensions of the lifeworld to 'get reproduced' is work, in other words, that an important number of everyday practices through which social cohesion, culture, and self are reproduced are work activities. He notes that modern society relies more and more on professionals for the reproduction of the functional elements of the lifeworld (Habermas 1984, vol. 2, 146–147), but the only aspect of the professionalization of symbolic reproduction that interests him is the reflective dimension, the fact that techniques of reproduction that were formulated and passed on in traditional ways take on the form of specialized, reflective forms of knowledge and technique. He does not note that if there are professionals, this is a clear indication that symbolic reproduction relies on work, that work therefore is not just about material reproduction and cannot be reduced to instrumental action implemented on moving bodies that can be manipulated (as he defined work earlier, see Habermas 1973, 8). As noted already, specific work is necessary, beyond everyday interactions, to sustain culture, society, and personality. Culture is reproduced by specialists, who actively remember and pass on foundational stories, myths, who specialize in representing the gods, or the national myths, who study the evolution of the common language and ensure its transmission. Social orders require the formulating and upholding of the laws and the norms of society, through the operations and policing of legal systems for instance. Personality is developed thanks to the work of carers, teachers, medical experts, who ideally provide the support for personal growth and self-confidence, but also ensure the passing on of cultural, social, and technical knowledge from expert to novice, from one generation to another. Communicative action *is* work, then, in the sense that there is specific work required to ensure that communicative actions have the requisite cultural, social, and psychological-cognitive resources to unfold with minimal success.

To sum up: work is one specific example of communicative action (one where technical discussions predominate, but which include constitutive normative and cultural elements), and communicative actions require specific work. We retrieve here, in the language of social theory, the key idea that work activities are needed for social reproduction generally, not just in the subsystem responsible for the material reproduction of society. What we are led to is the fundamental view that work designates activities that are part of the overall fabric of the lifeworld and that help to sustain this lifeworld, alongside other types of activities, but in their specific way, based on the specific structure of such activities. Following this understanding of work, we can now ask more precisely in what ways this particular type of social action is 'central' for the lifeworld and its inhabitants.

12.4 Social Centralities of Work

12.4.1 Effective Operations

First, following the suggestions of historians and anthropologists of techniques, a basic characteristic of work actions is their material, 'real-world' dimension, the fact that a distinctive feature of work is to produce some effect in the world, to be 'efficacious' in a real sense, by producing something or changing something in some respect, which, from some point of view, has value (Sigaut 2002 is particularly clear on this). Of course, it may well be that the value created is noxious, or superfluous, and there might well be some activities that are called work yet produce no real use value, as in the case of 'bullshit jobs.' Yet, these examples are no objection to the general feature of work described here; they are just bad instantiations of work as an efficacious action. We do not focus on the critique of current forms of work here, but on characterizing work in contrast with other forms of action. It seems difficult to argue against the idea that for society to be reproduced, many needs have to be fulfilled, and that this involves actions actually effectuating what is required for such fulfilment to be realized. If their computer breaks down while they write on the exaggerated significance given to work, post-work theorists will go to a shop to buy a new one, or have a specialist repair their existing one, thereby demonstrating the value that they place in reality on what work can achieve.

Another objection might refer to the passive and negative contributions to social reproduction we discussed in Section 10.3. Abiding by the mores and the laws of the community helps to reproduce it and these mores and laws in particular. Refraining from breaking laws and social rules is one way of participating to social reproduction, in 'negative' fashion. However, even though negative and passive modes of social action might have their role to play in the reproduction of the lifeworld, efficacious actions that create needed use value, or maintain a source of use value, are more basic, necessary conditions of it.

This indispensable material efficaciousness of work was well highlighted by Alfred Schutz, in a passage of his last magnum opus, *The Structures of the Lifeworld*. Schutz delineated the features of work precisely as this chapter attempts to do, namely through a comparison with other types of social action. 'All operation (...), as controlled corporeal conduct, in some way engages in the world. But not every operation changes the surrounding world in a way that is significant for the practical objectives of everyday life' (Schutz 1989 11). As a consequence of this focus on actual realization, work then is characterized by the fact that 'some determinate effect, a change in the natural and social world, was achieved by a plan of action.... (In work) change is not a purely accidental effect of action. It must rather be intended and inserted in the plan of action, whether or not the performance of the act succeeds' (Schutz 1989, 12). Schutz also made the point that in many cases work and communicative action are combined (Schutz 1989, 13) and he emphasized the mistake of restricting work to the 'economic sphere' narrowly conceived:

> This definition (of work), of course, includes productive activities in an economic sense, but it also includes all those forms of social action by which a change is made in the social world: declarations of love, marriages, baptism, court deliberations, the sale or even the collecting of postage stamps, revolutions and counterrevolutions.
>
> (12)

This list is of course provocative. It chimes with the wide and equally stunning set of examples listed by Charles and Chris Tilly in their characterization of work (1998, 22, see Section 10.1). We do not have to discuss the examples in these lists. What matters is that the sociologists formulated in decisive manner that society requires a lot more than just passive or negative forms of action to be effectively reproduced, and social reproduction requires a lot more work than just the production of goods for subsistence or the market.

12.4.2 Sustaining the Flows of the Lifeworld

If work is involved in the reproduction of society in general, in all of its 'spheres', then efficaciousness matters a lot. The hold of the 'metabolism' metaphor on theoretical imaginations is so strong, as is the reduction of work to 'the economic sphere' more broadly, it is difficult for us to acknowledge the pervasiveness of work efforts around us and how much we rely on them, individually and collectively. The world that surrounds every one of us is supported in every single one of its aspects and at every point in time by the efforts of ourselves and others to maintain it, ensuring the continuity of processes we all expect to be there. In the words of Marx and Engels at the start of the *German Ideology*:

> The first historical act is the production of the means to satisfy needs, the production of material life itself. This is an historical act which today, as thousands of years ago, *must daily and hourly be fulfilled merely in order to sustain human life*.
>
> **(Marx and Engels 1976, 42, emphasis JPD)**

In the reproduction chapter of *Capital*, volume one, Marx described social reproduction as 'the constant flux of society's incessant renewal' (1991 [1867], 716, section 9.3).

One way to emphasize this active, material, efficacious condition behind the maintenance of the lifeworld is to focus on the flows that make up everyday life. Everyday life is sustained by an indefinite number of flows that constitute it in its normality instant by instant: in no particular order, traffic flows, electricity flows, sewerage flows, water flows, information flows, the flows internal to individual bodies, and the flows of communications and interactions between bodies, and so on. Countless efforts are needed to actively uphold these flows, not just abstaining from preventing them or going along with them. We might rely on the binding force of language to maintain the social and cultural glue that keeps us together, as Habermas emphasized, but the force of the better reason has no efficacy if there is no physical infrastructure to allow this glue to stick, so to speak (from tunnels to human bodies and communication media), and if the actions agreed upon between the agents are not actually performed in the real world, through acts that do what they have to do for the actions to reach their goals (repair a pipe, control traffic, tend a wound, stock a supermarket aisle, show a child how 'their' and 'there' sound the same but mean different things, and so on).

This might all seem trivial, as Marx noted in the letter to Kugelmann already cited several times (Introduction, Section 10.1). And yet this is a trivial point most people take for granted, both in their everyday attitudes and even as scholars if they happen to be social philosophers or social theorists. It is a similar overlooking as when our bodies function well enough. We take our own metabolism and the social metabolism for granted, forgetting how much work is involved in sustaining them. This overlooking is none more blatant than in post-work theorists and automation enthusiasts who discount the infinite number of individual and collective efforts that are required to allow individual and collective lives to go on day after day. As soon as a flow we rely upon fails to occur though, we see all the work that was needed for it, let alone the work needed to restart it.

Work is socially central in a loose sense here, to the extent that it is an absolutely necessary condition of the lifeworld. Normative coordinations of action, and expressive assurances of sincerity are important modes of action coordination to be sure. But they are meaningless if they do not translate into 'operations' that implement the necessary changes in the real world, and thereby sustain the structures making up the reality of the common social framework. 'Operations' is the translation of *Wirken*, the term Alfred Schutz used to designate actions that engage with the world as opposed to purely internal acts. Work, we might say, is the kind of *Wirken* that is the necessary material condition of social reality, *Wirklichkeit.*

It is Husserl who introduced the concept of lifeworld which was taken up by Schutz to develop a phenomenological social theory. The most fundamental feature of the lifeworld, they both argued, is that it forms the unquestioned, pregiven layer that is the background of all individual experiences and intentionalities. For social individuals, it is the world in which all these experiences and intentionalities take place and which, in a way, makes them all relate to each other, just because they are part of it. The phenomenologists emphasized the extent to which this layer remains unthematized, both for everyday consciousness and indeed in theory. Husserl's seminal descriptions pointed already, if only in implicit fashion, to the effortful dimension that is entailed in maintaining this background framework day after day. He referred to it as 'Heraclitean flux' to emphasize the 'flow' character of it. He talked about it as

> the universal *operative* (*leistende*) life in which the world comes to be as existing for us constantly in flowing particularity (*in strömender Jeweiligkeit*), constantly 'pregiven' to us.
>
> **(Husserl 1970 [1936], 145, emphasis JPD)**

The metaphor '*strömende Jeweiligkeit*' is also an intriguing oxymoron. *Jeweiligkeit* means something like the fact-of-being-here-each-time. The world is here for us 'each time' (*jeweils*) as pregiven, it is that foundation on which all our intentionalities and actions rest and from which we draw each time we do something. And yet it is an 'each time'-givenness that is flowing, that flows minute to minute, day to day, year to year, from generation to generation. The material condition behind this temporal continuity making the world available for our existence is work, since work is what efficaciously ensures the flows of the lifeworld are maintained. Other types of social action secure particular dimensions of this flow, for instance cultural or moral understanding, but work is what ensures that the flows actually keep flowing. Some work ensures that the ongoingness of the social world is punctually effectuated (say technicians fix a burst pipe in the street), in the instant. Some work ensures this ongoingness will be secured tomorrow (when food is prepared today to be delivered tomorrow, as in the Roman *annona*, Section 11.3). Some work ensures the ongoingness will be secured next year (when public servants work on the nation's budget). And some work is long-term, as when newborns are trained over many years by many people into the different types of knowledge ensuring the future lifeworld remains connected to the present one.

We can see here that a crucial part of the unquestioned pregivenness of the lifeworld emphasized by Husserl and Schutz and by Habermas in their footsteps is the invisibility of the work that underpins all the systems and flows that provide the infrastructures, the frameworks, symbolic and material, for all of our everyday actions, experiences, and intentionalities. The normalcy of the everyday world is produced by cognitive schemes shared among members of a collective that allow it to function as a complex organization in complex interactions with its environments and within itself. Yet underneath these 'stocks of knowledge' that constitute the lifeworld (Habermas 1984, vol. 2, 138) that normalcy is held in existence primordially by work activities that actually make things happen and ensure that things endure.

12.4.3 'The Main Source of Social Solidarity'

The lifeworld is reproduced every day by the myriad actions of its members. Some of these actions reproduce it 'for real', as they carry out tasks required by this reproduction. If we look at this web of activities from the point of view of the agents involved, what comes to light are the twin concepts of cooperation and division of labour.

The two concepts are introduced here from the perspective of work as activity sustaining the lifeworld. Human beings owe their existence to a combination of their own actions and the actions of others. Their own actions directly bring them particular goods, but also produce goods for others (their family, a boss, customers). And the goods they consume (be they material or symbolic) are produced for them by themselves and by others. There is a direct analytical link between each producing for others and each consuming from others. No one is able to produce all the goods they require for their sustenance, where 'goods' and 'sustenance' are to be understood in the broadest sense, to include the need to be socialized, to be taught society's language and values for instance. Furthermore, human existence relies on general infrastructures that require dedicated work: building the temple, repairing the bridges, the roads, the mills, the airport, building the fortress and the schools, printing the dictionaries and the religious texts, and so on. So, everyone relies on everyone else for the particular goods they receive and for the public goods that are part of individual and collective reproduction. And as the life of individuals is reproduced through this all-out reciprocal interdependence, it is also the life of the collective as such that is reproduced at the same time. For instance, it is the collective's specific history, language, value system, and religion, that are reproduced through dedicated work.

From this point of view, individual and collective life rely on cooperation, everyone having their own 'operations', and sharing the latter's outcomes with everyone else. The term cooperation usually has a positive connotation, implying a prosocial attitude of the agents involved. Today, in the important fields of evolutionary theory and economics, cooperation is discussed alongside altruism (Fehr et al. 2002; Bowles and Gintis 2011). But at the basic level considered here, the term does not exclude negative affects. It is just a fact of human life that individuals have to 'work together' in order to sustain themselves, individually and as a collective. Many of them might dislike each other, and some groups within society might dislike other groups (for instance there might be class antagonism), but the structure of their needs imposes cooperation on them. When cooperation fails, the collective malfunctions and individual lives suffer.

Looking at society through this intricate web of interdependent needs and productive operations, a key feature associated with cooperation is the division of labour. Since everyone has only finite means available to fulfil all their needs (in terms of time, strength, skill, capital to invest for the requisite means of production, and so on), and since many needs rely on public goods to be satisfied (roads to transport material goods; schools to teach children, hospitals for the sick; cemeteries if the dead are buried together), everyone relies on everyone else for realizing particular tasks and fulfilling all of their needs (Brudney 2022). The overall social labour perforce has to be divided across all the individuals.

When it was said above that everyone has their own operations and shares the latter's outcomes with everyone else, this is of course an approximation. Many individuals do not contribute to social labour because they are physically or mentally unable to do so: the very young, older people who are too frail, people who have been seriously injured, people who have serious health issues. This rectification is not an objection to the image of work and its centrality presented in the book. The very notion of social reproduction entails that those who can work do so for each and every one, notably for those who are not able to work. Furthermore, given the extension of the notion of work for social reproduction, many people who do not work in the formal economy in fact do work and very often fulfil crucial positions in society: grandparents who care for young children whose parents are employed in the formal economy, volunteers who keep alive political organizations or environmental programmes, young people undertaking occupational training who prepare to make their own contribution, and so on.

If we return to the idea of interdependence through needs and of the work outputs that are shared to fulfil them, specialization is analytically entailed in this basic picture. Since every individual only has the ability to look after an infinitesimal part of the overall reproduction cycle, by necessity specialization arises as soon as labour is divided. In many societies, this specialization occurred along gender lines. In stratified societies, it occurred along status lines, with particular professions reserved for particular groups.

Of course, these three concepts of cooperation, division of labour and specialization have been discussed at length by social thinkers across the history of philosophy and the social sciences, from Plato to current evolutionary theorists and economists. If we restrict ourselves to classics in the Western tradition of social and political philosophy, key texts immediately come to mind, such as Plato's *Republic*, Adam Smith's *Wealth of Nations*, Hegel's *Philosophy of Right*, many passages in Marx, notably the 1844 'Comments on James Mill's Elements d'Economie Politique' (Marx 2000 [1844a]) and *The German Ideology* (Marx and Engels (2000 [1845–1846]), Durkheim's *Division of Labour in Society*, Dewey in many lectures and published texts (see Renault 2022 for a thorough discussion, including a wealth of textual references), all the way to Rawls, whose initial assumption in the different versions of his theory of justice is of society as a 'system of cooperation designed to advance the good of those taking part in it' (Rawls 1999, 4). Many other references could be added. For instance, as the previous chapter indicated, the idea of universal interdependence was explicitly thematized in medieval theology, from the eleventh century onwards, under the scheme of trifunctionality. We could lean on contemporary research in evolutionary theory, which emphasizes the importance of active cooperation in subsistence activities as a key factor in the evolution of the species (Fehr et al. 2002; Sterelny 2012, 2021). Or we could focus on the contribution made by Axel Honneth in contemporary critical theory, notably as he has emphasized the importance of interdependence via cooperation and the division of labour, in opposition to the system-theoretical oriented outlook of Habermas on questions of work (Honneth 1998, 2014; Herzog and Honneth 2014; Honneth 2023).

In the remainder of this chapter, in order to remain reasonably succinct, only the classical social philosophers just mentioned are cited. These philosophers use different methods and assumptions, emphasize many different aspects, and draw widely different conclusions, notably political conclusions, from the ideas of interdependence, cooperation, division of labour and specialization, from Plato's elitist, hierarchical order to Dewey's conception of fully democratic collective life. Yet despite all these differences, some core conceptual features emerge within this tradition, around the special role played by the core concepts in social life, which amount to different senses of work's social centrality.

Because a lot of work aims not at self-consumption or the care of others, but rather at the production of outputs to be exchanged so that some value can be obtained from the exchange (a desired good from barter, a profit for individual tradespeople, an income for waged workers, surplus value for owners of the means of production), it is tempting to view work through an individualistic and utilitarian lens, to equate work with economic concerns where each individual pursues their own good, attempts to satisfy their own utility and thereby relates to others only in instrumental fashion. But if work activities are considered from the point of view of the reproduction of the lifeworld, as 'productive life that creates life' as Marx called it ('*das produktive Leben ... ist das Leben erzeugende Leben*', 2000, 90), then the division of labour, the exchange of outputs that it enables, take on normative significance, not just a utilitarian one. Even in a capitalistic context, abstract value is created on the basis of use value. It is real needs that are fulfilled through production. Many of those needs might be 'false' or superfluous, a large part of the economic organization might be driven by the particular logics of capitalistic exploitation and valorization, but this does not gainsay the fact that even in this context, individual and collective lives are reproduced, even if in 'pathological' or unjust forms. The capitalistic context, while it is rightfully the main concern for social critique, can also obstruct the view regarding the conceptual relationship between work and the lifeworld. It is important to critique injustice and social pathologies, but this should not make us overlook the fact that despite all the flaws in its organization, it is work that sustains individual and collective life. From the perspective of the lifeworld's reproduction, what we see is a multitude of technically guided, effect-focused actions, whose aim and end result is the reproduction of individual lives and of the collective in some particular respect each time.

When work is viewed in this way, it becomes clear why many of the authors who have reflected on the division of labour have argued that it provides one of the strongest forms of social bond. If individuals rely on the work of others to have all of their needs fulfilled, including in the maintenance of the collective goods (material and symbolic) required for such a fulfilment, then work actions are always more than 'just' economic in the narrow, utilitarian sense of the term. They literally sustain life, thereby creating all-out existential dependence and interdependence. Through the division of labour, life is invested in all the individual work efforts, a massive expenditure of 'brains, nerves and muscles' reoccurs daily, to use Marx's expression. This life expenditure specifically aims at sustaining the life of the agents, of their close others and of the many anonymous others to whom they are related via collective organization, not only to ensure the consumption of each, but also to maintain the infrastructures and frameworks that are required for all these individual lives to continue.

Even in what is the most famous passage on the division of labour alongside book II of the *Republic*, namely Adam Smith's discussion of it in the second chapter of the *Wealth of Nations*, the dimension of solidarity that emerges from the idea of all-out interdependence is also present, even though the passage is reputed for establishing the self-centred, utilitarian point of view on work. As is well-known, the passage highlights the link between the division of labour and exchange: because an individual's needs cannot be satisfied by their work alone, each individual has to acquire the goods they need from others, and this occurs not through 'benevolence', but through 'trucking and barter', one person exchanging their surplus for the surplus of another. Yet underneath these exchange interactions, the reality is that each 'stands at all times in need of the co-operation and assistance of great multitudes', requires 'assistance' from its fellow creatures. 'Man has almost constant occasion for the help of his brethren', writes Smith. It is true that 'we address ourselves, not to their humanity, but to their self-love, and never talk to them of our own necessities, but of their advantages', yet these exchange interactions, because they help all to sustain their lives reciprocally, should be viewed as 'mutual good offices', which 'we stand in need of'. The foundation of work and the exchange of the outputs of work is all-out interdependence, which makes of all 'brethren' who stand in relation of 'cooperation' with each other. 'Brethren' is a strong metaphor that captures the normative dimension of productive cooperation and exchange: it highlights the depth and strength of the bond uniting the partners in exchange. As overall social labour is divided among all—Smith is directly implying with this term—and each takes charge of one part of the overall process according to their specialization, they thereby appear to each other as 'cooperators' sustaining each other's lives, just as members of a congregation who share the same faith support each other materially and spiritually. They are individuals united by what we might call a bond of life since it is about the reproduction of life and of the world in which those lives unfold through the expenditure of life. Underneath the cold, selfish calculations of exchanging individuals lie the strongest of social bonds, created out of existential necessity, since the fulfilment of needs is initially a question of life and death, and once survival is secured of a good or not-so-good life.

Hegel was decisively influenced by his reading of Smith. In a similar fashion to Smith, he highlighted how cooperation through the division of labour creates a form of universal interdependence and thereby becomes the root of 'ethical life'. It enforces a transfiguration of everyone's attitude to others and to society as a whole, from treating them as mere means towards the satisfaction of one's own needs (as in narrow economic theory), to seeing them as essential supports of one's life:

> In this dependence and reciprocity of work and the satisfaction of needs, subjective selfishness turns into a contribution towards the satisfaction of the needs of everyone else. By a dialectical movement, the particular is mediated by the universal so that each individual, in earning, producing, and enjoying on his own account, thereby earns and produces for the enjoyment of others. This necessity which is inherent in the interlinked dependence of each on all now appears to each individual in the form of universal and permanent resources in which, through his education and skill, he has an opportunity to share; he is thereby assured of his livelihood, just as the universal resources are maintained and augmented by the income which he earns through his work.
>
> **(Hegel 1991 [1821], 233)**

Strikingly, Dewey also used the New Testament trope of the 'brethren' to describe the sense of fraternity that arises from the interdependence rooted in the division of labour: 'This interdependence [is] the reality of altruism. I am my brother's keeper' (2016, 2, 73, cited by Renault 2022, 81).

One passage from Durkheim's *Division of Labour in Society* condenses in just a few lines the conception of work as reproduction of the lifeworld that is suggested here, while adding important features:

> the division of labour is the source – if not the sole, at least the main one – of social solidarity. Comte had already taken this view. Among all the sociologists, so far as we are aware, he was the first to point out that in the division of labour there was something other than a purely economic phenomenon. He saw in it 'the most essential condition of social life', provided that it was conceived of 'in all its rational extent, namely, as being applied to the whole range of our various activities of all kinds, instead of being limited, as is only too common, to mere material uses'. Considered from this viewpoint, he said: 'it leads one immediately to look not only at individuals and classes but also, in many respects, at different peoples, as

> participating at one and the same time, each following in its own fashion and to its own special, determined degree, in a vast common enterprise (*oeuvre*). It is one whose inevitable and gradual development links, moreover, those co-operating together at the present time with the line of their predecessors, whoever these may have been, and even to the line of their various successors. Thus, it is the continuous distribution of different human tasks which constitutes the principal element in social solidarity, and which becomes the primary cause of the scale and growing complexity of the social organism'.
>
> **(Durkheim 1984 [1896], 50–51)**

The citation by Durkheim of his illustrious predecessor is particularly telling. It introduces the idea of general social reproduction, which requires that work be considered not just from the narrow perspective of 'material use' but also encompassing 'all our operations'. It includes the idea of cooperation, of all members of society producing together the lifeworld that includes and supports them, 'an immense and common *oeuvre*', each contributing according to their specialized effort, in their 'respective mode and to a specific degree'. And it is a clear statement of the idea that work is the 'main source of social solidarity', provides the strongest bond binding the individuals together in a collective.

The text adds two insights, both conceptually entailed in the idea of the reproduction of the lifeworld. The first insight emphasizes the temporal nature of social solidarity, a feature we encountered with Husserl already. The very idea of reproduction refers to the mechanisms that allow society to maintain itself over time, minute by minute, day by day, year in year out, from one generation to the next. From the point of view of cooperation, the social bond therefore is not just synchronic but also diachronic. What binds generations to each other is not just the histories, language or values they share, the founding myths of the nation or its defining religion. 'Collective historical time' (Habermas 1984) is grounded in the fact that people cooperate with each other across the generations as they maintain the same lifeworld over time, notably its material infrastructures. This is another way of insisting on the fact that the lifeworld is not just a stock of linguistically articulated and stored knowledge, but '*operative* life' (Husserl), which requires material 'operations', to reuse Schutz's generic notion, and produces social bonds on the basis of those operations.

The second insight from Comte might sound far-fetched, a typical product of nineteenth-century industrial imagination, but it spells out a consideration still pertinent today (as Lukes emphasizes in his introduction to Durkheim 1984 [1896], xl–xlii). Human collectives have been inward-looking throughout time. Ethnographic records and evolutionary psychology stress how much a high degree of altruism towards in-group members is matched by hostility towards outsiders, as a distinctive feature of the species. In line with this feature, many work flows are bound by the borders of the community: exchanges of material goods within the collective usually far outweigh exchanges with individuals and groups from the outside; the work of socialization by definition is inward looking; the work of cultural reproduction is also largely internal and self-centred. And yet many work flows extend outside the bounds of the collective: individuals travel to other lands and establish material work exchanges with their homeland; raw material, tools, weapons, and special equipment are purchased outside the community; the division of labour and specialization extend beyond borders, linking professional groups. To some extent therefore, as the division of labour establishes a specific form of solidarity, work flows ground a kind of weak, universal social bond: one not based on a shared moral status, as in cosmopolitanism, but on the fact that cooperation extends beyond community borders. This bond is much weaker than in the case of an organized social collective because it is no longer about social reproduction in a directly obvious sense. In many cases (but not in all cases), the outside individuals and groups are related to in fairly contingent ways; other individuals and other groups could easily be used as interaction partners. All the rich cultural and moral layers linking members of the same collective need not be shared with these outsiders. But there is interdependence nonetheless, and a form of solidarity might arise from this. One concrete way to consider the normative aspect of these trans-border divisions of labour is when demands of justice in relation to work stress the need to consider entire value chains, which today often are transnational (Ferreras, Battilana, and Méda 2022). One way in which forms of exploitation can be put into place is precisely when workers in one country are protected to the detriment of other workers who are in the same value chain but live outside the national community of reference. Solidarity requires taking into account the entire division of labour in this particular sector of production.

At its most extended stretch, Comte suggests, humanity as a whole is included in a kind of giant division of labour, underpinning a work-based form of cosmopolitanism. Here the lifeworld to reproduce is simply planet Earth and the collective time is the entire history of the species. At a time when the very survival of humanity is at stake as a result of industrial development, this insight loses its speculative character and expresses reasonable normative demands. It speaks to our current predicament, where it is humanity as one collective of 'cooperators' that needs to get its act together if it wants to salvage its lifeworld and with it its own life.

Regardless of these two extra insights, the main point in this section is the idea that cooperation is 'the main source of social solidarity'. This vision of the division of labour as a deep root of solidarity might seem hopelessly idealistic and naïve, since social life seems to always be riven with tensions and conflicts between different groups. Isn't the division of labour one of the main structures through which all kinds of domination, exploitation, and oppression of some groups by others are expressed and entrenched, well before capitalism? Didn't many social struggles throughout history occur precisely around particular aspects of the collective organization of work? But social solidarity as it is discussed here fully accommodates the existence of tensions and open conflicts resulting from the organization of work and targeting aspects of this organization. This solidarity is a *de facto*, deep structure of social life, resulting from the fact that each relies on the others and the necessity of cooperation. Individuals and groups are brought together by the necessity to work together to sustain individual and collective lives. Whether they see it or not, whether they like it or not, as long as the collective is in existence and individuals draw their livelihood from it through sharing work outputs with each other, they all live in a state of all-out interdependence, each depends on all the others and on the collective as a whole. They are forced into solidarity, we might say. The injustice of domination, exploitation, and oppression through the organization of work is all the more unjust as work binds them all. The unfairness of privilege is precisely that some draw more benefits from cooperation than others, when all are in need of each other for their survival. Even though there is privilege and exploitation, none can extract themselves from the bond of cooperation, where cooperation just is the reciprocal exchange of work outputs for reciprocal benefit. We can employ a simple image to illustrate the inability of anyone to escape this bond of interdependence and forced cooperation. The ultra-rich need the roads built and repaired by the collective to drive their obscenely expensive cars, the metal from which the barbed wire at the top of their gated community's walls is made was not fabricated by them, they don't grow their own food, few of them produce their own electricity, none of them cleans their own house. The 'cooperation' in this case is wholly skewed, and yet there is a bond linking the ultra-rich and the poor workers servicing them, the bond of reciprocal reproduction. Challenging and potentially correcting the asymmetries in power and wealth between them is all the more effective and justified if there is indeed such a preexisting bond of reciprocity since such reciprocity by itself demands that the exchanges and the relationships be balanced and fair. Section 14.2 in the last chapter develops a meaning of politics precisely on this basis. On the other hand, when individuals realize the underlying solidarity that always already binds everyone to everyone else, what we have is the basis for genuine democratic practices, to which we turn in Section 14.3.

12.4.4 Recognition of Contributions

The notions of 'participation' and 'contribution' are two further concepts that are analytically entailed in the idea of cooperation through the division of labour. The historical and ethnographic record explored in the previous chapter showed that in many types of human societies, individual work efforts are evaluated by peers from this contributive point of view. In hunter-gatherer and horticulturalist societies, marriage partners are judged according to their work ethic and skill level. Good gardeners and good hunters are attracted to each other among the Achuar people and it is entirely acceptable for a woman gardener to leave a lazy hunter. In many hunter-gatherer societies expert skills directly translate into high social status. In Western antiquity, active contribution to social life was a strong expectation. Everyone had a job to do, idleness was universally condemned. In the tri-functional scheme, social hierarchy is tempered by an acknowledgement of the contribution of each estate to the common work, each according to their own calling. From the point of view of social reproduction, this rich historical evidence is not surprising: if everyone needs everybody else to sustain their individual life (the medieval lord knows very well they are not the one who grows and grinds the grain) and for the infrastructure everyone depends upon (the lords don't repair the roads, the mill or the common oven either, and they know this), then it is clear everyone contributes to reproduction, everyone's participation is required.

What changes through history and across cultures is the normative framework dictating who is entitled to contribute in what way, and the normative valence assigned to different types of contribution. The most common mode of organization for long periods of time is the sexual division of labour, assigning to genders different types of activities. The tropes of 'man the hunter' and 'woman the gatherer' are not universally true (in many societies men gather and care for children also, women are involved in technological work, see Waguespack 2005 on the activities of women in many hunter-gatherer societies). Despite this, it remains the case that in all societies recorded, some activities like big game hunting, or the use of heavy lethal weapons, are reserved for men and are the more highly valued social activities, while other activities are reserved for women and are less valued. This sexual division of labour, while particularly tenacious, has evolved and is today no longer taken for granted. In the trifunctional system, while the work of the 'labourers' has its place, it remains a lowly occupation. In modern, industrial society, a hierarchy of statuses parallels the increasing complexity of the division of labour, rating tasks and occupations on a range from the most esteemed to the least dignified, typically making a number of activities of social reproduction almost invisible, notably many activities of care. Professions, by contrast, manage to establish themselves as special occupations, granting their practitioners privileges, such as exemptionfrom competition or oversight in the fees they charge, their internal organizing of access, social status, and political influence.

Such a hierarchy of statuses that orders the division of labour into a normative scale is typically what Axel Honneth focused on in *The Struggle for Recognition* (1994). Honneth discussed the hierarchies structuring the modern divisions of labour under the 'third sphere of recognition', centred on demands by individuals and occupational groups to have their contributions to social reproduction recognized for their true worth. Honneth's now well-known theory of recognition vindicates the fundamental point already made by the classical social theorists and philosophers, that the continuing existence of a social order is not adequately explained just by reference to individual self-interest (as in rational choice theory), or a powerful Leviathan, or disciplinary or bio- power. Instead, a normative lens must be taken to account for the prosocial attitudes members of the collective display towards each other which ultimately provides the necessary condition for there being a social life in the first place. Along with the classical social thinkers, Honneth focused on the division of labour as one of the main institutional underpinnings of 'social solidarity', where the moral expectation of each member is the recognition of the contribution they make, individually and as part of an occupational group, to social reproduction. Honneth showed how the normatively laden public perceptions of occupations and activities, which rank the latter on a scale from the more to the less esteemed, is always contestable, as individuals and groups can feel unrecognized, unjustly overlooked or even despised, in their work contributions, and, if circumstances permit, actively challenge such perceptions. The recognitive lens implies that there is a direct correspondence between the structure of the recognition order at a given time, and the normative structure of the division of labour. The relationship between the two in fact is bidirectional: social status directs individuals from particular groups to particular work activities, and work activities define social status. Work is central in a critically troublesome sense here, to the extent namely that the normative structure of the division of labour gives a direct insight into the hierarchical structure of society more generally. Conversely, one of the main ways by which this normative order is contested is precisely through social conflict around the acknowledgement and valuation of particular work activities. This indicates a political dimension to the work of social reproduction to which we turn later in the book (Section 14.2.4).

12.4.5 Occupations

As Adam Smith demonstrated in the first pages of *The Wealth of Nations*, the division of labour leads naturally to specialization. Since every individual cannot fulfil all of their needs by themselves, and everyone is forced to concentrate on only some activities as their needs will be fulfilled by the activities of others, everyone is forced to specialize. Specialization in turn leads to the emergence of particular social bodies, namely the collectives of individuals who are engaged in the same line of work, complete similar tasks, learn and apply the same techniques, use the same tools and machines, produce the same kinds of outputs, enjoy the same social status on the basis of their occupation, share similar social fates on the basis of their place in the division of labour. In the previous chapter, we emphasized the significance for individuals of these occupational groups in ancient Rome and in the Middle Ages. Hegel, Durkheim, and Dewey all laid particular emphasis on the importance of these middle bodies for social theory. Dewey referred to them as 'occupations' and went as far as saying that the philosophy of society 'coincides with the philosophy of vocations, callings and occupations in life' (Dewey 2010, 1865). Durkheim like Hegel before him used the old term of 'corporations' and emphasized their transhistorical significance, which is noteworthy given that the goal of his first book was to highlight historical evolutions in the structure of social bonds. Durkheim argued that in complex human societies with a developed division of labour there is a functional necessity that individuals engaged in similar occupations form collectives with special bonds, beyond mere economic interest, which explains the repeated resurgence of corporations throughout time. Recent comparative history of work provides significant transcultural and transhistorical evidence for the psychological and sociological mechanisms that lead to the emergence of corporations in all kinds of cultural systems throughout human history (Lucassen et al. 2006, 2008). In turn, these occupational groups present different forms of 'social centrality'.

First, Hegel, Durkheim and Dewey highlight the special bond that occupational groups represent for their members, as 'second families' (Hegel 1991,

272; Durkheim 1986, 15–16). These are collectives in which individuals find not just the securing of their economic welfare, but also support when misfortunes hit or they go into old age. They are groups with a specific ethos, which mixes shared views of the world, similar values, active solidarity, all of which promote a sense of fraternity or 'brotherhood', as the corporations used to be called. Companions of a corporation are true 'brethren', to repeat Smith's term, as is attested in their active religious practices in Rome and in the Middle Ages. Crucially, Hegel and Durkheim base their view of such groups precisely on what distinguishes work actions from other social actions. It is precisely the sharing of particular productive practices, involving common knowledge, technical skills, and the sharing of theoretical and practical interests, which brings people together. The bodies and the minds of individuals in the same occupation undergo similar processes of education and face similar physical, psychological and social challenges. The moral, intellectual, and cultural threads that are distinctive of a corporation's ethos are anchored in a common way of engaging with the world via productive action. This bond based on activity cuts across regional and national borders. Individuals are brought together by what they do, not where they live or where they come from (Estlund 2003, 2005). Work is socially central in this case, inasmuch as it creates median bodies that provide a special kind of bond to others and a special kind of social identity for their members.

Second, both Hegel and Durkheim argue that occupational groups help to integrate individuals into the state. As Durkheim writes,

> A nation cannot be maintained unless, between the state and individuals, a whole range of secondary groups are interposed. These must be close enough to the individual to attract him strongly to their sphere of influence and, in so doing, to absorb him into the torrent of social life.
>
> **(Durkheim 1984, 27)**

This strikingly echoes the conception of 'ethical life' and the rational state in Hegel. This idea of 'mediation' can be understood in two senses. First, by providing a milieu of solidarity, corporations play a key educational, 'moralizing' (Durkheim) role. Within such groupings where solidarity is exercised daily and turns into an affect, individuals learn to integrate the needs and interests of others into their own ends. The selfish economic ends of single individuals are transfigured and turned towards collective ends, paving the way for life in the larger collective of society at large. Through the corporation, the individual 'belongs to a whole which is itself a member of society in general', and this ensures that 'he has an interest in, and endeavours to promote, the less selfish end of this whole' (Hegel 1991 [1821], 271). Or as Durkheim puts it: 'this attachment to something that transcends the individual, this subordination of the particular to the general interest is the very well-spring of *all* moral activity' (Durkheim 1984 [1896], 18, emphasis JPD). Dewey formulates similar thoughts in many of his writings. In *Democracy and Education* for instance, he recommends teaching science through its technical and occupational applications, not just because this shows its practical roots and demonstrates its concrete validity, but also because it underlies the 'social interests' and 'social ends' that are present in modes of working as they fulfil the needs of others (Dewey 1985 [1916], 287).

Because they provide a stable social basis for collective, organized action, professional groups also play a functional role in organizing political representation. For both Hegel (1991, 339–352) and Durkheim (1984, 28), the best way to bring problems arising at the level of society to the level of political consideration is through the channels provided by the different social-professional groups. As for Dewey, Renault (2022, 164–187) provides ample evidence of the importance of the representation of professional interests for real democracy, even though Dewey insists more than his two predecessors on the need to include other forms of 'association' into political representation.

In this case, work is socially central in a literal sense since particular work occupations lead to the creation of occupational groups, which become the mediating organs between atomized individuals and families on the one hand and the collective as a whole on the other. They are mediating organs in a moral (Durkheim), or an 'ethical' sense (Hegel), and also in a functional sense, when political representation is structured more or less directly along these professional groups.

12.4.6 Household Cooperation

If work is conceptualized as the activities enabling the production and reproduction of human life, then it matters to note that whatever normative framework and cultural understanding determines the structure of families at a particular time, it has been the case throughout human history, and it remains the case today, that the family unit is the primary locus in which individual lives are produced and reproduced. Today this is undoubtedly less true than has ever been the case in human history. A woman can bear a child on her own, a person can look after all of their needs without having a partner, an old person can be looked after in old age even without partner or close kin surrounding them. Yet even in relatively prosperous, technologically advanced societies, and even in our time when the family and the extended kin are no longer the basic units of social life, it remains the case empirically that overall, most lives are produced and reproduced in tight social units of more than one, where the labour of subsistence and care is divided between the members. This is a basic point to which no specific normative inflection needs to be assigned.

It is simply a fact of human evolutionary history (Goodenough 1980) that new members of the species are born, fed and looked after within social units that have a core nucleus centred around the collective of just a few adult partners. In the overwhelming majority, in unions usually recognized through the institution of marriage, the pairing is made up of two adults who are sexually involved, often (but not always) with proprietary rights in either direction. In some far less frequent cases, the core group in charge of the care of children is a consanguine union, made up of close kins. In most human cultures the young and the mature members of the family have their primary needs fulfilled to a large extent via the family. In many human cultures, these basic units are embedded in larger units structured by particular kinship rules. These larger kin groups add new dimensions and levels of social complexity to the division of labour ensuring the care of the young, the adult, and the old. But even in large kin groups, the basic pairings remain a functional core. Of course, many accidents can break up these pairings (death and divorce in particular), and human societies have invented all kinds of institutional solutions to remedy this so that care for the young in particular continues, at least minimally (in many cultures loss of a father is a very serious social accident), and society can be sustained over time as a result. Precisely, though, these are accidents, for which particular social solutions became necessary. Beyond the great variety of cultural and institutional rules defining families, the relations between genders and relations with broader kins, it remains the case that the family, the close union of a woman to her children and the help brought to them by closely associated males (the definition of the family proposed by Goodenough) is the social unit where individual lives in their overwhelming majority are produced and reproduced. And that makes work socially central in a decisive sense: beyond the general point that work ensures the reproduction of lifeworlds, it is notably work within families, divided between the family members, that ensures this reproduction. If we consider what work within families involves, it is clear that, just because of the function it has, namely, to tend to its members' everyday needs, this work will also have specific features compared to work outside families.

The reproduction perspective means that many different types of activities count as work, provided they fulfil some need as a result of a wilful effort to produce some value for someone. Among the many types of work activities, some stand out, namely those that are engaged in by individuals who have specialized in those activities. As we saw, specialization is a direct consequence of the division of labour in human society. A lot of the work of social reproduction is provided by people who are best at doing what is to be done, where 'best' is defined according to the level of theoretical and practical knowledge at the time, together with the cultural expectations defining productive excellence. Whatever 'best' means in each historical case, specialists are those who know how to reach that level of performance in the creation of particular use values. The corporations we considered in the previous section are collectives of such experts. It is interesting to consider the work that goes on in families from this point of view of specialization.

All families need to somehow provide the basic work that is required, each time depending on cultural expectations, for the reproduction of individual lives. In many cases, this work is provided not by specialists but by family members themselves. This includes the work that is needed, not just for the direct care of family members, but in relation also to the resources used by the family in its daily life: maintenance of housing, availability of means of transport, of means of communication, and so on. For privileged people, these infrastructure needs are tended to by others, by subordinates or by outside specialists. Rich or powerful people can use their wealth and influence to call on their dependents, their liege, their servants, their employees, or tradespeople, to fulfil several or indeed all the family's needs, to fix the roof, or indeed to breastfeed the infants and educate growing children. However, everyday life has many contingencies, and privileged people by definition are the minority. As a consequence, for most families at least some work around the home and some work for family members has to be performed by the family members themselves. Work in and for the family therefore makes of most people generalists who have to possess some of the basic technical skills and knowledge that are available in their current time. In pre-modern societies, technical knowledge and skills were broadly shared. In hunter-gatherer and in horticultural societies where the division of labour is not extensive, those who excel at particular tasks excel at tasks that everyone is supposed to master. Indeed, the general separation of the workplace from the family home is a recent phenomenon, emerging with the industrial mode of production. This means that in pre-industrialized societies people were both at the same time generalists and specialists. Even in modern society, however, many people are specialists in their professional occupation, but also have to be generalists in some respects as family members. This makes work socially central in another sense: in the vague sense, here, that most people in society, except for a few privileged ones, and those who cannot work, have a dual relationship to the work of reproduction: as generalists and as specialists. The division of labour does not apply to all work, a lot of work is very generally shared across many individuals in society, across most adults in any case. Apart from the very privileged and those who have severe impairments, some basic work tasks are almost universally shared. Even post-work theorists have to work on that account (see Hester and Srnicek 2023, who pinpoint this work as a blind spot in post-work theory).

Finally, work in families is central in yet another sense, to the extent namely that it is work within the family that directly reproduces society as such: namely, the work of social learning we mentioned several times already, involving knowledge of the language, norms, values, histories, theoretical, practical, and technical knowledges, underpinning collective life. A lot of social and cultural learning occurs through no explicit work, by children observing and imitating the adults. But not all social and cultural learning can happen in this way. Apprenticeship is a fundamental factor of human cultural evolution, allowing the passing on from generation to generation, and the continuous development, of the stock of knowledge that is constitutive of the lifeworld (Sterelny 2012). At least some aspects of apprenticeship require the specific efforts of one or several of the adults in the kin group, before it is taken care of outside the family in a formal setting. Dewey is of course the philosopher who in the tradition of Western philosophy put the most emphasis on the link between educational work in the family and formal educational work outside of it, as a decisive factor in the reproduction of a democratic society (Dewey 1985 [1916]). This work is socially central in a direct, functional sense: the work that families do in passing on knowledge of all kinds is an essential condition of social reproduction. The lifeworld cannot remain a world, an overarching framework for the many individual lives it harbours, if it is not reproduced as such. Beyond the idea of the 'moralizing' role played by families (Section 12.4.3 above), emphasized by Hegel and Durkheim, it is in this more basic, functional sense that families are 'the first root of the state', because of the work that goes on in them (Hegel 1991 [1821], 272).

12.4.7 Society's Infrastructure

In the passage from Durkheim quoted earlier and its citation of Auguste Comte, the last words in the last sentence point to another sense of work's centrality:

> it is the continuous distribution of different human tasks which constitutes the principal element in social solidarity, and *which becomes the primary cause of the scale and growing complexity of the social organism.*
>
> **(Durkheim 1986 [1916], 51)**

If Comte is correct, as Durkheim thinks he is, then:

> It is through the division of labour, or at least mainly through it, that the cohesion of societies would be ensured. *It would determine the essential characteristics that constitute them* [emphasis JPD].

On this view, the division of labour is 'central' not just in the sense that it provides the normative glue securing the cohesion of complex societies, the dimension that Durkheim's book investigates under the notion of 'social solidarity'. The second dimension mentioned here but not pursued in that book is that the division of labour is central in a 'constitutive' sense, to the extent first of all that the 'scope' of society is defined by how far in space work cooperation stretches, and secondly as the particular structure of that division of labour determines society's 'essential characteristics'.

Let us briefly explore these two dimensions. We noted earlier the blurriness of the boundaries separating one society from another. Value chains do not stop at national borders. Very early on in human history, exchange of precious commodities, of people, of technical know-hows, of knowledges, religions and myths connected human groups. However, it is also the case that, as Rawls for instance assumed in devising his theory of justice, society is a relatively enclosed system. Even today, at a time of extensive global exchanges, the great mass of work activities reproducing lifeworlds tend to be inward-looking. These activities are framed by cultural, moral, technical, legal, political traditions that are nationally or even regionally specific. Therefore, it seems correct to say that, even though borders are far from being hermetic and the boundaries separating human collectives are very undefined and porous, the 'social organism' extends as far as the division of labour does. The complex web of activities that reproduce a lifeworld reaches into and overlaps with other such webs in all kinds of ways, but the dimensions of these social webs are finite. Durkheim studied these particular dialectics via a review published in 1898 of a German book on 'political geography'. He noted that:

> the inner forces that constitute the life of a people are constantly advancing or retreating, according to whether they are increasing or decreasing, and the real frontier does likewise. For the same reason the frontier does not really consist of a line, but of a zone whose extent can be large, or less so. This is because it corresponds to the fact that the meeting of two bodies, whether they are social or not, gives rise to phenomena at the periphery that are very different from those that occur in inland areas in both. These phenomena require a certain space in which to develop. It is this space that is the true frontier. Thus, it is because it is something that is living that it possesses extensiveness, and is continually in the process of being transformed. Even the above does not highlight all the movements that play a role in the genesis of a frontier. As well as this tendency to isolation that impels people in contact with one another to withdraw into themselves, there is also a tendency to mingle together, to become involved with one another, to carry out exchanges.
>
> **(Durkheim 1986, 69)**

The passage highlights well the dialectic of inward activity and exchange with the outside. What is emphasized now, however, is the outcome of this dialectic: the 'extensiveness' of a social organism is finite and reaches as far as their division of labour does. Work is central in this case, in the sense that, through specialization and the division of labour, it determines the 'scale' of the lifeworld, its sheer quantitative, or geographical scope.

This dimension has a dynamic aspect, as Durkheim's citations, including the reference to Comte, indicate. If work is the set of activities that help to reproduce the lifeworld in all of its dimensions, then the way in which this web of work activities (including generalist and specialist work) is structured in fact can be viewed as the infrastructure supporting and nourishing the lifeworld as a whole. Looking at the division of labour in this way takes us very close to the outlines of a materialist social theory put forward by Marx and Engels at the beginning of the *German Ideology*. That famous passage can be read as making the same point as the French sociologists, namely that the division of labour determines the 'essential characteristics' of society:

> (The) mode of production must not be considered simply as being the reproduction of the physical existence of the individuals. Rather it is a definite form of activity of

> these individuals, a definite form of expressing their life, a definite mode of life on their part. As individuals express their life, so they are. *What they are, therefore, coincides with their production*, both with what they produce and *with how they produce*.
>
> **(Marx 2000 [1845], 177, translation altered)**

In the generic picture of human society presented in this passage, production is understood in a general sense, not just as production for the market but as 'production of life', reproduction of the current generation's life and production of the life of the next generation. This general sense of reproduction involves forms of cooperation, in particular specific organizations of the division of labour. The general organization of the 'production of life', Marx and Engels write, 'determines the conditions of society' (Marx 2000 [1845], 182). Taken at a general level, this directly echoes Durkheim's and Comte's claim that the nature of the division of labour also determines society's 'essential characteristics'. Work is central here in a *constitutive* sense, to the extent namely that the way in which it is organized, both technically and socially, provides the backbone of the collective and determines its particular structure. As we saw above, the normative order underpinning social relations, notably its hierarchical structure, is reflected and grounded in the organization of the division of labour. Now we see that the geographical organization of the collective is directly impacted by the way the activities of social reproduction are carried out concretely: how the countryside is utilized, shaped and potentially harmed; where cities grow and how far they extend; how 'town and country' relate to each other, and so on. Work as 'production of life' is the central infrastructure maintaining the lifeworld in existence and giving it its distinctive physical features in comparison with earlier iterations of the same lifeworld and in comparison with other lifeworlds.

The conclusion will extend this argument to suggest that the division of labour and the organization of the work of social reproduction also underpin the symbolic and cultural 'essential characteristics' of society, notably in the domains of science, art, and religion. For now, though, the next step is to study how the social centralities of work this chapter has delineated impact on individuals.

13
Facing Necessity

The previous chapter outlined different senses in which work is socially central. Underlying this social centrality of work was a basic thought, that of the social necessity of work, the simple idea that a lot of work is necessary for social reproduction, for the production and reproduction of individual and collective life. This necessity of work can refer to extensive historical, anthropological, and social-theoretical scholarship, as earlier chapters have shown. This necessity continues to exert its force today and in the foreseeable future, as Chapter 8 established. This chapter and the next continue to explore the implications of this necessity to work, first for individual people and then at the level of the collective.

The first section outlines the main ways in which work is linked to necessity in human life. This highlights a common problem with arguments against work's centrality: many of them ignore the many dimensions of necessity attached to work. Work is often taken for granted in theoretical debates, and because work is necessary in a number of ways, arguments that do not take into account all these aspects of necessity fail to be convincing. In the following sections, we outline how this perspective from necessity helps to explain in what different senses work is central for individuals.

13.1 The Necessity of Work

Let us first outline the different forms of necessity attached to the work of social reproduction. As a preamble, we might note how pervasive the necessity to work is. This was an obvious fact of human existence in premodern times, but it seems underappreciated in contemporary debates in social and political philosophy. It is as though the productive powers and technical feats of modern economies eroded the sense of how frail and needy we remain, such that theoretical discussions of justice, for instance, are conducted in a way that is detached from the many constraints of social reproduction. The basic intuition behind these final chapters is that discussions of work should not consider purely normative problems (perfectionist objections,

The Case for Work. Jean-Philippe Deranty, Oxford University Press. © Jean-Philippe Deranty (2024).
DOI: 10.1093/oso/9780192887146.003.0014

issues of freedom, equality and justice, and so on), but also keep in mind the sheer force of work's necessity, which ought to constrain normative debates. This echoes the general concern raised by James (2021), that the possibility of freedom only ever arises in the midst of 'practical necessity'. By bringing necessity to the foreground, this chapter aims to achieve further goals however: remaining aware of the necessity attached to work allows us to highlight new aspects of its centrality for individual and collective lives, in addition to the rich literature that already exists on the goods of work and the many links that have been established by theorists between work and politics.

13.1.1 Finitude

The first distinction to recall is between generalist work for self and kin, and specialist work for others. As the previous chapter established, most people have to work for themselves and their close others if they have any, using manual and technical skills available to everyone in society at that particular level of technological development. This is what Gorz referred to as 'work for oneself' (Gorz 1989, 153). This work is necessary simply to sustain one's life, the life of the members of the household, and the household itself, day in and day out. Very few people have the wealth or power to escape this necessity. Even postwork theorists have to purchase the food consumed in their household, prepare it, repair minor faults in their home, tend to minor injuries of their partners or older parents, teach their children basic social skills, and so on. This is a most banal, *everyday necessity*. As we noted in the previous chapter, this necessity is easily overlooked. Illich refers to it as 'shadow work' in reference to its invisibility within the value system of industrial, wage society (1980).

On top of such everyday work nearly everyone has to do, the division of labour and specialization bring with them extra layers of necessity. Total social labour, the putative overall amount of work efforts required to sustain the lives of individuals and the collective infrastructures is of necessity divided. This means that most individuals, on top of their generalist work for self and kin, also have to specialize in activities that others rely on and perform tasks others cannot perform themselves. The argument from finitude, that we only have finite time and finite personal resources to fulfil our many needs, simply means at first that each individual specializes in the sense that they do tasks others don't, and there is an exchange of outputs between them through the overall reproduction of the collective to which all belong. This is an exchange of outputs considered independently of any market mechanism, even though markets of course can facilitate the exchange. Social reproduction as such can be described as a giant exchange of individual work outputs, across all the spheres necessary for reproduction.

This necessity in specialization applies even in the case of Marx's vision of a 'society of associated producers', in which the division of labour enforced by capitalist work organization has been overtaken and the 'material elements' are in place for the 'development of the rich individuality which is all-sided in its production' (Marx 1973 [1857], 325; Heller 1976, 29). Even if in this new mode of social organization, 'each *can* become accomplished in any branch he wishes', and it 'becomes *possible* for me to do one thing today and another tomorrow, to hunt in the morning, fish in the afternoon, rear cattle in the evening, criticise after dinner' (Marx 2000, 185, emphasis JPD), the intrinsic temporal limitation everyone faces means that when I hunt in the morning, I can't fish at the same time, and when I fish in the afternoon, someone has to look after the cattle then. The possibility of multi-activity is premised on the social organization of total social labour, on the fact that 'society regulates the general production', which means precisely that it organizes who does what when. This basic dimension of necessity attached to the division of labour does not yet entail specialization in the sense of special training, acquiring specialist knowledge and skills. Many activities in that first sense of specialization might involve skills and knowledge available to all, or easily acquired by most. It's just that nobody can perform all the tasks that are required for the fulfilment of all their needs, even in the mythical abundance societies depicted by Sahlins. We might call this type of necessity the *necessity from finitude*.

Of course, for many work activities specialization means more than just focusing on a small set of tasks at a given time. In many cases, specialization does mean acquiring special theoretical and practical knowledge and special skills. The necessity attached to the division of labour in this case is *technical*: it is not just that we cannot do all the necessary tasks at once, it is also that we must have some particular knowledges and skills, and not others. Ultimately, it might come down to a question of time as well: with time, we might have learnt those skills and knowledges required to fulfil our needs. As Lady Katherine De Burg states in *Pride and Prejudice*: 'Had I practiced, I would have been a true proficient.' We might not have perfected those particular skills ever though, since we can rely on others, and some people are clearly better at particular tasks than others. I might count on others to do things they are better at than me, now or in any foreseeable future. Furthermore, everyone has activities they'd rather do and others they'd rather avoid. Even in Marx's vision of multisided individuality, the idea is not that everyone is equally good at all possible tasks, but rather that everyone should have the opportunity to engage in all the activities they might prefer. This possibility, however, does not take away the necessity to acquire the required technical knowledge and skills for each activity. Standards should not drop in the society of associated producers. Necessity here is the technical necessity to specialize, and relatedly, the necessity to depend on specialists for the performance of many tasks of social reproduction. Already in societies where all persons of the same gender are supposed to master the same skills in line with the structure of the sexual division of labour, some are better at some tasks than others. In societies where 'needs and means (to fulfil needs)', to use Hegel's useful formal terminology, have developed to a high degree of complexity, the majority of needs are fulfilled by specialists because they involve techniques and the learning of techniques only specialists can acquire, if only for questions of time. The necessity here is truly a technical one: we are compelled to rely on the technical know-that and know-how of others, which means in turn that most are under pressure to specialize, to learn special techniques, knowledges and know-how, precisely because others need the outputs produced by such technical knowledge. The simple notions of work for self and of the division of labour thus already highlight different layers of necessity attached to work, understood as active reproduction of individual and collective life: the *everyday necessity* to work; necessity *from finitude*; and *technical* necessity.

13.1.2 Natural Necessity

The necessity from finitude can be captured in other ways, which add further depth to the necessity of work. One such way is in biological and evolutionary terms. A common theme in philosophical anthropology is the incompleteness of the human being in comparison with other animals. The evolution of the species has not provided the human being with what other animals can rely on, namely an appropriate connection between perceptual capacities, motor abilities, behavioural reflexes and what the environment affords in terms of resources and challenges. The human being is a being 'born too early' and humanity a 'deficient life form' (Gehlen 1987). This is true phylogenetically and ontogenetically. Ontogenetically, a young animal requires protection, feeding and skill teaching for a relatively short period of time, until they can independently function in the tight system linking environment and instinctual behaviour. The human neonate is helpless in a much more extensive sense. They require years of dedicated protection, feeding, and training, before they can sustain themselves and act independently in their environment. At the level of the species, the lack of environmental specialization means that compensatory mechanisms had to be developed to ensure that the life form would survive.

Classical philosophical anthropologists like Arnold Gehlen and Helmut Plessner show the impact of under-specialization on all aspects of human biology, including perception, impulse reactions, motor behaviour, cognitive processing, and even sexuality. In every case, underspecialization which at first represents a significant threat to survival becomes an opportunity, as psychological and physical capacities are detached from pre-given schemata tightly connected to specific environments. Capacities are much more 'plastic' in the case of human animals: they can adapt to new objects, increase and diversify their range, are trainable, and can be improved indefinitely. This creates the biological conditions allowing humans to extend the scope of their interventions in the environment, both in terms of exploitation of a single environment and geographically, by populating environments across the entire planet. The plasticity of human capacities means that natural entities, including natural elements, can be studied and explored in more detached ways, and as a result can be turned into resources for survival, as sources of food, shelter, and clothing for basic biological needs, and into all kinds of artefacts for symbolic, cultural, and social needs. Eventually, the capacity for detached perception, for reflective and contemplative attitudes, and the multiple abilities of a hand detached from locomotion enabled the species to create tools that are interposed between human bodies and minds and natural entities. In turn, this drastically improved the extraction and shaping of utilities from the environment. In this naturalistic perspective, work, the ability to intervene instrumentally and efficaciously in the world, using particular techniques, is the direct outcome of humanity's specific biological, evolution-inherited abilities.

This evolutionary background signals another dimension of the necessity to work: work is necessary for that species to ensure its survival. Humans compensate for their lack of instinctual adaptation to their environment through work; or rather, work is *the human way* of adapting to the environment, by adapting the environment to human needs.

This latter necessity has been recognized in the philosophical tradition well before evolutionary theory and the modern philosophical anthropology inspired by it. Plato's retelling of the myth of Prometheus in *Protagoras* makes of *techne* a 'non-natural' gift to humanity after all the gifts of *physis* provided to animals have been handed out to all the other species and humans have been left out. In his 1496 *Oration on the Dignity of Man*, Pico Della Mirandola already formulated the idea of human being's essential incompleteness, which has to be compensated through work and in turn grants humans their superior productive power. As creator of the world and of all the species within it, God is the 'divine architect' and 'artificer', the supreme worker. Following his work of creation, God craves a creature that can witness the grandeur of his output. But all the natural orders have been filled, all the species already have their own essence without capacity to deviate from it. God creates human beings as the supernumerary species, the species without essence, who will make itself via its own activity, and on the basis of this independence, will be able to contemplate the world in all its diversity and majesty (Pico della Mirandola 2012 [1496], 7; cited in François 2022, 23).

In Marx, the idea is captured in the dialectic between natural, biological and historical, social needs (Heller 1976; Markus 1978; Honneth and Joas 1980, 18–24). Work is a necessity, first of all, to the extent that it helps to provide the '*necessities*' *of life*, the means to ensure the biological survival of the species. In the *Grundrisse* (1973 [1857], 325; see Section 7.2 in this volume), Marx speaks of work's 'natural paltriness' (*Naturbedürftigkeit*), which denotes the fact that work is humanity's specific way of ensuring the continuity of its life processes. Precisely because humans survive not through instinctual behaviour but through work (Marx 1991 [1867], 127), which involves an intentional, reflective attitude that incorporates knowledge into production, humans can act with increased efficiency, notably through the invention of tools and techniques adapted to different natural processes. With the increase in production, needs increase in their diversity, as Hegel already showed (1991 [1821], 228). New needs become part of what society deems 'necessary', defining the threshold between decent and indecent living (Heller 1976, 38; Geuss 2021, 16). The circle of needs expands and with it the circle of necessity: both what is deemed necessary for a truly human life, and the work that is necessary for fulfilling these needs. A new form of necessity, the necessity of social needs, replaces 'natural necessity'. This necessity of work continues to hold even in the emancipated society of associated producers. The passage from the *Grundrisse* continues: in this new phase of economic organization, 'natural necessity (*Naturnotwendigkeit*) in its direct form has disappeared because a historically created need has taken the place of the natural one'. But work continues to be necessary to fulfil historically created needs. The end of the anthropological narrative confirms what started it in the first place, namely 'natural necessity', *Naturnotwendigkeit*.

13.1.3 Social Necessity

Interdependence through the division of labour, which we explored in the previous chapter, also entails necessity: if we all rely on the exchange of our work outputs to fulfil our needs, then that means we necessarily rely on the work of each other for our survival, well-being, and flourishing. There is no escaping work for each other and exchange of work outputs. In turn, this social form of necessity entails separate dimensions.

Instead of looking at the division of labour in a horizontal way, as it were, on Smith's image of a web of exchanges from individual to individual (exchanging my products with the mythical baker), the division of labour can also be conceptualized in terms of each individual's relation to society as a whole (Geuss 2021, 18–21 draws the distinction clearly). This is a more realistic way of conceiving the division of labour. As soon as human collectives reach a certain demographic magnitude, and the division of labour crosses a threshold of complexity, the fulfilment of needs for each individual no longer seems well described as a multitude of one-to-one exchanges of outputs. That image is true at some level since it is individual efforts in the end that produce the outputs used by all. We are indeed tied to each other by our individual work efforts, through a bond of life as we said earlier. But from the point of view of how an individual person relates to the division of labour overall, the more accurate picture is different. The totality of work efforts in society, total social labour, produces a given amount of social wealth, namely the totality of use values, including cultural and symbolic goods and the maintenance of material and institutional infrastructures. Some of those use values can be transformed into value for exchange of course, but the point here is not the complex relation of use to exchange value, rather it is simply that the collective as a whole produces a certain amount of collectively produced wealth. For each individual, given the extreme limitations of our means compared to the multiplicity of our needs, getting access to that social wealth is the condition for survival and well-being. One way to access this wealth is through private property (Geuss 2021, 110–114): if by some institutional arrangement, we can lay claim to some of that wealth (obviously the scenario in capitalist societies), and if through this access we can fulfil all of our needs, then it is purely through private property that we ensure our survival and well-being. But for most individuals, this access via private property is not sufficient or indeed is not existent, as the majority of people rely mostly or even entirely on their work for their income. Next to the private title on socially produced wealth, which applies only to a few, it is work that provides the near universal claim to a portion of that wealth. By working if they are able to do so, by producing and reproducing a minute part of total social wealth, individuals can be said to participate in it, and this participation in overall social wealth entitles them to claim a portion of it. Later sections (14.2 and 14.3) take up the case of those who are not able to work, whether they lack the capacities for it or they have worked long enough and deserve retiring from work. The very notion of social reproduction entails support for those who are not able to work. And it should be remembered that work here is not waged work but all activities of social reproduction. For the majority of those who work in this sense (which includes many people outside and post- waged work), the view of the division of labour as a mediation between individuals and the collective turns cooperation (between each and everyone) into *participation* (of each in the whole). It is described clearly by Hegel in §199 of the *Philosophy of Right* (and used in rejuvenated form by Jaeggi 2017), and the aspect of necessity attached to it, a social form of necessity, well highlighted:

> the particular is mediated by the universal so that each individual, in earning, producing, and enjoying on his own account, thereby earns and produces for the enjoyment of others. This *necessity* which is inherent in the interlinked dependence of each on all now appears to each individual in the form of universal and permanent resources in which, through his education and skill, he has an opportunity to share; he is thereby assured of his livelihood, just as the universal resources are maintained and augmented by the income which he earns through his work.
>
> **(Hegel 1991 [1821], 233)**

Finitude, the vast discrepancy between our needs and our ability to fulfil them, which makes us utterly dependent on our 'brethren', translates here into the necessity for social inclusion through work. Marx spoke of this in terms of 'social mediation' (Marx 1973 [1857], 607). This social necessity connects with the necessity to learn particular skills and to specialize. It is a necessity that is felt in every human society, well before the advent of capitalist modernity. As pointed out, all individuals have to learn the skills and knowledge expected of everyone for the tasks of work-for-oneself and to specialize, as the division of labour requires at a given level of technological development. It is a necessity felt by children already, which drives the education and training systems, whether they are embedded in family structures and broader social relations, or they have become detached institutions. Hegel makes this point as well:

> The possibility of sharing in the universal resources—i.e. of holding particular resources—is, however, conditional upon one's own immediate basic assets (i.e. capital) on the one hand, and upon one's skill on the other.
>
> **(Hegel 1991 [1821], 233)**

Hegel notes uncritically that participation and sharing in total social wealth is underpinned by factors that favour some over others, namely those who hold some type of capital (financial or cultural) or have some form of innate superiority in skill acquisition. This point is thematized critically in the next chapter on the political implications of the necessity of work.

13.1.4 Human Neediness

As the evolutionary background makes clear, these different forms of necessity are all connected. They all stem from human beings' extreme vulnerability, which makes them utterly dependent on others and on artificial, non-instinctual modes of action for their survival. We are back to the theme of finitude, but having reviewed some of the main ways in which this finitude is expressed, the term now has a more encompassing sense. It denotes a state of the human being as such, an ontological characteristic of the species and its members, their extreme dependence, their being exposed to lack, suffering, and the threat of death. German has kept from older Northern European languages a small word that captures all these meanings in one, denoting the radical exposure of human beings: *Not*. The term is of the same family as the English '*need*'. Humans are inherently needy, exposed to want and lack, to the possibility of misery and distress. These negative connotations are all related to the idea of 'natural necessity', *Naturnotwendigkeit*, as Hegel and Marx employ the term.

Natural necessity has an important modal dimension that is underappreciated in contemporary political theory: this is necessity because human beings cannot escape such an ontological state. This modality adds to the notion's tragic dimension: the state humans *cannot* escape is one of exposure, to hunger, cold, disease, emotional distress of all kinds, to want and to suffering generally, and ultimately to the tragic certainty of our own death, the death of those we care about as well as the death of all the other beings with whom we share the gift and the fate of life.

Work in this context is a necessity in a double sense. It is the necessary response (in the modal sense of *notwendig*) to want and misery, the primary way to alleviate them for a while at least, to survive, and to flourish perhaps, in some sense and for some time. Work is necessary (*notwendig*) to alleviate necessity (*Not*). But work is itself a form of *Not*, of misery, as it is always toil in some way, at least as the breaking of rest, as the opposite of idleness and leisure, as being almost always duller and more serious than play, as always including some imposition. To the *necessity to work* might be added the *necessity of work*, that is, the necessity that is entailed in work itself, as the response to *Not*.

To capture this ontological depth of the concept of necessity and work's imbrication in it, it is useful to turn to a philosopher who attempted precisely to unveil the metaphysical roots of modern life, that is, the ultimate existential stakes, the chances for spiritual loss and redemption and the confrontation with reality, that are to be found in key experiences of modernity. In *Gravity and Grace*, Simone Weil dedicated an entire chapter to the notion of 'necessity'. In the following passage, she linked work explicitly to the negative features of the human condition that were just highlighted:

> Relentless necessity, wretchedness, distress, the crushing burden of poverty and of labour which wears us out, cruelty, torture, violent death, constraint, disease—all these constitute divine love. It is God who in love withdraws from us so that we can love him. For if we were exposed to the direct radiance of his love, without the protection of space, of time and of matter, we should be evaporated like water in the sun; there would not be enough 'I' in us to make it possible to surrender the 'I' for love's sake. Necessity is the screen set between God and us so that we can be. It is for us to pierce through the screen so that we cease to be.
>
> (Weil 2002, 33)

The point in citing this passage is that, beyond Weil's tragic theology, it articulates in a compelling way the intuition that runs through the end of the book. That is, that there is a double condition for real freedom: first, to not ignore the *Not* that characterizes human existence, to acknowledge it, as an ineliminable constraint on human organizations for instance; and second, that freedom, therefore, consists precisely in facing necessity. As this chapter and the next will seek to show, it is the double necessity of work, arising from the three dimensions we highlighted (intrinsic finitude, evolutionary legacy, and social dependency), that make work indispensable, 'central', for our psychological development and in the collective organization of human communities. As we review the psychological and political centrality of work, from the point of view of work's double necessity, we will also repel the last remaining objections.

13.2 Facing Necessity

Emphasizing the many dimensions of necessity attached to work helps to dispel the perfectionist worries that were summarized in Section 8.3.

There are 'goods' attached to work, if one insists on using this language, but these need not be understood in a perfectionist sense. Rather than being central because they would be elements of the good life that anyone ought to favour, the 'goods' of work instead can be thought of as positive effects that can emerge in favourable circumstances from the necessity (*Notwendigkeit*) to engage in work, and from facing the necessity (*Not*) of work. These good effects of work resulting from the facing of necessity are what this chapter attempts to outline. On such an approach, the instrumentalist worry is not an objection: the 'goods' delineated in the remainder of this chapter are indeed produced by work, work is therefore 'instrumentally' important in this sense and is not itself a good. But acknowledging the inherent 'instrumentality' of work does not negate its importance, on the contrary. As we will see, the view from necessity coupled with the definition of work as technical activity of social reproduction shows why it is through work most eminently that individuals have the highest chance of achieving these 'goods'. More specifically, what will be shown is that correctly organized work (where the core features of such organization are specified in the next chapter) is the necessary condition for achieving features of subjectivity that are structurally required for leading a free and flourishing life. The argument is not normative, it is not that work ought to be viewed as one privileged element of a good life, but it is an ontological, or descriptive argument, that there are features about work as a response to necessity and as a kind of technical and social activity that lead, in good circumstances, to constitutively positive features of human selves.

This view from necessity coupled with the conception of work as activity of reproduction also undercuts the pluralism worries entailed in anti-perfectionist objections. If the thesis defended is that work is 'central' in a constitutive sense, as a privileged medium for the development of subjective capacities that are themselves conditions of freedom and flourishing, then the problem with ranking subjective preferences raised by the internal and external pluralism objections, while legitimate in other contexts, is not relevant in this case. It is very reasonable to argue that all kinds of goods enter a well-lived human life, and that many people attach more value and significance to other forms of experience and relationships than work. The centrality of work defended in this book has nothing to object to these two claims. As the book acknowledges unreservedly, centrality does not mean exclusivity. Central here means irreducibly constitutive: the claim is that there are structural features inherent in activities of work, related to the fact they enable an efficient facing of necessity, which make work that is organized in good enough conditions an indispensable medium of freedom and self-development, and consequently a condition for any reasonable conception of flourishing. Being serious about the necessity to work and thus the inescapability of work, means that work is initially beyond preferences, and an argument will be mounted to show that independent of subjective preferences, work has 'goods' attached to it (when correctly organized) that are invaluable for human subjects. It is true that some individuals might value work as part of their own bundle of preferences, while others would rather avoid working. For the latter, the necessity to work and the necessity of work undoubtedly represent greater imposition than for the former. But it should be remembered that work here is not waged work, but work viewed as intentional, technical activity to produce useful outcomes, which includes many more activities than just work for a wage. Once work is viewed in this way, the seemingly draconian conclusion about goods of work being achieved even for those who would rather not work loses much of its sinister aspect, since 'not working' usually means not being engaged in waged work. The chapter tries to show what it is in the features of work activities that make them conducive to self-development. This undercuts the internal pluralist worry raised specifically by Arneson when he emphasized the many senses in which work might be meaningful. Individuals might have their own preferences about work, but the argument will point to features of work that matter beyond, or underneath those preferences.

One source of confusion in discussions of the 'goods of work' is that they are often linked to a distributivist conception of justice. In such a conception, justice is the fair distribution of the benefits and burdens of living together, and a key prerequisite in outlining the principles ensuring such fair distribution is neutrality towards conceptions of the good. The distribution should be fair, independently of people's personal preferences regarding work. Including the goods of work in the bundle of goods to be distributed (as Gheaus and Herzog 2016 typically do), or worse still, as Rawls did with his early condemnation of 'idlers' (see Section 8.2), assuming that contribution through work is an underlying condition of participation in the fair system of distribution, contradicts the very basis of a just society since it favours one conception of the good (where work features) over others. The perspective from necessity establishes the significance of work for individual and collective life, the 'goods of work', in a different way than the distributivist one. It begins by saying that work cannot be escaped, for all the reasons listed above. It then shows how, dialectically, facing this necessity, individually and collectively, can promote freedom and other important aspects of human life, or instead produce different forms of injustice and unfreedom. These important aspects of human life that work can support are not 'goods', in the sense of metaphorical commodities to be distributed fairly. If work is a necessity, the justice question is not whether or how it should be distributed but how it should be organized fairly, given that it has to be organized. The shift in approach turns on the initial background conception of work. If work is conceptualized as the overall reproduction of society, rather than the source of wealth or a personal preference, then the primary question is no longer how overall social wealth ought to be divided up and allocated in relation to people's preferences. Instead, the focus is on the collective organization of the work efforts, and how each individual finds their fair place in it.

From the point of view of necessity, the distributivist take on the 'goods of work' is problematic because it tends to overlook the extent to which work is necessary, and the sheer amount of work that is needed for the reproduction of lifeworlds. The focus on the distribution of goods that does justice to individual preferences takes for granted that the lifeworld will be there at all times. Just like economic theories that take for granted natural resources and amenable environments from which economic action is to draw *ad libitum*, theories of distributive justice take for granted that someone will do the work to maintain the social environments in which people can do 'as they wish'. In Van Parijs, who offers the most sophisticated account of distributivist justice on perfectly antiperfectionist assumptions, the preference for work is translated as preference for a career or for money over leisure. This conceptualizes work narrowly as the source of individual utilities. But a lot of work is unpaid and not institutionalized in a profession and yet utterly necessary for social reproduction. Even in a market economy the point of work ultimately is not to make money, but to produce use-values, to sustain the lifeworld and the lives within it. Of course, in capitalist societies, this point disappears from view, both in practice, in the motivations of many agents (except for those who offer care for free), and in many theoretical accounts (except for those who contrast capitalist production and social reproduction). But when reflecting on why work is needed and why it matters, we don't have to confuse overall social wealth with the amount of exchange value produced in the formal sectors of the economy, which immediately obfuscates all the work that goes on to maintain subsistence, well-being and provide the possibilities for flourishing.

At this juncture, one might wonder: emphasizing the necessity of work, the necessity to work and work being itself a form of *Not*, is that not a strange way to go about 'making the case' for it? The all-out vulnerability we humans are under, which forces us to work and which work puts us under, the urgency of bodily needs and of our minds' cravings that force us to undergo long, complex courses of action to produce use values, the comprehensive reliance on close and anonymous others stemming from our ever-multiplying needs, our utter dependency on material infrastructures and social processes whose complexity no one can fully muster, the hierarchies work places us under, both external and internal to work organizations, how could all of this heteronomy, opening up manifold avenues for domination and mental and physical misery be anything but something to alleviate, to avoid, to try and overcome? How could we ever be happy, flourishing, or free through work, given all the layers of imposition, physical, emotional, moral, social, and spiritual, work is about and is itself made up of?

The simple line taken in this book is that the response to these worries can be found in their very formulation. If work is truly a 'realm of necessity', in the many senses the previous section has outlined, as the response humans give to necessity which makes it itself a form of necessity (both a necessary response and a form of *Not*), then it is pointless to argue against it, simply because there is no point arguing against necessity. If work is necessary, it is illusory to aim to move 'post' it. A realistic view of the human species, of human history and of human societies to date shows that it is unrealistic to claim to move 'beyond' work.

An important theoretical point emerges from reminding ourselves of our radical vulnerability. Mainstream political philosophy was born at the end of the Fordist years, at a time in Western, industrialized nations when, for a few countries at the core of capitalist development, the main economic trends could give the impression that humanity had finally conquered the age-old condition of scarcity and struggle for existence. The way in which economic issues are debated in the distributivist or allocative approaches to justice, which came to define the discipline henceforth, at least in its mainstream English-speaking variant, implies that, for these kinds of approaches, issues of production have been resolved. In the background of the complex schemes for fair distribution stands the assumption that there will always be plenty to distribute. This unpronounced assumption reflects within specialized theory the profligacy of the late 1960s and early 1970s, the naïve view that technological power backed by accelerating scientific progress, coupled with the presumption of inexhaustible natural resources and infinitely pliable environments, would henceforth secure processes of wealth creation well beyond what is required for the satisfaction of everyone's needs, now and for all future times. All that remained to resolve with such assumptions of proficiency was the fairness of the distribution of primary goods, in such a way that this distribution would not undermine the levels of economic efficiency and productivity that had been reached. Today, as human-induced climate catastrophe urgently demands a reorganization of economic activities, as value chains and supply chains become increasingly disrupted by the folly of new wars, the unleashing of zoonoses, and coming climate extremes are bound to increase disruptions manyfold, the brief parenthesis in the sense of human frailty that a few countries could indulge in for a few decades should have evaporated. Necessity has returned with a vengeance we might say, even though many theorists and philosophers writing in rich countries who so far have remained shielded from the first signs of the catastrophes to come still seem to struggle to integrate this factor in their writing. With the return of necessity, the necessity to think about how to organize work, and what work is necessary, has also returned. The dramatic situation in which we find ourselves reminds us of our *Not*, and that we respond to *Not* through work. The theoretical point, then, is that awareness of necessity brings with it a different approach to political philosophy, and work is directly implicated in this awareness, as the necessary response humans bring to necessity.

This thought applies directly to debates in the post-work literature. Post-work theorists standardly argue that it is not work itself, productive or creative activity, they argue against, but work as a contemporary 'condition' (Danaher 2019a), in other words, waged work in a capitalist setting, and with it the particular ideology, the 'work ethic' or the 'work dogma' that comes with it. From the perspective of necessity though, this distinction is not satisfactory. If work is indeed necessary (in all the senses outlined), then 'post-work' does not seem the right approach. It is simply unrealistic to argue for post-work society if work is necessary. Rather, if work is necessary, the necessary answer to necessity, then the worry should be about how best to organize this necessity. We might well work less, work differently, and work for other goals than the ones defined by capitalist settings, we might want to abolish the current work ethic, but none of that equates with moving 'beyond work'.

The first response to the worry about emphasizing necessity in making the case for work is thus that it does not seem a good idea to remain overly idealistic and ignore the facts of necessity when doing social and political theorizing. Yet this realistic response does not have to end up in a pessimistic outlook about the chances for human happiness, flourishing and freedom. Work is our fate, but that fate need not be one made up solely of misery, dependence and heteronomy. In fact, the very necessity that work is about and that work itself is can be shown to harbour the conditions for the special 'goods' or benefits that can be attached to work, and for the path towards freedom that work can represent. The next chapter will be dedicated to the collective aspects of work necessity. Here, the perspective is on the individual and we can already make general points about freedom and self-development from this point of view.

13.2.1 Strengthening Subjective Life

Not only is it unrealistic to want to take necessity out of human life, but the acknowledgement of necessity does not have to lead to a depressed view of the human predicament. We don't concede much by recognizing that we are creatures of necessity. For instance, an accurate image of freedom views it not as the opposite of necessity, but rather as growing out of necessity, as a way of coming to terms with necessity, cognitively and practically. This thought can rely on a long and venerable philosophical tradition, from the Stoics to Spinoza. In formal terms, a basic Hegelian point is to doubt any definition that characterizes a concept by simply opposing it to its contrary notion. In the context of contemporary work debates, the temptation to understand freedom as pure release from any bond of necessity is well visible in Gorz's seminal writings, as his depiction of 'autonomy', a term that is at the heart of his critiques of pro-work policies, seems to be synonymous with detachment from all and any kind of dependence, whether social or material. This is in line with his grounding in Sartrean existentialism, and the latter's maximalist conception of freedom as self-constitution. Even writings that defend the idea that work can be reconciled with autonomy, like Adina Schwartz's oft-cited 1982 article, propound an unrealistic, maximalist vision of autonomy as perfect independence. Arguably, freedom and necessity should not be opposed frontally, but rather freedom, for human beings at least, has to be a freedom that is gained within necessity, that arises out of necessity as it were.

A more 'dialectical' conception of freedom as the active facing of necessity can be found in the writings of another one of the great existentialist phenomenologists, namely in Merleau-Ponty's work. Merleau-Ponty's consistent focus on the 'ambiguity' characteristic of human agency was based precisely on the reciprocal links between necessity and freedom. As he writes for instance in a 1946 article republished in *Sense and Non-Sense*, the strength of existential philosophy is that in it the human being 'no longer appears as a product of his environment or an absolute legislator but emerges as a product-producer, the locus where necessity turns into concrete liberty' (Merleau-Ponty 1964 [1946], 134; see also this page in *Phenomenology of Perception*, 2012 [1945], 174). This dialectic expresses a key principle of human freedom existentialist philosophers found encapsulated already in famous formulations about the scope of human agency in Marx's *German Ideology* ('circumstances make human beings just as much as human beings make circumstances' 2000, 189), or in the *18th Brumaire*: 'Human beings make their own history, but they do not make it just as they please; they do not make it under circumstances chosen by themselves, but under circumstances directly encountered, given, and transmitted from the past' (Marx 2000, 329; see Deranty 2016).

Applied to work, this insight translates into a vision of human life where the work of necessity, the necessity to work and the necessities built into work, can be conduits of freedom. And if, as we take it below, real freedom is understood as the external and internal conditions of self-agency, then the same dialectical thought can be extended to flourishing andhappiness. What this means for post-work debates is that, if there is indeed a necessity to work, it is not by unrealistically escaping work that we might achieve happiness, flourishing and freedom, but rather by meeting it upfront, unless of course we manage to have others face necessity for us, instead of us, an option we discuss below, which is clearly unjust. Indeed, as we will now try to show, not only can major existential 'goods' be obtained through the work of necessity, but the work of necessity is in fact a privileged way to achieve them.

The dialectical relations between necessity and freedom, and between the work of necessity and self-realization, have been explored at length by interpreters of Marx, notably to gauge the meaning of the famous passage in volume 3 of *Capital*, where Marx appears to oppose the realm of freedom and the realm of necessity. Some read the passage as contradicting Marx's vision expressed in many other texts which outline the freedom-enhancing powers of meeting the challenges of necessity (Klagge 1986; Kandiyali 2014). Others (Sayers 2006; James 2017) read the *Capital* passage as being consistent with earlier passages, notably from the 1844 *Economic-Philosophical Manuscripts* and from the *Grundrisse*. In these exegetical discussions, the goods of work arising from facing necessity are threefold: developing one's capacities, contributing to the good of others, and thereby developing communal life. Work is central to building a truly humane society as it is the active way of caring for others, thereby creating a community based on solidarity (Tyssedal 2023). Rather than rehearsing these arguments and providing its own take on the *Capital* passage, this chapter instead seeks to retrieve these three fundamental 'goods', as well as additional ones, by following the guiding thread that was presented in the introduction already and has been pursued throughout the book, namely to articulate the goods and the bads of work by considering what distinguishes it as a particular kind of activity within human life.

In trying to show how work activities entail structural features which mean that,when organized well enough, they provide the conditions for agency and self-development, the chapter relies on a rich vein of psychological writings on work in France in the last few decades, around the work of Christophe Dejours (see Dejours 2009 for a survey of the main themes in his *oeuvre*; Dejours and Deranty 2010 for a succinct defence of the centrality of work;

Dejours et al. 2018, for the significance of this tradition in contemporary philosophy of work), Yves Clot (1999, 2014), Pascale Molinier (2006, 2013) and a new generation of scholars inspired by their work. In Deranty (2009, 2010), the reader can find presentations of the main themes and arguments in this tradition. Here, rather than repeating the arguments put forward by these psychological theorists to demonstrate and study the importance of work for human subjectivity, the argument highlights the psychological centrality of work from a more abstract, philosophical point of view, using the perspective from necessity as its entry point. Only a few key concepts and arguments from Dejours' writings especially are mobilized to help in this task.

Dejours' model of the impact of work on human subjectivity is a 'dynamic' one, that is, a conception of subjectivity that puts the emphasis on the developmental process by which subjectivity gradually forms over time, through defining experiences linked to key relationships: relationships of the maturing psyche to the body from which it gradually detaches itself, and constitutive relationships to significant others. This focus on development is justified by the assumption that the psychic structures that are put into place through it play a large role in determining the future behavioural patterns and forms of experience and self-relation of the mature subject.

An important emphasis resulting from the dynamic, developmental perspective is the view that psychic identity is an inherently unstable formation, on account firstly of psychic blind spots and structural contradictions resulting from psychological development itself, and secondly because of the never-ending pressures that are exerted on this subjectivity by internal and external demands: demands stemming from the metabolic, notably sexual, systems in the subject's body; and demands stemming from the environment, notably from the different social interactions in which the subject lives. The psychic balance the subject aims to maintain while dealing with those demands, on the basis of the psychic construct inherited from childhood, is intrinsically fragile and can be undone in a number of ways. Work is one of those situations where psychic constructs are under stress, not just for contingent reasons because work can be tiresome, boring, or organized in such a way that other people (management, clients) make life difficult for the working subject. Beyond these challenges attached to work as a result of the content of tasks or work's organization, work is structurally challenging, Dejours shows, because of the gap ergonomists have highlighted between the way the work process is supposed to unfold, the prescribed form of work tasks, and what it actually takes to realize these tasks. The multiple contingencies that define any situation in which a task is to be fulfilled mean that it is often impossible to achieve the work performance simply by following prescriptions. Many tasks are intrinsically difficult in any case, require some level of skill, or assumed knowledge, or mastery of machines, or technical processes. As a result of all this, except in cases where work is just routine performance of simple tasks (for instance in generalist work in the home), work in many cases involves the possibility of failure for working subjects. And most work involves some form of suffering, not just because it has intrinsic negative aspects (if only because it is experienced as boring or even meaningless), but also because the gap between prescription and performance entails the possibility of failure as soon as the tasks are not very simple or routine.

In many cases, we can in fact bridge the gap between prescription and realization. We can apply the relevant knowledge, gain the knowledge required, apply or learn a skill, use or learn to use a machine and fulfil the prescribed tasks. We can adapt to new situations, to unanticipated challenges, to unforeseen breakdowns, and to unplanned mishaps. When this occurs, the working subject has improved her knowledge, skill, technical ability, or interpersonal dexterity, has demonstrated creativity, ingenuity, inventiveness, practical or communicational or emotional intelligence, which in most cases mobilizes some form of theoretical insight.

In these situations where the gap between prescription and performance has been breached, a general psychodynamic benefit often occurs in the background, on top of the development of practical and theoretical intelligence. By overcoming the fear of failure, by countering the suffering inherent in work's difficulties, the fragile psychic construct can come out strengthened from the work effort. Work challenges, like other social or material challenges, can easily disrupt fragile psychic identities. But work challenges can also strengthen subjectivity because in meeting them, the self develops internal resources, cognitive, bodily, emotional, affective, which can translate into greater resilience and self-confidence. These resources then should be seen as forms of self-development, not just because distinct skills and capabilities have been improved upon or added to the arsenal of skills possessed by the subject, but also, more fundamentally, because they mean that the self as self, the subject in her own self-relating, has increased self-mastery, has become more assured of herself. The self gives shape to herself by developing subjective resources, as it were. Subjective life hardens itself, strengthens itself in successful work performances. The ergonomic challenges built into work tasks can thus have a positive developmental impact, they can foster self-development, not just the development of capabilities, but the development of the self herself, a strengthening of psychic life that makes the self more resilient towards challenges, both external and internal.

An apt Hegelian image that helps to articulate the idea of self-development as an active form of freedom is his definition of freedom as 'being at home in one's other' (see Honneth 2015 for a clear exposition but focused only on a human 'other'; Patten 1999; Gleeson and Ikaheimo 2019 for the same idea in terms of 'concrete freedom'; Deranty 2021a). Bringing this view of freedom in communication with the idea of self-development translates Dejours' dynamic conception of subjectivity into the following picture: living one's life involves being caught up in all kinds of material, interpersonal, and social interactions. In order to avoid being alienated in those interactions, individuals require a whole range of capacities, different types of knowledge to draw on, as well as cognitive, emotional and bodily skills to apply and use these knowledges appropriately. Capacities on this view are powers the subject exercises by mobilizing her psychic and bodily resources. These exercises of subjective power enable the subject to maintain a sufficient level of control in interactions. Cognitive resources ensure the situation is not befuddling, the subject knows what is going on and what contextually relevant information to apply. Practical and social skills enable the subject to do what has to be done, taking into account what is expected in the situation, her own goals and intentions and the threats and affordances that are present in the context. Emotional resources enable the subject to not be overwhelmed by the situation. The reference to emotional resources is key, because one major source of 'alienation', of being overwhelmed by situations, is internal. It is not just that there might be a lack of sufficient resources to deal with the complexity of a situation, but one's own 'inner demons' and 'hang-ups' mean the situation presses on blind spots in that particular person's psyche, such that another person with similar levels of physical or cognitive abilities would be able to deal with it, but that first person cannot. Her psychic construct is specifically targeted by the context, as a result of her subjective construction.

This model allows for a graduated scale of 'free interactions with one's others'. Subjective life that is sufficiently in charge of itself is not just capable of withstanding internal and external challenges, which is a negative way of defining subjective health. If subjective resources allow it and interactions are sufficiently well navigated, the subject can also positively engage with challenges, which means that the subject might thrive in these interactions, that is, develop subjective resources further and increase the sense of self, which will be expressed in affects such as a sense of security, comfort, self-confidence, resilience, and inner strength (Deranty 2022). This is a conception not just of psychological balance but also of freedom, because, negatively speaking, the challenges have not overwhelmed the subject, the subject was not alienated in interactions, and positively speaking, the subject has for a while at least made her immediate world a world in which she is 'at home', in which for instance her goals can be realized, her actions have meaning. In the field of contemporary philosophical discussions, the model of freedom this articulates is a 'positive' one, where freedom is not defined as the absence of interference or domination, but rather, taking the subject's efforts as the main perspective, as the positive ability to deal with all the interactions one is involved in while living one's life. This 'positive' conception of freedom is a scaled and minimalist one; it defines freedom as a 'good enough' level of control and self-control in given situations. As a result, it is not beset by the problems that are raised by defenders of 'negative' accounts (typically liberal and republican conceptions of freedom), against conceptions emphasizing self-determination, self-realization, or authenticity. The core idea is simply of a strong enough psychic life, not the realization of human essence, or the full deployment of rationality in one's life plan, or fully corresponding to one's true self. It is about having the sufficient amount of inner strength required to navigate life with minimal autonomy, dealing with internal pressures and external challenges sufficiently well.

Such an approach to work is invaluable because it combines a detailed ergonomic model of work activities with a detailed psychodynamic model of subjectivity, the combination of which delivers convincing descriptive tools to study the psychic impact of work and leads to the idea of the centrality of work for human subjects. However, the idea that work situations are paramount in making us face the gap between prescription and performance is not explicitly justified by Dejours and the other French psychologists of work. In other words, the necessity of work (work as *Not*) is well accounted for, but the necessity to work is largely taken for granted. It is important to stress and delineate clearly this necessity if the centrality of work is to be fully defended from a psychodynamic perspective. This is because in activities chosen by the self outside of a work context (leisure activities and hobbies), there is often also a gap between prescription and performance: in learning an instrument for one's pleasure, in playing games with others, in gardening at home, and so on. In such situations, there are also technical standards to abide by, procedures to follow, tools, instruments or machines to learn to use. The subject can easily fail in learning the violin or growing beautiful roses. However, the full developmental effect of activities arises only in situations in which fulfilling the task truly puts the subjective identity at stake. And this occurs when there is necessity attached to the task, when the subject has no way of avoiding the task and what it takes to realize it. You can always abandon a game that is too hard or too boring for you, you can adjust the rules if you wish, and you can stop learning the violin if you don't see any meaningful progress and you're not enjoying it. There is no consequence attached to being a poor gardener, apart from disappointment (if you are growing vegetables because it feeds your family, then it is work). The necessity attached to work amplifies the personal stakes of failure and success dramatically, and with them, the psychodynamic impact.

It could be objected that for many people, work that is experienced as being too hard or too boring or too dangerous, or meaningless, can also be renounced. Slaves and people in economic dependency do not have that option, but others do. But before the work was abandoned for any of these reasons, the tasks that it involved were engaged in. In those situations, the subject experienced the pressures inherent in fulfilling the tasks.

If we focus on these pressures, we see that, adding to the general necessities that were enumerated in the previous section, more specific task-related necessities arise from the ergonomic dimension. Work aims to address a need by producing some added value, which means that the ultimate judgement on the validity of the activity's output, and in turn the activity's meaning, is in the hands of the user, often a different person than the agent herself. The very notion of 'use value' introduces a level of necessity, namely that the output does have true value. And this value is defined by a judgement that escapes the producer. If the user is the same as the producer, unless the producer lies to themselves, they will have to judge that their work did not produce a valuable output if that is the case. Additionally, all work, even work involving simple tasks, has a technical dimension, which implies the correct application of some technical gesture or process. This means that those who know about the tasks also pass judgement, implicitly or explicitly. This is another dimension of necessity: the necessity to complete the tasks in a technically sound way. Even if the worker has an idiosyncratic way of fulfilling the task, their technique has to prove itself in the output. Indeed, as we saw in Section 12.3, there is a cultural dimension to technical efficiency, which means that the work gestures need to abide by technical expectations lest they be rejected. Finally, a lot of work occurs in formal organizations with hierarchies, which means that the working activity is controlled and supervised by external authorities, a third dimension of necessity surrounding the task aspect of work.

All these constraints surrounding the completion of work tasks are simply not felt in other contexts. In the case of work, if the task is not completed, usually in a specified time, if the outcome is not of the expected quality, if the technical standards are not met, and if the processes and procedures are not followed, negative consequences ensue, which can be serious for the self and potentially for others. Some form of disappointment all the way to severe distress (in the case of care work, Molinier 2013) is expressed by those who expected the work's outcomes. For the worker, legal repercussions might arise, admonishments from managers, the reprobation of co-workers or other professionals or of the broader community, material punishment, such as loss of income or dismissal. These repercussions follow and matter because work matters. Whether we judge the reasons for it are good or not, the work was set up with the tasks it involves because some need was supposed to be met by it, someone expected the outcome from it.

For the subject herself, there is arguably an inner compulsion to do the task well and therefore a negative psychological outcome in waiting if this is not the case. We can make sense of this aspect by referring to the natural necessity inherited from our evolutionary past, which has rendered humans hard-wired to practical success, attracted to activity and to seeing activities through to the end. Self-determination theory (Ryan and Deci 2017) provides strong confirmation from another strand of psychological research, to make sense of the ample phenomenological evidence that there is an inherent motivation for humans to achieve a task, and conversely inherent displeasure in not being able to achieve or see through what we set out to do. As Dejours frequently argues in line with self-determination theory, rather than trying to find external incentives or pressuring mechanisms to motivate people to work, organizations should ensure they don't destroy and instead promote the intrinsic motivation to work and to work well (see Coutrot and Perez 2022, 96–100, for concrete corporate initiatives along these lines).

All these repercussions of not fulfilling the task are part of the overall *Not*, the all-out vulnerability work puts us in. As such, they increase the stakes in attempting to fulfil the task: this looming background builds up the fear of failure and in turn provides the psychodynamic rewards, the developmental benefits, when we overcome its threats. By contrast, the stakes of not winning at a game with friends, of sucking at learning the violin, of not being able to grow vegetables for fun, are likely to be a lot less intense than in a work context. The psychodynamic benefit in case of success will be all the more diminished. Of course, an individual can invest a lot emotionally or existentially in doing something, and they might not need the external consequences of failure to feel the pressure of succeeding at the tasks. But arguably this is a rare occurrence and in fact, precisely because the task lacks necessity, the amount of psychic investment in those cases might be laughable. If you can't learn the violin properly, just give up on it. If you never win at chess against your friend, this should not lead you to feel depressed. It is empirically doubtful that most people feel as much psychological impact from failure at hobbies compared to failure at work. There is no need to invoke a particular ideology of work to explain this contrast. The stakes surrounding the fulfilment of work tasks, and the very definition of what those tasks are about (fulfilling needs) are a large part of the answer, even if in some situations an added ideological element, a particular version of the work ethic, might add to the dramatic stakes of work.

13.2.2 Work and Play

The sign that necessity dramatically increases the developmental impact of work by contrast with other contexts of action can be seen in the way we engage in hobbies. As soon as we are serious about a leisure activity and we want to truly learn, we put ourselves in a situation that resembles a work situation. For most people, self-motivation and self-learning are not enough: we willingly put ourselves under the command of an external authority who provides not just expert advice and demonstrations of competent action, but also an external voice that represents precisely the heteronomous controls we are placed under in work situations, someone to give us homework, to impose deadlines, to test our learning development, to reprimand us if we have been lazy. Thus, apart from exceptional individuals who are capable of self-motivation and organizing their own learning, we all recognize de facto that real development occurs only when two key conditions are in place: when we actually face our limits and make a real effort to overcome them (bridging gaps); and when there are stakes in not doing this, represented and enforced by an external authority. We all acknowledge the old motto Hegel recalls in the *Phenomenology of Spirit* in relation precisely to the link between work and freedom: 'fear of the Lord is the beginning of wisdom'.

There is much talk today of the 'gamification' of work, the introduction of game features into waged work (competition between co-workers, targets to reach, personal and company records, live league tables, and so on), and even of actual games in formal work contexts, for the purpose of team building, maintaining worker motivation and increasing productivity (Le Lay 2022). What is less noted is the extent to which games, playing, often take on work dimensions and more generally, how work is the implicit reference point for playing and many leisure activities. This is visible already in the phenomenon we just mentioned: many people deliberately choose to put themselves in work-like situations in their hobbies, by hiring someone who tells them what to do, how to do it, and when to do it by. People do this because they know this is the condition for truly learning and improving at particular tasks.

That work is the reference point for serious leisure is confirmed by the professionalization that affects many hobbies and leisure activities today. Most hobbies and leisure activities have their professional counterparts. When it comes to physical activity and sport, there is no endeavour, however arcane or pointless (curling, the indefinitely diverse ways to run down a slope on skis or swim back and forth in a pool) that does not have its professional league. The same applies to all the games where different levels of skills can be acquired so that it makes sense to rank people in a non-random way and there is a clear scale of progression. Chess, go, all kinds of card games, and all kinds of bowling games (bocce, pétanque, pinball), have their professional competitions, with players earning their living by playing. Of course, playing video games and playing online are now lucrative forms of work, and even broadcasting and commenting on one's own online playing, even if one is not very good at it, have become professional occupations.

These professionalized forms of game and play reveal important aspects of human attitudes to task performance. Professional leagues exist because there is interest from the public: the games draw audiences, who are happy to pay to see people play, and to whom advertisers can market their products. There is clearly a deeply anchored, powerful attraction in seeing 'brethren' achieve the highest level of skill at a particular activity. In spectator sport, it is solely the display of skill that is of interest, since the outcome of those activities is meaningless when it comes to primary human needs. The only need that is fulfilled here is the pure need to complete tasks, to 'bridge gaps' as well as possible, and the shared pleasure of witnessing expert demonstrations of practical, bodily, emotional and cognitive intelligence. These games become work for those who engage in them professionally of course. All of this shows how tenuous the line is between play and work, and how work is the model for playing in many ways, something well delineated by Dewey already (1985 [1916], 202–214). Professionals teach lay people how to improve themselves in their leisure activities, and lay practitioners' ideal is to reach the level of professionals. But professionals are typically people who have made a free activity that one can abandon at any moment (a leisure) into a necessary one. In doing so, they accepted to subject themselves to the necessities that come with achieving tasks seriously: disciplines of learning, which imply disciplines of the body and of the mind, external disciplines enforced by others (in their case, coaches and trainers, doctors, and officials of all kinds), and indeed the discipline required to fulfil the needs of those to whom the activity is ultimately addressed, the paying audience. Whatever one thinks of the professionalization of games and leisure activities (one could easily see it as a symptom of capitalist pathology), what this striking and overwhelming feature of contemporary societies demonstrates is that there is continuity between play and work and what makes work the reference point for playing is precisely the embrace of necessity.

Of course, highlighting the benefits of facing necessity is highly ambivalent. All the heteronomous pressures surrounding work performances easily make of work an experience of unfreedom. One key lesson of self-determination theory is precisely how easy it is to undermine the intrinsic nature of workers' motivations, notably if autonomy is undermined, but also if external rewards take over in the motivation for acting. It is most likely because they already recognized how easily working leads to heteronomy, and not just because of the way it was socially organized in their time, that ancient philosophers equated work with slavery and freedom with the release from the necessity to work. As Chapter 6 explored, the sadistic irony the German fascists displayed in linking work with freedom has made it a difficult motto to defend today. All those heteronomous pressures identified as characteristics of activity in work contexts can undeniably be a source of alienation and withering of the self, physically, emotionally, existentially, and even cognitively. In his critical writings on the impact of neoliberal work, Dejours shows how the specific types of compulsion created by neoliberal management techniques undermine the moral powers of individuals, enlisting passive and sometimes even active contributions in the demise of others (Dejours 1998).

And yet the fact that the line is fine between autonomy and heteronomy, between freedom and alienation, is not a valid reason to reject the argument that the facing of necessity is the true source of self-development and of freedom understood as the capacity to withstand and thrive in interactions. The very notion of necessity demands that it should not be ignored. If necessity cannot be avoided, then it is by facing it, not by ignoring it, that we can realistically develop our powers and thereby acquire some relative level of internal and external autonomy, being at home within our own self and in our environments. Over against this, freedom and thriving should not rely on the fantasy of a happy state where somehow necessity would not exist, or by relying on a social organization that amounts to displacing the necessity to work onto others. Facing necessity is the path to freedom, in a general, conceptual sense, and also, more specifically, because the encounters with all the heteronomous pressures identified above arguably provide privileged paths towards psychic development, and thereby to a form of internal freedom that can manifest itself in free interactions with the world.

13.2.3 The Goods of Facing Necessity

There is now abundant literature on 'the goods of work', from a variety of theoretical paradigms, whether in the expanding literature on meaningful work (Yeoman 2014; Veltman 2016; Yeoman et al. 2019), which draws on a number of traditions and key references, notably Aristotle, or, as mentioned earlier, in the ongoing research on Marx's rich conception of work, notably in the continuing discussion of how to articulate the 'realm of freedom' and the 'realm of necessity'. A paper by Anca Gheaus and Lisa Herzog (2016) usefully details the main benefits of work discussed in the literature. Unsurprisingly, the three goods already encountered in the discussion of Marx and self-determination theory reappear in, but with community and recognition now distinguished as separate ones. Their list then includes excellence, contribution, community, and recognition. The simple argument defended here, which adds a new layer to this literature, is that work is indeed indispensable for reaching such goods, but not just because modern people as a matter of fact spend a lot of time in paid work as Gheaus and Herzog explain. Rather, work brings with it important 'goods', because of the manifold necessity attached to it, of which the necessity to earn an income is only one among many other aspects. Arguing as Gheaus and Herzog do leaves their argument open to criticism by post-work theorists (for instance Danaher 2019a), that in another social organization, the same goods would be obtained outside of work, and since waged work is under threat of automation and waged work is the source of many individual and social ills, listing goods that might possibly be obtained from other sources than work amounts to a poor defence of its centrality. Instead, the point defended here is that the 'goods' of work are structurally attached to it because it is a particular kind of activity, and we understand this all the better if we take the perspective from necessity, in the many senses of the term that were highlighted earlier on.

The first 'good' of work that we encountered (Section 13.2.1) was actually freedom, for which an original characterisation was proposed. With the help of Dejours it was shown why the necessities attached to work can explain dialectically why it is work that allows us to develop subjectively, in terms of distinct skills and capacities, but also more fundamentally, in terms of a minimally unified and sufficiently resilient subjective life. The dimension of freedom emphasized is internal, the capacity to be in charge of oneself as a subject and to draw on one's subjective resources to maintain balance and possibly grow in life interactions. The previous chapter also showed how work creates specific social bonds and can thus be viewed as the root structure of human communities. Bringing these insights together, we can now add that these collectives arise out of necessity (we have to work, individually and together) and yet are a requirement for individual freedom. The next chapter will study under what conditions these bonds of necessity can become the vehicle for collective freedom. The present section highlights in more detail how work necessity translates into different 'goods' for individuals, keeping in mind the proviso expressed earlier about the non-perfectionist and non-distributivist sense in which this metaphorical expression is used here.

By facing everyday necessity through generalist work, we sustain our everyday existence and that of our close ones. This is the baseline for any account of freedom: bodies and minds are born, nurtured, and taken care of day in and day out. Against Arendt, there is no reason to describe this generalist work under a different term, since generalist work in the home and care for individuals also involve intentional production of useful outputs according to technical standards. By facing social necessity through specialist work, we help sustain the flows of the life world, we do our bit to sustain the community. From this double facing of necessity, we rightfully claim a form of recognition from our peers, as contributors to the common good (Gomberg 2007; Noonan 2020). The output of our work might be deemed problematic (say if we produce cigarettes and smoking is viewed as a nefarious economic activity), but this is clearly a case where the ambivalence of work is at play. Conflict over the interpretation of the social value of work outputs implies precisely that work ought to make a contribution. In many cases, however, the social value of the work is clear, even if the pay does not follow social recognition. When this happens, a rightful good of work (contribution) becomes the basis for political claims (adequate recognition, whether symbolic or material), which the next chapter takes up. Here, the simple point that is being made is that the imposition placed on us to take our place in the division of labour becomes a source of social recognition, which can arguably lead to a form of psychic rewards and become a major feature of one's identity. Indeed, Marxist scholars emphasize (Kandiyali 2020; Tyssedal 2023) how much contribution is a major, independent 'good' of work, which explains why many people willingly accept to do work they don't find fulfilling because the sense of making contributions to the lives of others is in itself an intrinsic motivation. From an empirical point of view, even in premodern societies, this value of contribution existed (Chapter 11). The interpretation of individual contribution to the common good might well have changed enormously throughout history, as Honneth shows in describing the modern principle of achievement (1995b), but the basic idea of work as an individual effort that is recognized and indeed is expected from individuals to help sustain the collective, is a trait that comes across consistently in the historical and ethnographic records.

More specifically, a valuable work effort meets a specific form of recognition from the specific other to whom a use value was provided. Even in a market exchange, even when money is the medium for social interactions, this kind of recognition, expressed in forms of thankfulness, can still exist (Ikäheimo 2022 on gratitude). Many people still say thank you when work has provided them with a good or a service, even though they paid for it.

When the work has been performed according to technical standards, the worker can benefit from another highly specific kind of recognition, namely recognition from peers and members of the same occupation. Again, this is a form of recognition that can be witnessed across the historical record, well before the rise of 'modernity'. Dejours describes this as being the beneficiary of a 'judgment of beauty', when peers recognize the technical value, the 'crafty' quality of the contribution (Dejours 2012; Deranty 2012).

The contribution to the work collective attracts another special form of recognition when it has enabled the group as a whole to perform a complex act or to produce a complex output. Here the recognition is from peers for a collective achievement.

And recognition can come from those who supervised the work, who might have directed the work process, just as a conductor can be thankful to every member of the orchestra for a symphony well played and might have special thanks for a few instrumentalists among all the others, who gave the performance a special moment.

Even the owners of the means of production might express thankfulness for the work of their employees, and once again, despite the transaction being legalistic and financially mediated, the employees might receive this thankfulness as an addition to their identity, as clearly occurs standardly in many workplaces.

All these different types of recognition, however, arise specifically from the successful performance of efforts that manage to abide by the multiple constraints arising from the expectations of users, peers and superiors regarding usefulness, timeliness, correct technical application, and so on. In other words, when recognition is granted by others for successful work actions—and of course in many cases such recognition is lacking or inadequate—a part of this recognition is an acknowledgement that the working subject navigated all the constraints attached to work, that they were able to face necessity and not be overwhelmed by it, and that they came out victorious, for this one time at least, from the challenge. In every positive recognition of a job well done and of a useful contribution, however minute or apparently simple the task, there is the acknowledgement by fellow humans that this working individual faced the fate all have to face—to go toe to toe with Gorgonian necessity-, and exhibited the human capacity to withstand the encounter.

One 'good of work' identified by classical social philosophers but not singled out as such in recent accounts is the good of personal identity, the idea that work has such an impact on self-development that, when it is engaged in the form of a long-term occupation, it comes to define the person in her specific attributes, including her worldview (see Kohn and Schooler 1982 and 1983 for influential empirical confirmations). This was already clearly outlined by Hegel in the *Philosophy of Right.* The theory of estates has a macro-economic dimension, designating the division of work across different branches of production, and mapping the needs to be fulfilled. But it also has sociological and psychological dimensions, considering the significance for individuals of their involvement in this organization. Through their inclusion in particular sectors of the economy, Hegel writes in §207, individuals attain 'determinate particularity' and thereby 'actuality', in other words, their full reality as individuals, their 'determinate' content. As the previous sections in his book make clear, this 'determinate particularity' includes specific sets of cognitive and practical knowledge and skills (§197), and even specific modes of relating to social and natural environments (§203–205). The theory of corporations (§251–253) confirms these different elements and adds a moral outlook to them.

As Renault shows (2022, 125–127), the significance of work for the actual content of individual subjectivity was also highlighted, in similar terms, by Dewey across his writings. One aspect emphasized by Dewey is that work gives content to personality notably through the integration of capacities that would otherwise remain disconnected:

> A calling is also of necessity an organizing principle for information and ideas, for knowledge and intellectual growth. It provides an axis which runs through an immense diversity of detail; it causes different experiences, facts, items of information to fall into order with one another. The lawyer, the physician, the laboratory investigator in some branch of chemistry, the parent, the citizen interested in his own locality, has a constant working stimulus to note and relate whatever has to do with his concern. He unconsciously, from the motivation of his occupation, reaches out for all relevant information, and holds to it. The vocation acts as both magnet to attract and as glue to hold. Such organization of knowledge is vital, because it has reference to needs; it is so expressed and readjusted in action that it never becomes stagnant. No classification, no selection and arrangement of facts, which is consciously worked out for purely abstract ends, can ever compare in solidity or

> effectiveness with that knit under the stress of an occupation; in comparison the former sort is formal, superficial, and cold.
>
> **(Dewey 1985 [1916], 319; Renault 2022, 126)**

This passage is particularly noteworthy, for several reasons. Firstly, Dewey lists being a parent and a concerned citizen as 'callings' like other formal occupations. Callings are occupations, literally modes of occupying the mind and the body (types of *Wirken* Schutz would say), which provide direction and meaning to existence. Since callings are concretely defined by the performance of particular tasks, these 'vocations' (Dewey uses the terms synonymously) are also types of work. This confirms making generalist and specialist work two genres of the same kind. Secondly, Dewey contrasts the coordination of knowledges, and given his focus in the rest of the book he clearly has the coordination of skills in mind as well, when such coordination is guided by the aims and values of a particular 'vocation', with the development and integration of knowledge and skills in the abstract, that is, outside a work context. When knowledges and skills are developed and applied within the framework of meaningful work activities, Dewey argues, this is infinitely superior to the alternative context. This is so, first, because the determinate goals of the work activities provide meaningful direction to knowledge and skill acquisition; they represent the 'magnet' for cognitive development. And second, work activities constitute the 'glue' allowing the personality to develop harmoniously. Crucially, Dewey notes that the developmental power inscribed in work activities arises not just from their framing and coordinating force, but also, and primordially, from the 'stress' they put on knowledge and skill, in other words, the necessity they bring to the latter's acquisition and application. This necessity in turn comes precisely from the fact that work ultimately is about fulfilling needs, and the many sides of necessity that are involved in need fulfilment. These are striking confirmations and extensions of points made earlier in the chapter.

This passage from Dewey alerts also to another good of work that is overlooked in contemporary accounts. The necessity attached to work forces an acknowledgement of reality that is harder to achieve in 'abstract' knowledge. Knowledge that is developed 'under the stress' of work, Dewey states, is 'so expressed and readjusted in action that it never becomes stagnant'. If we elaborate on this view using the analyses above, we might say that the necessity to produce an output that is satisfactory, to use techniques and processes correctly, to abide by social and ethical standards in the production of the output, all the necessities surrounding the performance of tasks force the working subject to take reality into account. That knowledge can never become 'stagnant' in a work context means amongst other things that it must constantly acknowledge the reality of situations. By contrast, knowledge developed and acquired outside of work contexts is 'formal, superficial and cold': absent the 'stress' of having to abide by all the necessities surrounding work, it very easily detaches itself from the complexities and fluctuations of reality.

It is justified here to speak of a 'transcendental' power of work, in the Kantian sense of the term (Deranty 2010). This power can be highlighted from another perspective, namely by using arguments of cognitive psychology and social epistemology. It is only too obvious that the human mind has a strong propensity to avoid facing reality. From ancient moral philosophers to the classical metaphysicians of the seventeenth century, all the way to contemporary psychologists, many scholars have emphasized and studied the innumerable logical fallacies and cognitive biases the human mind is prone to fall into. These make us disregard evidence that contradicts our prejudices, exaggerate some facts and ignore others, project into reality what we fear or desire, and so on. By forcing us to face what prevents a smooth realization of our intentions, work contexts force us to take some features of reality seriously, and actually deal with them. The idea behind this good of work is well captured in a passage from Simone Weil's *Gravity and Grace*: 'What is real in perception and distinguishes it from dreams, is not the sensations, but the necessity enshrined in these sensations "Why these things and not others?" "Because that is how it is"' (Weil 2002 [1947], 53). Dejours makes this confrontation with what resists the mechanistic application of preexisting knowledge the source of true knowledge. Science, he argues, is a formalization of knowledge that has its origins in failures of established knowledge, and work contexts are privileged places where such failures are experienced. Another quote by Simone Weil formulates this idea clearly: 'A test of what is real is that it is hard and rough (*dur et rugueux*)' (Weil 2002, 53). The necessity built into work forces us to endure the challenge of the real. This is hard and rough: it takes us out of our comfort zone and puts us 'under stress'. But it is the condition for knowing reality, as we are so easily disposed and indeed so tempted to look past the real and create our own fantasy worlds where all our biases are confirmed and our intentions magically realized.

Of course, in many work contexts, the propensity of the human mind to wander and ignore reality goes on unabated. Indeed, work contexts can develop their own, specific forms of fallacious thinking. Dejours highlights psychological defence mechanisms at the level of workplaces or even entire industries, for instance when workers have to face serious risks to their well-being (Dejours 1980). He has studied concrete examples of dysfunctional workplaces, where people's sense of reality, whether of external reality or the reality of ethical expectations at the time, was severely damaged, due to deleterious forms of management and work organization (Dejours and Bègue 2014). In his famous study of an accident in the US Navy, Ed Hutchins highlighted how even in the most controlled and apparently emotion-free of work contexts, a ship of the US Navy, irrational forms of behaviour might develop (Hutchins 1995). And, of course, workplaces are rife with social biases that cause discrimination against people on the basis of their ethnic background, culture, sexuality, age, or gender (Vallas 2012).

And yet all of this only shows that human psychology remains operative in work contexts, which is unsurprising. It does not speak against the idea that the necessity built into work forces us to face reality. As a matter of fact, a lot of work is successful in fulfilling orders, many workplaces do produce the outputs they were tasked with producing, and individual workers get the job done. When this happens, it has to be, by definition, because the challenges of performing the tasks were met. Even for generalist work, but more so for specialist work, this involves learning particular forms of theoretical and practical knowledge. In many cases, actually performing the tasks requires more than simply applying prescribed knowing or know-how. When gaps have to be bridged between prescription and performance, the features of reality that prevent the task from being completed have to be identified, understood, circumvented or used favourably. This might require a special understanding or even an original interpretation of a physical process, of a legal issue, of a psychological trait in a colleague or a customer or a boss, of a person's specific bodily or emotional needs. Whatever makes the realization of the task tricky, we have to face the hard and rough challenge of reality's resistance and acknowledge it in order to deal with it. Hegel's motto, 'fear of the lord is the beginning of wisdom', is applied by him to describe the way human consciousness becomes aware of a deep truth about itself, in its relation to others. This idea can be generalized here: against the powerful inclination of human minds to ignore reality and engage in wishful thinking, work forces us to acknowledge what there is.

Maria Jahoda spoke of the 'tie to reality' as one of the benefits of work that unemployed people can no longer enjoy (Jahoda 1981, 1982). This notion of a 'tie to reality' expands the idea of the 'transcendental' power of work, to generalize from what we learn *at* work to what we learn *through* work. For example, much of what each one of us knows about the social world, regarding economic realities, aspects of the legal or political systems, or the different parts of the cultural or education systems, arises from how we come across them in social life. Yet it is in work contexts that these complex environments are likely to be faced in more informative ways. Of course, if we have a car accident, we might be involved with the justice system and will have access to it in this way. And we might read about any of those aspects mentioned, learn about them out of interest, or have knowledgeable persons among our acquaintances tell us about them. But personal experience and hearsay are weak starting points for truly knowing about all the complex systems that surround us. As Dewey made the point in the quote above, work contexts provide the vantage point from which we view reality, and because of all the layers of necessity built into them, there is always a part in work contexts where you just cannot cheat with reality. Some of the knowledge acquired at work and through work might be very partial, fragmented, or biased. But the part of that knowledge that touches the reality of our work needs to be based in fact if we are to effectively overcome the resistance to our efforts. Through this, we have true access to some dimensions of complex social reality. And the same argument applies for other aspects of reality.

This section has shown how the fate of having to face necessity for individuals can bring with it all kinds of 'goods', some of which have been identified from other perspectives already, and others which are less well recognized in classical and contemporary scholarship. The original feature of the goods that were discussed here was that they were shown to emerge from the facing of necessity. The next chapter considers what facing necessity means for a collective, in particular how the collective organization of the facing of necessity engenders other forms of necessity, with their own inherent benefits and burdens.

14
Organizing Necessity

Taking up the perspective from necessity introduced in the previous chapter allows us to consider the collective, political dimensions of work in a new light. In a way comparable to the individual level, the political centrality of work emerges all the more forcefully if we see work as a necessary response to necessity, this time a collective one.

14.1 The Collective Response to Necessity

The individual and the collective aspects of having to face necessity are intimately entwined. A large part of the necessity individuals have to face in work comes from their dependence on others: the dependence on other workers whose own contributions are often an intrinsic part of the individual work effort; on the addressees of work efforts, whose judgement determines the value of the work output, including through their purchase of it; on other experts who define and judge the technical viability of the work effort; and more generally, on the different types of social necessity that force us to work, our inherent finitude and the fact that we owe our very survival and our well-being, the realization of our goals and life chances, to our inclusion in a collective. Conversely, precisely because individual work efforts are so interwoven, in their aims, in the processes that deliver outputs of all kinds, and in the conditions underpinning these processes, notably through the reliance on institutions and material infrastructures, the collective as such also has to face necessity, as a collective.

This collective response to necessity is an organization of the work of necessity, a complex combination of social processes, institutional and material mechanisms that coordinate and support the individual efforts producing the outputs needed for the reproduction of individual and collective life. This collective coordination embraces many different fields and objects, starting with basic material issues, for instance, securing access to energy and raw materials and food. It includes, among many other aspects, the acquisition, development, and transmission of technologies, or the social

The Case for Work. Jean-Philippe Deranty, Oxford University Press. © Jean-Philippe Deranty (2024).
DOI: 10.1093/oso/9780192887146.003.0015

mechanisms underpinning the allocation of the work to be done among particular individuals and groups of individuals, for instance, who does the work of care. These social mechanisms, in turn, mix economic, social and cultural aspects: the different markets enabling the exchange of goods and services, including labour markets; the systems of the different occupations and professions, how they are socially ranked and rewarded through different classes of remunerations (wages, fees, piece-work payment, the direct exchange of services, barter, gifts, and so on); which groups access different occupations and professions; the cultural representations underpinning the hierarchy of activities, from the most prestigious to those types of activities to which contempt or even stigma and taboo are attached; and so on.

Many dimensions of the collective organization of work can be questioned from the point of view of freedom, for instance, the relative subjection of workers in formal work organizations, the more or less subtle domination exerted through the gendered division of labour, and at the most general level, the compulsion on most to work in order to live. Similarly, many dimensions of the collective organization of work can be questioned from the point of view of justice, in terms of fairness and equality: for instance, the distribution of the benefits and burdens of different types of work; the distribution of the outputs of work and of the wealth created by work; the relative differences between the incomes derived from work; the relative returns given to work efforts compared to forms of rent based in privilege and private property; the hierarchy of occupations, to which both financial and social benefits accrue; how social hierarchies are both reflected in and entrenched by the hierarchy of occupations. Literature in political philosophy has explored all these issues at length. Marxist scholarship, of which we studied a large sample in Chapter 3, obviously has had lots to say on the injuries to freedom and justice in modern work organizations. As we saw in Chapter 10, feminist scholarship has questioned the fairness of economic organizations and cultural representations underpinning divisions of labour, from a variety of theoretical perspectives. Following Rawls, mainstream political philosophy has engaged with many of the issues just listed, regarding the fair distribution of income and work outputs, access to valued professions (Arnold 2012), and freedom in the workplace (Hsieh 2005, 2008a, 2008b). There is a rich strand of republican literature on issues of freedom and justice in relation to work, both at the macro-level of the organization and distribution of work and its rewards (Gourevitch 2013, 2014), and at the level of the workplace (Gonzalez-Ricoy 2014; Anderson 2015, 2017; Breen 2015, 2017; Breen and Hirvonen 2021). Recognition theory has maintained a constant interest in normative and critical issues about collective organizations of work

(Honneth 1995b, 2012, 2015, 2017; Renault 2007; Smith 2009, 2012, 2019; Deranty 2012; Deranty and Renault 2012; Smith and Deranty 2012a, 2012b; Angella 2016), including at the workplace level (Honneth 1995a; Dejours et al. 2018; Deranty and Renault 2022). Just as with the individual dimension, however, conceptualizing the division of labour from the perspective of necessity provides an original, sideways perspective, one in which the force of necessity starkly increases existential and political stakes and thereby highlights the importance of work in a refreshed way.

The collective response to the necessity of work creates an added layer of necessity, an institutional, organizational one, on top of the other necessities that force us into work and that constitute work. The generic social dependency we live in as a result of our finitude, which leads to the division of labour and the need for social inclusion, takes on a specific shape in accordance with the ways social labour is organized. This overall organization functions largely as a necessity for the individuals. It is a necessity for individuals, first because it is the frame of their existence, to which changes can be brought only through considerable political and cultural action. And throughout human history, these organizations have been based largely on the domination of the majority by a minority who set the terms of the organization in their favour (Anderson 2015; Hunnicutt 2024). However, this added layer of necessity, organizational necessity, is a form of necessity not just because it expresses and entrenches social domination, but more basically, because it is itself a response to necessity, the collective way of dealing with necessity. The collective response to necessity draws from its origin, namely the facing of necessity, the power it imposes upon the individual. For instance, the discipline imposed on each new generation to take their place in the overall social system, a system whose spinal cord is the division of labour, is not an invention of modern capitalism, but a necessity in all human societies.

Just as with the experience of work for individuals, the 'hard and rough' compulsion that is intrinsic to the collective response to necessity, the urgency with which it imposes itself on each and all, precisely because of its urgency and unavoidability, makes it at the same time a highly ambiguous normative aspect of existence. Precisely because the organization of work is experienced as a social fate, the demands it makes on people across its different coordinates are highly conspicuous. The necessity that is built into the organization of necessity creates *pressure points* at the different junctures where this organization exerts its power over individuals and groups within society. These demands are felt in unmistakable ways, firstly because they impact deeply on minds and bodies, and secondly because, as they determine the identity, well-being and status of individuals and groups, the latter cannot but compare their fate to that of others in relation to all these things and in relation to work itself. As a result, at each one of those pressure points, the very necessity of this socially organized, second-order necessity is open for questioning and challenging (Deranty and Renault 2012 for an early model of this approach). Countless examples throughout history illustrate this ambivalent aspect of the organization of work, the way in which it is both a necessity that imposes itself on socialized individuals and groups, and at the same time, precisely because of its non-suppressible character, a fact of life which people can question, challenge, and attempt to reject and transform. Of course, the sheer magnitude of structures of domination and the weight of tradition often mean that organized forms of necessity can remain in place for long periods of time and can last generations. The historical record, however, shows comprehensively that even the most severe forms of organized necessity have met with resistance, rejection, and attempts at transformation.

This is a very simple historical point to make, and yet another point that is easily overlooked in discussions on work. It needs to be raised in particular as a response to post-industrialist arguments (Section 8.1). The post-industrial motto in the sociology of the late 1970s had a lasting legacy and still operates in the background as an authoritative sociological reference in the rejection of the centrality of work. Reference to the post-industrial phase of capitalism in Kathi Week's *The Problem of Work*, for instance, plays an important role in her overall argument. As we saw, besides the description of changes in the structure of capitalist production in core countries, the post-industrial paradigm also entails as one of its key planks a rejection of the view that work-centred class struggle is the main driver of political change. The problem with this part of the post-industrial reference is that it invites observers to unduly extend the context-bound analyses of the 1970s outlining the rise of new social movements and the demise of Taylorist and Fordist work-centred politics, into a vision that is more general and temporally open, concluding to the ultimate disconnect between work and progressive politics. What was an empirical description of a shift in political organization and political demands is turned into a blanket ban on the very capacity of work in late capitalism to mobilize collective movements for the improvement of the social-economic conditions of the majority. Habermas' call in 1990 to 'think socialism afresh', that is, to reject the political centrality of work for a socialist programme, was a spectacular expression of this post-industrial vision (see also Castells 1997, 360). Against this, it is important to highlight, that, as a matter of fact, work has never ceased to be a major catalyst of collective mobilization in the last five decades, with constantly shifting foci, following the changing fault lines in the experiences of injustice, domination and exploitation (see for instance Chhachhi 2014 and Bieler and Nowak 2021 for recent labour struggles in the Global South; Silver and Zhang 2009 for China). To name one historical movement which had long-lasting repercussions, notably in theoretical debates on work, and that ironically coincided with the emergence of the post-industrial paradigm, the wages for housework collective had work, the work performed by women, as its central problem and mobilizing factor. It is telling that Kathi Weeks is deeply inspired by this movement, and yet, because of her post-work premise, has to admonish it for its work-centredness. This points to a persistent feature of post-work analyses: since their premise is that work is an obsolete value, they tend to focus their political lens away from labour struggles, and overlook the general political significance such tstruggles can have, not realizing that they often have implications well beyond the particular sector or the particular interests they emerge from, which can challengeentrenched structures of the social organization, as the wages for housework movement did (see Dinerstein and Pitts 2021 for a detailed critique along those lines). In contrast, the joint perspective from necessity and social reproduction illuminates the potential for political conflict that is inscribed in the collective organization of work, that is, the questioning of different aspects of the overall distribution and organization of the work of necessity, the work enabling the reproduction of the lifeworld and of the lives it supports.

14.2 Questioning the Organization of Necessity

It is worthwhile canvassing the main ways in which the necessity of organized necessity can be questioned. This provides first an original way of considering how the justice inherent in collective organizations of work can be problematized, and thereby shed a different light on areas already thoroughly studied by countless empirical and normative enquiries. It also prepares the ground for the 'turning around' of necessity into freedom, this time at the level of collectives, in the section that follows. As we will see, collective answers to the question of how to organize the work of necessity fairly are an essential part of securing freedom in necessity.

14.2.1 Which Work Is Necessary?

The first questioning of an existing organization of necessity simply asks whether particular kinds of work are *actually* necessary. This questioning of the very necessity of socially mandated work is at the heart of many current forms of resistance to, and of refusal of, work. It might concern the needs that work fulfils, which might be harmful to individuals, like cigarette smoking, or craving for unhealthy food, or to the community at large, like the spreading of misleading forms of information. If the work is demonstrably useful, the questioning of necessity might regard the amount of work that is demanded: that some work is necessary for the outputs it produces for particular needs might be accepted, but the amount of work that an organization of work requires of particular people to produce those outputs might be disputed (Spencer 2022). This concern captures much of post-work theory's complaint, which is not that some work might be needed to some extent, but rather that it takes up too much of our time (Frayne 2015; Turner 2024). What is at issue then is that *so much* work might be necessary for some. The rejection of the necessity of some work is at its starkest when workers feel they are involved in a 'bullshit job' (Graeber 2018). Such jobs are egregious precisely because social forms of necessity (the compulsion with which work is accompanied, including in its concrete organization on the job) are deployed for activities that are the very opposite of necessary, and are not just expendable, but downright useless. In all these cases, however, the questionings of the necessity of work are based on the assumption of what a good justification for work would be if it was indeed necessary. And as a matter of fact, a lot of work actually is such and does produce use values that are genuinely needed. These questionings of work, therefore, are not refusals of work *tout court*, but refusals of those types of work that pass for necessary but are not.

14.2.2 Is Work for Value Necessary?

A more specific way to make the organization of necessity contentious is to challenge the necessity of work when it is organized with the creation of exchange value as its driving motivation, rather than for uses that would be genuinely needed. This is one sense in which to interpret the critique of a society in which we 'live to work instead of working to live'. A specific questioning of necessity therefore targets the necessities that are attached to the capitalist mode of production.

In order to live, we must reproduce individual lives and the life of the collective, and for that, we must produce use values, and so we must work. Indeed, in order to be able to address future hazards and contingencies (technological, economic, environmental challenges), in order to look after members of the collective who cannot work or can no longer work, in order to fulfil the needs of new members, in order to exchange with other groups so as to acquire goods and services our collective cannot produce, and in order to maintain and improve the existing productive apparatus, we also need to produce a surplus, on top of the use values necessary for present needs (Marx 2000 [1875], 613). This is just to recall the simple point already elaborated in earlier chapters (notably in Sections 10.1 and 12.4.2) that the reproduction of the lifeworld involves different temporalities, and, because of this, a lot of work is in fact necessary on top of the production of use values for the present day and the next. Similarly, work just has to be organized. It has to be organized materially in terms of underlying infrastructures; economically in terms of the coordinating of supply and demand, at the macro-level of national economies, of entire industries and value-chains; and at the micro-level of individual workplaces through technical divisions of labour. The social and economic division of labour at the level of society, and the necessity of management, that is, of the technical organization of complex work process, are not capitalistic inventions, but functional necessities of the organization of work (Marx 1991 [1867], 470–480 on the division of labour at the social level, and Marx 1991 [1867], 449, on the management function at the level of individual firms). But if the point of work is not to produce necessary use values (the sum of necessary and surplus product), but rather to ensure there is ever more value created ad infinitum, then the necessities attached to the material, macro-, and micro-organizations of work become questionable and open to criticism and rejection. The questionability of capitalistic necessities stems from the fact that it is in principle always possible to produce more value, by working, or making others work, longer and more intensively; and all the technological, material and organizational processes by which value is produced can be indefinitely 'rationalized', intensified and extensified (see Green 2007 for an authoritative sociological account regarding affluent societies in the 2000s). Yet all this work and surplus work of creating value for the sake of it might be necessary in a capitalist framework but is not necessary from the point of view of what a lifeworld and the individual lives it hosts require. The organization of work in such a setting serves to create private wealth, not the collective wealth that is the sum of necessary and surplus products.

One complication stems from the fact that abstract value relies on use value: for commodities to be exchanged, they have to promise to fulfil some need, even if just a social need of keeping up with the Jones' (Marx 1991, 131: 'nothing can be a value without being an object of utility'). And as a matter of fact, some of the values produced in capitalistic conditions are necessary, to the extent that these values attach to goods or services that fulfil needs. Even if they are caught in the abstraction of the valorization process, many commodities fulfil needs and have their use. Even if the bread is produced under capitalist conditions, it does feed those who eat it. And yet even this necessity grounded in use can be questioned in a capitalistic system, and as a matter of fact is regularly questioned by consumer groups and social movements (Honneth 2014, 198–222 for an original focus on this relatively underexplored aspect). First, because of the incessant drive to create value, the capitalist mode of production creates countless unnecessary, luxury needs, 'false needs', and noxious needs. Luxury needs are needs that might appear necessary once they have become 'social needs' (Hegel 1991, 229) yet could easily be relinquished without much harm to individuals, for instance, if compared with other forms of social life where these needs did or do not exist. False needs are needs created solely for the purpose of producing abstract value. Noxious needs are needs that require use values to be satisfied, which occasion some damage to individuals or the collective, either through their very consumption (alcohol, gambling), or because the work required to produce them is damaging, for instance, if it creates unnecessary pollution harming human health, or it destroys parts of the natural environment and affects non-human species. All these needs define use values which can be questioned as being genuine utilities. Second, even if some use values produced through capitalistic work are deemed necessary, they often do not justify all the effort it takes to produce them as these use values are treated as mere means for the end of valorization. Some of these efforts arise from the imperative to produce more, or more cheaply, than the competitors, to secure and to increase profit for private interest. This surplus effort comes with the work ideology denounced by post-work theorists with good justification. However, implicit in the criticism that capitalism makes us live to work rather than making life itself the priority, is the recognition of necessity. In order to live we need to work. Work that sustains life, truly necessary work is not something we can wish away (Deranty 2022). Indeed, as we saw, many goods can be attached to it for individuals. And as we will see in the next section, it is the backbone of a free community.

The *reductio ad necessitam* of the quest for abstract value that has just been outlined might appear very naïve from the point of view of economic theory. First, questioning the necessity in the organization of work might seem to amount to an unrealistic questioning of economic necessity itself, namely the rationality governing the mechanisms underpinning the organization of production and distribution in response to consumption demands. There is no denying this kind of rationality: some macro-economic organizations produce more general wealth than others, however it is counted, through gross domestic product or other measures. Some types of workplace organizations are more efficient than others, produce more outputs, or produce more cheaply, or produce outputs in higher demands, for reasons explained by economic theory. From the point of view of relative price and margins, output, and consumer demand, there just are more or less rational ways to organize work. This rationality expresses a form of necessity that cannot be ignored, or taken for granted, just as political theory ought not to take for granted all the work that is required, as a matter of fact, to reproduce lifeworlds. Not taking for granted the very fact of economic necessity means accepting that one has to take into account economic realities in organizing work, the mechanisms that dictate prices, and so on. There is no escaping the necessity of aiming to be economically sound in the organization of work. In strictly economic terms, the necessity of being economically rational, whether it is expressed in terms of market shares, of profitability, debts and bankruptcy, or in non-market terms, in terms of the viability and performance of production chains, comes from the fact that inefficiency is 'punished', translates into deleterious outcomes (insolvency, underinvestment, supply issues, underconsumption), and efficiency is rewarded (investment capacity, full consumption, multiplier and productivity effects, 'O-ring' effect, see Section 7.3). Inefficiency is also normatively problematic because it means wasting resources, starting with the wasting of human work itself.

If economic necessity has to be acknowledged and integrated into the macro- and micro-organizations of work, where does this leave the questioning of necessity that was just intimated? Aren't processes of 'rationalization' in production and distribution methods intrinsic to the attempt at being economically rational and achieving full economic efficiency? If this general point seems difficult to object to, then isn't the attempt at finding ever new ways of creating profit, of winning the economic competition, through constant technological, organizational innovation, what economic rationality dictates? But these are precisely what capitalistic economic methods aim to achieve. One might thus fear that the questioning of necessity advocated in this section, which targeted the quest for abstract value over use value, simply negates economic necessity. And since economic necessity cannot be overlooked, that would mean that the questioning of value creation in the name of use value would in fact be misdirected, based on a naïve view of what it takes to produce use value (namely a competitive market economy).

Such a worry, however, is only valid if the necessity built into the capitalist mode of production is equated with all economic necessity. The two, however, need to be kept apart. Under capitalist conditions, many forms of economic behaviour are necessary if one wants to be able to hold one's part in the general game and not go under. Marx's three volumes of *Capital* can be read as the comprehensive and painstakingly detailed analysis of all the many forms of necessity economic agents are subjected to under capitalist conditions, for instance attempting to lengthen the working day, intensify the work process through organizational and technological 'rationalization', and so on. But these economic rules are necessary only within capitalism. We might say that this is a context-specific or social form of economic necessity. Other modes of production would have their own social form of economic necessities, the rules by which agents have to act in order to stay in the game in their own social order. Besides such context-specific forms of economic necessity, there is a more formal sense of economic necessity, a second-order one, if one will: namely, the fact that in any given social order, some economic necessity exists, which simply states that, within that context, some organizations of work are economically efficient and rational and others are less so, or not at all. It is well beyond the scope of this book to investigate whether some content can be given to this formal principle and whether it is independent of contexts. It might well be that there are basic economic rules, which remain formal enough but link together some specific concepts, for instance, supply, demand, relative production times, price of labour, and size of the markets, on the basis of which some content can be given already to the basic idea that in any collective organization of work, not everything goes, that some organizations of work, whatever their social-political context, are more efficient than others, and that organizations of work that deny this formal economic necessity are bound to fail economically. The key point is that it is conceptually possible to take seriously the idea of economic necessity without thereby robbing oneself of the ability to criticize an organization of work geared solely to the pursuit of abstract value, with use-value only the means to the end of valorization. The tension between use values, the reproduction of the lifeworld, and capitalistic imperatives can be raised without rejecting the necessity to consider economic realities. Indeed, current capitalism is evidently destructive of lifeworlds. The laws of accumulation as they are currently set up are antithetical to necessary work, understood as the work necessary for social reproduction. In other words, there is a direct contradiction today between capitalistic necessity and the genuine necessity of work.

A second economic worry about questioning the necessity of work for abstract value, as opposed to use value, stems not from the focus on capitalism, but more generally from the idea that the accumulation and redistribution of wealth, beyond the mere meeting of necessity, is a material condition for cultural and social development. Value creation, one might argue, is a necessary condition for cultural, scientific and artistic development, because this is what allows the creation of a surplus out of which surplus work of invention, innovation and creation beyond mere work of necessity for basic needs can arise. But all it takes to avoid this problem is to be clear about the different kinds of work that the reproduction of the lifeworld requires, or synonymously the different dimensions of reproduction that require work. As the point was made earlier, the necessary work of reproduction includes work that reproduces the lifeworld culturally and symbolically and work that ensures that a surplus is produced, not just to ward off hazards and contingencies the collective is bound to face, but also to invest in innovations of all kinds. Once again, the fact that the capitalist mode of production requires constant innovation as a functional imperative should not be misinterpreted as meaning that only that mode of production can secure innovation. Any social system in principle can organize its own work collectively to ensure surpluses are produced with which innovation and creations of all kinds are supported.

14.2.3 Unsustainable Work

As just said, a major deleterious consequence of capitalist inversion is its unsustainability. The valorization process makes abstract value the sole intrinsic good. All other realities are treated instrumentally, human reality as labour power and consuming power, natural environments and non-human beings as resources and as dumping grounds. Intrinsic to capitalism is an unsustainable mode of production, which impacts work directly. If work is necessary in the sense that it is what helps sustain the lifeworld in its flows and with it the lives of its members, then work that is organized in such a way that it undermines the natural preconditions of the lifeworld is in direct contradiction with its primary necessity. We have here a striking example of an organization of work that imposes social necessities (the first of which is the necessity to work to survive) on the basis of a false necessity. The necessity that capitalism assumes, that work is necessary for social and individual reproduction, is a false necessity because it is articulated in a way that in fact intrinsically undermines the lifeworld work is supposed to maintain. Post-work theorists are correct in rejecting damaging work, but this rejection is premised on a more fundamental affirmation of work, the work that actually produces necessary use values, which cannot be done away (Foster 2017).

14.2.4 Injustice in the Collective Organization of Work

Another major way that the necessity of work can be and is in fact often questioned concerns the fairness of its organization. The issue with this organization is not just the classical liberal-egalitarian question of the fairness all things considered of the distribution of primary goods. From the point of view of organized necessity, a more basic question needs to be asked before the fairness of distribution, namely who works and who doesn't. Before equality of opportunity or equality of outcomes or welfare are considered, the first issue of equality is *equality before necessity*. In most social systems, some exceptions are granted to certain individuals and often to entire groups, allowing them to avoid working even though they could. This always means that the share of work needed for the reproduction of the lifeworld falls on others who have to do their own share and take on the extra share not performed by those who don't work but could. From the point of view of justice before necessity, these arrangements are unfair.

In societies that are organized on some version of a functional scheme, for instance the distinction between those who fight, those who pray and those who labour, it is conceivable that the estates of those who are not '*laboratores*' in fact might be seen to be working from the point of view of the reproduction of the lifeworld. The initial function of the feudal lord was to protect his lieges and the population on his territory and to pass justice. The taxation system was premised on this vision of an exchange of services (Le Goff 1982, 264–266; Duby 2010, 119–123). Similarly, the clergy could be seen to perform the most important work of social reproduction, by maintaining the lines of communication between the earthly and the heavenly worlds and by securing the purity of the former (Duby 2010, 157–185). From this point of view, the tripartite scheme could not be interpreted simply as an example of ideological justification exempting privileged social classes from work. By the time of the French Revolution, however, and in fact consistently before that, it was not clear to large masses of the peasant and the urban populations that the classes exempt from work on the land or from craftwork were doing any necessary work themselves (274–278). The consistent recurrence of worker strikes, tax rebellions, and urban and peasant revolts (Kohn 2004, 2006) testifies to that. The fact that taxes were often the trigger for rebellion is symptomatic: it shows that the working classes no longer considered that the contract between the different orders had been upheld, of each doing their work as was required for the benefit of all (Foucault 2015 on the 1639 'Nu-Pieds' revolt in France).

In modern societies, it is private property that is the ground for privilege and exemption from work. Property in the means of production, in land, in real estate or in more abstract entitlements allows the wealthy to receive a rent on the back of other people's work and to exempt themselves from the necessity to work (Christophers 2022 for the UK). Of course, many wealthy people do work, and some work a lot. This is not surprising, given that work is among other forms of necessity an inner necessity inherited from our evolutionary history. But in societies where wealth is a ground for social privilege, it provides the opportunity to avoid facing the work of necessity if one wishes to.

Here we can retrieve and adapt arguments made by scholars who defend the idea of a 'participation income' (Atkinson 1996) or 'civic minimum' (White 2003): that is, that social payments ought not to be granted universally on a minimum basis, as a baseline allowing people to make their own life choices like defenders of a UBI argue, but rather that such payments ought to be tied to a direct contribution made to social reproduction by those who are able. In the debates surrounding participation income (Pérez-Muñoz 1996 for a good synthesis), a premise is clearly articulated (in particular by Birnbaum 2011), which chimes in well with the perspective taken in the book. This is the focus on all the work that is required, whether formally included in the market economy or 'informally' conducted, to ensure the reproduction of the lifeworld. Because many activities are required for society as a whole to function and for individual lives to be supported, it would be exploitative for some to decide not to contribute through their own effort and still expect all the goods, processes, and infrastructures required for their individual and collective life to be provided, which would be the output of the work of others. Against Van Parijs' argument for a UBI, Birnbaum thus argues for an ethos of reciprocal contribution. The same argument can be generalized to those who, through their wealth or their property rights, can exempt themselves from the work of reproduction.

One might object that through their consumption, their investment and the taxes they pay, the non-working rich contribute to the lifeworld in their own ways. They support the work of others through the consumption of the latter's work outputs, through the payment of wages to the employees in whose enterprises they have shares, by hiring people who provide them with the services they are not prepared to take charge of themselves, like the tending of their gardens, the grooming of their dogs or the care of their children. For this objection to be valid, it would have to be the case that the amounts spent by the wealthy correspond at least roughly to the amount of effort non-wealthy persons have to put in to produce an equivalent output through their work. How is such an equivalent to be calculated? A ready answer, of course, is through market mechanisms and the equivalences that the abstract medium of money enables, notably between prices and wages. In an ideal, neoclassical scenario, the price of a worker's labour power matches what other agents are prepared to pay for the service they require. However, a large body of economic theory suggests that such a theoretical balance is highly unlikely. We can rely here on critical discussions in the theory of the wage (Adams 2020 for a clear presentation that cites the leading references, notably Manning 2003). Classical, Marxist, and institutionalist critiques of the neoclassical model in wage theory highlight the asymmetries in labour markets, starting with the dependency on earning a wage in the first place, to reject the idea that wage rates represent the correct equilibrium between supply and demand. Instead, employer market power means that wages tend to be under the level at which reproduction is secured. This critical view of equilibrium models of wages can be extended and applied to the discussion here. In the reality of class societies, including capitalist ones, the wealthy can use their wealth to assert political power over other classes, which translates directly into them receiving the outputs from the work of others for a fraction of what a fair equivalent would actually represent. From the point of view of work, this signals a form of general social exploitation, exploitation in a technical, Marxian sense (Renault 2023) but also in the more mundane sense in which it is discussed in participation debates, where wealth allows a minority to exempt themselves from the necessity experienced by everyone else. Wealth and power are not just shields against social necessity but also escapes from it, they afford the ability to deflect the facing of necessity onto others. The mechanisms for this avoidance of necessity are the same as when the wealthy exempt themselves from the risk of death in times of war, by buying out their lot if they are conscripted.

Equality before necessity is not just about who has and who does not have to face necessity. It is also about the fairness with which the organization of necessity recognizes efforts to meet it. Once again, the view from necessity adds an original dimension to these classical issues, which are addressed at length in other disciplines, from other, established angles. In economic theory, as we just saw, the issue of wage differentials is explained via ideal equilibrium models between demand and supply of labour, whilst on the critical side the focus is on the extent to which power asymmetries distort perfect market conditions. In recognition theory, the issue is whether ideological representations about particular occupations allow some of them to receive a premium from their privileged position in the social imaginary, while others suffer from a misrecognition or even a denial of recognition of their achievements (Honneth 1995b). In these approaches, the fairness of distribution is evaluated internally as it were, assessing how rules behind the allocation of financial and symbolic capital reflect power relations between groups. The view from necessity suggests a new insight into the fairness of the collective organization of work, which is encapsulated in the following question: to what necessity does a particular occupation respond? From the perspective that this question opens up, the issue of justice becomes: how is the collective organization of work commensurate with the degree to which an occupation addresses an aspect of work necessity? This question reflects an intuition that is commonly shared: that many of the jobs that are essential to social reproduction attract financial and even symbolic rewards that are a lot less than those awarded to occupations which fulfil needs that are essential to only a few or might not even be essential at all, for instance in the spectacle industry (sport or movie stars), or that merely aim to create abstract value (financial industry, real estate industry). An argument might be made for the creation of abstract wealth if it is a means to ensure a surplus for the collective, but in a capitalist context, the accumulation of value is primarily for the purpose of private interests. As such, the material and symbolic rewards that go to workers in spectacle and speculative industries are inversely proportional to their contribution to the reproduction of the lifeworld. From the point of view of necessity, the inversion of values in the rewarding of work is clear to see.

Beyond the issue of the premium put on valorization over social reproduction in capitalist settings, the interpretation of 'achievement' also shifts when necessity is concerned. Some occupations might entail some degree of technical achievement but are less necessary than others regarding the reproduction of the lifeworld. The capacity to run over ten hurdles in less than thirteen seconds is less necessary than the ability to teach children with special needs. Of course, this example is a caricature: part of the reproduction of the lifeworld involves symbolic reproduction, in which many elements cannot be declared necessary from an external, objective point of view, but rather are more or less essential depending on particular worldviews and visions of the good. Art for instance, or the knowledge of history, are viewed as essential in some lifeworlds, whereas sporting accomplishments seem more essential in others. In the former lifeworld, part of the social surplus will be diverted to support the work of art educators, creators, and organizers, or the work that preserves and communicates heritage, as this would all be considered necessary work. In the latter, art might be viewed as superfluous, something that private interest might choose to support but not something the public ought to, but sport might be seen as an essential part of the lifeworld, rightfully claiming part of the social surplus. Even in the absence of objective criteria that would help to define an external viewpoint to decide which symbolic activities are necessary, it remains the case that a lot of work clearly is absolutely essential to the reproduction of the lifeworld. However, the work of 'essential workers' is often underpaid and undervalued. Because of its necessity, such work ought to be fairly rewarded as a principle of justice.

Finally, the classical egalitarian worry about the fair distribution of primary goods can be raised from the point of view of necessity: given that work is a strain on mind and body, and of necessity, a form of imposition, is itself a form of *Not*, at the very least the point of work, that it is a response to necessity, should lead to fair outcomes for those who engage in it. Unfair distribution is unjust not just for reasons explained by a particular theory of justice, but also because it is an unfair reward for the imposition that all those who work face equally.

14.2.5 Unfreedom in the Collective Organization of Work

In this context, issues of freedom are intrinsically linked to the issues of equality. Breen (2019) is a good reference point to study this, as it helpfully distinguishes the different dimensions of freedom tied to meaningful work according to the three main approaches in contemporary philosophy, in terms of positive self-realization, autonomy, and non-domination.

Inequality in facing necessity is also an issue of freedom: some who have power and wealth, who are born in privileged families, might be entirely released from the need to contribute through work. For all the others, there is no such freedom. On the model presented here, this freedom to escape the necessity to work and the necessity of work is not only unjustified on the grounds of equality, but also an ambivalent form of freedom since it means foregoing the possibility of self-development which is entailed in taking on meaningful work. Indeed, as we made the point already, many who could financially avoid work in fact don't, precisely because they know that it is through work they will find meaning, social connection, and self-development, and they might value making their own contribution to the collective.

For all those who cannot escape work, a key issue of autonomy is occupational choice: whether the individual has a say in how they will make their own contribution to the work of social reproduction. This is a political issue to the extent that individual choices are significantly determined by social and economic conditions, which shape the objective pathways towards occupations and careers that are open to individuals belonging to different social groups and also because these conditions combined with cultural representations influence the range of choices individuals from underprivileged groups consider and the decisions they make about their own lifepaths. Giving individuals the real opportunity to choose their work is a basic demand of freedom and since this ability depends on social structures over which the collective has agency, it translates into concrete demands for equality: from the equality of opportunity as a principle of justice (as theorized by Rawls for instance), to the dismantling of cultural prejudices about who can do what work, all the way to an equalizing of conditions (Gomberg 2007). Even though he rejected the call for equalization and endorsed a high degree of inequality in labour market outcomes for individuals, we can note that, in the passage on occupational choice in the *Philosophy of Right*, Hegel clearly articulated the conceptual link between individual freedom and the 'inner necessity' of having to take one's place within the collective organization of work (1991 [1821], 237).

The perspective from necessity also grants a fresh view on issues of freedom as non-domination in relation to work. First, a questioning of the very necessity with which a particular organization of work is enforced can be raised, as it was raised regarding the necessity of particular kinds of work (in Section 14.2.1 above). Granted, some form of organization is needed, formally investing power in managers and supervisors, as well as in organizational hierarchies (different work ranks) and professional hierarchies of seniority or technical ability (graded levels of expertise). If these hierarchies and the different levels and kinds of command that come with them are anchored in the overall response to necessity, they might be acceptable, even necessary in the sense of being unavoidable. As we recalled, Marx acknowledged the necessity of managerial functions from the point of view of the technical division of labour. But once again, the argument from necessity is double-edged: any claim of power over others that is not grounded in the technical response to necessity becomes an ideological necessity, in other words, is and can be denounced as arbitrary and unjustified. More specifically, it can be denounced as an unjustified form of domination.

This applies in particular to capitalist work arrangements. The creation of exchange value relies on the creation of use value on the principle that 'nothing can be a value without being an object of utility'. Discounting for the sake of simplicity the complications that come with luxury, false, and noxious needs, this means that some part of the capitalist process of production does meet the challenge of necessity, even if it does so only as a means to its end of value creation (when meeting necessity should, in fact, be the end). To that extent, some of the power exerted by those who are hired by the owners to organize production is justified from the point of view of necessity. As a matter of fact, many needs are fulfilled in capitalism, and the different forms of management that help accomplish this are therefore partially justified. However, the point of capitalist production is not the fulfilment of needs, but rather the creation of value. Therefore, despite the partial justification of managerial power, to the extent that capitalists hire specialists specifically to increase value, the power granted to these specialists is undue: both in its origin (property as opposed to usefulness) and in its scope, since it goes beyond the sole purpose of justified management, which is to organize production and ensure it is efficient.

Another issue of freedom that relates to the collective organization of work stems from the fact that the facing of necessity can, under certain circumstances, be a vector of self-development for individuals, or instead produce a form of self-withering and of alienation, of the self from the world, from others and indeed from itself. Self-development can be viewed as a condition of freedom, on the model that was outlined in reference to Dejours' writings (Section 13.2.1). The issue of equality in facing necessity is thus also whether the work of facing necessity is organized in such a way that individuals can engage in self-development, or the opposite. Classical studies have highlighted the importance of 'just fit' between the worker and their job (Muirhead 2007), and how the deep impact of work on autonomy makes work an issue of justice (Schwartz 1982; Roessler 2012). We can see here that the perspective from necessity provides an original, critical angle which adds to these arguments. The justice of work arrangements hangs not just on the fact that work has such a deep developmental impact that it becomes an intrinsic component of autonomy, the underlying condition of any flourishing life. It also stems from the fact that different work arrangements entail a differential apportioning of the capacities for self-development. There might be an unequal distribution of the chance to develop concrete freedom through work.

14.3 Achieving Freedom Together

Based on all the dimensions that have been outlined so far, at least three different ways can be highlighted in which work can be said to be highly significant in a political sense: first, as the collective condition for individual well-being and flourishing; second as the collective response to the pressure points that the organization of work creates; and third as the source of citizenship and civic participation. These are three different ways in which work enables people to achieve freedom collectively.

14.3.1 Politics of Self-development

Work is politically significant firstly because of its impact on individual lives and because of the ability of the collective to influence this impact. At this level, a political conclusion is drawn from all the arguments about the importance of work for individual self-development.

Because work is about facing many layers of necessity, it can easily become an experience that overburdens individual abilities: physically, emotionally, intellectually, and indeed morally. Work can disrupt and destroy people's bodies and mental health; it can damage relationships that matter to them. Work can also warp the moral sense and inculcate harmful habits. This occurs notably when dysfunctional work organizations lead to compensatory behaviour that expresses itself in bullying of some individuals or in sexist or racist discrimination, or when managerial culture destroys workplace solidarity and insulates people from each other and destroy basic forms of empathy and solidarity, as Dejours has shown and theorized extensively (Dejours 1998, 2010, 2015; Dejours and Bègue 2014). On the other side, as the case was made, work is an irreplaceable condition for self-development, precisely because it forces us to deal with necessity and face reality. In forcing us to mobilize our capacities to overcome obstacles, work that is sufficiently supportive gives people the opportunity to further develop their knowledges and skills and, in the process, increase their resilience. Work is thus intrinsically ambivalent when it comes to individual self-development.

If work can thus either damage and destroy individuals or be the conduit for their personal growth and concrete freedom, then the conditions in which work is set up, which directly influence the impact it has on individuals, are crucial. The collective organization of work is significant first because work is so impactful on individuals and yet cannot be avoided. Since individual flourishing, understood in the psychosomatic sense delineated above and not in the maximalist sense of Aristotelian *eudaimonia*, depends directly on contexts for which the collective is ultimately responsible, we have here a first sense of the political significance of work. The first sense in which people can achieve freedom together is by collectively ensuring that each individual can develop their own freedom through their work.

This first aspect of work's political significance transpires throughout Marx's writings and might have been a fundamental inspiration for him throughout his life (Geras 1983). His view of a free collective is precisely that it is one that gives everyone the opportunity to be free, in the sense of full self-development. Here we can note already in anticipation of the argument presented in Section 14.3.3 below, that this collective conditioning of individual self-development dialectically brings out a higher, moral development within the collective itself. As the *Communist Manifesto* famously expressed it: 'the free development of each is the condition for the free development of all' (2000, 262). In other words, when the collective organization of work makes it possible for each to develop their capacities and thus their freedom (taken here in the sense of concrete freedom), what is made possible thereby at the same time is a full development of moral sense across society, from which practices of solidarity and equality can arise to ensure that all are able to 'freely develop'. From a community riven with antagonisms, the collective has developed into a true 'association'.

This political significance of work translates concretely into measures to protect and expand the institutional and organizational conditions that enable work to remain a source of self-development. These measures are taken through legal and legislative processes. They usually result from industrial action and social movements that manage to translate demands from the ground at the level of collective decision-making.

Against this first sense of work's political significance, one might counter that the argument underpinning it is very general and that, as soon as one attempts to state more precisely what this legal and legislative work might entail in respect to concrete features of work organization, one encounters difficulties that might be practically impossible to overcome. In order to justify legal and legislative interventions in concrete work organizations, substantial evidence would be required to establish the links between features of this organization and self-development. But given the diversity of subjective expectations and psychological profiles and the diversity of work contexts, how could concrete legal or legislative requirements ever achieve the goal of enabling subjective development and preventing injuries to it? In his recent book, Honneth raises precisely this kind of scepticism towards approaches that rely on 'goods of work' to critique contemporary forms of work (2023). Several considerations can be brought up to respond to this objection.

As we saw in Section 13.2.1, a large amount of empirical scholarship, including by Dejours and his research teams, provides precise and overlapping insights into the relationship between the concrete conditions of work organization and individual well-being. How can all this knowledge be operationalized 'politically', in the sense given to the term in this sub-section, that is, as the collective responsibility to ensure self-development through work? While it is difficult to specify the kinds of work arrangements that need to be in place to allow each and every one to have the opportunity to freely develop at their work, it is a lot less difficult to determine forms of work organization that are highly likely to make this opportunity impossible for most people (there will always be exceptions, individuals who thrive in stressful or even toxic environments). If we take as a guiding thread the assumptions that led to the idea of work as a conduit of self-development, namely that it is such a conduit because it forces subjects to face tasks that require the mobilization of their subjective resources to be completed, including interpersonal ones, then a number of conditions that make this impossible immediately come into view. In the organization of the work process, work cannot possibly be a conduit for self-development if the tasks involved are technically too simple or too difficult, too repetitive or changing all the time, physically or emotionally too draining or not exerting enough. When the gap between prescription and performance is very narrow, there is no room to mobilize creativity and develop practical intelligence, so some level of initiative is required (see Arneson 1987 already for a clear articulation of these points). This formulates negative or threshold requirements for self-development. These thresholds can be overseen and controlled in a number of ways by collective agencies: in a direct fashion, at the level of the workplace if spaces exist where the organization of the labour process can be collectively discussed and controlled; at the industry level, by professional associations and trade unions that can report, alert, and if granted legal and statutory power, intervene in particular workplaces and at sector level; and at the general collective level, through legislative work that puts in place work, health, and safety standards, as well as national controlling agencies (Anderson 2015 and 2017 on the scope for legislative and legal overseeing of workplaces).

Similarly, if the relationship with managers and other coworkers is one of diffidence and lack of cooperation, then once again there is every chance that the developmental potential of work will be undermined, even if the task components have the required level of complexity and variety. This is the case not just in situations where bullying or other forms of workplace dysfunction is at play, but also when dysfunctional work relations get in the way of proper recognition by expert others and by management, as symbolic rewards from them are expected by workers for successful task completion (see Section 13.2.3). While policy against bullying and clear violations of physical and emotional integrity can be legislated, the role of the polity in other forms of dysfunctional management is not as straightforward. It is difficult at first to name institutional channels by which interpersonal work environments can be improved, bad practices denounced, and good practices defended. In many cases, it will not be the role of the collective to intervene. Equally, however, nefarious work relations on the ground can arise not just from problematic practices by the individual actors involved, but also from structural, macro-economic, and ideological factors that frame workplace interactions. Dejours' critique of contemporary management has identified the universal use of performance evaluation and total quality controls as two strategies of modern management that lead directly to dysfunction in workplaces, notably as they undermine solidarity and real cooperation (Dejours 1998, 2006). Beyond internal and 'horizontal' forms of mitigation and intervention at the initiative of workers, unions, and managers themselves, there is an important place for collective intervention in this respect as well. The links between practice on the ground and what institutional recourse is possible can be quite varied, it is difficult to be specific and comprehensive here. What matters is the in-principle possibility of collective intervention in management dysfunctions. This intervention might be legal and involve criminal prosecution in cases where existing laws are demonstrably broken, but it can also be legislative and 'cultural', when a systemic pattern of management practices across industries can be identified as harming workers. One spectacular recent example of such collective intervention involving a legal and a legislative response has been the trial and condemnation of higher executives at the French company Télécom for 'institutionalized workplace bullying', and corresponding work in the French parliament, following a spate of suicides that had been triggered by a particularly brutal shift in the company's reorganization (see the special issue of *Travailler*, Lelay 2021). In the most general terms, the balance of power between capital and labour at the level of the polity would have a direct impact on the scope of possible legal and legislative interventions in those management practices that can be shown empirically to lead to deleterious interpersonal work environments.

Other aspects of work that likely disrupt the possibility of work being a conduit for self-development are more directly linked to the collective organization, namely those that tie the social meaning of work acts to their role in social reproduction. Work that is detrimental to aspects of collective life, either because it damages some individual lives within the collective, or because it produces negative externalities, will likely prevent some workers at least, to find their work a conduit of concrete freedom. The same argument is true of work that makes no real contribution to social reproduction. Conversely, if the work clearly contributes to social reproduction but is not recognized as such, or its value is not well recognized in the eyes of those who perform it, then once again some of the potential positive impact of that work on people's identity is unduly limited. In all these cases, it is at the level of the community as a whole that issues need to be rectified, and this occurs standardly in the life of modern polities. The value and necessity of destructive industries is constantly problematized, increasingly so in recent years as climate catastrophe becomes a serious threat. Struggles for the recognition of valuable contributions and for their proper reward are consistent features also.

One key aspect of this collective recognition of a valid contribution concerns the way material conditions that provide the concrete context in which work is performed, the terms of employment and income in the case of waged work, translate into social reality the recognition that accrues to every such contribution. One way to criticize the increased economic precarity that is spreading today is not just from a general psychological point of view, in relation to existential needs of security and stability in one's life, but also in terms of how working conditions affect these needs specifically, because of the specific structure of the work of facing necessity. If a work contract is too insecure, for instance, does not specify a precise number of work hours per week, or tenure is not permanent, or income is too low, then the expenditure of mental, physical, and emotional energy that the work acts represent is merely for day-to-day subsistence. The work of facing necessity remains bound to necessity, which prevents work from promoting self-development. There is every chance that precariousness, because of the burden it places on workers, robs of its developmental potential even work that might otherwise be interesting and challenging to an individual in terms of the content of the tasks and its meaningfulness for the individual or the collective. The freedom-as-inner-development perspective makes a case against precarious work that is more specific than one prosecuted with reference to general issues of existential security, justice or equality. Needless to say, the collective has many avenues at its disposal to intervene in the material conditions framing work activities. The democratic route, however, is itself impacted by the organization of work. This is a second way to understand the political centrality of work, to which we now turn.

14.3.2 Democratic Work

This second level at which the collective organization of necessity can be a conduit for freedom is situated at the pressure points identified in the previous section. These, to recall, are social spaces where particular forms of necessity are faced by individuals and groups, in such a way that these facings of necessity do not appear fair to them: for instance if necessity does not seem equally shared among all who should face it, or the symbolic or material goods and bads associated with these facings are not fairly distributed, or because freedom is limited in ways that cannot be justified by the challenge of necessity.

Necessity can be transformed into freedom from this second perspective when those questionings are answered, when something is done about inequality and limitations of freedom in the collective organization of work, or about the value of work efforts or the conditions of activities being meaningful to workers. From this particular perspective, 'freedom in necessity' denotes an ideal state where everyone accepts as justified the work they have to do and the conditions in which they are made to do it: everyone thinks the work they do and the work that others do has real social value, they and others do their fair share, they do it in ways that make sense to them, and the power others exert over them, based on this organization of work, is justified. If, like many in contemporary political theory, we are sceptical about the usefulness of an ideal state in political theory, we can think of 'freedom in necessity' from this viewpoint rather in a dynamic, antagonistic, and transformative sense. In this alternative formulation, value, justice, freedom, and equality are principles appealed to in attempts to correct the injustices that erupt at the different pressure points in the collective response to necessity. 'Freedom in necessity' in this sense means struggle, the denunciation of wasteful work, injustice and inequality, attempts at empowerment and transformation of situations of inequality and unjustified domination (Deranty and Renault 2007; Renault 2019 for modelling of this sense of politics). Since the collective response to necessity is itself a necessity, a second-order necessity, freedom in necessity at this level literally means the attempts to assert freedom and equality within (second-order) necessity.

The normative principle fuelling such attempts, both in terms of the procedures they consistently translate into, and the kind of end result they aim to achieve, is democracy. The questioning of collective necessity at the different pressure points that the organization of work imposes to individual and collective life is driven by the democratic concern that everyone who has a stake in this organization (everyone involved in social reproduction, those who can work and those who can't but rely on it) should reasonably agree with the particulars of it, and that the organization and its outcomes should favour no one all things considered (Young 1979). Everyone who is able should do their fair share of the necessary work, in fair conditions, and should receive a fair amount of social benefits, material and symbolic, as a result of doing their part in social reproduction. Since the fundamental principle is social reproduction, part of the necessity to work includes supporting those who for some reason are not able to work. As we discussed (Section 14.2.4), this does not include those who could work but choose not to. However, given the wide extension of what the work of social reproduction involves, in fact, many people work, even if it isn't in the formal economy. Given that social reproduction is the fundamental perspective from which work is viewed here, the democratic demand encompasses all those who are part of collective life, those who can and those who cannot work.

The expression that can be given to the questioning of necessity via democratic procedures issues in forms of freedom in two ways. First, the challenging of (second-order) necessity is in and of itself an assertion of freedom, even if the assertion is not successful in achieving its aims. Second, when an organization of work has been democratically accepted, the embrace of necessity translates into a classical form of autonomy, where the rule that each and every one has to abide by has been agreed to by them. Following Rousseau's classical motto according to which obedience to a rule to which one agrees is freedom, we might say that embracing a necessity in a way that has been chosen or at least agreed to is in itself a form of freedom. There is no rejecting necessity if it is a genuine necessity. Freedom, however, is not negated by it, if the collective organization to meet its challenges has been approved by all involved.

These thoughts apply already in small groups where there is a division of labour and organization of work. In a family, for example, the necessity of work creates many pressure points, r who does what tasks, whose time is taken up by them, who endorses the mental burden of caring for the others, financially, materially, and emotionally, and so on. If that work of necessity is organized in such a way that every member of the family unit has been genuinely heard and the burden is fairly divided, then everyone understands why their time and effort are taken up when they have to do tasks. Arguably, the work of necessity becomes an autonomous act in that case. Of course, a lot is assumed under this reference to being 'genuinely' heard. In a patriarchal setting where women are supposed to do most or all the work of physical and emotional care, what appears as an individual agreeing to a division of labour in fact might only reflect them having internalized an ideology that translates into them doing more work, or more burdensome work, than they would in a more egalitarian setting. This concern has been taken up in feminist theories of autonomy (Mackenzie and Stoljar 2000). However important that concern is, though, it introduces a complication when the democratic principle has to be implemented in practice, but not an objection to the principle itself. Indeed, taking into account the multiplicity of pressure points imposed by the necessity to work, it might be the case that members of a family decide freely among each other and each in their own name, that some will 'specialize' in the work of care in the home, while other 'specialize' in the work of financial care through waged work. They might do this in full recognition of the differential value attached to these works within their society, or the differential rewards and possibilities for self-development attached to different tasks and take this into consideration in their deliberation. In this ideal scenario, this family's organization to face its own necessities would transform necessity into autonomy. Indeed, we could surmise that the autonomy gained by each member in transforming necessary work into work willed by oneself and with others would strengthen the solidarity within that family, and potentially improve the quality of the care each provides to the others.

At the level of a larger community, what gives concrete shape to this form of freedom is economic democracy. Economic democracy is the idea that a society can only be truly democratic if the organization of work is included in the range of objects over which there is deliberation. The idea of economic democracy is usually defended from the point of view of the conditions of real democracy. An eminent philosopher who throughout his life included work and the economic organization within the realm of democratic decision-making was John Dewey. Dewey extended the scope of democratic action to the organization of work, out of concern for what happens when social life is split between its political dimension, where citizens are supposed to be actively engaged, and economic life where they are denied autonomy (Cukier 2018; Renault 2022). Most recently, Axel Honneth has returned to these arguments and defended at length the idea that real democracy requires a fair division of labour (Honneth 2023). The discussion here draws on these earlier arguments but adds to them the perspective of work as necessity, and more specifically the necessity to organize necessity. Economic democracy is required not just in the name of a thriving democratic collective life. The demand that the different parts of the collective organization of work be justified arises from the ground so to speak, namely from the experience of necessity, from the many burdens those who have to work can feel at each one of the pressure points highlighted earlier. The notion of economic democracy in its most expansive sense relies precisely on what was argued earlier in this section, namely that each one of those social spaces, in which some aspect of collective organization is at play and directly impacts individual life, is in principle up for grabs in public criticism, and something to be taken up in collective decision-making. Only by providing the opportunity to all, and most particularly to those who are personally involved, to have a say on a sore point in the organization of necessity, is there a chance that the necessity of the organization of work at that point is no longer imposed as a form of domination, or presented as an inevitable, or natural necessity (as manager power is depicted in capitalist settings for instance), but rather as something that those involved can endorse and thereby engage in freely. At each pressure point, only if democratic processes ensure each can in principle agree with the way the collective facing of necessity is organized, does this collective organization have a chance to not lead to unfreedom or injustice. This is a 'negativistic' way to mobilize the rich literature on economic democracy. Economic democracy is thus the way to ensure the collective response to necessity is not itself a necessity that negates the freedom and rightful claims of individuals. When this occurs, when this collective response is democratic, we have classically a case where necessity turns into freedom: it is precisely because a challenge was put to the collective, and the collective can answer that challenge in ways that promote active participation of each, that freedom comes out strengthened. Work is politically central in this particular sense, because the democratic response here is a response to necessity, in other words, a response to something that just has to be taken up and responded to. Once again, it is the very necessity built into work that makes it so normatively salient, in this case politically salient.

This democratic grounding of the collective organization of work includes, as said, all aspects of the collective organization of work. Democratic enquiry questions what work is necessary, which entails considering the type of goods and services to produce, and the technologies to use. Democratic control can be exercised also over negative externalities of production processes. Following on from the aspects of the questioning of necessity that were highlighted in the previous section, this democratic enquiry embraces also more specialized aspects of work, including the labour process itself, management techniques, the prerogatives of management and the rights of workers. And of course, it concerns the distribution of the benefits accruing to contributions to social reproduction, taking into consideration past contributions for those who can no longer work, and including those who are not able to work in the distribution of the goods of social cooperation.

This collective control over the different aspects of the collective organization of work occurs at different levels. It occurs first at the level of the entire polity, through legal and legislative work, through the establishment and reform of the laws of contracts, of corporations, of labour, through national control agencies and through public debate over the value of different forms of production. It occurs also at the level of industries and economic sectors. Here, trade unions and social-professional associations play key mediating roles, not just in helping to implement legal and statutory control, but also in bringing crucial information from the ground to central decisional centres. All modern thinkers of economic democracy have emphasized the political role of professional associations and trade unions (for Dewey, see Renault 2022, 167–170). And crucially, models of economic democracy entail some form of workplace democracy. There is no scope here to articulate the links between economic and workplace democracy. Cukier (2018) provides a convincing critical synthesis of three key models (Dewey, Beatrice and Sidney Webb 1897, and Karl Korsch 1977), which have explored this articulation at length. Vrousalis (2019) has analyzed in detail the links between the two. Against objections from an alleged necessity built into capitalistic economic laws, some sophisticated studies show the feasibility of economic democracy and the kind of alternative economic necessity it gives rise to (Schweikart 2011; Hahnel 2021).

On a critical note, a key aspect of capitalism, notably in its recent neoliberal variant, is specifically about de-democratization in relation to work, both at a general level and at the level of workplaces. At the general level, de-democratization means that the collective organization of work has been gradually detached from democratic control. This has occurred in the realm of theory, with the transformation of mainstream economic theory from political economy to a universal theory of decision-making detached from concrete contexts. In practice, the wresting of the collective organization of work from democratic control has occurred through mutually reinforcing mechanisms: decisions being handed over to experts, to independent institutions like central banks, to alleged neutral agencies, like rating agencies. The financialization of capital plays its role in this trend, as financial indicators and the interests of financial markets increasingly narrow the scope of collective action and dictate the course it takes (Durand 2017).

14.3.3 Work as a Condition of Politics

As we emphasized throughout the second part of the book, with their work and by exchanging their work outputs, individuals support themselves, the people closest to them, but also strangers they know nothing about, and the collective as such. At the heart of social life, one of the strongest bonds connecting members of the collective is the sharing of vulnerability and all-out interdependence, which are met with cooperation and the organization of this cooperation through the division of labour. As we saw in Section 12.4.3, this investment of individual life resources to support individual and collective life via the division of labour has led some of the most influential social thinkers to call it 'the main source of solidarity'. Because it is one of the main roots of the bond uniting the members of a collective, the collective organization of work is highly significant for politics, perhaps even 'central'. It is significant not just as one of the most important objects of political decision-making, across the many dimensions the previous section outlined. The multi-sided organization of work is even *a condition* of politics, since politics is the collective making decisions about itself, and the organization of work is not only the material condition of its existence and reproduction but also, arguably, secures the bond bringing individuals together into such a collective and therefore in a sense constitutes this collective.

This constitutive power of the organization of work in relation to politics is reflected in two main dimensions, which come to light if we focus on the structure of the organization of work or instead on the bond it creates between citizens. The first dimension is *institutional*: the way in which work is collectively organized impacts significantly on the structure of politics, the way the collective makes decisions about itself. This link is already thematized in Plato's *Republic*, the first great book of political philosophy in the Western tradition. In this first ideal theory of justice, political functions directly reflect the occupational structure. Of course, the model is utterly anti-democratic. In this case, the institutional centrality of work is used as an argument to explain why only a few (those whose work is pure knowledge) are in fact truly deserving of political life in the strict sense. The modern counterpart to Plato's *Republic* is Hegel's *Philosophy of Right*. In that book, the structure of political institutions is once again fully tethered to the structure of the division of labour, but this articulation includes all citizens in principle. The exclusion of a large number of people, the 'rabble', from genuine participation in 'ethical life' is noted but not endorsed, it is in fact a pathology of the market economy (1991, 266). Precisely, this pathology contradicts the condition of politics, which is inclusion through work. Active citizenship in Hegel's view should not be based on ethnic origins, wealth or personal worth, but on contribution to social cooperation (1991, 272–273). The polity for him is best viewed, not as an aggregate of atomically separated individuals brought together by the invisible hand of intertwined self-interests, but rather as a community organized in social spheres (the family and civil society) and united in the state, which three spheres provide the institutional frames for constitutive aspects of the individuals' freedom. Each one of those spheres is characterized by specific kinds of work: the work of reciprocal support, care and primary education in families (1991, 209–231); the work of social contribution in civil society (227–239); the work of higher-order integration, both functional and 'spiritual' (cultural and affective), in the community as a whole (282–302). This higher-order integration that is achieved by the work of state institutions is concretely organized through the classical separation of governmental powers, and these powers are rooted in the collective organization of work in the two other major spheres of life (family and society). Political representation, which underpins the exercise of legislative power, mirrors the structure of the division of labour: first in the composition of parliament into two chambers, and second as the election of representatives is concretely administered on the basis of the occupational structure. This ensures that knowledge of social reality in all its complexity, notably the many interconnections between the different sectors of social reproduction, can be taken up into political deliberation (1991, 339–353; Deranty 2001).

The structure of executive power also reflects the structure of the division of labour (1991, 330–331). This ensures that the decisions taken at the highest level of the executive match the needs of social reality on the ground and in turn that they are applied appropriately, taking into consideration the specific needs and rights of the different sectors of society. Hegel thus constantly emphasizes the tight structural parallels between the organization of work and the organization of political powers. This is to ensure not just functional efficacy, but also that the rights of both particular bodies and individuals in civil society and the rights of the state are equally considered and safeguarded. The political system in Hegel's vision of the state is thus an emanation and higher-order integration of the many sub-systems making up the organization of work in civil society. Hegel's political theory still provides a useful formal model to understand how work is politically 'central' in an institutional sense.

The second, related way, in which the collective organization of work is constitutive of political life, results from the transformation of the dispositions individuals acquire through their involvement in the organization of work into *civic dispositions*. By this are meant the affects people develop and the attitudes they take towards the collective and towards other people with whom collective life is shared, and with whom therefore decisions about this life have to be reached.

As we saw in Section 14.2, there are many ways in which the bond of interdependence linking everyone to everyone else via the division of labour can be skewed, such that some do not do their fair share, receive more than they ought to, or have unjustified power over others. As a result, the experience of work can be one of domination, oppression, and exploitation for many or indeed for the majority. When this is the case, it might well happen that the dispositions acquired at work translate into civic dispositions that are negative in view of what is required for effective democratic participation. For example, frustrations resulting from the experience of injustice and unfreedom might be redirected towards particular classes of people, in perverse variations of class struggle or because psychological mechanisms crystallize resentment nourished by bad work experiences into forms of discrimination. In some cases, injustice and ill-being at work might establish distrust among all co-citizens and lead some groups to nourish political affects and engage in political actions directed against the collective itself. Dejours (1998) has shown convincingly the destructive effects of dysfunctional workplaces, both for the moral sense that ought to be displayed in the workplace and more broadly regarding the concern for others that is a prerequisite of a well-functioning polity.

However, as noted also, even if such tensions and conflicts exist as a result of an unjust and pathological organization of work, it remains the case that each is dependent on everybody else for their existence. Such interdependence is a deep structure of social life, from which nobody can escape as long as they draw their livelihood from the sharing of work outputs with others. Underneath inequality and injustice, individuals and classes are forced into a fundamental form of solidarity from the point of view of reproduction. For politics, as it is analysed here, this means that even though unjust and pathological organizations of work might undermine the civic connection between members of the collective, that connection remains a reality immanent within it. Indeed, injustice and pathologies in the organization of work are all the more nefarious for perverting civic dispositions and civic connections that ought to grow from work-based solidarity. However, except in extreme cases of societal dysfunction, which undeniably can and have happened throughout history, these perversions of civic life resulting from work's dysfunctions are not sufficient to render the link between primary solidarity based on necessary cooperation and civic life redundant.

This is why the arguments put forward by some of the most influential political philosophers (including from the point of view of law, Estlund 2003, 2005), highlighting the civic significance of work-based interactions and experiences, should not be read as idealistic or utopian projections of what ought to be or might happen in some distant future, but rather as description of an inherent dimension of modern societies. This immanent political potential of work can be destroyed if its organization becomes overly unjust and pathological. But it remains a potentiality because of the significance of work for individuals and for the structure of the collective. Hegel's approach to social theory provides a model here as it seeks to capture the 'effective reality' (*Wirklichkeit*) of modern institutional mechanisms underneath the apparent chaos of social and political phenomena. Such descriptions are not articulations of an *ought*, but pinpoint deep structures in the organization of society.

Hegel also offers a model for the dispositional dimension of work's political significance. He already made the case that occupational groups ('corporations') are the social spaces in which 'ethicality' is concretely achieved, that is, the comprehension by individuals that the realization of their aims and preferences depends on interactions with other citizens that are not limited to self-interested transactions and instead requires that they take into account the needs of others and of the collective itself. This is why he states multiple times that the corporation is the second 'ethical root' of the state (1991, 272). As we saw (Section 12.4.5), Durkheim's emphasis on the trans-historical durability of professional bodies has much in common with Hegel's social theory on this point. Dewey is another seminal reference here (see Honneth 1998, and Renault 2022, 164–187 for the range of relevant texts), with many texts by him highlighting the debilitating effects of hierarchical workplaces for democratic life, and conversely the educative power of work for democratic habits. After him, major contemporary theorists of democracy such as Carole Pateman (1970) and Robert Dahl (1985) have expounded at length the argument that democracy is more than just an arrangement of political institutions, requires specific dispositions in citizens, that those dispositions are cultivated and practised in pre-political social spaces, and that places of work are particularly significant for the development of these dispositions. A germane strand can be found among Marxist and socialist political philosophers, based on Marx's notion of a free polity as 'an association of free producers'. Following Marx, a common theme in socialist and Marxist theories of non-alienated politics is the foundational role played by solidarity, the concrete care citizens demonstrate toward each other, which is expressed eminently in work activities. To cite just three recent contributions, we find this idea in Gomberg's notion of contributive justice (Gomberg 2007), in Cohen's elucidation of the socialist ideal as entailing not just fair distribution but also dedication to a 'community principle' (Cohen 2009), and in Honneth's articulation of 'the idea of socialism' (Honneth 2017), as political materialization of 'social freedom' (Honneth 2015). Honneth's latest magnum opus (2023) is a thorough exploration of the negative and positive impacts on individuals of experiences resulting from the concrete organization of work and how they influence their civic participation and the quality of political deliberation. A republican version of this theme is articulated in Elizabeth Anderson's seminal text on equality in the workplace (2015).

These theoretical proposals all point to the logics of reciprocity and reinforcement that link the attitudes individuals adopt in their work efforts and in their civic life. In delivering work outcomes, people aim to achieve not just personal utility. They also intend to deliver a good with social value, which means both something they know the collective recognizes as valuable (a genuine use value) and something that will be of use to someone in the collective. They are aware of, and fully intend, the capacity of work to support concrete individual lives (which they may or may not know personally) and the life of the collective itself. This deliberate other- and collective-directedness of the individual work effort makes it already a political gesture since it is a wilful attempt to support the collective as such, to the extent of one's abilities. Indeed, according to this viewpoint, everyone knows that everyone is engaging in work in this way, namely *attempting* to support each other and the group. The interdependence in this case is not just material and utilitarian (the baker and the shoemaker needing each other's outputs), but also an interlinking and reinforcement of good wills and prosocial attitudes. When this collective makes decisions about itself, at the properly political moments in its collective life, it does so in the full knowledge that it has come together as the joint outcome of all those individual efforts that wilfully produced a life together. This necessarily impacts the nature of collective deliberation, notably deliberation about the organization of collective work. If the collective is genuinely understood by all as the joint outcome of everyone's 'operations', then everyone will be entitled to have a say on what these operations should be about, how they should be organized and how their outputs should be distributed. This includes those who are not able to provide any 'operations' (but recall the wide extension of work from the point of view of social reproduction), since the principle at play is the reproduction of the collective by itself, with all its members included. In this situation, people achieve freedom together in an emphatic sense. They strive to meet necessity together, which entails all the material efforts to create the lifeworld in which all the single, individual lives are sustained and combined, and all the efforts to collectively organize and regulate this lifeworld that has been created and is being maintained together.

Conclusion

Transcending Necessity

To make the case for work, the second part of the book emphasized the *Not* of the human condition and the many-sided necessity that it entails, notably the necessity and the *Not* that work itself is, as the necessary response to *Not*. Yet humans also have the power to transcend necessity. As Marx suggested, humans belong to two realms. One way to understand this is by saying that once the response to necessity has been secured, we can turn our attention towards things that matter independently of issues of survival and of material well-being. Even if work is 'central' because it provides what is necessary, other things will also be 'central' in a different way, namely non-instrumentally, because we value them for what they are, not for what they bring to us as a response to some need of necessity. From the point of view of the ends pursued, the essential instrumentality of work (Section i.2) seems to make it a subordinate dimension of existence, compared with the things that matter in and of themselves. This is a standard argument in post-work theory, which inspired Lafargue's defence of idleness, was at the heart of Gorz's vision of full autonomy, and has been reformulated in many recent post-work writings (for instance in particularly clear fashion by Frase 2016, and Hester and Srnicek 2023).

The 'case for work' the book has advocated questions the assumptions behind this argument. If work is central in all the senses that have been delineated, at psychological, social and political levels, then it is far more than just a material basis for activities that could be pursued without further connection to it. To begin with, because of this multidimensional centrality, many people find their work activities intrinsically valuable and meaningful and use their leisure time as respite rather than a way to 'transcend' work. It would be egregious to argue that in all cases these are examples of adaptive preferences or ideological illusions. As Sections 5.3 and 13.2.2 have argued, the line between play and work is very porous. As soon as people are serious about a leisure activity or a hobby, they begin to treat it like

The Case for Work. Jean-Philippe Deranty, Oxford University Press. © Jean-Philippe Deranty (2024).
DOI: 10.1093/oso/9780192887146.003.0016

work. Work is a paradigm example of a teleological activity involving skill and technique, which humans are intrinsically drawn to, as is testified by the success of professional sports and games, and the many representations of work in entertainment and artistic representations. Indeed, many passages by Marx have been cited, notably in Section 7.2, and there is ample Marxian scholarship, which demonstrates that he did not conceive of the two-realms metaphor as indicating a rigid separation between different spheres of life and different times of existence. As we saw, the ideal of the 'rich individuality' for him, is one which is 'as all-sided in its production as in its consumption, and whose labour also therefore appears no longer as labour, but as the full development of activity itself' (1973 [1857], 325). In short, the multi-dimensional centrality of work means that, though it is at first a response to necessity, it is often intrinsically valuable to people in many different ways.

Nevertheless, the case for work should not be taken to mean that, according to it, human life is, or ought to be, all work and no play. Even if humans can derive many 'goods' from having to face necessity, and even if the shared facing of necessity and the collective organizing of necessity bring them together in many senses, it is a fact that humans also experience, enjoy, talk about, and reflect on many things beyond work. What does the 'case for work' have to say about things that 'transcend' necessity, in the sense that they do not seem to be themselves responses to necessity?

Three different types of such things immediately come to mind. First, there are ways of being, acting, and interacting besides work which humans value for themselves, for example love, friendship, playing, being active just for the joy of it, such as engaging in sports activities. Second there are values which matter intrinsically, such that no further reason is required for trying to achieve them or for enjoying them: typically, what is entailed in the Good, the True, and the Beautiful. Many people enjoy knowledge for the sake of it and feel an expansion of self and of their human powers in acquiring more knowledge in all kinds of areas. Many people enjoy natural or artistic beauty as a pursuit for which no further 'for the sake of' is required. The contemplation of a beautiful landscape or of great paintings, or the deep immersion in a film that moves us are beyond the realm of instrumentality characterizing the world of work. And for many philosophers, the everyday intuition is true that doing good, respecting others, are intrinsically valuable attitudes, without needing to consider the consequences of acting in this way. Finally, a third kind of thing that seems valuable beyond instrumental reasons are 'transcendent' entities which provide a larger frame of meaning within which our finite condition can make sense: a God if we believe in such things, the infinity of the natural order, or 'Being'.

The dialectical view of necessity inspired by Hegel opens the window on the many connections that tie together the 'realm of necessity' and those other realms beyond necessity, and it helps to answer the final objection that these realms beyond necessity seem to suggest. To avoid going into complex exegetical considerations, these close connections between necessity and what transcends it can be simply outlined by elaborating on an image Hegel uses in several passages of his lectures on art and on religion to demarcate the two 'realms'. This is the metaphor of the 'Sunday of life', a metaphor that captures in figurative form the meanings entailed in the notion of 'sabbath' (Hunnicutt 1979, 2024):

> For our actual worldly doings, we have a number of workdays, during which we are concerned with our particular interests and our worldly goals, (our needs, pleasures, and satisfaction) in general. Then there is Sunday, when all these things are set aside, when we collect ourselves, live for ourselves, i.e. for our true essence and for the essential higher nature that is within us, released from our absorption in necessary business and labor of every kind. Free from labor and in contemplative mood, we raise ourselves above everyday life.
>
> **(Hegel 1984, 92–93; 2018, 826–827)**

For our purposes, this passage can be read as discussing not just religion, but more broadly all the other aspects of human existence beyond 'the realm of necessity' that were outlined a moment ago. Inasmuch as we have to work, we are in the realm of the conditioned, of never-ending 'mediatedness' (Section i.2). But there are spheres of human life that are concerned with the unconditioned, that is, with states of being, modes of doing, and with entities that matter intrinsically. In Hegel's system, art, religion, and philosophy (the theory of theoretical enquiries) are the three main ways to talk about these objects and experiences of 'unconditionality', in relation to the Beautiful, the Good, and the True. In Chapter 5, we encountered the notions of 'festivals' and 'cult' to denote these dimensions that are celebrated when we move beyond the banality of the everyday and consider our place in the world in absolute ways.

Yet Hegel uses this image of the Sunday of life, and sets up this contrast, precisely to 'overcome' the opposition dialectically, that is, to show the essential relations that connect religious, artistic, and theoretical experiences and practices to everyday life. This overcoming relies on a famous aspect of dialectic, namely the unity of identity and difference. This is the idea that, precisely because they differ *from* each other, conceptual differences also relate *to* each other. Each refers to the other that it is not to be what it is. Differences are united conceptually, to the precise extent that they differ. Moreover, any complex entity entails both conceptual unity and differences. Identity requires differentiation and differences are united in conceptual identity. Applying these two formal schemas to the two realms of the everyday and the transcendent and continuing to speak figuratively to avoid an overly abstract analysis, we arrive at the following point: there can be a Sunday of life only because all the other days of the week preceded it. Sunday makes sense only as the last of all the other days of the week. Or to say the same thing differently: it is the same person and the same community that work on the days of the week and that 'live for themselves', 'collect' themselves and celebrate on the 'sabbath' and during 'festivals'. The dialectical point is that Sunday's life is not separate from weekly life, but is a transfiguration of it, and is therefore linked to it for its content. And as the book has shown, work is central 'during the week', in the many ways that were outlined in the last chapters, that is: work 'makes or breaks' the person; when it is sufficiently meaningful and fairly organized it gives her strength, knowledge, skills, and resilience; it sustains the lifeworld materially and connects everyone socially; and it is at the centre of collective decision-making. If Sunday is the transfiguration of the other days of the week, but the other days of the week are centrally organized around work, then Sunday is the transfiguration of work itself in a sense, it owes its content to work in some way. It is a time of reflection, contemplation, and higher elaboration on 'material' that has been made real by work.

Another dimension of dialectic is the idea that in complex systems, the more basic constituents and processes 'make up' the whole in a bottom-up relationship, but are also constituted top-down by the higher-level processes of which they are the constituents. This applies also to the relation between the sphere of everyday work and the sphere of the 'Sundays' of life. Not only is the content of 'transcendent' ways of being and doing already constituted in the immanence of everyday life, reciprocally the ways of working are informed and determined by the ways selves and the community self-represent, by the highest values and metaphysical views that provide individuals and their community with ultimate meaning. To take an example from what has been a thread in this book, the ways Achuar women work in their gardens and Achuar men hunt in the forest are directly influenced by their ontological beliefs and spiritual practices. But what makes Achuar society in a real, material sense, what produces and reproduces Achuar people and their community are the practices in which this circle of activity and beliefs is effectively enacted, which are work activities.

To see what all this means concretely we can ask what it is that we do, value, and ponder on our metaphorical 'Sundays'.

On Sundays, we often rest and do nothing. This is fine, except that, on a fair organization of society, we had to work the rest of the week (if we are able to), to then do nothing on the last day. The right to idleness is not an objection to the centrality of work if that centrality is premised on necessity. There might well be a right to idleness, but because there is no escaping necessity, it can only be limited.

On metaphorical Sundays, we might also contemplate or celebrate aspects of who we are as a community, a nation, or a culture, in religious or civic forms of 'cult'. But what is it that makes a community, a nation, or a culture 'objective', to use Hegel's term, that is, effectively real? As we saw, it is the work of material and cultural reproduction. To use another Hegelian image, which was reprised by Schutz (Section 12.4.1), effective reality (*Wirklichkeit*) is a product, a *Werk*, which in the case of human society means that it has been actively produced and reproduced by material and symbolic work (Chapter 10). The people who celebrate themselves celebrate who they are and who they are is what they have made of themselves through work. This is made visible in celebratory festivals when the community comes together as the latter is often represented through the different occupations and 'estates' which form it. The order of celebrations often reflects the social organization of work. This was typically the case in Rome with the place reserved to the *collegia* (Section 11.3). When the celebration concerns the very existence of the community, after a revolution gave it its independence for instance (Independence Day in the USA), or its new constitutional identity (14 July in France), or after a war ended (Remembrance Day in Australia), it is the work of those who defended the community that is the focus, and this time the order of celebrations reflects the specific division of labour that organized the armed forces and their allied services. Community 'festivals' thus celebrate the work that has allowed the community to exist and continue.

Following Hegel, we might also say that on metaphorical Sundays, we typically engage in forms of discourse, cognition, and experience that are 'unconditioned' or 'absolute' and that deal with 'transcendent' objects: religious, artistic, and theoretical activities and experiences concerned with supreme beings, beautiful or entertaining artefacts and pure, that is non-applied, knowledge.

Let us consider science and art first. The dialectical point is that the transcending *of* necessity makes transcending essentially related to what it transcends and an *actual* transcending of necessity is only ever the transcending *of an actual* necessity. Transcending discourses, practices, and experiences are intrinsically related to the specific immanence that they transcend. The simplest way to verify this in the case of art, science, and philosophy (the science of science for Hegel) is sociological and institutional. The very existence of people dedicating themselves principally to creating art or engaging in theoretical enquiries relies on a specific organization of the division of labour which makes room within itself for these activities. The institutional ways in which those practices concretely unfold are also dependent on many other dimensions of social organization: how those activities are financed, how the occupations are internally organized, how they are viewed by the rest of society, and so on. When we consume knowledge or works of art or entertainment goods just for the pleasure of knowing, of experiencing beauty or for fun, we feel that we rise above the trivial concerns of our humdrum lives (to speak like Lina Lamont in *Singing in the Rain*). And that might be true from our point of view as consumers of these goods. But we shouldn't forget that these goods are themselves products of work, made by people who worked, and the work that produced these 'transcendent' goods is itself part of the division of labour, which means that it was supported in all kinds of ways by the work of many others. Indeed, many stories and visual representations are specifically about aspects of work, where the occupational or professional identity of the protagonists matters, or the labour process itself is the heart of the representation (as in heist and detective films for instance).

But the dependence of transcendence on what it transcends goes deeper. To begin with, this dependence is technological and material: science and art rely constitutively on the artefacts and infrastructures available at the time for the creation, production, distribution, and consumption of their outputs. To rely constitutively means that scientific and artistic activities are impacted in the very content of what they can produce by their technological environment, through the material channels and media enabling the production and distribution of outputs, and the empirical methods of enquiry and expression made possible by them. The tools, machines, and material infrastructures are not neutral carriers of meanings, as if the latter could have been created by pure minds in any other environment. Instead, technology is directly implicated in the meanings that are created, it constrains and partly determines what can be thought, said, and expressed. But technology is an output of the work that goes on in the immanence of social life, even if independent scientific and aesthetic knowledge and values are also harnessed in this process (which simply confirms the bottom-up/top-down dialectic). This means that when we enjoy knowledge in an 'absolute', unconditioned way, or a piece of art or entertainment just for the beauty or the fun of it, those 'transcendent' entities, in fact, emanate from and to a large extent reflect the world of work we think we escape by enjoying them, because of their deep reliance on existing technology.

More fundamentally still, the generalized conception of social reproduction, which means that work, as the work of social reproduction, encompasses all dimensions of individual and collective lives, entails that the collective makes itself and its lifeworld. A key concern in the book (Chapter 12) has been to emphasize the ongoing, material efforts it takes to produce and reproduce individual and collective lives in all their features. Implied in this holistic vision of work, therefore, is the idea that the work of social reproduction includes the work of scientific and artistic production. The point here is not simply that science and art are forms of work. Beyond the idea of 'absolute' discourses being themselves part of the division of labour, the point here is that, as a collective organizes its work and thereby creates and maintains its own lifeworld, it creates symbolic languages, like formalized knowledge and aesthetic representations, as part of that process. Looked at it this way, science and art emerge from the organization of work, from the collective work effort, as two of its outputs among all the others. This image is only partly correct, since these languages are largely autonomous. They have their own internal dynamics such that they can be taken up and further developed by people from other lifeworlds who speak these same languages. But given that they have to be maintained and developed by real people who exert real efforts to do so within real lifeworlds, the dependence of these 'absolute' modes of knowing and speaking on the immanence of social life remains a fact. And such dependence is not merely material, because the people who work to develop these languages have been born, bred, educated, and socialized in particular lifeworlds, which involves the reproduction of symbolic and social structures. Despite being highly formal, these languages reflect the lifeworld from which their speakers have emerged, however mediated this 'reflection' is. Hegel's conception of the 'absolute' discourses of art, religion, and science is precisely that they are the transfiguration in self-referential, thematic languages of the 'subjective' and 'objective' practices and discourses that make up the lifeworlds in which they are rooted. That people from different lifeworlds can speak the same 'absolute' languages (can enjoy the same kinds of artworks, pray to the same god, collaborate in the same sciences), is based on the human ability to transplant oneself into new lifeworlds and on the fact that many human lifeworlds have much in common.

What about religious and metaphysical contemplations? How could they be related to the rest of the working week? In fact, if we remember that work is a most acute experience of necessity (Section 13.1), we have a candidate idea for understanding why it can be a privileged source of metaphysical enquiry, for questioning the ultimate reasons behind things, why there is something rather than nothing, why we do whatever we do, and what is the point of existing at all. Work represents an immediate affective and cognitive experience of the dimensions of the necessary, the real, the possible, and the impossible. The 'pressure points' that work puts us under are privileged grounds for asking for ultimate reasons and the meaning of what we do. It is not by chance, therefore, or because of an idiosyncratic feature of modern experience, that Camus singles out an experience of work (rolling a boulder up a hill) as the paradigm example of the absurd. Rather than viewing the figure of Sisyphus as a metaphor for the absurdity of work, we might instead read it as the insight that a root of metaphysical discovery, next to the death of others and the thought of our own death, is experiencing necessity in work. This is not to reduce religious or spiritual contemplation to the work of facing and organizing necessity. Qua activities, contemplation, meditation andadoration are undoubtedly different from the material activities of facing necessity. Yet once again, it would be a mistake to conclude from this that the human being is split and is only truly human in those former activities. The meditating and praying being is also a working being, and the relationship between these parts is not one of true ends relating to instrumentally useful material means, but rather the transfiguration of thoughts and affects that arose to a large part (given the psychological and social centrality of work) from work.

What about supreme beings who transcend humanity through their wisdom or power or 'love'? Hegel's gesture of conducting the conceptual study of art and religion through their history and not just in formal, analytical terms already suggested that these two areas of human practice, experience, and discourse are essentially tied, both in terms of their content and for the fundamental motivations behind them, to their social, historical background. One of his most famous disciples, Ludwig Feuerbach, adopted this viewpoint and elaborated the first comprehensive theory of religion as an emanation of the needs of historical people (Deranty 2021b). Here is not the place to venture into such complex questions. It is sufficient to remind ourselves of the conceptual point behind the metaphor of the Sunday of life, namely that transcendence is only ever transcendence of a given immanence. The people who believe in transcendent entities and engage in cultic practices to beseech and honour them are the same people who face the *Not* of human existence and the *Not* of work during the week. It is the same bundles of affects, drives, fears, hopes, cognitive, and physical powers that face the challenges of necessity and pray to the gods. And it is the same collective that organizes this facing of *Not* via the division of labour and that marks out a special sphere in which fears and hopes can be answered in ultimate terms, with specialist workers dedicated to these tasks. The Hegelian insight is that this common ground between work and religion should be taken seriously.

A similar thought applies to Nature as a vast reality in which finite beings like us contemplate their finitude and experience all-encompassing belonging. A privileged (but of course not exclusive) experience of our limits is in the facing of necessity through work. This experience, precisely because it is 'hard and rough' (Section 13.1), also puts us in touch with reality in ways that are incontrovertible. The very idea of connections and interconnections within and between areas of reality is not just thought of or imagined in work. It is felt in the flesh, both as a problem, because these interconnections create all kinds of difficulties, and as a resource, because it is thanks to interconnections that we can rely on features of the world and the work of others for our own work and the fulfilment of our needs. Yet again, the dualistic image of our predicament that seems so evident turns out to be conceptually problematic, in this case the idea that the contemplation of nature occurs in an entirely separate sphere of human thought and experience compared to the trivial concerns of work. The being who contemplates nature is a being who was already immersed in it thoroughly, with all the others, through the work of necessity.

Finally in the times when they don't work, many people enjoy doing things that matter more to them than work, preferring to 'eat, pray, love', to use another figurative catchphrase, or rather, since religion was already mentioned, 'eat, play, love'. 'Love' might refer to all relationships to significant others that are deeply important to the self through different stages of their life history. In this broad sense, 'love' is clearly just as 'central' as work (which is precisely Dejours' thesis, 2009 for instance), it makes and breaks us just as much as work. Even if they might not be as existentially significant as 'love', other relationships, experiences and activities might also matter a lot. Yet it is, once again, the same person who, in the majority of cases, will work, is working, or has worked, and who also likes to eat, play and love. Given that for many people, subjectivity and identity are developed through work, the latter is more than just an instrumental, material basis for activities and experiences external to it. When individuals 'transcend' their work in activities and experiences they value intrinsically, they do this on the basis of everything work has made of them, for better and for worse. The content and the structure of work impact the content and structure of life outside work. The dialectical point is precisely to hold separation and connection together. There is no denying the value for many people of life outside work, but this transcendence of work remains connected through many ties, psychological, social and material, to the organized world and the personal experiences of work. The argument also applies at the level of society. The lifeworld, in which non-work activities and outside work experiences unfold, is the same lifeworld that is organized as a division of labour and is reproduced by work. On that 'objective' side, therefore, hobby and leisure activities rely so much on all the work producing the infrastructures and implements these activities require, the latter's contents are also determined by work, to a significant degree at least. To cite just one example: chess is not being played today as it was played even twenty years ago. The basic rules have not changed, but many other dimensions of the game have been altered by the move to online playing and advances in computing, which have affected tactics and strategies and the very experience of the game.

Intrinsically enjoyable experiences and intrinsically valuable entities outside of work matter a lot to us, for sure. But the life that craves these experiences and that engages with those entities is the same life that has the power and the responsibility to sustain individual existence and the common lifeworld, by exercising its capacity for intelligent, purposeful activity. Work is the part of our existence through which we play our role in shaping the reality of our own lives and the lives of others, including those we care about. Work makes us an active part of the world and of society and connects us with both. The stakes entailed in these connections, for us and for others, explain why work matters so much.

Bibliography

Acemoglu, Daron, and Pascual Restrepo (2018) 'Artificial Intelligence, Automation, and Work'. In *The Economics of Artificial Intelligencec*, edited by Ajay Agrawal, Joshua Gans, and Avi Goldfarb, pp. 197–236. Chicago: University of Chicago Press.

Acemoglu, Daron, David Autor, Jonathon Hazell, and Pascual Restrepo (2020) 'AI and Jobs: Evidence from Online Vacancies', National Bureau of Economic Research, Working Papers no. 28257.

Adams, Zoe (2020) *Wage and the Law: A Critical Perspective*. Oxford: Oxford University Press.

Adorno, Theodor (1967/1968) 'Sociology and Psychology' (Part I) and (Part II), *New Left Review* 46 and 47.

Adorno, Theodor (2005) *Minima Moralia*. London: Verso.

Adorno, Theodor, and Max Horkheimer (2002) *Dialectic of Enlightenment*. Translated by Edmund Jephcott. Redwood City: Stanford University Press.

Aglietta, Michel (2001) *A Theory of Capitalist Regulation: The US Experience*. London: Verso.

Agrawal, Ajay, Joshua Gans, and Avi Goldfarb (eds) (2019) *The Economics of Artificial Intelligence: An Agenda*. Chicago: University of Chicago Press.

Althusser, Louis (2011) *Sur la reproduction*. Paris: Presses Universitaires de France.

Anderson, Elizabeth (2015) 'Equality and Freedom in the Workplace: Recovering Republican Insights', *Social Philosophy and Policy* 31(2): 48–69.

Anderson, Elizabeth (2017) *Private Government: How Employers Rule Our Lives (and Why We Don't Talk about It)*. Princeton: Princeton University Press.

Anderson, Elizabeth (2023) *Hijacked: How Neoliberalism Turned the Work Ethic against Workers and How Workers Can Take It Back*. Cambridge: Cambridge University Press.

Angella, Marco (2016) 'Work, Recognition and Subjectivity: Relocating the Connection between Work and Social Pathologies', *European Journal of Social Theory* 19(3): 340–354.

Angier, Tom (2016) 'Aristotle on Work', *Revue Internationale de Philosophie* 70(4): 435–449.

Applebaum, Herbert (1992) *The Concept of Work*. New York: SUNY Press.

Arendt, Hannah (1958) *The Human Condition*. Chicago: The University of Chicago Press.

Arendt, Hannah (1961) *Between Past and Future*. New York: Viking Press.

Arendt, Hannah (1963) *Eichmann in Jerusalem. Report on the Banality of Evil*. New York: Viking Press.

Aristotle (1944) *Politics*. Translated by Horace Rackham. Cambridge, Mass.: Harvard University Press.

Aristotle (1961) *Metaphysics*, Books I–IX, Books X–XIV. Translated by Hugh Tredennick. Cambridge, Mass.: Harvard University Press.

Aristotle (1999) *Nicomachean Ethics*. Translated by Terence Irwin. Indianapolis: Hackett Publishing.

Arneson, Richard (1987) 'Meaningful Work and Market Socialism', *Ethics* 97(3): 517–545.

Arneson, Richard (1999) 'Human Flourishing versus Desire Satisfaction', *Social Philosophy and Policy* 16(1): 113–142.

Arneson, Richard (2000) 'Perfectionism and Politics', *Ethics* 111(1): 37–63.

Arneson, Richard (2009) 'Meaningful Work and Market Socialism Revisited', *Analyse & Kritik* 31(1): 139–151.

Arnold, Samuel (2012) 'The Difference Principle at Work', *Journal of Political Philosophy* 20(1): 94–118.

Arntz, Melanie, Terry Gregory, and Ulrich Zierahn (2016) ' The Risk of Automation for Jobs in OECD Countries: A Comparative Analysis', OECD Social, Employment and Migration Working Papers No. 189.

Arntz, Melanie, Terry Gregory, and Ulrich Zierahn (2019) ' Digitization and the Future of Work: Macroeconomic Consequences', Institute of Labour Economics, Paper No. 12428.

Aronowitz, Stanley, and Jonathan Cutler (1998) *Post-Work: The Wages of Cybernation*. London: Routledge.

Aronowitz, Stanley, and William DiFazio (1994) *The Jobless Future*. Minneapolis: Minnesota University Press.

Arruzza, Cinzia (2013) *Dangerous Liaisons: The Marriages and Divorces of Marxism and Feminism*. Milton Keynes: Merlin Press.

Arthur, Chris (2004) *The New Dialectic and Marx's 'Capital'*. Leiden: Brill.

Atkinson, Anthony (1996) 'The Case for a Participation Income', *The Political Quarterly* 67(1): 67–70.

Autor, David (2015) 'Why Are There Still So Many Jobs? The History and Future of Workplace Automation', *Journal of Economic Perspectives* 29(3): 3–30.

Autor, David, and Michael Handel (2013) 'Putting Tasks to the Test: Human Capital, Job Tasks, and Wages', *Journal of Law and Economics* 31: 59–96.

Axster, Felix, and Nikolas Lelle (eds) (2018) *'Deutsche Arbeit'. Kritische Perspektiven auf ein ideologisches Selbstbild*. Göttingen: Wallstein Verlag.

Bakker, Isabella (2007) 'Social Reproduction and the Constitution of a Gendered Political Economy', *New Political Economy* 12(4): 541–556.

Ball, Kirstie (2018) 'Workplace Surveillance: An Overview'. In *Surveillance Studies: A Reader*, edited by Torin Monahan and David Murakami Wood, pp. 269–272. Oxford: Oxford University Press.

Barratt, Edward (2004) 'Foucault and the Politics of Critical Management Studies', *Culture and Organization* 10(3): 191–202.

Barratt, Edward (2008) 'The Later Foucault in Organization and Management Studies'. *Human Relations* 61(4): 515–537.

Bastani, Aaron (2018) *Fully Automated Luxury Communism*. London: Verso.

Bataille, Georges (1988 [1967]) *The Accursed Share: An Essay on General Economy, vol. 1: Consumption*. Translated by. Robert Hurley. New York: Zone Books.

Bataille, Georges (1997) *The Bataille Reader*. Edited by Fred Boting and Scott Wilson. London: Blackwell.

Benanav, Aaron (2020) *Automation and the Future of Work*. London: Verso.

Bhattacharya, Tithi (ed.) (2017) *Social Reproduction Theory: Remapping Class, Recentering Oppression*. London: Pluto Press.

Baudrillard, Jean (1975) *The Mirror of Production*. New York: Telos Press.

Bauman, Zygmunt (1989) *Modernity and the Holocaust*. Ithaca: Cornell University Press.

Bauman, Zygmunt (1998) *Work, Consumerism and the New Poor*. London: Open University Press.

Beadle, Ron (2019) 'Work, Meaning and Virtue'. In *The Oxford Handbook of Meaningful Work*, edited by Ruth Yeoman, Catherine Bailey, Adrian Madden, and Marc Thompson, pp. 73–87. Oxford: Oxford University Press.

Beadle, Ron, and Kevin Knight (2012) 'Virtue and Meaningful Work', *Business Ethics Quarterly*: 22(2), 433–450.

Beauvoir, de Simone (2010 [1949]) *The Second Sex*. New York: Vintage Books.

Bell, Daniel (1973) *The Coming of Post-Industrial Society: A Venture in Social Forecasting*. New York: Basic Books.

Bellofiore, Ricardo (2018) 'Taking up the Challenge of Living Labour: A "Backwards-Looking Reconstruction" of Recent Italian Debates on Marx' Theory of the Capitalist Mode of Production'. In *The Unfinished System of Karl Marx*, edited by Judith Dellheim, and Frieder Otto Wolf, pp. 31–89. London: Palgrave Macmillan.

Bellofiore, Ricardo, and Roberto Fineschi (eds) (2009) *Re-Reading Marx: New Perspectives after the Critical Edition*. London: Palgrave.

Bellofiore, Ricardo, Guido Starosta, and Peter Thomas (eds) (2013) *In Marx's Laboratory. Critical Interpretations of the Grundrisse*. Leiden: Brill.
Benanav, Aaron (2022) *Automation and the Future of Work*. London: Verso.
Bennett, Judith (2007) *History Matters: Patriarchy and the Challenges of Feminism*. Philadelphia: University of Pennsylvania Press.
Bennholdt-Thomsen, Veronika (1988) 'The Future of Women's Work and Violence against Women'. In *Women: The Last Colony*, edited by Maria Mies, pp. 11–30. London: Zed Books.
Benton, Margaret (1969) 'Political Economy of Women's Liberation', *Monthly Review* 21(4): 13–27.
Berg, Heather (2014) 'An Honest Day's Wage for a Dishonest Day's Work: Reproductivism and Refusal', *Women's Studies Quarterly* 42(1/2): 161–177.
Berg, Justin, Jane Dutton, and Amy Wrzesniewski (2013) 'Job Crafting and Meaningful Work'. In *Purpose and Meaning in the Workplace*, edited by Bryan Dik, pp. 81–104. American Psychological Association, No. 248.
Berger, Thor, Chinchih Chen, and Carl Benedikt Frey (2017) 'Cities, Industrialization and Job Creation: Evidence from Emerging Countries', Oxford Martin School, 1–25.
Bhattacharya, Titthi (2017) *Social Reproduction Theory: Remapping Class, Recentering Oppression*. London: Pluto Press.
Bieler, Andreas, and Jörg Nowak (2021) 'Labour Conflicts in the Global South: An Introduction', *Globalizations* 18(8): 1323–1334.
Birnbaum, Simon (2011) 'Should Surfers Be Ostracized? Basic Income, Liberal Neutrality, and the Work Ethos', *Politics, Philosophy and Economics* 10(4): 396–419.
Black, Bob (1986) *The Abolition of Work and Other Essays*. Port Townshend: Loompanics.
Blanchot, Maurice (1988 [1983]) *The Unavowable Community*. Translated by Pierre Joris. New York: Station Hill Press.
Blanchot, Maurice (2015 [1980]) *The Writing of the Disaster*. Translated by Anne Smock. Lincoln: University of Nebraska Press.
Blok, Vincent (2014) 'Reconnecting with Nature in the Age of Technology', *Environmental Philosophy* 11(2): 307–332.
Boland, Tom, and Ray Griffin (2023) 'The Future of Work Guaranteed: Assembling NEETs in the Apparatus of the Welfare State', *Organization* 30(5): 873–891.
Bond, Sarah (2016) 'Currency and Control: Mint Workers in the Later Roman Empire'. In *Work, Labour and Professions in the Roman World*, edited by Koenradd Verboven, and Christian Laes, pp. 227–245. Leiden: Brill.
Bond, Sarah (2019) 'Work and Society'. In *A Cultural History of Work: Antiquity*, edited by Ephraim Lytle, pp. 127–142. London: Bloomsbury.
Bonefeld, Werner (2010) 'Abstract Labour: Against Its Nature and on Its Time', *Capital & Class* 34(2): 257–276.
Bonefeld, Werner (2014) *Critical Theory and the Critique of Political Economy*. London: Bloomsbury.
Bonefeld, Werner, and Chris O'Kane (eds) (2018) *Handbook of Critical Theory*. London: Sage.
Bowles, Samuel, and Herbert Gintis (2011) *A Cooperative Species. Human Reciprocity and its Evolution*. Princeton: Princeton University Press.
Bowring, Finn (2002) 'Post-Fordism and the End of Work', *Futures* 34(2): 159–172.
Breen, Keith (2007) 'Work and Emancipatory Practice', *Res Publica* 13: 381–414.
Breen, Keith (2012) *Under Weber's Shadow: Modernity, Subjectivity and Politics in Habermas, Arendt and MacIntyre*. London: Routledge.
Breen, Keith (2015) 'Freedom, Republicanism, and Workplace Democracy', *Critical Review of International Social and Political Philosophy* 18(4): 470–485.
Breen, Keith (2017) 'Non-Domination, Workplace Republicanism, and the Justification of Worker Voice and Control', *International Journal of Comparative Labour Law and Industrial Relations* 33(3): 419–440.
Breen, Keith (2019) 'Meaningful Work and Freedom. Self-realization, Autonomy, and Non-domination in Work'. In *The Oxford Handbook of Meaningful Work*, edited by Ruth Yeoman,

Catherine Bailey, Adrian Madden, and Marc Thompson, pp. 51–72. Oxford: Oxford University Press.
Breen, Keith, and Jean-Philippe Deranty (eds) (2021a) *The Politics and Ethics of Contemporary Work: Whither Work?* London: Routledge.
Breen, Keith, and Jean-Philippe Deranty (2021b) 'Whither Work? Politics and Ethics of Contemporary Work'. In *The Politics and Ethics of Contemporary Work. Whither Work?*, edited by Keith Breen and Jean-Philippe Deranty, pp. 1–15. London: Routledge.
Breen, Keith, and Jean-Philippe Deranty (2024) 'Work and the Work Ethic: A Critique of Post-work Arguments'. In *Debating a Post-Work Future: Perspectives from Philosophy and the Social Sciences*, edited by Denise Celentano, Michael Cholbi, Jean-Philippe Deranty, and Kory Schaff, pp. 131–150. London: Routledge.
Breen, Keith, and Onni Hirvonen (2021) 'Workplace Democracy and Republican Freedom'. In *The Politics and Ethics of Contemporary Work: Whither Work?*, edited by Keith Breen and Jean-Philippe Deranty, pp. 178–199. London. Routledge.
Brentano, Lujo (1923) 'Puritanismus und Kapitalismus'. In *Lujo Brentano, Der Wirtschaftende Mensch*, pp. 364–370. Berlin: Felix Meiner.
Bresson, Alain (2016) *The Making of the Ancient Greek Economy: Institutions, Markets, and Growth in the City-States*. Princeton: Princeton University Press.
Brewer, Rose (1993) 'Theorising Race, Class and Gender'. In *Theorising Black Feminisms: The Visionary Pragmatism of Black Women*, edited by Stanlie James and Abena Busia, pp. 13–30. London: Routledge.
Brückner, Wolfgang (1988) 'Arbeit macht frei'. Herkunft und Hintergrund der KZDevise. Opladen: Otto-von-Freising-Vorlesungen der Katholischen Universität Eichstätt.
Brudney, Daniel (1998) *Marx's Attempt to Leave Philosophy*. Cambridge, Mass.: Harvard University Press.
Brudney, Daniel (2022) 'On Productivity Holism', *European Journal of Philosophy*, online first.
Brynolfsson, Erik, and Andrew McAfee (2011) *Race against the Machine*. Lexington: Digital Frontier Press.
Brynolfsson, Erik, and Andrew McAfee (2014) *The Second Machine Age: Work, Progress, and Prosperity in a Time of Brilliant Technologies*. New York: Norton.
Brynjolfsson, Erik, Daniel Rock, and Chad Syverson (2019) 'Artificial Intelligence and the Modern Productivity Paradox: A Clash of Expectations and Statistics'. In *The Economics of Artificial Intelligence*, edited by Ajay Agrawal, Joshua Gans, and Avi Goldfarb, pp. 23–60. Chicago: University of Chicago Press.
Bryson, Valerie (2003) *Feminist Political Theory. An Introduction*. London: Palgrave Macmillan.
Buggeln, Mark, and Michael Wildt (2014) *Arbeit im Nationalsozialismus*. Oldenburg: De Gruyter.
Bughin, Jacques (2020) 'Artificial Intelligence, Its Corporate Use and How It Will Affect the Future of Work'. In *Capitalism, Global Change and Sustainable Development*, edited by Luigi Paganetto, pp. 239–260. New York: Springer.
Burch, Ernest (2006) *Social Life in Northwest Alaska. The Structure of Inupiaq Eskimo Nations*. Fairbanks: University of Alaska Press.
Burford, Alison (1972) *Craftsmen in Greek and Roman Society*. Cambridge: Cambridge University Press.
Caffentzis, George (1999) 'The End of Work or the Renaissance of Slavery? A Critique of Rifkin and Negri', *Common Sense* 24: 20–39.
Canovan, Margaret (1978) 'The Contradictions of Hannah Arendt's Political Thought', *Political Theory* 6(1): 5–26.
Carchedi, Guglielmo (2007) 'A Comment on Bonefeld's "Abstract Labour: Against Its Nature and on Its Time"', *Capital & Class* 35(2): 307–309.
Carchedi, Guglielmo (2009) 'The Fallacies of "New Dialectics" and Value-Form Theory', *Historical Materialism* 17: 145–169.
Carter, Chris (2008) 'A Curiously British Story: Foucault Goes to Business School', *International Studies of Management & Organization* 38(1): 13–29.

Castells, Manuel (1997) *The Power of Identity. The Information Age: Economy, Society and Culture*, Vol. II. Oxford: Blackwell.
Celentano, Denise (2019) 'Automation, Labour Justice, and Equality', *Ethics and Social Welfare* 13(1): 33–50.
Celentano, Denise, Michael Cholbi, Jean-Philippe Deranty, and Kory Schaff (2024) *Debating a Post-Work Future: Perspectives from Philosophy and the Social Sciences*. London: Routledge.
Chalcraft, David, and Austin Harrington (eds) (2001) *The Protestant Work Ethic Debate*. Liverpool: Liverpool University Press.
Chamberlain, James (2018) *Undoing Work, Rethinking Community: A Critique of the Social Function of Work*. Ithaca: Cornell University Press.
Chamoux, Marie-Noëlle (1994) 'Sociétés avec et sans concept de travail', *Sociologie du Travail* 36: 57–71.
Chapman, Anne (1982) *Drama and Power in a Hunting Society. The Selk'nam of Tierra Del Fuego*. Cambridge: Cambridge University Press.
Chessell, Darren (2018) 'The Jobless Economy in a Post-work Society: How Automation Will Transform the Labor Market', *Psychosociological Issues in Human Resource Management* 6(2): 74–79.
Chhachhi, Amrita (2104) 'Introduction: The "Labour Question" in Contemporary Capitalism', *Development and Change* 45(5): 895–919.
Cholbi, Michael (2018a) 'The Desire for Work as an Adaptive Preference', *Autonomy* 4: 1–17.
Cholbi, Michael (2018b) 'The Duty to Work', *Ethical Theory and Moral Practice* 21(5): 1119–1133.
Christophers, Brett (2022) *Rentier Capitalism. Who Owns the Economy and Who Pays for It?* London: Verso.
Cicero (1991) *On Duties*. Cambridge: Cambridge University Press.
Clark, Samuel (2017) 'Good Work', *Journal of Applied Philosophy* 34: 61–73.
Cleaver, Harry (2000) *Reading Capital Politically*. Austin: AK Press.
Cleaver, Harry (2017) *Rupturing the Dialectic. The Struggle against Work, Money, and Financialisation*. Austin: AK Press.
Clifton, Judith, Amy Glasmeier, and Mia Gray (2020) 'When Machines Think for Us: The Consequences for Work and Place', *Regions, Economy and Society* 13: 3–23.
Clot, Yves (1999) *La Fonction psychologique du travail*. Paris: Presses Universitaires de France.
Clot, Yves (2014) *Travail et Pouvoir d'Agir*. Paris: Presses Universitaires de France.
Cohen, Gerald Allan (2000 [1978]) *Karl Marx's Theory of History: A Defence*. Princeton: Princeton University Press.
Cohen, Gerald Allan (2009) *Why Not Socialism?* Princeton: Princeton University Press.
Cohen, Josh (2018) *Not Working: Why We Have to Stop*. London: Granta.
Collins, Patricia Hill (2000) *Black Feminist Thought*. London: Routledge.
Coutrot, Thomas, and Coralie Perez (2022) *Redonner du sens au travail. Une aspiration révolutionnaire*. Paris: Seuil.
Cravey, Alta (1998) *Women and Work in Mexico's Maquiladoras*. London: Rowman & Littlefield.
Cukier, Alexis (2018) *Le Travail démocratique*. Paris: Presses Universitaires de France.
Cupcea, George, and Rada Varga (2018) *Social Interactions and Status Markers in the Roman World*. Oxford: Archeopress.
Cutts, Joshua (2019) 'Herbert Marcuse and "False Needs"', *Social Theory and Practice* 45(3): 353–370.
Dahl, Robert (1985) *A Preface to Economic Democracy*. Berkeley: University of California Press.
Dalla Costa, Mariarosa, and Selma James (1972) *The Power of Women and the Subversion of the Community*. Bristol: Falling Wall Press.
Danaher, John (2017) 'Will Life Be Worth Living in a World without Work? Technological Unemployment and the Meaning of Life', *Science and Engineering Ethics* 23: 41–64.
Danaher, John (2019a) *Automation and Utopia: Human Flourishing in a World without Work*. Cambridge, Mass. Harvard University Press.

Danaher, John (2019b) 'In Defence of the Post-Work Future: Withdrawal and the Ludic Life'. In *The Future of Work, Technology and Basic Income*, edited by Michael Cholbi and Michael Weber, pp. 99–116. London: Routledge.

Danaher, John (2021) *Automation and the Future of Work*. In *Oxford Handbook of Digital Ethics*. Oxford: Oxford University Press.

Daniels, Arlene Kaplan (1987) 'Invisible Work', *Social Problems* 34(5): 403–415.

David, Paul (1990) 'The Dynamo and the Computer: An Historical Perspective on the Modern Productivity Paradox', *American Economic Review* 80(2): 355–361.

Davidson, Donald (2002) *Essays on Action and Events*. Oxford: Clarendon Press.

Davis, Angela (1972) 'Reflections on the Black Woman's Role in the Community of Slaves', *The Massachusetts Review* 13 (1/2): 81–100.

De Robertis, Francesco Maria (1971) *Storia delle Corporazioni e del Regime Associativo nel Mondo Romano*. Bari: Adriatica Editrice.

Dean, Mitchell (2009) *Governmentality. Power and Rule in Modern Society*. London: Sage.

Dean, Mitchell (2015) 'Foucault and the Neoliberalism Controversy'. In *The Sage Handbook of Neoliberalism*, edited by Damirn Cahill, Melinda Cooper, Martijn Konings, and David Primrose, pp. 40–54. London: Sage.

Dejours, Christophe (1980) *Travail, usure mentale* (4th edition, 2015). Paris: Bayard.

Dejours, Christophe (1998) *Souffrance en France: La banalisation de l'injustice sociale*. Paris: Seuil.

Dejours, Christophe (2006) *L'Evaluation du travail à l'épreuve du réel. Critique des Fondements de l'évaluation*. Paris: INRA Editions.

Dejours, Christophe (2009) *Le Travail vivant*, 2 volumes. Paris: Presses Universitaires de France.

Dejours, Christophe (ed.) (2010) *Observations Cliniques en psychopathologie du travail*. Paris: Presses Universitaires de France.

Dejours, Christophe (2012) 'From Psychopathology to the Psychodynamics of Work'. In *New Philosophies of Labour: Work and the Social Bond*, edited by Nicholas. Smith and Jean-Philippe Deranty, pp. 209–250. Leiden: Brill.

Dejours, Christophe (2015) *Le Choix. Souffrir au travail n'est pas une fatalité*. Paris: Bayard.

Dejours, Christophe (2018) *Le Facteur humain* (7th ed.). Paris: Presses Universitaires de France.

Dejours, Christophe (2021) *Ce qu'il y a de meilleur en nous: travailler et honorer la vie*. Paris: Payot.

Dejours, Christophe, and Florence Bègue (2014) *Suicide et travail: que faire?* Paris: Presses Universitaires de France.

Dejours, Christophe, and Jean-Philippe Deranty (2010) 'The Centrality of Work', *Critical Horizons* 11(2): 167–180.

Dejours, Christophe, Jean-Philippe Deranty, Emmanuel Renault, and Nicholas Smith (2018) *The Return of Work in Critical Theory: Subject, Society, Politics*. New York: Columbia University Press.

Delphy, Christine (1984) *Close to Home: A Materialist Analysis of Women's Oppression*. Armherst: University of Massachusetts Press.

Deranty, Jean-Philippe (2000) '"The Son of Civil Society": Tensions in Hegel's Account of Womanhood', *Philosophical Forum* 31(2): 145–162.

Deranty, Jean-Philippe (2001) 'Hegel's Parliamentarianism: A New Perspective on Hegel's Theory of Political Institutions', *Owl of Minerva* 32(2): 107–133.

Deranty, Jean-Philippe (2009a) *Beyond Communication. A Critical Study of Axel Honneth's Social Philosophy*. Leiden: Brill.

Deranty, Jean-Philippe (2009b) 'What Is Work? Key Insights from the Psychodynamics of Work', *Thesis Eleven* 98(1): 69–87.

Deranty, Jean-Philippe (2010) 'Work as Transcendental Experience: Implications of Dejours' Psychodynamics for Contemporary Social Theory and Philosophy', *Critical Horizons* 11(2): 181–220.

Deranty, Jean-Philippe (2012) 'Cooperation and Expression as Norms for a Contemporary Critique of Work?'. In *New Philosophies of Labour: Work and the Social Bond*, edited by Nicholas Smith and Jean-Philippe Deranty, pp. 151–179. Leiden: Brill.

Deranty, Jean-Philippe (2013) 'Cartographie critique des objections historicistes à la centralité du travail', *Travailler* 30(2): 17–47.
Deranty, Jean-Philippe (2015) 'Historical Objections to the Centrality of Work', *Constellations* 22(1): 105–121.
Deranty, Jean-Philippe (2016) 'Lost Paradigm: The Fate of Work in Post-War French Philosophy', *Revue Internationale de Philosophie* 70: 491–511.
Deranty, Jean-Philippe (2021a) 'The Body of Spirit: Hegel's Concept of Flesh and its Normative Implications', *Hegel Bulletin* 42(1): 39–56.
Deranty, Jean-Philippe (2021b) 'Feuerbach, Ludwig'. In *The Encyclopedia of Philosophy of Religion*, edited by Stuart Goetz and Charles Taliaferro, pp. 899–907. London: Wiley-Blackwell.
Deranty, Jean-Philippe (2022) 'Post-work Society as an Oxymoron: Why We Cannot, and Should Not, Wish Work Away', *European Journal of Social Theory* 25(3): 422–439.
Deranty, Jean-Philippe, and Thomas Corbin (2024) 'Artificial Intelligence and Work: A Critical Review of Recent Research from the Social Sciences', *AI & Society* 39(2): 675–691.
Deranty, Jean-Philippe, and Michael Olson (2019) 'The Work of Art in the Age of its Digital Distribution', *Angelaki* 24(5): 104–123.
Deranty, Jean-Philippe, and Emmanuel Renault (2007) 'Politicising Honneth's Ethics of Recognition', *Thesis Eleven* 88: 92–111.
Deranty, Jean-Philippe, and Emmanuel Renault (2012) 'Arbeit als Ort von Ungerechtigkeit und Herrschaft. Die Grenzen der zeitgenössischen politischen Philosophie', *Deutsche Zeitschrift für Philosophie* 60(4): 573–593.
Deranty, Jean-Philippe, and Emmanuel Renault (2022) 'Democratising Work from Below: Beyond Workplace Republicanism'. In *The Politics and Ethics of Contemporary Work: Whither Work?*, edited by Keith Breen and Jean-Philippe Deranty, pp. 150–165. London: Routledge.
Derrida, Jacques (1989) *Of Spirit: Heidegger and the Question*. Trans. G. Bennington and R. Bowlby. Chicago: Chicago University Press.
Descola, Philippe (1994) *In the Society of Nature: A Native Ecology in Amazonia*. Translated by Nora Scott. Cambridge: Cambridge University Press.
Descola, Philippe (1996) *The Spears of Twilight. Life and Death in the Amazon Jungle*. Translated by Janet Lloyd. New York: The New Press.
Descola, Philippe (2013) *Beyond Nature and Culture*. Translated by Janet Lloyd. Chicago: University of Chicago Press.
Descola, Philippe (2021) *Les Formes du visible*. Paris: Seuil.
Dewey, John (1985 [1916]) *Democracy and Education: The Middle Works of John Dewey, 1899–1924*, volume 9. Carbondale: Southern Illinois Press.
Dewey, John (2010) *Class Lectures*, volume 1. InteLex, electronic edition.
Dill, Bonnie Thornton (1979) 'The Dialectics of Black Womanhood', *Signs* 4(3): 543–555.
Dinerstein, Ana Cecilia, and Harry Pitts (2021) *A World beyond Work? Labour, Money and the Capitalist State between Crisis and Utopia*. Bingley: Emerald Publishing.
Donaldson, Sue, and Will Kymlicka (2019) 'Animal Labour in a Post-Work Society'. In *Animal Labour: A New Frontier of Interspecies Justice?*, edited by Chris Blattner, Kendra Coultner, and Will Kymlicka, pp. 207–228. Oxford: Oxford University Press.
Dreyfus, Hubert (1995) *Being-in-the World: A Commentary on Heidegger's Being and Time, Division I*. Cambridge, Mass.: MIT Press.
Dreyfus, Hubert (2014) *Skilful Coping: Essays on the Phenomenology of Everyday Perception and Action*. Oxford: Oxford University Press.
Duby, Georges (1982) *The Three Orders: Feudal Society Imagined*. Translated by Arthur Goldhammer. Chicago: University of Chicago Press.
Duby, Georges (2010) *Le Moyen Age*. Paris: Fayard.
Durand, Cédric (2017) *Fictitious Capital: How Finance Is Appropriating Our Future*. London: Verso.

Durkheim, Emile (1984 [1896]) *The Division of Social Labour in Society*. Translated by Wilfred Halls. London: Palgrave Macmillan.
Durkheim, Emile (1986) *Durkheim on Politics and the State*. Edited by Anthony Giddens. Redwood City: Stanford University Press.
Dyer-Witheford, Nick, Atle Mikkola Kjøsen, and James Steinhoff (2019) *Inhuman Power: Artificial Intelligence and the Future of Capitalism*. London. Pluto Press
Ebben, Mauren (2020) 'Automation and Augmentation: Human Labor as Essential Complement to Machines'. In *Maintaining Social Well-Being and Meaningful Work in a Highly Automated Job Market*, edited by Shalin Hai-Jew, pp. 1–24. Hershey: IGI Global.
Eistenstadt, Shmuel (1964) 'Social Change, Differentiation and Evolution', *American Sociological Review* 29(3): 375–386.
Eisenstadt, Shmuel (1968) *The Protestant Ethic and Modernization: A Comparative View*. New York: Basic Books.
Eisenstadt, Shmuel (ed.) (1970) *Readings in Social Evolution and Development*. Oxford: Pergamon Press.
Eleb, Ingo (2018) 'Helmut Reichelt and the New Reading of Marx'. In *Sage Handbook of Frankfurt School Critical Theory*, edited by Beverley Best, Werner Bonefeld, and Chris O'Kane, pp. 367–385. London: Sage.
Elster, John (1985) *Making Sense of Marx*. Cambridge: Cambridge University Press.
Elster, John (1986) 'Self-Realization in Work and Politics: The Marxist Conception of the Good Life', *Social Philosophy and Policy* 3(2): 97–126.
Ekkehardt, Ernst, Rossana Merola, and Daniel Samaan (2019) 'Economics of Artificial Intelligence: Implications for the Future of Work', *IZA Journal of Labor Policy* 9(1): 1–35.
Engels, Friedrich (2010 [1884]) *Origins of the Family, Property and the State*. London: Penguin.
Estlund, Cynthia (2003) *Working Together: How Workplace Bonds Strengthen a Diverse Democracy*. Oxford: Oxford University Press.
Estlund, Cynthia (2005) 'Working Together: Crossing Color Lines at Work', *Labor History* 46(1): 79–98.
Estlund, Cynthia (2021) *Automation Anxiety: Why and How to Save Work*. Oxford: Oxford University Press.
Etzler, John Adolphus (1842) *The Paradise within the Reach of All Men, Without Labour, by Powers of Nature and Machinery: An Address to All Intelligent Men*. London: J. Cleave.
Etzrodt, Christian (2008) 'Weber's Protestant-Ethic Thesis, the Critics, and Adam Smith', *Max Weber Studies* 8(1): 49–78.
Faitini, Tiziana (2023) *Shaping the Profession: Towards a Genealogy of Professional Ethics*. Leiden: Brill.
Faye, Emmanuel (2009) *Heidegger: The Introduction of Nazism into Philosophy in Light of the Unpublished Seminars of 1933–1935*. New Haven: Yale University Press.
Faye, Emmanuel (2012) 'Being, History, Technology, and Extermination in the Work of Heidegger', *Journal of the History of Philosophy* 50(1): 111–130.
Federici, Silvia (1995) 'Wages against Housework'. In *The Politics of Housework*, edited by Ellen Malos, pp. 187–194. Cheltenham: New Clarion.
Federici, Silvia (2012) *Revolution at Point Zero: Housework, Reproduction, and Feminist Struggle*. Brooklyn: PM Press.
Fehr, Ernst, Urs Fischbacher, and Simon Gächter (2002) 'Strong Reciprocity, Human Cooperation, and the Enforcement of Social Norms', *Human Nature* 13(1): 1–25.
Feldman, Alex (2019) 'Power, Labour Power and Productive Force in Foucault's Reading of Capital', *Philosophy and Social Criticism* 45(3): 307–333.
Felten, Edward, Manav Raj, and Robert Seamans (2019) 'The Occupational Impact of Artificial Intelligence: Labor, Skills, and Polarization', NYU Stern School of Business.
Felten, Edward, Manav Raj, and Robert Seamans (2021) 'Occupational, Industry, and Geographic Exposure to Artificial Intelligence: A Novel Dataset and its Potential Uses', *Strategic Management Journal* 42(12): 2195–2217.

Ferguson, Susan (2019) *Women and Work: Feminism, Labour, and Social Reproduction.* London: Pluto Press.
Ferreras, Isabelle (2017) *Firms as Political Entities. Saving Democracy through Economic Bicameralism.* Cambridge, Mass.: Harvard University Press.
Ferreras, Isabelle, Julie Battilana, and Dominique Méda (2022) *Democratise Work. The Case for Reorganising the Economy.* Chicago: University of Chicago Press.
Fine, Cordelia (2010) *Delusions of Gender: How Our Minds, Society and Neurosexism Create Difference.* New York: W.W. Norton.
Fine, Cordelia (2017) *Testosterone Rex: Myths of Sex, Science and Society.* New York: W.W. Norton.
Finley, Moses (1999 [1973]). *The Ancient Economy.* Berkeley: University of California Press.
Firth, Raymond (1967) *The Work of the Gods in Tikopia.* London: Athlone Press.
Firth, Raymond (2002 [1957]) *Man and Culture: An Evaluation of the Work of Malinowski.* London: Routledge.
Fischbach, Franck (2023) *Marx with Spinoza: Production, Alienation, History.* Translated by Jason Read. Edinburgh: Edinburgh University Press.
Fischbach, Franck, and Emmanuel Renault (eds) (2022) *Philosophie du Travail: Activité, Technicité, Normativité.* Paris: Vrin.
Fischbach, Franck, Anne Merker, Pierre-Marie Morel, and Emmanuel Renault (2022) *Histoire Philosophique du Travail.* Paris: Vrin.
Fisher, Elizabeth (1979) *Woman's Creation. Sexual Evolution and the Shaping of Society.* Maidenhead: McGraw Hill.
Fitzpatrick, Tony (2004) 'A Post-Productivist Future for Social Democracy?', *Social Policy and Society* 3(3): 213–222.
Fleming, Peter (2015) *The Mythology of Work. How Capitalism Persists Despite Itself.* London: Pluto Press.
Fleming, Peter (2019) 'Robots and Organization Studies: Why Robots Might Not Want to Steal Your Job', *Organization Studies* 40(1): 23–38.
Flohr, Miko (2016) 'Constructing Occupational Identities in the Roman World'. In *Work, Labour and Professions in the Roman World*, edited by Koenraad Verboven and Christian Laes, pp. 147–172. Leiden: Brill.
Foltz, Bruce (1995) *Inhabiting the Earth: Heidegger, Environmental Ethics, and the Metaphysics of Nature.* New York: Prometheus Books.
Ford, Martin (2015) *Rise of the Robots.* New York: Cornell University Press.
Ford, Martin (2021) *Rule of the Robots: How Artificial Intelligence Will Transform Everything.* London: Basic Books.
Ford, Nick (2016). *Abolish Work: A Lazy Exposition of Philosophical Ergophobia.* https://archive.org/details/AbolishWorkALazyExpositionOfPhilosophicalErgophobia.
Foster, Richard Bellamy (2017) 'The Meaning of Work in a Sustainable Society: A Marxian View', *Monthly Review* 69(4): 1–14.
Foucault, Michel (1977 [1975]) *Discipline and Punish: The Birth of the Prison.* Translated by Alan Sheridan. London: Penguin.
Foucault, Michel (1978 [1976]) *The History of Sexuality. Volume I: Introduction.* Translated by Robert Hurley. New York: Random House.
Foucault, Michel (1982) *Ethics: Subjectivity and Truth: Essential Works of Foucault, 1954–1984: Power*, vol. 1. New York: New Press.
Foucault, Michel (1988 [1961]) *Madness and Civilisation. A History of Insanity in the Age of Reason.* Translated by Richard Howard. New York: Vintage Books.
Foucault, Michel (1989 [1966]) *The Order of Things: An Archaeology of the Human Sciences.* Translated by Alan Sheridan. London: Routledge.
Foucault, Michel (2001 [1974]) 'Truth and Juridical Forms'. In *Essential Works of Foucault, 1954–1984: Power*, vol. 3. New York: New Press.
Foucault, Michel (2008 [1978–1979]) *The Birth of Biopolitics.* Translated by Graham Burchell. London: Palgrave Macmillan.

Foucault, Michel (2015 [1972–1973]) *The Punitive Society. Lectures at the Collège de France.* Translated by Graham Burchell. London: Palgrave Macmillan.
François, Arnaud (2022) *Le Travail et la vie.* Paris: Herman.
Frase, Peter (2016) *Four Futures: Life after Capitalism.* London: Verso.
Fraser, Nancy (1985) 'What's Critical about Critical Theory? The Case of Habermas and Gender', *New German Critique* 35: 97–131.
Fraser, Nancy (2014) 'Behind Marx's Hidden Abode: For an Expanded Conception of Capitalism', *New Left Review* 86: 55–72.
Fraser, Nancy (2017) 'Crisis of Care? On the Social Reproductive Contradictions of Contemporary Capitalism'. In *Social Reproduction Theory: Remapping Class, Recentering Oppression*, edited by Tithi Bhattacharya, pp. 21–36. London: Pluto Press.
Fraser, Nancy (2022) *Cannibal Capitalism.* London: Verso.
Fraser, Nancy, and Rahel Jaeggi (2018) *Capitalism. A Conversation in Critical Theory.* Cambridge, Mass.: Polity Press.
Frayne, David (2015) *The Refusal of Work: The Theory and Practice of Resistance to Work.* London: Zed Books.
Frayne, David (2016) 'Critiques of Work'. In *Handbook of the Sociology of Work and Employment*, edited by Stephen Edgell, Heidi Gottfried, and Edward Granter, pp. 616–633. London: Sage.
Frayne, David (2024) 'The Post-Work Imagination'. In *Debating a Post-Work Future: Perspectives from Philosophy and the Social Sciences*, edited by Denise Celentano, Michael Cholbi, Jean-Philippe Deranty, and Kory Schaff, pp. 61–86. London: Routledge.
Freedman, Estelle (2017) *The Essential Feminist Reader.* New York: Modern Library.
Frey, Carl Benedikt, and Michael Osborne (2017) 'The Future of Employment: How Susceptible Are Jobs to Computerisation?' *Technological Forecasting and Social Change* 114: 254–280.
Freyssenet, Michel (1999) 'The Emergence, Centrality and End of Work', *Current Sociology* 47(2): 5–20.
Friedan, Betty (1963) *The Feminine Mystique.* New York: W.W. Norton.
Furnham, Adrian (1990) *The Protestant Work Ethic: The Psychology of Work-Related Beliefs and Behaviours.* London: Routledge.
Gardiner, Jean (1979) 'Women's Domestic Labor'. In *Capitalist Patriarchy and Female Work*, edited by Zillah Eisenstein, pp. 173–189. New York: Monthly Review Press.
Garver, Valerie (2019) *A Cultural History of Work in the Medieval Age.* London: Bloomsbury.
Gehlen, Arnold (1987) *Man: His Nature and Place in the World.* Columbia: Columbia University Press.
Gentile, Dario, Elettra Gentili, and Glenda Stimilli (eds) (2018) *Italian Critical Thought. Genealogies and Categories.* London: Rowman & Littlefield.
Georgieff, Alexandre, and Anna Milanez (2021) 'What Happened to Jobs at High Risk of Automation?', OECD Social, Employment and Migration Working Papers No. 255.
Geras, Norman (1983) *Marx and Human Nature: Refutation of a Legend.* London: Verso.
Geuss, Raymond (2021) *A Philosopher Looks at Work.* Cambridge: Cambridge University Press.
Gheaus, Anca, and Lisa Herzog (2016) 'The Goods of Work (Other than Money!)' *Journal of Social Philosophy* 47(1): 70–89.
Giddens, Anthony (1992) 'Introduction'. In Max Weber, *The Protestant Ethics and the Spirit of Capitalism*, pp. vii–xxiv. London: Routledge.
Gilham, Jonathan, Lucy Rimmington, Hugh Dance, Gerard Verweij, Anand Rao, Kate Barnard Roberts, and Mark Paich (2018) 'The Macroeconomic Impact of Artificial Intelligence'. *Pricewaterhouse Coopers Report.*
Gimenez, Martha (2000) 'What's Material about Materialist Feminism? A Marxist Feminist Critique', *Radical Philosophy* 101: 18–28.
Gleeson, Loughlin, and Heikki Ikäheimo (2019) 'Hegel's Perfectionism and Freedom'. In *Perfektionismus der Autonomie*, edited by Douglas Moggach, Nadine Mooren, and Michael Quante, pp. 163–182. Leiden: Brill.

Godelier, Maurice (1980) 'Work and Its Representations: A Research Proposal', *History Workshop Journal* 10: 164–174.
Godelier, Maurice (1986 [1982]) *The Making of Great Men: Male Domination and Power among the New Guinea Baruya*. Cambridge: Cambridge University Press.
Godelier, Maurice (2007) *Au Fondement des sociétés humaines. Ce que nous apprend l'anthropologie*. Paris: Albin Michel.
Gomberg, Paul (2007) *How to Make Opportunity Equal? Race and Contributive Justice*. Oxford: Blackwell Publishing.
González-Ricoy, Inigo (2014) 'The Republican Case for Workplace Democracy', *Social Theory and Practice* 40(2): 232–254.
Goodenough, Ward (1980) *Description and Comparison in Cultural Anthropology*. Cambridge: Cambridge University Press.
Gorz, André (1980) *Ecology as Politics*. Montreal: Black Rose Books.
Gorz, André (1982) *Farewell to the Working Class: An Essay on Post-Industrial Socialism*. London: Pluto Press.
Gorz, André (1985) *Paths to Paradise: On the Liberation from Work*. London: Pluto Press.
Gorz, André (1989) *Critique of Economic Reason*. London: Verso.
Gorz, André (1994) *Capitalism, Socialism, Ecology*. London: Verso.
Gorz, André (1999) *Reclaiming Work: Beyond the Wage-Based Society*. Oxford: Polity.
Gorz, André (2018) *Ecologica*. London: Seagull Books.
Gourevitch, Alex (2013) 'Labour Republicanism and the Transformation of Work', *Political Theory* 41(4): 591–617.
Gourevitch, Alex (2014) *From Slavery to the Cooperative Commonwealth*. Cambridge: Cambridge University Press.
Graeber, David (2018) *Bullshit Jobs: A Theory*. New York: Simon & Schuster.
Gowdy, John (ed.) (1998) *Limited Wants, Unlimited Means: A Reader on Hunter-Gatherer Economics and the Environment*. Washington DC: Island Press.
Gramsci, Antonio (1992) *Selection from the Prison Notebooks*. New York: International Publishers.
Granter, Edward (2009) *Critical Social Theory and the End of Work*. London: Routledge.
Granter, Edward (2021) 'Critical Theory and the Post-Work Imaginary'. In *Experiencing the New World of Work*, edited by Jeremy Aroles, François-Xavier de Vaujany, and Karen Dale, pp. 204–226. Cambridge: Cambridge University Press.
Granter, Edward, and Jeremy Aroles (2023) 'Crisis and Utopia: André Gorz and the End of Work', *Journal of Classical Sociology* 23(2): 211–228.
Green, Francis (2007) *Demanding Work: The Paradox of Job Quality in the Affluent Economy*. Princeton: Princeton University Press.
Gruetzemacher, Ross, David Paradice, and Kang Bok Lee (2020) 'Forecasting Extreme Labor Displacement: A Survey of AI Practitioners', *Technological Forecasting and Social Change* 161: 120323.
Gruetzemacher, Ross, Florian Dorner, Niko Bernaola-Alvarez, Charlie Giattino, and David Mannheim (2021) 'Forecasting AI Progress: A Research Agenda', *Technological Forecasting and Social Change* 170: 120909.
Guy-Sheftall, Beverly (ed.) (1995) *Words of Fire: An Anthology of African-American Feminist Thought*. New York: The New Press.
Habermas, Jürgen (1971) *Toward a Rational Society. Student Protest, Science and Politics*. Translated by Jeremy Shapiro. Boston: Beacon Press.
Habermas, Jürgen (1972) *Knowledge and Human Interests*. Translated by Jeremy Shapiro. Boston: Beacon Press.
Habermas, Jürgen (1973) 'Labour and Interaction: Remarks on Hegel's Jena Philosophy of Mind'. In *Theory and Practice*. Translated by John Viertel, pp. 142–169. Boston: Beacon Press.
Habermas, Jürgen (1973) *Theory and Practice*. Translated by John Viertel. Boston: Beacon Press.
Habermas, Jürgen (1979) *Communication and the Evolution of Society*. Translated by Thomas McCarthy. Boston: Beacon Press.

Habermas, Jürgen (1984) *The Theory of Communicative Action*, volume 1: 'Reason and the Rationalisation of Society'. Thomas McCarthy. Boston: Beacon Press.
Habermas, Jürgen (1985). *The Theory of Communicative Action*, volume 2: 'Lifeworld and System: A Critique of Functionalist Reason'. Thomas McCarthy. Boston: Beacon Press.
Habermas, Jürgen (1990) 'What Does Socialism Mean Today? The Rectifying Revolution and the Need for New Thinking on the Left', *New Left Review* 83: 3–21.
Habermas, Jürgen (1994) 'The New Obscurity: The Crisis of the Welfare State and the Exhaustion of Utopian Energies'. In *The New Conservatism: Cultural Criticism and the Historians' Debate*, edited by Jürgen Habermas and Shierry Weber Nicholsen, pp. 48–70. Cambridge, Mass.: MIT Press.
Hackman, Richard, and Greg Oldham (1974) *The Job Diagnostic Survey: An Instrument for Diagnosing Jobs and Evaluating Job Redesign Projects*. Department of Administrative Sciences: Yale University.
Hahnel, Robin (2021) *Economic Democratic Planning*. London: Routledge.
Hall, Timothy (2011) 'Reification, Materialism and Praxis: Adorno's Critique of Lukacs', *Telos* 155: 61–82.
Hamacher, Werner (1996) 'Working through Working', *Modernism/Modernity* 3(1): 25–50.
Hamilton, Alastair (2000) 'Max Weber's The Protestant Work Ethic and the Spirit of Capitalism'. In *The Cambridge Companion to Weber*, edited by Steven Turner, pp. 151–171. Cambridge: Cambridge University Press.
Hardt, Michael, and Antonio Negri (2001) *Empire*. New Haven: Harvard University Press.
Harley, Sharon, and The Black Women and Work Collective (eds) (2002) *Sister Circle: Black Women and Work*. New Brunswick: Rutgers University Press.
Hartmann, Heidi (1979) 'The Unhappy Marriage of Marxism and Feminism: Towards a More Progressive Union', *Capital & Class* 3(2): 1–33.
Hartmann, Martin, and Axel Honneth (2006) 'Paradoxes of Capitalism', *Constellations* 13(1): 451–458.
Haudricourt, André-Georges (1987) *La Technologie science humaine. Recherches d'histoire et d'ethnologie des techniques*. Paris: Maison des Sciences de l'Homme.
Hawkes, Kristen (1990) 'Why Do Men Hunt? Benefits for Risky Choices'. In *Risk and Uncertainty in Tribal and Peasant Economies*, edited by Ed Cashdan, pp. 145–166. Boulder: Westview.
Hawkes, Kristen, and James O'Connell (1981) 'Affluent Hunters? Some Comments in Light of the Alyawara Case', *American Anthropologist* 83: 622–626.
Hawkes, Kristen, James O'Connell, and Nicolas Blurton Jones (2018) 'Hunter-Gatherer Studies and Human Evolution: A Very Selective Review', *American Journal of Physical Anthropology* 165: 777–800.
Hegel, G. W. F. (1984) *Lectures on the Philosophy of Religion*. Berkeley: University of California Press.
Hegel, G. W. F. (1991 [1821]) *Elements of the Philosophy of Right*. Translated by Hugh Barr Nisbet. Cambridge: Cambridge University Press.
Hegel, G. W. F. (2018 [1826]) *Vorlesungen über die Philosophie der Kunst*. Hamburg: Felix Meiner.
Heidegger, Martin (1962) *Being and Time*. Translated by John Macquarrie and Edward Robinson. Oxford: Blackwell.
Heidegger, Martin (1991) *Nietzche, volumes 1 and 2*. Translated by David Farrell Krell. San Francisco: HarperCollins.
Heidegger, Martin (1999) *Contributions (from Enowning)*. Translated by Parvis Emad. and Kenneth Maly. Bloomington: Indiana University Press.
Heidegger, Martin (2001 [lecture course of winter 1933]) *Being and Truth*. Translated by Gregory Fried and Richard Polt. Bloomington: Indiana University Press.
Heidegger, Martin (2003) 'Overcoming Metaphysics'. In *The End of Philosophy*. Translated by Joan Stambaugh. Chicago: University of Chicago Press.

Heidegger, Martin (2009 [1934 summer course]) *Logic as the Question Concerning the Essence of Language*. Translated by Wanda Torres Gregory and Yvonne Unna. New York: State University of New York Press.
Heidegger, Martin (2013 [lecture course winter 1933]) *Nature, History, State*. Translated by Gregory Fried and Richard Polt. London: Bloomsbury.
Heidegger, Martin (2014 [lecture course winter 1934]) *On Hegel's Philosophy of Right*. Translated by Andrew Mitchell. London: Bloomsbury.
Heidegger, Martin (2014 [1935]) *Introduction to Metaphysics*. Translated by Gregory Fried and Richard Polt. Yale University Press.
Heinrich, Michael (2004) *An Introduction to the Three Volumes of Karl Marx's Capital*. New York: Monthly Review Press.
Heinrich, Michael (2013) 'The "Fragment on Machines": A Marxian Misconception in the *Grundrisse* and Its Overcoming in *Capital*'. In *Marx's Laboratory. Critical Interpretations of the Grundrisse*, edited by Ricardo Bellofiore, Guido Starosta, and Peter Thomas, pp. 197–213. Leiden: Brill.
Heller, Agnes (1976) *The Theory of Need in Marx*. London: Allison and Busby.
Herzog, Lisa, and Axel Honneth (2014) *Der Wert des Markts. Ein ökonomisch-philosophischer Diskurs vom 18. Jahrhundert bis zur Gegenwart*. Berlin: Suhrkamp.
Hester, Hellen (2018) *Xenofeminism*. Cambridge: Polity.
Hester, Helen, and Will Stronge (2020) *Toward Post-work Studies: Identifying Misconceptions in an Emerging Field. Autonomy*. https://autonomy.work/portfolio/post-workmisconceptions2/.
Hester, Helen and Nick Srnicek (2023) *After Work: A History of the Home and the Fight for Free Time*. London: Verso.
Hodgkinson, Tom (2004) *How to Be Idle*. London: Hamish Hamilton.
Hoffmann, Maja, and David Frayne (2023) 'Ecological Postwork Theory'. In *Elgar Encyclopedia of Environmental Sociology*, edited by Christine Overdevest, pp. 188–194. Cheltenham: Edward Elgar Publishing.
Holloway, John (2010) *Crack Capitalism*. London: Pluto Press.
Holloway, John, Fernando Matamoros, and Sergio Tischler (eds) (2009) *Negativity and Revolution: Adorno and Political Activism*. London: Pluto Press.
Honneth, Axel (1991) *The Critique of Power: Reflective Stages in a Critical Social Theory*. Translated by Kenneth Baynes. Cambridge, Mass: MIT Press.
Honneth, Axel (1995a) 'Work and Instrumental Action: On the Normative Basis of Critical Theory'. In Axel Honneth, *The Fragmented World of the Social: Essays in Social and Political Philosophy*, pp. 15–49. New York: SUNY Press.
Honneth, Axel (1995b) *The Struggle for Recognition: The Moral Grammar of Social Conflicts*. Translated by Joel Anderson. Oxford: Polity.
Honneth, Axel (1998) 'Democracy as Reflexive Cooperation: John Dewey and the Theory of Democracy Today', *Political Theory* 26(6): 763–783.
Honneth, Axel (2012) 'Labour and Recognition: A Redefinition'. In Axel Honneth, *The I in We: Studies in the Theory of Recognition*, pp. 56–74. Cambridge: Polity.
Honneth, Axel (2014) *Freedom's Right: The Social Foundations of Democratic Life*. Translated by Joseph Ganahl. New York: Columbia University Press.
Honneth, Axel (2017) *The Idea of Socialism: Towards a Renewal*. Translated by Joseph Ganahl. Cambridge: Polity.
Honneth, Axel (2023) *Der Arbeitende Souverän: Eine Normative Theorie der Arbeit*. Berlin: Suhrkamp.
Honneth, Axel, and Hans Joas (1988) *Social Action and Human Nature*. Translated by Raymond Meyer. Cambridge: Cambridge University Press.
Honneth, Axel, and Hans Joas (eds) (1991) *Communicative Action: Essays on Jürgen Habermas' Theory of Communicative Action*. Cambridge, Mass.: MIT Press.
hooks, bell (1984) *Feminist Theory: From Margin to Center*. Cambridge, Mass.: South End Press.

hooks, bell (2000) *Feminism Is for Everybody: Passionate Politics.* Cambridge, Mass.: South End Press.
Horgan, Emilia (2021) *Lost in Work: Escaping Capitalism.* London: Pluto Press.
Horkheimer, Max (1947) *Eclipse of Reason.* Oxford: Oxford University Press.
Horkheimer, Max (2002) *Critical Theory: Selected Essays.* New York: Continuum.
Howard, Michael (2015) 'Exploitation, Labor, and Basic Income', *Analyse & Kritik* 37(1): 281–304.
Hsieh, Nien-hê (2005) 'Rawlsian Justice and Workplace Republicanism', *Social Theory and Practice* 31(1): 115–142.
Hsieh, Nien-hê (2008a) 'Workplace Democracy, Workplace Republicanism, and Economic Democracy', *Revue de Philosophie Économique* 8(2): 57–78.
Hsieh, Nien-hê (2008b) 'Justice in Production', *Journal of Political Philosophy* 16(1): 72–100.
Hull, Gloria, Patricia Bell Scott, and Barbara Smith (eds) (1982) *All the Women Are White, All the Blacks Are Men, but Some of Us Are Brave. Black Women's Studies.* Old Westbury: The Feminist Press.
Hunnicutt, Benjamin Kline (1979) 'The Jewish Sabbath Movement in the Early Twentieth Century', *American Jewish History* 69(2): 196–225.
Hunnicutt, Benjamin Kline (1988) *Work without End.* Philadelphia: Temple University Press.
Hunnicutt, Benjamin Kline (2013) *Free Time: The Forgotten American Dream.* Philadelphia: Temple University Press.
Hunnicutt, Benjamin Kline (2024) 'A History of Work as Lived Experience'. In *Debating a Post-Work Future: Perspectives from Philosophy and the Social Sciences*, edited by Denise Celentano, Michael Cholbi, Jean-Philippe Deranty, and Kory Schaff, pp. 41–60. London: Routledge.
Hurka, Thomas (1993) *Perfectionism.* Oxford: Oxford University Press.
Husserl, Edmund (1970 [1936]) *The Crisis of European Sciences and Transcendantal Phenomenology.* Translated by David Carr. Evanston: Northwestern University Press.
Hutchins, Ed (1995) *Cognition in the Wild.* Cambridge, Mass.: MIT Press.
Hwang, Tim (2018) 'Computational Power and the Social Impact of Artificial Intelligence', arXiv: 1803. 08971
Ikäheimo, Heikki (2022) *Recognition and the Human Life-Form: Beyond Identity and Difference.* London: Routledge.
Illich, Ivan (1980) 'Shadow Work', *Philosophica* 26(2): 7–46.
Illouz, Eva (2007) *Cold Intimacies: The Making of Emotional Capitalism.* Oxford: Polity Press.
International Labor Organization (2018) 'The Impact of Technology on the Quality and Quantity of Jobs'. Global Commission on the Future of Work.
Jaeggi, Rahel (2017) 'Pathologies of Work', *Women's Studies Quarterly* 45(3/4): 59–76.
Jaeggi, Rahel (2018) *Critique of Forms of Life.* Cambridge, Mass.: Harvard University Press.
Jahoda, Maria (1981) 'Work, Employment, Unemployment: Values, Theories and Approaches in Social Research', *American Psychologist* 36(2): 184–191.
Jahoda, Maria (1982) *Employment and Unemployment: A Social-Psychological Analysis.* Cambridge: Cambridge University Press.
James, David (2017) 'The Compatibility of Freedom and Necessity in Marx's Idea of a Communist Society', *European Journal of Philosophy* 25(2): 270–293.
James, David (2021) *Practical Necessity, Freedom, and History: From Hobbes to Marx.* Oxford: Oxford University Press.
James, Selma (1973) *Sex, Race and Class.* Brooklyn: Petroleuse Press.
Jaros, Stephen (2000) 'Labor Process Theory: A Commentary on the Debate', *International Studies of Management and Organization* 30(4): 25–39.
Joas, Hans (1991) 'The Unhappy Marriage of Hermeneutics and Functionalism'. In *Communicative Action: Essays on Jürgen Habermas' Theory of Communicative Action*, edited by Axel Honneth and Hans Joas, pp. 97–118. Cambridge, Mass.: MIT Press.
Jones, Jacqueline (1985) *Labor of Love, Labor of Sorrow: Black Women, Work and the Family, from Slavery to the Present.* New York: Basic Books.

Joshel, Sarah (1992) *Work, Identity, and Legal Status at Rome: A Study of the Occupational Inscriptions.* Norman: University of Oklahoma Press.

Joyce, Patrick (1987) (ed.) *The Historical Meanings of Work.* Cambridge: Cambridge University Press.

Jünger, Ernst (2017 [1932]) *The Worker.* Translated by Bogdan Costea. Evanston: Northwestern University Press.

Just, Daniel (2016) 'A Biopolitics of Immaterial Labor', *Political Studies* 64(2): 401–416.

Kandiyali, Jan (2014) 'Freedom and Necessity in Marx's Account of Communism', *British Journal for the History of Philosophy* 22(1): 104–123.

Kandiyali, Jan (2017) 'Marx on the Compatibility of Freedom and Necessity: A Reply to David James', *European Journal of Philosophy* 25(3): 833–839.

Kandiyali, Jan (2018) 'Schiller and Marx on Specialization and Self-Realization'. In *Reassessing Marx's Social and Political Philosophy: Freedom, Recognition, and Human Flourishing*, edited by Jan Kandiyali, pp. 239–260. London: Routledge.

Kandiyali, Jan (2020) 'The Importance of Others: Marx on Unalienated Production', *Ethics* 130(4): 555–587.

Kandiyali, Jan, and Paul Gomberg (2024) 'Communism Should Not be Post-Work'. In *Debating a Post-Work Future: Perspectives from Philosophy and the Social Sciences*, edited by Denise Celentano, Michael Cholbi, Jean-Philippe Deranty, and Kory Schaff, pp. 177–196. London: Routledge.

Kant, Immanuel (2017) *Metaphysics of Morals.* Translated by Mary Gregor. Cambridge: Cambridge University Press.

Kaplan, David (2000) 'The Darker Side of the "Original Affluent Society"', *Journal of Anthropological Research* 56 (3): 301–324.

Karakilic, Emrah (2022) 'Why Do Humans Remain Central to the Knowledge Work in the Age of Robots? Marx's Fragment on Machines and Beyond', *Work, Employment and Society* 36(1): 179–189.

Kelly, Robert (1995) *The Foraging Spectrum: Diversity in Hunter-Gatherer Lifeways.* Washington: Smithsonian Institution Press.

Kicillof, Axel, and Guido Starosta (2007) 'On Materiality and Social Form: A Political Critique of Rubin's Value-Form Theory', *Historical Materialism* 15(3): 9–43.

Kicillof, Axel, and Guido Starosta (2011) 'On Value and Abstract Labour: A Reply to Werner Bonefeld', *Capital and Class* 35(2): 295–305.

Kimball, Bruce A. (2010) *The Liberal Arts Tradition: A Documentary History.* Lanham: University Press of America.

Klagge, James (1986) 'Marx's Realms of "Freedom" and "Necessity"', *Canadian Journal of Philosophy* 16(4): 769–778.

Knights, David, and Hugh Willmott (1989) 'Power and Subjectivity at Work: From Degradation to Subjugation in Social Relations', *Sociology* 23(4): 535–558.

Kohn, Melvin, and Carmi Schooler (1982) 'Job Conditions and Personality: A Longitudinal Assessment of Their Reciprocal Effects', *American Journal of Sociology* 87(6): 1257–1286.

Kohn, Melvin, and Carmi Schooler (1983) *Work and Personality: An Inquiry into the Impact of Social Stratification.* Norwood: Ablex Publishing.

Kohn, Samuel (2004) *Popular Protest in Late Medieval Europe.* Manchester: Manchester University Press.

Kohn, Samuel (2006) *Lust for Liberty. The Politics of Social Revolt in Medieval Europe, 1200–1425.* Cambridge, Mass.: Harvard University Press.

Komlosy, Andrea (2018) *Work: The Last 1,000 Years.* London: Verso.

Konitzer, Werner, and David Palme (2016) *'Arbeit', 'Volk', 'Gemeinschaft'. Ethik und Ethiken im Nationalsozialismus.* Frankfurt am Main: Campus Verlag.

Kornhauser, Arthus (1962) ‚Toward an Assessment of the Mental Health of Factory Workers: A Detroit Study', *Human Organization* 21(1). 43–46.

Korsch, Karl (1977) *Politische Texte: Arbeitsrecht für Betriebsräte*. Hamburg: Europäische Verlaganstalt.
Korsgaard, Kristin (2008) *The Constitution of Agency: Essays on Practical Reason and Moral Psychology*. Oxford: Oxford University Press.
Krause, Sharon (2013) 'Beyond Non-Domination: Agency, Inequality, and the Meaning of Freedom', *Philosophy & Social Criticism* 39(2): 187–208.
Kurtz, Donald (1994) 'Winnowing the "Great Kalahari Debate"; Its Impact on Hunter-Gatherer Studies', *Political and Legal Anthropology Review* 17(10): 67–80.
Kuruma, Samezo (1957) *Theory of the Value-Form and Theory of the Exchange Process*. Tokyo. Tokyo: Iwanami Shoten.
Kymlicka, Will (2002) *Contemporary Political Philosophy*. Oxford: Oxford University Press.
Labb, Mickael (2022) 'Le travail chez Simone Weil: réalité, subjectivité, liberté'. In *Histoire Philosophique du Travail*, edited by Franck Fischbach, Anne Merker, Pierre-Marie Moral, and Emmanuel Renault, pp. 309–328. Paris: Vrin.
Lafargue, Paul (2012 [1883]) *The Right to be Lazy*. Chicago: Charles Kerr.
Lahire, Bernard (2011) *The Plural Actor*. London: Wiley.
Landemore, Helen, and Isabelle Ferreras (2016) 'In Defense of Workplace Democracy: Towards a Justification of the Firm-State Analogy', *Political Theory* 44(1): 53–81.
Lane, Marguerita, and Anne Saint-Martin (2021) 'The Impact of Artificial Intelligence on the Labour Market: What Do We Know So Far?'. OECD Social, Employment and Migration Working Papers no. 256.
Laslett, Barbara, and Johanna Brenner (1989) 'Gender and Social Reproduction: Historical Perspectives', *Annual Review of Sociology* 15: 381–404.
Lazarsfeld, Paul, and Anthony Oberschall (1965) ‚Max Weber and Empirical Social Research', *American Sociological Review* 30(2): 185–199.
Le Goff, Jacques (1980) *Time, Work and Culture in the Middle Ages*. Chicago: University of Chicago Press.
Le Goff, Jacques (1982) *La Civilisation de l'occident médiéval*. Paris: Flammarion.
Lee, Richard (1979) *The !Kung San: Men, Women, and Work in a Foraging Society*. Cambridge: Cambridge University Press.
Lee, Richard, and DeVore, Irene (eds) (1968) *Man the Hunter*. London: Routledge.
Legrand, Stéphane (2007) *Les Normes chez Foucault*. Paris: Presses Universitaires de France.
Le Lay, Stéphane (ed.) (2021) 'Le jugement France Télécom : un tournant juridique historique?', *Travailler* 46: 7–164.
Le Lay, Stéphane (2022) *Jouez! Le travail à l'ère du management distractif*. Paris: CNRS Editions.
Lelle, Nikolas (2016) '"Hinter dem Ruf nach deutscher Arbeit verschanzt sich die Volksgemeinschaft". Überlegungen zu einem vernachlässigten Element des Nationalsozialismus'. In *Schiefheilungen. Zeitgenössische Betrachtungen über Antisemitismus*, edited by Charlotte Busch, Martin Gehrlein, and Tom David Uhlig, pp. 179–200. Wiesbaden: Springer.
Lelle, Nikolas (2019) 'Arbeit, (Un)Freiheit, Tod. Erwiderungen von Jean Améry, Primo Levi und Tibor Wohl auf die KZ-Devise "Arbeit macht frei"', *Zeitschrift fur Geschichtswissenschaft* 67: 538–551.
Lelle, Nikolas (2022) *Arbeit, Dienst und Führung: Der Nationalsozialismus und sein Erbe*. Berlin: Verbrecher Verlag.
Lerner, Gerda (1986) *The Creation of Patriarchy*. Oxford: Oxford University Press.
Leroi-Gourhan, André (1943) *L'Homme et la matière*. Paris: Albin Michel.
Leroi-Gourhan, André (1945) *Milieu et techniques*. Paris: Albin Michel.
Lévinas, Emmanuel (1979) *Totality and Infinity*. Translated by Alphonso Lingis. Leiden: Martinus Nijhoff.
Levine, Andrew (1995) 'Fairness to Idleness: Is There a Right Not to Work?' *Economics and Philosophy* 11: 255–274.
Lewis, Kyle, Will Stronge, Jack Kellam, and Lukas Kikuchi (2023) 'The Results Are In: The UK's Four-Day Week Pilot'. *Autonomy*, https://autonomy.work/wp-content/uploads/2023/02/The-results-are-in-The-UKs-four-day-week-pilot.pdf.

Liesen, Laurette (2017) 'Women, Behavior, and Evolution: Understanding the Debate Between Feminist Evolutionists and Evolutionary Psychologists', *Politics and the Life Sciences* 26(1): 51–70.
Lips-Wiersma, Marjolein, and Sarah Wright (2012) 'Measuring the Meaning of Meaningful Work: Development and Validation of the Comprehensive Meaningful Work Scale (CMWS)', *Group & Organization Management* 37(5): 655–685.
Lis, Catharina, and Hugo Soly (2016) 'Work, Identity and Self-Representation in the Roman Empire and the West-European Middle Ages: Different Interplays between the Social and the Cultural'. In *Work, Labour and Professions in the Roman World*, edited by Koenraad Verboven and Christian Laes, pp. 262–290. Leiden: Brill.
Little, David (1970) *Religion, Order and Law*. Oxford: Oxford University Press.
Livingstone, James (2017) *Fuck Work*. London: Verso.
Lucassen, Jan (ed.) (2006) *Global Labour History: A State of the Art*. Lausanne: Peter Lang.
Lucassen, Jan (2021) *The Story of Work: A New History of Humankind*. New Haven: Yale University Press.
Lucassen, Jan, Tine De Moore, and Jan Luiten van Zanden (eds) (2008) *The Return of the Guilds*. Cambridge: Cambridge University Press.
Lukács, György (1972 [1923]) *History and Class Consciousness: Studies in Marxist Dialectics*. Translated by Rodney Livingstone. Cambridge, Mass.: MIT Press.
Lytle, Ephraim (ed.) (2019) *Cultural History of Work: Antiquity*. London: Bloomsbury.
Lytle, Ephraim (2019) 'Introduction'. In *Cultural History of Work: Antiquity*, edited by Ephraim Lytle, pp. 1–18. London. Bloomsbury.
MacIntyre, Alasdair (1979) 'Social Science Methodology as the Ideology of Bureaucratic Authority' In *Through the Looking Glass: Epistemology and the Conduct of Enquiry*, edited by Maria Falco, pp. 42–58. Lanham: University Press of America.
MacIntyre, Alasdair (2007) *After Virtue* (3rd ed.). London: Duckworth.
MacIntyre, Alasdair (2016) *Ethics in the Conflicts of Modernity*. Cambridge: Cambridge University Press.
Mackenzie, Catriona, and Nathalie Stoljar (eds) (2000) *Relational Autonomy: Feminist Perspectives on Autonomy, Agency and the Social Self*. Oxford: Oxford University Press.
Mackinnon, Catherine (1989) *Toward a Feminist Theory of the State*. Cambridge, Mass.: Harvard University Press.
Mackinnon, Malcolm H. (1988) 'Calvinism and the Infallible Assurance of Grace', *British Journal of Sociology* 39(2): 143–177.
Malinowski, Bronislaw (2014 [1922]) *Argonauts of the Western Pacific*. London: Routledge.
Manning, Alan (2003) *Monopsony in Motion: Imperfect Competition in Labor Markets*. Princeton: Princeton University Press.
Marcuse, Herbert (1966 [1955]) *Eros and Civilization. A Philosophical Inquiry into Freud*. New York: Beacon Press.
Marcuse, Herbert (1970 [1941]) *Reason and Revolution: Hegel and the Rise of Social Theory*. New York: Beacon Press.
Marcuse, Herbert (2002 [1964]) *One-Dimensional Man: Studies in the Ideology of Advanced Industrial Society*. London: Routledge.
Marcuse, Herbert (2007) *Art and Liberation*. London: Routledge.
Márkus, György (1978) *Marxism and Anthropology: The Concept of Human Essence in the Philosophy of Marx*. Assen: Van Gocum.
Márkus, György (2011) 'Beyond the Dichotomy Praxis and Poiesis'. In *György Márkus, Culture, Science, Society: The Constitution of Cultural Modernity*, pp. 37–57. Leiden: Brill.
Martin, Bernd (ed.) (1989) *Martin Heidegger und das dritte Reich*. Darmstadt: Wissenschaftliche Buchgesellschaft.
Marx, Karl (1973 [1857]) *Grundrisse: Introduction to the Critique of Political Economy*. Translated by Martin Nicolaus. London: Penguin.
Marx, Karl (1981 [1894]) *Capital*, volume 3. Translated by David Fernbach. London: Penguin.

Marx, Karl (1988 [1861–1863]) *Economic Manuscripts*, volume 30. London: Lawrence & Wishart.
Marx, Karl (1991 [1867]) *Capital*, volume 1. Translated by Ben Fowkes. London: Penguin.
Marx, Karl (2000) *Selected Writings*. Oxford: Oxford University Press.
Marx, Karl (2000 [1844a]) 'On James Mill'. In Karl Marx, *Selected Writings*, pp. 124–133.
Marx, Karl (2000 [1844b]) Economic and Philosophic Manuscripts of 1844. In Karl Marx, *Selected Writings*, pp. 83–121.
Marx, Karl (2000 [1875]). 'Critique of the Gotha Program'. In Karl Marx. *Selected Writings*, pp. 610–616.
Marx, Karl, and Friedrich Engels (2000 [1845–1846]) The German Ideology. In Karl Marx, *Selected Writings*, pp. 175–208.
Marx, Karl and Friedrich Engels (2010) *Letters 1868–1870*. Marx and Engels Collected Works, volume 43. London: Lawrence and Wishart.
Mason, Paul (2015) *Postcapitalism. A Guide to our Future*. London: Penguin.
Mauss, Marcel (1973 [1936]) 'Techniques of the Body', *Economy and Society* 2: 70–88.
McCarthy, Thomas (1978) *The Critical Theory of Jürgen Habermas*. Cambridge, Mass.: MIT Press.
McKinlay, Alan (2013) 'Managing Foucault: Genealogies of Management', *Management & Organizational History* 1(1): 87–100.
McKinlay, Alan, and Ken Starkey (1998) 'Managing Foucault: Foucault, Management and Organisation Theory'. In *Foucault, Management and Organisation Theory*, edited by Alan McKinlay and Ken Starkey, pp. 1–13. London: Sage.
Méda, Dominique (1995) *Le Travail une valeur en voie de disparition*. Paris: Aubier.
Méda, Dominique and Vendramin, Patricia (2017) *Reinventing Work in Europe*. London: Palgrave Macmillan.
Merleau-Ponty, Maurice (1946 [1964]) *Sense and Non-Sense*. Translated by Hubert Dreyfus and Patricia Allen Dreyfus. Evanston: Northwestern University Press.
Merleau-Ponty, Maurice (2012 [1945]) *Phenomenology of Perception*. Translated by Donald Landes. London: Routledge.
Mezzadri, Alessandra (2019) 'On the Value of Social Reproduction', *Radical Philosophy*, 2(4): 33–41.
Mezzadri, Alexandra (2020) 'The Informal Labours of Social Reproduction', *Global Labour Journal* 11(1): 156–163.
Mies, Maria (1982) *The Lace Makers of Narsapur: Indian Housewives Produce for the World Market*. London: Zed Books.
Mies, Maria (1986) *Patriarchy and Accumulation on a World Scale: Women and the International Division of Labour*. London: Zed Books.
Mies, Maria (1988) *Women: The Last Colony*. London: Zed Books.
Mies, Maria, and Zandana Shiva (2014 [1993]) *Ecofeminism*. London: Zed Books.
Mokyr, Joel (2018) 'The Past and the Future of Innovation: Lessons from Economic History', *Explorations in Economic History* 69: 13–26.
Molinier, Pascale (2006) *Les Enjeux psychiques du travail*. Paris: Payot.
Molinier, Pascale (2013) *Le Travail du care*. Paris: La Découverte.
Monahan, Torin, and David Murakami Wood (2018) *Surveillance Studies: A Reader*. Oxford: Oxford University Press.
Morris, William (1993 [1884]) *News from Nowhere and Other Writings*. London: Penguin.
Mueller, Gavin (2021) *Breaking Things at Work*. London: Verso.
Muirhead, Russell (2007) *Just Work*. Cambridge, Mass: Harvard University Press.
Mukhopadhay, Carol, and Patricia Higgins (1988) 'Anthropological Studies of Women's Status Revisited: 1977–1987', *Annual Review of Anthropology* 17: 461–495.
Mumby, Dennis, Robyn Thomas, Ignasi Martin, and David Seidl (2017) 'Resistance Redux', *Organization Studies* 38(9): 1157–1183.
Münch, Richard (1982) 'Talcott Parsons and the Theory of Action. II. The Continuity of the Development', *American Journal of Sociology* 87(4): 771–826.
Munro, Kirstin (2019) 'Social Reproduction Theory, Social Reproduction and Household Production', *Science and Society* 83(4): 451–468.

Murphy, James Bernard (1993) *The Moral Economy of Labour*. New Haven: Yale University Press.

Musgrave, Richard (1974) 'Maximin, Uncertainty and the Leisure Trade-off', *Quarterly Journal of Economics* 88: 632–653.

Nancy, Jean-Luc (1986) *The Inoperative Community*. Translated by Peter Connor, Lisa Garbus, Michael Holland, and Simona Sawhney. Minneapolis: University of Minnesota Press.

Nancy, Jean-Luc (2000) *Being Singular Plural*. Translated by Robert Richardson and Anne O'Byrne. Redwood City: Stanford University Press.

Negri, Toni (1991 [1973]) *Marx Beyond Marx. Lessons on the Grundrisse*. Translated by Michael Ryan, Mauricio Viano, and Harry Cleaver. London: Pluto Press.

Negri, Antonio (2009) 'An Italian Rupture: Production against Development', *diacritics* 39(3): 21–27.

Nicholson, Linda (1999) 'Feminism and Marx: Integrating Kinship with the Economic'. In Linda Nicholson, *The Play of Reason*, pp. 29–42. Ithaca: Cornell University Press.

Nieswandt, Barbara (2022) 'Automation, Basic Income and Merit'. In *Politics and Ethics of Contemporary Work: Whither Work?*, edited by Keith Breen and Jean-Philippe Deranty, pp. 102–120. London: Routledge.

Nietzsche, Friedrich (1968 [1901]) *The Will to Power*. Translated by Reginald John Hollingdale and Walter Kaufman. New York: Vintage Books.

Nietzsche, Friedrich (1989 [1887]) *The Genealogy of Morals*. Translated by Walter Kaufman. New York: Vintage Books.

Nietzsche, Friedrich (1996 [1878]) *Human, All Too Human: A Book for Free Spirits*. Translated by Reginald John Hollingdale. Cambridge: Cambridge University Press.

Nietzsche, Friedrich (2001 [1882]) *The Gay Science*. Translated by Josefine Nauckhoff. Cambridge: Cambridge University Press.

Nietzsche, Friedrich (2006 [1883–1885/1888]) *Thus Spoke Zarathustra. A Book for None and All*. Translated by Adrian Del Caro. Cambridge: Cambridge University Press.

Noonan, Jeff (2020) 'Luddites, Labor, and Meaningful Lives: Would a World without Work Really Be Best', *Journal of Social Philosophy* 51(3): 441–456.

Nun, Jose (2000) 'The End of Work and the "Marginal Mass" Thesis', *Latin American Perspectives* 27(1): 6–32.

Nussbaum, Martha (2011) 'Perfectionist Liberalism and Political Liberalism', *Philosophy & Public Affairs* 39(1): 3–45.

Nussbaum, Martha (2012) *Women and Human Development*. Cambridge: Cambridge University Press.

O'Connor, Brian (2018) *Idleness: A Philosophical Essay*. Princeton: Princeton University Press.

O'Doherty, Damian, and Hugh Willmott (2001) 'Debating Labour Process Theory: The Issue of Subjectivity and the Relevance of Post-Structuralism', *Sociology* 35(2): 457–476.

Offe, Claus (1985) *Disorganised Capitalism. Contemporary Transformations of Work and Politics*. Cambridge: Polity Press.

Offe, Claus (1996) *Modernity and the State: East, West*. Cambridge: Polity Press.

Oliva, Antonio, Oliva Angel, and Ivan Novara (eds) (2020) *Marx and Contemporary Critical Theory. The Philosophy of Real Abstractions*. London: Palgrave Macmillan.

Ott, Hugo (1988) *Martin Heidegger. Unterwegs zu seiner Biographie*. Frankfurt am Main: Campus Verlag.

Parfit, Derek (1984) *Reasons and Persons*. Oxford: Oxford University Press.

Parsons, Talcott (1991 [1951]) *The Social System*. London: Routledge.

Parsons, Talcott, and Robert Freed Bales (1953) *Working Papers in the Theory of Action*. Glencoe: Free Press.

Pateman, Carole (1970) *Participation and Democratic Theory*. Cambridge: Cambridge University Press.

Pateman, Carole (1988) 'The Patriarchal Welfare State'. In *Democracy and the Welfare State*, edited by Amy Gutmann, pp. 231–260. Princeton: Princeton University Press.

Patten, Alan (1999) *Hegel's Idea of Freedom*. Oxford: Oxford University Press.

Pérez-Muñoz, Cristian (1996) 'A Defence of Participation Income', *Journal of Public Policy* 36(2): 169–193.
Pettinger, Lynne (2019) *What's Wrong with Work?* Bristol: Bristol University Press.
Pfannebecker Mareile, and Jason Smith (2020) *Work Want Work. Labour and Desire at the End of Capitalism*. London: Bloomsbury.
Pico della Mirandola, Giovanni (2012 [1496]) *Oration on the Dignity of Man: A New Translation and Commentary*. Francesco Borghesi, Michael Papio, and Massimo Riva. Cambridge: Cambridge University Press.
Pieper, Joseph (1998 [1948]) *Leisure, the Basis of Culture*. Translated by Alexander Dru. South's Bend: St Augustine's Press.
Plato (2013) *The Republic*. Translated by Christopher Emlyn-Jones nd William Preddy. Cambridge, Mass.: Harvard University Press.
Polt, Richard (2014) 'Hitler the Anti-Nihilist? Statehood, Leadership, and Political Space in Heidegger's Seminar of 1933–34', *European Review* 22(2): 231–243.
Polt, Richard (2019) *Time and Trauma. Thinking through Heidegger in the Thirties*. Lanham: Rowman & Littlefield.
Porcher, Frédéric (2002) 'Nietzsche, penseur du travail?' In *Histoire Philosophique du Travail*, edited by Franck Fischbach et al., pp. 269–288. Paris: Vrin.
Postone, Moishe (1993) *Time, Labor, and Social Domination*. Cambridge: Cambridge University Press.
Povinelli, Elizabeth (1994) *Labor's Lot: The Power, History, and Culture of Aboriginal Action*. Chicago: University of Chicago Press.
Purdy, Mark, and Paul Daugherty (2016) 'Why Artificial Intelligence Is the Future of Growth', *Accenture*. Available at: dl.icdst.org/pdfs/files2/2aea5d87070f0116f8aaa9f545530e47.pdf
Quinn, Naomi (1977) 'Anthropological Studies of Women's Status', *Annual Review of Anthropology* 6: 181–225.
Raffnsøe, Sverre, Andrea Mennicken, and Peter Miller (2019) 'The Foucault Effect in Organization Studies', *Organization Studies* 40(2): 155–182.
Rawls, John (1974) 'A Reply to Alexander and Musgrave', *The Quarterly Journal of Economics* 88(4): 633–655.
Rawls, John (1988) 'The Priority of Right and Ideas of the Good', *Philosophy and Public Affairs* 17: 251–276.
Rawls, John (1996) *Political Liberalism*. New York: Columbia University Press.
Rawls, John (1999) *A Theory of Justice* (revised ed.). Cambridge, Mass.: Harvard University Press.
Read, Jason (2003) *The Micropolitics of Capital*. New York: SUNY Press.
Renault, Emmanuel (2007) 'Reconnaissance et travail', *Travailler* 18: 119–135.
Renault, Emmanuel (2018) 'Travail et interaction. Origines et implications d'une distinction'. In *Dialogues avec Jürgen Habermas*, edited by Isabelle Auber and Jean-François Kervégan, pp. 117–128. Paris: CNRS Editions.
Renault, Emmanuel (2019) *The Experience of Injustice. A Theory of Recognition*. New York: Columbia University Press.
Renault, Emmanuel (2022) *Dewey et le travail*. Paris: Vrin.
Renault, Emmanuel (2023) *Abolir l'exploitation. Expériences, théories, stratégies*. Paris: La Découverte.
Rice, Christophe (2013) 'Defending the Objective List Theory of Well-Being', *Ratio* 26, 196–211.
Rifkin, Jeremy (1995) *The End of Work: The Decline of the Global Labor Force and the Dawn of the Post-Market Era*. New York: Putnam Publishing.
Roberts, Michael James (2019) 'Twilight of Work: The Labor Question in Nietzsche and Marx', *Critical Sociology* 45(2): 267–280.
Robertson, Ivan, and Cary Cooper (2011) *Well-Being: Productivity and Happiness at Work*. London: Palgrave Macmillan.
Rockmore, Tom (1992) *On Heidegger's Nazism and Philosophy*. Oakland: University of California Press.

Roessler, Beate (2012) 'Meaningful Work: Arguments from Autonomy', *The Journal of Political Philosophy* 20(1): 71–93.
Rose, Julie (2016) *Free Time*. Princeton: Princeton University Press.
Rosser, Gervase (2015) *The Art of Solidarity in the Middle Ages*. Oxford: Oxford University Press.
Rubin, Isaak (1972 [1923]) *Essays on Marx's Theory of Value*. Detroit: Black and Red.
Russell, Bertrand (1932) 'In Praise of Idleness', *Harper's Magazine*.
Ryan, Richard, and Edward Deci (2017) *Self-Determination Theory: Basic Psychological Needs in Motivation, Development, and Wellness*. New York: Guilford.
Sahlins, Marshall (1974) *Stone Age Economics*. New York: de Gruyter.
Sahlins, Marshall (1998 [1972]) 'The Original Affluent Society'. In *Limited Wants, Unlimited Means: A Reader on Hunter-Gatherer Economics and the Environment*, edited by John Gowdy, pp. 5–41. Washington DC: Island Press.
Sakolsky, Ron (2009 [1992]) 'Disciplinary Power, the Labor Process, and the Constitution of the Laboring Subject', *Rethinking Marxism* 5(4): 114–126.
Salzinger, Leslie (2003) *Genders in Production: Making Workers in Mexico's Global Factories*. Oakland: University of California Press.
Saniee, Iraj, Sanjay Kamat, Subra Prakash, and Marcus Weldon (2017) 'Will Productivity Growth Return in the New Digital Era', *Bell Labs Technical Journal* 22: 1–18.
Sapirstein, Philip (2019) 'Work, Skill and Technology'. In *A Cultural History of Work in Antiquity*, edited by Ephraim Lytle, pp. 95–112. London: Bloomsbury.
Sayers, Sean (2006) 'Freedom and the "Realm of Necessity"'. In *The New Hegelians: Politics and Philosophy in the Hegelian School*, edited by Douglas Moggach, pp. 261–274. Cambridge: Cambridge University Press.
Sayers, Sean (2011) *Marx and Alienation: Essays on Hegelian Themes*. Basingstoke: Palgrave Macmillan.
Scanlon, Thomas (1998) *What We Owe Each Other*. Cambridge, Mass.: Harvard University Press.
Schatz, Holger, and Andrea Woeldike (2001) *Freiheit und Wahn deutscher Arbeit. Zur historischen Aktualität einer folgenreichen antisemitischen Projektion*. Hamburg: UN-Rast Verlag.
Scheidel, Walter, Ian Morris, and Richard Saller (eds) (2007) *The Cambridge Economic History of the Greco-Roman World*. Cambridge: Cambridge University Press.
Schiller, Friedrich (2005) *Letters on the Aesthetic Education of Man*. Translated by Reginald Snell. New York: Continuum.
Schmidt-am-busch, Hans-Christoph (2001). *Hegel's Begriff der Arbeit*. Berlin: De Gruyter.
Schneider, Michael (1999) *Unterm Hakenkreuz. Arbeiter und Arbeiterbewegung, 1933 bis 1939*. Bonn: Dietz Verlag.
Schutz, Alfred (1989) *The Structures of the Life-World*, volume 2. Translated by Richard Zaner and David Parent. Evanston: Northwestern University Press.
Schwartz, Adina (1982) 'Meaningful Work', *Ethics* 92(4): 634–646.
Schweikart, David (2011) *After Capitalism*. Lanham: Rowmann and Littlefield.
Scoville, James (2001) 'The Taylorisation of Vladimir Illich Lenin', *Industrial Relations* 40(4): 620–626.
Searle, John (1995) *The Construction of Social Reality*. New York: The Free Press.
Sedgwick, Peter (2007) *Nietzsche's Economy: Modernity, Normativity and Futurity*. London: Palgrave Macmillan.
Sennett, Richard (1998) *The Corrosion of Character: The Personal Consequences of Work in the New Capitalism*. New York: W. W. Horton and Company.
Sewell, Graham, and Barry Wilkinson (1992) "Someone to Watch over Me': Surveillance, Discipline and the Just-in-Time Labour Process', *Sociology* 26(2): 271–289.
Shaw, Christopher (1991) 'William Morris and the Division of Labour: The Idea of Work in *News from Nowhere*', *Journal of William Morris Studies* 9(3): 19–30.
Shaw, Stephanie (1996) *What a Woman Ought to Be and Do*. Chicago: University of Chicago Press.
Sigaut, François (1990) 'Folie, réel et technologie', *Techniques et Culture* 15: 167–179.
Sigaut, François (1999) 'Deux Leçons d'Haudricourt', *Techniques et Culture* 33: 185–187.

Sigaut, François (2002) 'La Formule de Mauss', *Techniques et Culture* 40: 143–168.
Silver, Beverly, and Lu Zhang (2009) 'China as an Emerging Epicenter of World Labor Unrest'. In *China and the Transformation of Global Capitalism*, edited by Ho-Fung Hung, pp. 174–187. Baltimore: Johns Hopkins University Press.
Simmel, Georg (1989) *Gesamtausgabe*, volume 2: *Aufsätze 1887 bis 1890*. Frankfurt am Main: Suhrkamp.
Simmel, Georg (2004 [1907]) *The Philosophy of Money*. Translated by Tom Bottomore and David Frisby. London: Routledge.
Sinnicks, Matthew (2021) '"We Ought to Eat in Order to Work, Not Vice-Versa": MacIntyre, Practices and the Best Work for Humankind', *Journal of Business Ethics* 174: 263–274.
Smith, Adam (1999 [1776]) *The Wealth of Nations*. London: Penguin.
Smith, Bonnie (2004) *Women's History in Global Perspective*. Chicago: University of Illinois Press.
Smith, Jason (2020) *Smart Machines and Service Work: Automation in an Age of Stagnation*. London: Reaktion Books.
Smith, Nicholas (2009) 'Work and the Struggle for Recognition', *European Journal of Political Theory* 8(1): 46–60.
Smith, Nicholas (2012) 'Work as a Sphere of Norms. Paradoxes and Ideologies of Recognition'. In *Recognition Theory as Social Research. Investigating the Dynamics of Social Conflict*, edited by Shane O'Neill and Nicholas Smith, pp. 87–108. London: Palgrave Macmillan.
Smith, Nicholas (2017) 'Arendt's Anti-Humanism of Labour', *European Journal of Social Theory* 22(2): 175–190.
Smith, Nicholas (2019) 'Work as a Realm of Social Freedom'. In *The Politics and Ethics of Contemporary Work: Whither Work?*, edited by Keith Breen and Jean-Philippe Deranty, pp. 16–30. London: Routledge.
Smith, Nicholas, and Jean-Philippe Deranty (eds) (2012a). *New Philosophies of Labour: Work and the Social Bond*. Leiden: Brill.
Smith, Nicholas, and Jean-Philippe Deranty (2012b) 'Work, Recognition and the Social Bond: The Renaissance of a Paradigm'. In *New Philosophies of Labour: Work and the Social Bond*, edited by Nicholas Smith and Jean-Philippe Deranty, pp. 1–38. Leiden: Brill.
Smith, Nicholas, and Jean-Philippe Deranty (2012c) 'Work and the Politics of Misrecognition', *Res Publica. A Journal of Legal, Moral and Social Philosophy* 18: 53–64.
Sohn-Rethel, Alfred (1971) *Warenform und Denkform*. Frankfurt: Europäische Verlagsanstalt.
Sohn-Rethel, Alfred (1978) *Intellectual and Manual Labour: A Critical Epistemology*. London: Palgrave Macmillan.
Solms-Laubach, Franz Graf zu (2007) *Nietzsche and Early German and Austrian Sociology*. Berlin: Walter de Gruyter.
Sombart, Werner (2015 [1911]) *The Jews and Modern Capitalism*. Mansfiled: Martino Fine Books.
Spencer, David (2022) *Making Light Work: An End to Toil in the Twenty-First Century*. Oxford: Polity.
Spittler, Gerd (1990) 'La Notion de travail chez les Kel Ewey', *Revue du Monde Musulman et de la Méditerranée* 57: 189–198.
Spittler, Gerd (2016) *Anthropologie der Arbeit: Ein ethnographischer Vergleich*. Lausanne: Springer.
Squicciarini, Mariagrazia, and Jacopo Staccioli (2022) 'Labour-Saving Technologies and Employment Levels: Are Robots Really Making Workers Redundant?', OECD Science, Technology and Industry Policy Papers 124.
Srnicek, Nick, and Alex Williams (2015) *Inventing the Future: Postcapitalism and a World without Work*. London: Penguin Random House.
Stabel, Peter (2019) 'Workplace Cultures'. In *A Cultural History of Work in the Medieval Age*, edited by Ephraim Lytle, pp. 85–98. London: Bloomsbury.
Standing, Guy (2016) *The Precariat: The New Dangerous Class*. London: Bloomsbury.
Sterelny, Kim (2012) *The Evolved Apprentice*. Cambridge, Mass.: MIT Press.
Sterelny, Kim (2021) *The Pleistocene Social Contract. Culture and Cooperation in Human Evolution*. Oxford: Oxford University Press.

Storey, David (2015) *Naturalizing Heidegger: His Confrontation with Nietzsche, His Contributions to Environmental Philosophy*. New York: SUNY Press.
Strangleman, Tim (2007) 'The Nostalgia for Permanence at Work? The End of Work and Its Commentators', *The Sociological Review* 55(1): 81–103.
Suzman, James (2022) *Work: A Deep History from the Stone Age to the Age of Robots*. London: Penguin.
Susskind, Daniel (2020) *A World without Work: Technology, Automation and How We Should Respond*. New York: Metropolitan Books.
Susskind, Richard, and Daniel Susskind (2015) *The Future of the Professions: How Technology Will Transform the Work of Human Experts*. Oxford: Oxford University Press.
Tilly, Charles, and Chris Tilly (1998). *Work under Capitalism*. London: Taylor & Francis.
Toupin, Louise (2018) *Wages for Housework*. London: Pluto Press.
Tran, Nicolas (2016) '*Ars* and *Doctrina*: The Socioeconomic Identity of Roman Skilled Workers (First Century BC–Third Century AD)'. In *Work, Labour and Professions in the Roman World*, edited by Koenraad Verboven and Christian Laes, pp. 246–261. Leiden: Brill.
Tronti, Mario (2019 [1965]) *Workers and Capital*. Translated by David Broder. London: Verso.
Turner, Ben (2024) 'Post-Work and the Problem of Recognition: A Defence of Working Time Reduction'. In *Debating a Post-Work Future: Perspectives from Philosophy and the Social Sciences*, edited by Denise Celentano, Michael Cholbi, Jean-Philippe Deranty, and Kory Schaff, pp. 240–261. London: Routledge.
Tyssedal, Jens Jorund (2023) 'Good Work: The Importance of Caring about Making a Social Contribution', *Politics, Philosophy & Economics*, OnlineFirst, 18 January 2023.
Uno, Kozo (1980) *Principles of Political Economy. Theory of a Purely Capitalist Society*. Translated by T. Sekine. Brighton: Harverster Press.
Vallas, Steven Peter (2012) *Work. A Critique*. Cambridge: Polity Press.
Van Parijs, Philippe (1991) 'Why Surfers Should Be Fed: The Liberal Case for an Unconditional Basic Income', *Philosophy & Public Affairs* 20(2): 101–131.
Van Parijs, Philippe (1995) *Real Freedom for All. What (if Anything) Can Justify Capitalism?* Oxford: Oxford University Press.
Vatin, François (1993) *Le travail. Économie et physique, 1780–1830*. Paris: Presses Universitaires de France.
Veltman, Andrea (2010) 'Simone de Beauvoir and Hannah Arendt on Labor', *Hypathia* 25(1): 55–78.
Veltman, Andrea (2016) *Meaningful Work*. Oxford: Oxford University Press.
Verboven, Koenraad (2016) 'Guilds and the Organisation of Urban Populations during the Principate'. In *Work, Labour and Professions in the Roman World*, edited by Koenraad Verboven and Christian Laes, pp. 173–202. Leiden: Brill.
Verboven, Koenraad (2019) 'Workplace Cultures'. In *A Cultural History of Work in Antiquity*, edited by Ephraim Lytle, pp. 73–94. London: Bloomsbury.
Verboven, Koenraad, and Christian Laes (eds) (2016) *Work, Labour and Professions in the Roman World*. Leiden: Brill.
Verboven, Koenraad, and Christian Laes (2016) 'Work, Labour, Professions. What's in a Name?' In *Work, Labour and Professions in the Roman World*, edited by Koenraad Verboven and Christian Laes, pp. 1–19. Leiden: Brill.
Vernant, Jean-Pierre (2006) 'Work and Technological Thought'. In Jean-Pierre Vernant, *Myth and Thought among the Greeks*, pp. 263–320. Translated by Janet Lloyd Jeff Fort. New York: Zone Books.
Vincent, Jean-Marie (1987) *Critique du Travail. Le Faire et l'Agir*. Paris: Presses Universitaires de France.
Vogel, Lise (1983) *Marxism and the Oppression of Women: Toward a Unitary Theory*. Leiden: Brill.
Vogler, Candace (2002) *Reasonably Vicious*. Cambridge, Mass.: Harvard University Press.
Vrousalis, Nicholas (2019) 'Workplace Democracy Implies Economic Democracy', *Journal of Social Philosophy* 50(3): 259–279.

Waguespack, Nicole (2005) 'The Organization of Male and Female Labor in Foraging Societies: Implications for Early Paleoindian Archaeology', *American Anthropologist* 107(4): 666–676.
Wajcman, Judy (2017) 'Automation: Is It Really Different This Time?', *British Journal of Sociology* 68(1): 119–127.
Wallman, Sandra (1980) 'Social Anthropology of Work', *Current Anthropology* 21(3): 299–314.
Webb, Beatrice, and Sidney Webb (1897) *Industrial Democracy*. London: Longmans, Green & Co.
Weber, Max (1961) *General Economic History*. Translated by Frank Knight. Mineola, NY: Dover Publications.
Weber, Max (1978) *Economy and Society*. Oakland: University of California Press.
Weber, Max (1992) *The Protestant Ethic and the Spirit of Capitalism*. Translated by Talcott Parsons. London: Routledge.
Weeks, Kathi (2011) *The Problem with Work: Feminism, Marxism, Antiwork Politics, and Postwork Imaginaries*. Durham: Duke University Press.
Weil, Simone (2002 [1947]) *Gravity and Grace*. Translated by Emma Crawford and Mario von der Ruhr. London: Routledge.
Weiner, Annette (1977) *Women of Value, Men of Renown*. Brisbane: University of Queensland Press.
Weiner, Annette (1988) *The Trobrianders of Papua New Guinea*. Fort Worth: Harcourt Brace Jovanovich.
White, Stuart (1997) 'Liberal Equality, Exploitation, and the Case for an Unconditional Basic Income', *Political Studies* 45(2): 312–326.
White, Stuart (2003) *The Civic Minimum. On the Rights and Obligations of Economic Citizenship*. Oxford: Oxford University Press.
Widerquist, Karl (2006) 'Who Exploits Who?', *Political Studies* 54(3): 444–464.
Wilde, Oscar (2001 [1891]) *The Soul of Man under Socialism and Selected Critical Prose*. London: Penguin.
Wilson, Andrew, and Miko Flohr (eds) (2016) *Urban Craftsmen and Traders in the Roman World*. Oxford: Oxford University Press.
Wilson, Elizabeth (1977) *Women and the Welfare State*. London: Tavistock Publications.
Wilson, Shaun (2004) *The Struggle over Work: The 'End of Work' and Employment Alternatives in Post-Industrial Society*. London: Routledge.
Wolin, Richard (1993, 2nd edition) *The Heidegger Controversy: A Critical Reader*. Cambridge, Mass.: MIT Press.
Wolin, Richard (2022) *Heidegger in Ruins: Between Philosophy and Ideology*. New Haven: Yale University Press.
Wood, Allen (2004) *Karl Marx*. London: Routledge.
Wrzesniewski, Amy, and Jane Dutton (2001) 'Crafting a Job: Revisioning Employees as Active Crafters of Their Work', *The Academy of Management Review* 26(2): 179–201.
Yeoman, Ruth (2014) *Meaningful Work and Workplace Democracy: A Philosophy of Work and a Politics of Meaningfulness*. London: Palgrave Macmillan.
Yeoman, Ruth, Catherine Bailey, Adrian Madden, and Marc Thompson (2019) *Oxford Handbook of Meaningful Work*. Oxford: Oxford University Press.
Young, Iris Marion (1979) 'Self-Determination as Principle of Justice', *Philosophical Forum* 11(1): 30–46.
Young, Iris Marion (1990) *Justice and the Politics of Difference*. Princeton: Princeton University Press.
Young, Iris Marion (2002) 'Autonomy, Welfare Reform, and Meaningful Work'. In *The Subject of Care: Feminist Perspectives on Dependency*, edited by Eva Feder Kittay and Ellen Feder, pp. 40–60. Lanham: Rowman & Littlefield.
Zafirovski, Milan (2019) 'A Neglected Gap in the Weber Thesis? The Long Economic Lag of Capitalism from Protestantism', *Social Science Information* 58(1): 3–56.
Zimmerman, Michael (1990) *Heidegger's Confrontation with Modernity: Technology, Politics and Art*. Bloomington: Indiana University Press.
Zuidevart, Lambert (2007) *Social Philosophy after Adorno*. Cambridge: Cambridge University Press.

Index

For the benefit of digital users, indexed terms that span two pages (e.g., 52–53) may, on occasion, appear on only one of those pages.